The Presidents We Imagine

❖ STUDIES IN AMERICAN THOUGHT ❖
AND CULTURE

Series Editor

Paul S. Boyer

The Presidents
We Imagine

*Two Centuries of White House Fictions
on the Page, on the Stage,
Onscreen, and Online*

Jeff Smith

THE UNIVERSITY OF WISCONSIN PRESS

The University of Wisconsin Press
1930 Monroe Street, 3rd Floor
Madison, Wisconsin 53711-2059

www.wisc.edu/wisconsinpress/

3 Henrietta Street
London WC2E 8LU, England

Copyright © 2009

1   3   5   4   2

Printed in the United States of America

Library of Congress Cataloging-in-Publication Data
Smith, Jeff.
The presidents we imagine : two centuries
of White House fictions on the page, on the stage, onscreen, and online / Jeff Smith.
p.   cm.—(Studies in American thought and culture)
Includes bibliographical references and index.
ISBN 978-0-299-23184-2 (pbk.: alk. paper)
ISBN 978-0-299-23183-5 (e-book)
1. American literature—20th century—History and criticism.
2. Political fiction, American—History and criticism.
3. Presidents in literature.
4. Political plays, American—History and criticism.
5. Presidents in motion pictures.
I. Title.   II. Series.
PS228.P6S65   2009
700′.45873099—dc22
2008039542

To my parents,

ROBERT *and* MARGYE,

and my sister,

ELLEN

Contents

Illustrations

Acknowledgments

This project would not have been possible without the help of James Lastra and Deborah Nelson of the University of Chicago Department of English Language and Literature and Neil Harris of the Departments of History and Art History. Their wide-ranging expertise, which encompasses literature, film, television, and other arts and media as well as many historical periods, enabled me to range widely as well, and their comments on drafts and many other suggestions were invaluable all along the way.

Also invaluable, especially in identifying works to be studied, were the many librarians on "Fiction_L," the national e-mail list maintained by the Morton Grove, IL, Public Library's "Webrary" (http://www.webrary.org). Others whose efforts enabled me to go forward include Gerald Graff of the University of Illinois at Chicago; Janice Knight, Michael Murrin, Elizabeth Helsinger, Justin Steinberg, and Tim Merrill of the University of Chicago; and Paul Frommer, Kathie Heine, Marie Bishop, and other members and staff of the University of Southern California's Center for Management Communication. My colleagues Lee Cerling, Lucy Lee, and Judith Whitman took a particular interest in this work, suggested ideas, and/or read parts of the book in draft, and Shirley Maxey, my department chair during the project's early stages, was both strongly supportive and instrumental in clearing the way for it. Series editor Paul S. Boyer of the University of Wisconsin–Madison Department of History, Gwen Walker of the University of Wisconsin Press, and their colleagues saw the book through to publication, and I'm grateful for their many very helpful suggestions as well.

I've had more outstanding teachers at every level of my education than anyone has a right to expect. Those whose particular influence can be felt in this book include Robert Ferguson, Howard Suber, Robert Silberling, Gerald Isenberg, Mel Piehl, Warren Rubel, and the late Gerald

Mast, Wayne C. Booth and Joseph M. Williams. I hope my work does credit to their superb instruction.

At a critical stage of this project's development, I had the immense benefit of a Fulbright Fellowship that allowed me to teach topics related to it at the American University in Bulgaria. For this, I am deeply indebted to Professor Dr. Julia Stefanova, Executive Director, Rada Kaneva, Program Officer, and the other members of the Bulgarian-American Commission for Educational Exchange. This commission and its staff do a marvelous job of administering the Fulbright program in Bulgaria, as well as the Fulbright International Summer Institute, which I have also been privileged to attend. The national Fulbright staff in Washington, D.C., was also very helpful to me and, of course, should be congratulated for running the best educational exchange program on the planet, a program that has always represented America at its finest. My work at the American University in Bulgaria was a great experience as well, and for that I want to thank not only the students in my courses but President Michael Easton, Provost Ann Ferren, Dean Steven Sullivan, Andrew White and my other faculty colleagues, Nikolina Ivanova-Bell and her colleagues in the AUBG library, and Elena Bardarova, Nevena Yaneva, and everyone else on an unfailingly helpful university staff.

Equally important was the stimulating company of my fellow Fulbright Scholars and local friends. This community was for me what Hemingway's moveable feast was in 1920s Paris. For making it that, and for their friendship and interest in my work, my thanks go to Georgi Djartov, Boyan Dobrev, Brian Grandjean, Brad Guarino, Jean Lee, Sunnia Ko, Maria Kotseva, Jon and Amy Kuiken, Brian McAllester, Phred Mileski, Sarah Perrine, Magdalena Rahn, Adriana Stefanova, Christina Tahchieva, Julia Terlinchamp, Konstantina Vasileva, Tiago Villenueva, Matt Ziems, and everyone else in our large circle of Bulgarian and American comrades and traveling companions.

The original inspiration for this book was a dinner conversation one Presidents Day, with my friends and fellow scholars Deborah Kearney and Kristin Leuschner, and I'm very grateful to them for giving me the idea and for the many other ways in which they've supported me and the project. Deborah Kearney's help was essential, too, in preparing and checking the manuscript. At various times, Andrew and Ruth Mackinlay, Kathy Finn, Marilda Ribeiro Rosa, Linda Blum, Cory Smith (and Betsy, Michael, and Holly), Sharon King and Curt Steindler, Susi Mowson and Graham Weymouth (and Jasper and Timothy), Rebecca

Pallmeyer and Dan McAdams, David Morris, and numerous other friends and acquaintances—and, of course, my family, to whom this book is dedicated—also made useful suggestions, helped me clarify my thinking, or otherwise contributed to the effort.

Finally, for publishing articles and sponsoring presentations of mine on the topics here, I'm grateful to the *European Journal of American Culture*; to the American Humor Studies Association, its journal *Studies in American Humor,* and those who attended the association's special session at the 2004 Modern Language Association convention; and to Milena Katsarska and the Department of British and American Studies at the University of Plovdiv. I hope this book will help further and widen the conversations begun in those forums.

The Presidents We Imagine

Introduction

Presidents in the American Imagination

On the morning of Election Day 2000, CNN's website carried a feature story speculating on what the soon-to-be-chosen new president might learn from reading about the presidency in books. "Interestingly," wrote Books Editor Todd Leopold as he surveyed the field, "almost all works about presidents are biographical and autobiographical. Outside of a handful of thrillers, presidents—even fictional presidents—seldom appear as characters in novels." To explain this surprising fact, Leopold quoted Fred I. Greenstein, a presidential historian: "Perhaps the role doesn't lend itself to imaginative embellishment," Greenstein suggested.[1]

Of all the many miscounts that would mar that long day (and the weeks that followed), this one was far from the most damaging. But to say that CNN understated the number of fictional presidents would itself be a huge understatement. The presidency is something that Americans are continually imagining and re-imagining, not just in novels but in movies, stage plays, TV series, and every other storytelling form and medium.

In this, of course, they are not unique. All nations and all peoples tell stories about leaders; from Gilgamesh, Fu Xi, and Agamemnon to King David, King Arthur, and King Lear, such stories are the starting points of most of the world's literary traditions. And whether the leaders are real or imagined, whether they are kings and queens, gods, warrior heroes, mythical founders, or, today, prime ministers and presidents, stories about them are often projections of the nation itself—of people's hopes and fears for it, of their sense of its strengths, weaknesses, righteousness, and guilt.

Indeed, in one view, a nation *is* its stories. Walt Whitman offered a classic expression of this idea in his famous lecture on the death of Abraham Lincoln. The importance of that event, said Whitman, was not just historical or political, but poetic. "The immeasurable value and meaning of that whole tragedy lies, to me, in senses finally dearest to a nation," said Whitman, which for him were "the imaginative and artistic senses—the literary and dramatic ones." Lincoln was a figure to rival those of ancient epics, his war and his death the sources of "a great literature" yet to be written. They were "a cement to the whole people," Whitman declared, a guarantee that "America, too," would have stories of its own as great as Homer's and Shakespeare's.[2]

In the running argument over whether America could produce great literature—a common worry in the nineteenth century—Whitman's view that it would has long since prevailed. Less well settled is the importance of such literature to a nation's political life. A poet and storyteller like Whitman might naturally assign it a lofty role, but for the most part, works of art and imagination still tend to be walled off from other pursuits, treated as something apart from the "real" world of politics and commerce. Historians might consult them as evidence along with other documents of the past, and the better works might be admiringly studied for insights into some vague "human condition" that transcends particular histories and countries. Seldom, though, are mere stories viewed as constituent elements, building blocks, of the concrete historical circumstances in which we find ourselves actually living. They are difficult to mine for quantifiable data, and their typical focus on individual characters and actions tends to obscure—or at most, gesture toward—the economic interests and other big, abstract material forces that the social sciences are best geared to explain.

Yet even where such forces are clearly at work, so is something else. Consider the events about which Whitman was speaking. Obviously the Civil War was in part a clash of economic systems. But economic systems don't leave home to slog through mud and shoot at each other; only people do that, and they do it only if they're persuaded of a number of things. They have to see themselves as part of a group under some kind of threat, and they have to see the people they're shooting at as agents of the group posing that threat. Even if they're acting merely on their "interests," in the narrowest sense of costs and benefits, those interests somehow have to register in their minds. The people in question have to come to believe that forces and entities they cannot actually see could cause things to happen that would, in the end, do them palpable harm.

To take risks as terrible as those in war, moreover, most of them would have to believe that more is at stake than mere interests. They would want to see themselves as contributing to something nobler, some greater community or cause—the Union, the South, "freedom," their "rights," "the future," "our way of life"—that had come to feel real and urgent to them even if it could not be directly seen. "The Union" is not a concrete thing to be carried in the knapsacks of those fighting for it; it must be conjured in their imaginations, made to sound in "the mystic chords of memory," as Lincoln put it. And that is most likely to happen if the person guiding the effort (and making the speeches about mystic chords) is perceived to be not merely some random individual with a gift for fine phrasing but a projection in some form of the embattled community itself.

In short, people are moved to act by what's in their minds. And whatever else that might include—whatever ideals, ideologies, powerful symbols, shared beliefs, even mass delusions—it must also include some notion of themselves and others as participants caught within and struggling to shape a chain of events: that is, as characters in an unfolding story. This is at least as true in politics as anywhere else. Political leaders, ideas, and systems gain power, for good or ill, by telling stories that large numbers of people find persuasive: History is moving inexorably toward a proletarian utopia; our people are a master race destined to rule the world; we're on a mission to build the New Jerusalem, a shining city on a hill; our forefathers gave their lives for this ground, and we will defend it to our dying breath. Updating Whitman, one current theory holds that the nation itself is such a story, or a collection of them. Nations are *Imagined Communities*, says political historian Benedict Anderson in his influential book of that title. They come into existence only when people from diverse, previously unrelated classes and tribes join together to make one, which in turn requires them to see it in their minds. And the vehicles of such collective imagining—two of the developments most important to the rise of the "postcolonial" nationalism familiar today—are the novel and the newspaper. Since the eighteenth century, in Anderson's view, popular literature and the mass media have been the sources of Whitman's "cement to the whole people." They are the "technical means," says Anderson, whereby individuals come to see themselves *as* a whole people, as moving through time in company with others whom they never meet but, nonetheless, acknowledge as fellow citizens—fellow participants in the same shared story.[3]

In making this point Anderson invokes literary criticism, specifically the great critic Erich Auerbach's classic study of the "representation of reality": the ways in which changing literary styles and techniques reflect changing conceptions of reality itself. In Anderson's view, the modern nation is an invention made possible by the same new ways of imagining reality—the same new conceptions of space, time, society, and power—that Auerbach uncovered in the history of imaginative literature.[4] Other analysts, too, have seen the technical means of storytelling as tightly linked to those of nation-building and governing. Edmund S. Morgan's *Inventing the People: The Rise of Popular Sovereignty in England and America* argues that "the people," along with related concepts like political representation and "the consent of the governed," are complex fictions developed in the course of various seventeenth- and eighteenth-century political struggles (including the American Revolution). To be successful, government "requires the acceptance of fictions, requires the willing suspension of disbelief," Morgan writes, and "The political world of make-believe mingles with the real world in strange ways, for the make-believe world may often mold the real one."[5]

In fact, there is a growing body of scholarship—often grouped under the broad heading of "cultural studies"—devoted to the many features of real history and lived experience that are brought into being through acts of collective imagining, inventing, constructing, representing, and memory. Recent books, to name just a few examples, have examined the cultural processes involved in *Imagining India, Imagining Tomorrow,* and *Imagining the Modern City*; in *Inventing Beauty, Inventing Human Rights,* and *Inventing Wyatt Earp*; in *Constructing Masculinity, Constructing Childhood,* and *Constructing the Self*; in *Representing Jazz, Representing Race,* and *Representing Sport*; and in the shaping of various events and institutions *in American Memory*: Watergate, the civil rights movement, Independence Hall, and, of course, Lincoln and the Civil War. Cultural historians have also charted the changing and always "contested" uses of the images of other presidents besides Lincoln—notably George Washington,

Thomas Jefferson, and Richard Nixon—as well as the fluid meanings attached to other culturally iconic figures and character types like the Indian, the mother, the killer, the hillbilly, the teenage girl, Jesus, and Elvis Presley.[6]

But although selected presidents and other national institutions, including the U.S. Constitution and the Supreme Court, have been subjects of studies focused on their role in the "cultural imaginary" (as it is sometimes called), the presidency itself and the character type "president" have not been. This is surprising for a number of reasons. First, as discussed further below, the number of works featuring fictional presidents is huge. Contrary to the historian quoted by CNN, the presidency lends itself very well to "imaginative embellishment" if we judge from the amazing array of novels, films, and other fictional stories in which it plays an important role.

Second, and partly explaining these large numbers, the question is not merely one of "embellishment," as if the real presidency simply exists and writers then make up stories about it. As we will see, Americans have been imagining and telling stories about presidents since before there *were* presidents. Like any human invention, the presidency had to be imagined before it could be created—and the earliest imaginings drew quite explicitly on what Alexander Hamilton, its chief architect, called "resources even from the regions of fiction."[7] By *fiction* Hamilton meant something like "lies": false claims from opponents about how the presidency would work in practice (as opposed to his own supposedly true account). Understood more broadly, though, Hamilton's remark simply notes the unavoidable. If nations themselves are imaginative constructions, their leadership is even more so. Rulership of any kind is an essentially metaphorical act, a community's projection of authority onto an individual in much the same way that love is metaphorically projected through a red rose. In the past, kings ruled by virtue of such metaphors as "divine right" and "the king's two bodies." It was said that the king had both a physical being, or "body natural," and a kingly presence, or "body politic." The political body was even called a *persona ficta*—literally, a fictional person—and was imagined as outliving any given king.[8] But eventually that fiction lost its power to persuade. It became too difficult to suspend disbelief in some immortal, hereditary right to rule that attaches itself to certain individuals temporarily, yet for life.

And with that, the basis for authority shifted. Americans consider it one of their great political achievements to have understood, and rejected, the fictive quality of kingly rule. Their founding declaration was a kind of exposé, an effort to demystify that rule and dispel the fiction by submitting "facts" to "a candid world." Governments, said the Declaration of Independence, are not divine creations but "are instituted among men" for the people's own purposes and by their consent. The people make them, and can therefore re-imagine and remake them when the need arises.

As Morgan explains, though, "the consent of the governed" was another fiction, as was the "people" that allegedly gave that consent. Granted, these fictions have proven robust. A phrase like *the American people* is in regular use across the political spectrum; political leaders, commentators, and speechwriters who agree on nothing else agree in assuming that there is an entity of that name that exists apart from any actual living Americans, that ordained the Constitution in the 1780s yet survives to this day, and that wants and needs various things as it looks to the future (which we know because politicians on all sides are forever telling us what "the American people want"). The fiction of "we, the people" is so strong that even critics of a given national project will often be heard accepting ownership of it—as when antiwar activists complain that "we" invaded Iraq and "we're" killing innocent civilians there, even though the activists themselves personally did nothing of the kind. And the notion that presidents legitimately hold office by virtue of representing the people is deeply enough held to have survived many apparent refutations—including, spectacularly, the 2000 election, when the office was awarded to the candidate who indisputably *lost* the popular (i.e., people's) vote. Significantly, in foreclosing the effort to count votes from actual people, the Supreme Court did not claim that the outcome it was mandating was the people's choice. Instead, the fictive quality of the enterprise was briefly acknowledged and thrown open to view: The Chief Justice called it "perhaps delusive" to search for the people's will through accurate vote counting, and the justice whose order stopped the count went even further, citing the need for legitimacy and "the public acceptance democratic stability requires" as reasons *not* to continue that search.[9] The people, he seemed to be saying, need their fictions.

Whether they needed the particular fiction that George W. Bush had been duly elected is another question, but the broader point was not obviously false. Not only was the presidency born in storytelling, but familiar stories have continued to exert their pressures on it, helping set the terms and expectations on which real presidents must then act. Those terms, moreover, are continually being re-negotiated. Like citizens of other democracies, Americans formulate their ideas about where, how, and by whom the nation should be led in a multitude of never-ending debates, a great (or not so great) national discussion whose many sites include political meetings and campaigns, committee hearings and courtrooms, news reporting and commentary, Internet "blogs" and "chat rooms," and countless private conversations of all kinds. In this discussion, stories are central. When a citizen, politician, or commentator says "America is going to the dogs" or "Ronald Reagan was a great president" or "I'll fight for the middle class" or "This candidate wants to be the next JFK," some story is being invoked—some larger confection of events, scenarios, causes and effects, heroes and villains, and happy or unhappy endings—apart from which the statement would have no meaning. And as the great discussion proceeds, it generates demands on the presidency that register in election results, opinion polls, party platforms, and political speeches—but also in novels, movies, and other works of the imagination, including some that have explicitly political purposes and many others that claim to have none.

The premise of this book, then, is that imaginings of presidents, like imaginings of the nation itself, are not just significant artifacts of America's cultural history, and not just reflections of the conflicting fears, hopes, and beliefs of its people(s)—though they are very importantly those things too. But beyond reflecting, they also *participate* in the ongoing "fiction" that is America. They are grounds of its existence, one layer of the soil out of which the nation has grown. The stories that Americans tell and have told about presidents are part of what makes America the nation that it is.

This being the case, it follows that the stories that demand to be studied are not just those dealing with presidents who have actually lived. Especially insofar as the fiction precedes and helps create the reality, it is at least as important to consider presidents who are *wholly* fictional—those who arose in the first place in storytellers' minds. Up until now, critics have devoted occasional attention to individual novels, movies, and other works in which such presidents appear, and even more occasionally they have focused on how those works treat the presidents in question. But there has never been a literary or cultural history of such works as a group, as a narrative genre or super-genre in its own right.

To be honest, I originally set out to fill that gap under the same misimpression as CNN: that presidents rarely appear as substantial characters in fiction or film. I thought, therefore, that it should be possible to survey, or at least catalog, virtually every such work in existence. That assumption did not last long. Because imagination is a central feature of the presidency and its development over time, such works range far beyond the "handful of thrillers" that CNN's editor apparently had in mind. Indeed the thrillers alone are far more than a handful: there are thousands of them, and virtually any one picked at random will as likely as not feature a fictional U.S. president. Though sometimes those presidents appear in minor roles or "offstage," often they are major characters. And that is only one genre and one medium. Further complicating matters, many speculative works posit American leaders who are not called "president," perhaps because the government is imagined to be transformed in some basic way; and still other works, especially satires, offer identifiable real presidents thinly disguised in other characters or roles. Even defining the term narrowly, there are too many fictional presidents even to list.[10]

Defining the term narrowly, however, also risks making the task too narrow. The term *fictional president* is almost as difficult to draw boundaries around as the term *fiction*. Histories and biographies claim to be true, yet they too rely on storytelling devices of all kinds. For the great majority of Americans who have never met a president, let alone known one well, knowledge of presidents is inevitably mediated through stories and pictures, and because these are representations they are always to some degree fictive. Even in his own memoirs, a president is an imagined character—perhaps especially there, in fact. Conversely, there may be more commitment to factual reporting in the story of a fictional president than in a work depicting a president who actually existed. Philip Roth's novel *The Plot Against America*, for instance, imagines Charles Lindbergh as president. That never happened, yet *The Plot Against America* is considerably more "realistic" and documentary-like than Roth's absurdist satire *Our Gang*, even though the latter is based on the real presidency of Richard M. Nixon.[11]

And if fictions can be found outside works that are so labeled, they are also correctly sought nowadays outside the boundaries of literature altogether. Even very broadly defined—expanded to include film, television, comic books, and other storytelling vehicles—the term *literature* covers only some of the many mechanisms of the cultural imaginary. It's inadequate, for instance, in describing satire, which is in part a literary mode but in part the manifestation of an attitude by whatever

means. When Yippie protesters in the 1960s make a pig their presidential "nominee," or when a captured Indian dresses and acts in exaggerated "presidential" styles (a story retold here in chapter 2), such acts of
performance art, or "guerilla street theater" as the Yippies called it, give
us presidents at least as imaginative and/or imaginary as anything in a
typical novel or film. Recognizing this, contemporary literary criticism
has cast its net wider, reaching beyond books and stories to study extra-
literary expressions and "communicative acts" of all kinds.[12] But even
this broadened effort might not capture every imaginative product worth
considering. If a video-game simulation allows you to "run for president" yourself, or to play-act presidential decision making, the game's
outcome and even its story-hero (the "game persona" or "player character") could be described as an imagined or fictional president despite
being neither authored nor even "communicated" in any usual sense.

Instead of "fictional presidents," therefore, what seemed to be
needed—and what the chapters that follow try to provide—was a study
of "presidential fictions": selected works in various media, along with
other acts of imagination, in which American presidents and the presidency figure importantly as characters, motifs, literary devices, or ways
of making meaning. If we cannot examine every such fiction, we can
nonetheless account for key developments and discover some recurring
themes. We can see how imaginings of the presidency have evolved over
time, and consider how they might contribute to our understanding of
the presidency as culturally contested ground, a scene of struggle over
the political values and meanings that come to be attached to national
leaders and their efforts. And by exploring the many ways in which
America has been "led" by imagined as much as by real presidents, we
can better understand America's real politics, public life, and evolving
national identities.

Because a history like this extends over more than two hundred
years, it encompasses numerous developments in politics, in storytelling
modes, and in media technologies, each of them working changes on the
others. In some cases constructing a certain kind of story has been a way
of trying to solve a real-life political problem, while in others the power
of particular stories has added to the pressures driving real events. The
chapters that follow attempt to track this interplay through successive
periods. The representation of political reality, like the representation of
reality itself, has evolved through identifiable phases, with each one
bringing to the fore a new cluster of leading themes and concerns—a

distinctive set of problems in the *political* imaginary, along with characteristic ways of using narrative resources to answer them. The related but separate problems of creating and legitimizing a new kind of republican leadership, as described in chapter 1, variously called for both the use and the avoidance of the new conventions of novelistic realism. Later, the rise of party and opposition politics, along with sectional and other divisions in the young republic and elite nervousness at the specter of mass democracy, produced the "low" comic figures and satirical doubles discussed in chapter 2. Such figures prepared the way for depictions of presidents with psychological depth—a point that was reached, however, only with Lincoln, whose place in the nation's history seemed to call for a character with a subtle interior history of his own. Chapter 3 describes the treatment of Lincoln as a character in the years following the Civil War, as well as the panoply of fictional presidents created in response to the disappointments of the Gilded Age and the hopes of the Progressive Era.

Chapter 4 deals with the period of the Great Depression, whose disastrous effects seemed to call for leaders who could reach deeply enough into citizens' lives to solve their everyday problems. But a reach that deep could easily become totalitarian control, a fear expressed in several important fictions of the time. And the "personal" presidency that took shape in the 1930s—first in fiction and *then* in reality—was also subject to human frailties and foibles. Anxieties about this yielded whole genres of fiction and film in the decades following. The Cold War culture and counterculture described in chapter 5 probed the possibilities and limits of the human, including the fragile human being in whose hands the fate of the planet seemed to rest. And in the confessional culture of recent years, with the dignity-defying intimacies and criss-crossings of the real and "virtual" discussed in chapters 6 and 7, the range of imaginings has proliferated, and the fictions at times have turned back on themselves. The result of these latest developments, as reviewed in chapter 7 and the book's conclusion, has been to highlight the many ways in which an office invented in storytelling continues to operate on terms set down in the cultural imaginary.

Over the course of this trajectory, and in part under the impact of successive waves of emerging new media, fictional depictions of presidents have become ever more varied. Long a part of the nation's political history, they are also a colorful record of it, and one that has largely been overlooked. But their role and importance go beyond merely recording.

New fictional themes and styles often do not so much "reflect" developments in actual politics as anticipate and even help them along. Political life imitates art; writers and artists turn political fears and hopes into characters, projecting into them some vision of what the nation is or needs. Such were the acts of imagining that created the presidency in the first place. Presidents have represented America since 1789, but even before that, Americans were representing presidents — as they have continued to do ever since.

1

Imagining a President

George Washington and His Fictional Predecessors

❖

Here the writers against the Constitution seem to have taken
pains to signalize their talent of misrepresentation. Calculating
upon the aversion of the people to monarchy, they have endeav-
ored to enlist all their jealousies and apprehensions in opposition
to the intended President of the United States; not merely as the
embryo, but as the full-grown progeny, of that detested parent.
To establish the pretended affinity, they have not scrupled to
draw resources even from the regions of fiction.

Alexander Hamilton, *Federalist* 67

❖

America began appearing in European literature before more than
a handful of Europeans had ever been there. By one account,
Shakespeare's *The Tempest* is a vision of America circa 1611. One might
call it a literary "reworking" of early travelers' reports, except that
those reports were already products of a literary imagination. Fictions—
well-established, even ancient, stories and storytelling styles—were involved in imagining, indeed perceiving, even something as big, visible,
and solid as a continent.[1]

The presidency, at first, was not big, visible, or solid; it was a new, in some ways unprecedented, creation, designed for a government that no one had yet seen operate. It therefore should not surprise us—even if it did surprise and disgust Alexander Hamilton, one of the presidency's chief proponents—that attempts to imagine it led into "the regions of fiction": the culture's already existing stock of images and narratives. Nor should it surprise us that much of that stock, too, had been imported from abroad. The stories that Americans would come to tell about presidents grew out of stories that influential Britons had already been telling, at least a half-century before there even *was* a United States of America.

The "Robinocracy" and the Patriot King: British Forerunners of the Fictional Presidency

Anglo-American politics is conventionally traced through a line of constitutional reforms and arrangements reaching back at least to Magna Carta in 1215. But the continuous evolution toward modern party politics really begins with the "Glorious Revolution" and the new parliamentary monarchy it gave rise to in the late seventeenth and early eighteenth centuries. The British Parliament of Queen Anne's time was split between two loose alliances that came to be known as Whigs and Tories, and this basic structure—two dominant, more or less equally matched parties, one governing and one in opposition, seeking mandates and occasionally trading places through elections—not only migrated to America but has persisted, with surprisingly few changes, ever since.

Broadly speaking, the Whigs were the party of the rising mercantile and commercial classes, and of the two they were the more successful party, ruling Britain for much of the eighteenth century and standing most firmly in the line of descent that leads to the parties and politics familiar today. But their opponents, the Tories, could claim another distinction: They and their sympathizers included a number of prominent authors, among them Henry Fielding and, most famously, the circle of "Augustan Age" poets who included Jonathan Swift, Alexander Pope, and John Gay. There was literary talent on the other side too; Daniel Defoe was a key propagandist for the Whig regime, and his *Robinson Crusoe* is sometimes read as a parable of the new mode of self-made industriousness associated with Whig politics. But the opposition's writers, the famous group that came to be known as the "Tory Wits," ensured that what the Tories lost in political power they made up in wit—which meant that what was bad for the conservative cause politically was good for English literature. Responding to what Swift denounced as "a base, corrupted, wicked age," an age in which "a dunce might govern for a dozen years together," the Tory Wits got busy writing satirical, thinly fictionalized portraits of those dunces. And the most notorious of these, in their view, was the longtime Whig leader Robert Walpole. The success of Walpole's new brand of politics can be measured not just by his twenty-one years in power but by the rise of what, in effect, was a new kind of government: Walpole was Britain's first "prime" minister and the first official resident of 10 Downing Street.[2]

For many years Walpole's leading opponent was the Tory politician and propagandist Lord Bolingbroke. Besides gathering around him the Tory Wits, Bolingbroke published an opposition newspaper, *The Craftsman*, so-called because it was devoted to exposing and lampooning the "crafty" methods of Walpole and his Whig associates. To their conservative critics, these methods were not a new mode of legitimate politics; they were simply "corruption," an unholy alliance of government with money. Walpole's administration was unapologetically friendly to certain class interests, and among its many "projects"—for the Tory Wits, a term of abuse—were such familiar modern mechanisms of government and finance as paper credit, stock trading, and a national debt. Defenders of this program justified it in the same terms political leaders routinely use today: it was the route to national prosperity. But to the Tories it was a "Robinocracy" or rule of thieves, a boon only to bankers, brokers, speculators, financiers, and their political henchmen. Robbin' "Robin" Walpole's reign as "Robinarch" was lamentable evidence, Bolingbroke charged, that "The power of money, as the world is now constituted, is real power."[3]

For Bolingbroke, the answer to the grimy reality of the Robinocracy was "The Idea of a Patriot King." The Patriot King, a paragon of "liberty and good government," would rule above party, revive the forgotten spirit of the constitution, and make "public virtue and real capacity" once again the basis of political power. By dispelling the "mystery" that the schemers and powerbrokers had made of politics, he would give the government back to the nation they had robbed and duped. Partisan strife, therefore, would come to an end. "A Patriot King is the most powerful of all reformers," Bolingbroke wrote, "for he is himself a sort of standing miracle, so rarely seen and so little understood, that the sure effects of his appearance will be admiration and love in every honest

Lockit, the corrupt prison warden (Peter Bayliss, *left*) and Peachum, the dishonest businessman and fence (Stratford Johns, *right*), explain to the highwayman Macheath (Roger Daltry) how a gang of thieves and criminals is "like the Great." From a 1983 BBC-TV production of *The Beggar's Opera*.

breast, [and] confusion and terror to every guilty conscience." The rule of money and power divides and corrupts the whole nation, but the Patriot King would restore "concord," reforming not just the government but the people too: "A new people will seem to arise with a new king."[4]

While awaiting this happy event, the Augustan poets mocked the Robinarch and his cronies in satires that included Swift's *Gulliver's Travels* and Pope's *The Dunciad*.[5] But it was John Gay's *The Beggar's Opera* that created characters so transparently based on Walpole's government that the name of one of those characters, "Bob Booty," became a nickname for Walpole. The musical style that Gay pioneered, a light-comic opera based on popular ballads, is often cited as a forerunner of modern musicals. But this "low" style also reflected the Tories' low view of the new governing clique of "gamesters and lawyers," as one of Gay's lyrics put it. These the play analogized to a cynical crime boss and his outlaw gang of drunken gamblers and thieves. Apparently stung by the portrayal, the real-life leaders reflected in characters like Peachum, Lockit, and Macheath (a spelling that includes the word *cheat*) saw to it that Gay was not permitted to stage a sequel. But *The Beggar's Opera* itself stayed in almost continuous production, appearing somewhere every year for nearly the next century and a half. From its first New York performance in 1750 onward, it was also frequently produced in America.[6]

What makes all this relevant to the American presidency is not just the fact that *The Beggar's Opera* was said to be George Washington's favorite play.[7] Lord Bolingbroke and his gifted friends lost the political argument; all Western nations today, not least the United States, are governed by descendants of the Robinocracy. But whatever its failures in practice, the Tory vision has held up well in the politics of the imagination. The criminals of *The Beggar's Opera* were prototypes of a class of characters that would often reappear, especially in American political fiction and drama. Bolingbroke had warned that under the new finance-based party politics, "some cabal or other will draw the whole wealth of the nation and the whole power of the state to itself," and American political storytellers have never ceased to agree.[8] As we survey their works in the coming chapters, we will see many incarnations of that scheming cabal. We will find it attempting, again and again, to manipulate politics, seize power, and corrupt a nation that is more dependent than most on believing that it lives by ideals. But we will also see the cabal in regular confrontation with versions of the Patriot King. That three-century-old ideal is one that Americans can still recognize today, in no small part because it has served as a template for so many writers and filmmakers. Patriot Kings, as Bolingbroke envisioned them, were "the most uncommon of all phenomena in the physical or moral world," a source of benefits "like those which poets feign."[9] But they have not been uncommon at all in the literary and cinematic world. There, poets have been feigning them ever since.

"From the Regions of Fiction": The Constitutional Framing Debates

By the time America's leaders came to write the U.S. Constitution, Bolingbroke's vision was among many that informed their discussions.[10] So were legends of Patriot King–type heroes. Prominent among these were two defenders of the ancient Roman republic, Cato and Cincinnatus. Former officers of George Washington's army called themselves the "Society of the Cincinnati," and Cato's avid following among Augustan and American politicians was reflected both in political essayists' frequent use of the pseudonym "Cato" and in the popularity of Joseph Addison's 1713 *Cato: A Tragedy,* yet another play that was said to be Washington's favorite. (To boost his bedraggled troops' morale, he had it staged at Valley Forge.)

But whether drawn from history and legend or simply made up for the purpose, stories played a central role in the constitutional framing and ratification debates. The presidency could not exist without first being imagined, and to describe how it might succeed or fail in practice required envisioning "characters" and "scenes," as advocates on both sides of those debates frankly put it. And even after the office had come to life in the person of Washington, writers and artists had to come to grips with it as a living reality. They were called upon to put the presidency into recognizable shape for a public whose view of it was bound to depend not just on Washington himself, but on Washington's story: the narratives through which his acts and achievements would become widely known.

But what shape *would* be recognizable, and what sorts of imaginings would strike readers of the time as plausible and compelling? Since we are speaking of stories, these questions go to the relationship between the political and the literary. The political problem, of course, was to frame an institution suitable for ruling a republic. And what was a republic? James Madison, writing as "Publius," sought to define the term in *Federalist* 39: "a government which derives all its powers directly or indirectly from the great body of the people, and is administered by persons holding their offices during pleasure for a limited period, or during good behavior."[11] In earlier notes to fellow Constitutional Convention delegates, Madison had also identified the political "vices" that a good republic would try to correct:

> In absolute Monarchies, the prince is sufficiently neutral towards his subjects, but frequently sacrifices their happiness to his ambition or his avarice. In small Republics, the sovereign will is sufficiently controuled from such a sacrifice of the entire Society, but is not sufficiently neutral towards the parts composing it.[12]

For Madison, then, the task for designers of a republic was twofold. The power of rulers had to be limited by ensuring that it came from the people; but it also had to be, one might say, "neutralized" by ensuring that it came from and benefited the *great body* of the people, not some separate or privileged caste.[13]

The literary problem arose from the fact that the same period that saw the emergence of republican institutions was also a period of transition, even revolution, in literary and rhetorical styles, as new modes became available in which to address a newly empowered, democratized public. This, however, entailed new choices, as older modes did not immediately disappear. By the late eighteenth century, a key choice facing the writer of stories was the choice between a more or less "realistic" style—a style associated with the growing popularity of that recent literary development, the novel—or the older styles that have been variously described as classicism, neoclassicism, the Ciceronian or "grand" style, the epic and romance traditions, or, in one well-known analysis, "literary traditionalism" generally.[14] *Neoclassicism* is a particularly useful term, suggesting as it does what these impulses had in common and, at the same time, traditionalist narrative's kinship with oratory. The neoclassical mode emphasized linguistic elegance or "decorum," historical or "type" characters, and general or universal subjects. Realism, by contrast, affirmed the growing literary stature of individuality, uniqueness, unadorned language meant to be "purely referential," and plots that "had to be acted out by particular people in particular circumstances."[15]

We might suppose that realism, with its focus on characters of the middling classes and a society resembling the reader's own, was the more "republican" mode—a literary counterpart to the political triumph of the common man. Indeed, theories of realism and the novel have generally traced them to the same social changes that drove the American and French revolutions.[16] But the truth is more complicated. A closer look at the ways the presidency was written about, pre- and post-Washington, shows that the task of explaining and legitimating the new office called for *both* realistic and traditional/neoclassical narrative forms. And perhaps most surprisingly, it called for them in reverse order: The new, realistic mode was essential to the "pre-selling" of the presidency, while the older narrative styles were, much like George Washington himself, recalled to the nation's service once the problem had turned to placing a real man in a real office.

Even more than most aspects of the framing and ratification debates, the debate over the proposed new executive was, for obvious reasons, a clash of ideas about human nature and power. Again and again the Constitution's "federalist" proponents and "antifederalist" critics appealed to what they claimed were universal truths in these matters, truths that would determine how the presidency wound up working regardless of the best intentions of its creators. At the Constitutional Convention, Benjamin Franklin warned his colleagues against the frightening prospect of an American "Pharaoh"—a figure whose rule would follow a logic that would end by "enslaving the people":

> [A]ll history informs us, there has been in every State & Kingdom a constant kind of warfare between the governing & governed: the one striving to obtain more for its support, and the other to pay less. . . . Generally indeed the ruling power carries its point, the revenues of princes constantly increasing, and we see that they are never satisfied, but always in want of more. The more the people are discontented with the oppression of taxes; the greater need the prince has of money to distribute among his partizans and pay the troops that are to suppress all resistance, and enable him to plunder at pleasure.

The presidency as Franklin saw it taking shape at the convention dangerously promised its occupants both pre-eminence and profit, thus drawing together the two greatest political temptations: "the love of power, and the love of money." Unless the element of profit were removed (Franklin proposed that presidents earn no salaries), the office would attract not "the wise and moderate" but, instead, "the bold and the violent, the men of strong passions and indefatigable activity in their selfish pursuits." And the sorry result would be "great convulsions" and "the most violent effects . . . the bustle of cabal, the heat of contention, the infinite mutual abuse of parties, tearing to pieces the best of characters."[17]

Elbridge Gerry also saw dangers ahead, especially if the choice of president were left to the people:

> A popular election in this case is radically vicious. The ignorance of the people would put it in the power of some one set of men dispersed through the Union & acting in Concert to delude them into any appointment. [Gerry] observed that such a Society of men existed in the Order of the Cincinnati. They are respectable, United, and influencial. They will in fact elect the chief Magistrate in every instance, if the election be referred to the people. [Gerry's] respect for the characters composing this Society could not blind him to the danger & impropriety of throwing such a power into their hands.[18]

Gerry's reference to the Cincinnati implied that even the proven, virtuous leadership of Washington might not be proof against a cabal—a "set of men . . . acting in Concert." Although he later served the new government in Congress and as vice president, Gerry was concerned enough about such dangers that he refused to sign the proposed Constitution.

Franklin went ahead and did sign it; his American Pharaoh was hypothetical but Washington was real, and Franklin found in him reason to believe that America would always produce selfless leaders—three or four, anyway, in any given era.[19] The antifederalists put the odds much lower. "[F]or the first president, and, perhaps, one in a century or two afterwards," wrote "the Federal Farmer," the nation might find "a great and good man, governed by superior motives." But that was most unlikely; a cabal comprised of "the servile supporters of his wishes" will be the outcome "with nine tenths of the presidents."[20] Others were even more pessimistic. One pseudonymous antifederalist, "An Old Whig," thought the odds of a virtuous president were one in *a hundred million.* Echoing Franklin's fears of "great convulsions" and "most violent effects," the Old Whig described "a scene of horror and confusion" as the country descended into military dictatorship. "Let us suppose," he wrote, that a future leader was, like Washington,

> a favorite with his army, and that they are unwilling to part with their beloved commander in chief—or to make the thing familiar, let us suppose a future president and commander in chief adored by his army and the militia to as great a degree as our late illustrious commander in chief; and we have only to suppose one thing more, that this man is without the virtue, the moderation and love of liberty which possessed the mind of our late general—and this country will be involved at once in war and tyranny.

For the Old Whig, the more likely model was not Washington but another famous general and politician—the one whom Cato, the virtuous Roman, had tried to stop:

> We may also suppose, without trespassing upon the bounds of probability, that this man may not have the means of supporting, in private life, the dignity of his former station; that like Caesar, he may be at once ambitious and poor, and deeply involved in debt. Such a man would die a thousand deaths rather than sink from the heights of splendor and power, into obscurity and wretchedness.

Probability, in the Old Whig's view, foretold future Caesars—presidents who would cling desperately to the office because losing it would be "a shock almost too great for human nature to endure."[21]

Like most good stories, the antifederalists' narratives were meant not just to inform their listeners but to move them. At the Virginia ratifying convention, Patrick Henry repeated the warning against military dictatorship and then, according to the convention record, "strongly *and pathetically* [i.e. feelingly] expatiated on the probability of the president's enslaving America, and the horrid consequences that must result."[22] The threat this sort of rhetoric posed to the Constitution was not lost on its advocates. What could stop the new plan from being ratified, they knew, were not just alternative political philosophies and interests, but their opponents' ability to conjure up vivid characters and compelling stories. Responding effectively, therefore, would demand more than just dry explanations of the vesting clause or the enumerated powers in Article II. The federalist writers would have to become literary critics, unmasking the unscrupulous willingness of the antifederalists to "draw resources even from the regions of fiction." And they would have to refute those "shameless" stories by telling a more forceful story of their own.[23]

When he took up the pen of "Publius" in turn, therefore, Alexander Hamilton spoke of the Constitution's critics not just as political adversaries, but as *artists*—albeit "wicked" ones whose "devices" and "unwarrantable arts" were put to the service of frightening and misleading the public. The "talent of misrepresentation" he denounced in them included a gift for spinning "extravagant" stories, tales that "disfigure" the presidency by conjuring up "counterfeit resemblances." Summarizing their work, Hamilton offered this mocking review of the presidents imagined in antifederalist writing:

> He has been decorated with attributes superior in dignity and splendor to those of a King of Great-Britain. He has been shown to us with the diadem sparkling on his brow, and the imperial purple flowing in his train. He has been seated on a throne surrounded with minions and mistresses; giving audience to the envoys of foreign potentates, in all the supercilious pomp of majesty. The images of Asiatic despotism and voluptuousness have scarcely been wanting to crown the exaggerated scene. We have been almost taught to tremble at the terrific visages of murdering janizaries; and to blush at the unveiled mysteries of a future seraglio.[24]

What offended and worried Hamilton was the emotional appeal of his opponents' exaggerated scene making—its desire and potential to make its audience "tremble" and "blush." But, intriguingly, this rejoinder does not dismiss the fictive devices. Instead it turns them back on their authors, taking the images they've already created and deliberately high-lighting details: the throne, the diadem, the imperial purple. It suggests that to *fully* visualize this fearful despot would make Hamilton's point, revealing just how unlikely such a figure would be in the American context.

To explain how, instead, the presidency actually would work, Hamilton soon turned to constructing his own characters and plots. But compared to his opponents' tales, his little narratives seemed to be composed in a different key altogether. In defense of the proposed term of four years, for instance, Hamilton spoke of its effect on a president's "consciousness." A four-year term would put "the prospect of annihilation" far enough in the future to keep it from improperly influencing a man with "a tolerable portion of fortitude," since "he might reasonably promise himself, that there would be time enough before it arrived, to make the community sensible" of the propriety of his measures. Granted, as he neared the end of that term, and the public's verdict, it was likely that

> his confidence, and with it his firmness, would decline; yet both the one and the other would derive support from the opportunities which his previous continuance in the station had afforded him, of establishing himself in the esteem and good-will of his constituents. He might, then, hazard with safety, in proportion to the proofs he had given of his wisdom and integrity, and to the title he had acquired to the respect and attachment of his fellow-citizens.[25]

Compared to the epic figures and grandiose rhetoric of the anti-federalists—or even of Franklin, a man of an earlier generation—Hamilton's prose here is workaday, his imagined president a character of modestly "novelistic" size: someone with a recognizable interior life, with worries and doubts, with calculations and perhaps even moods that change over time.

Further, Hamilton argued, even the kinds of motives his opponents invoked, like the urge for fame, would have the good effect of encouraging a president to "undertake extensive and arduous enterprises for the public benefit"—but only *if* "he could flatter himself with the prospect of being allowed to finish what he had begun." If he couldn't, said Hamilton, then those same motives

> would, on the contrary, deter him from the undertaking, when he foresaw that he must quit the scene before he could accomplish the work,

and must commit that [work], together with his own reputation, to hands which might be unequal or unfriendly to the task. The most to be expected from the generality of men, in such a situation, is the negative merit of not doing harm, instead of the positive merit of doing good.[26]

The issue, in other words, wasn't whether the individuals who would seek the presidency would wish to glorify themselves; that might even be a virtue. (Hamilton called the love of fame "the ruling passion of the noblest minds.") The real issue was how well the office was designed to accommodate these natural impulses. If it were term-limited or in some other way poorly constructed, the presidency could swallow up its occupant's ambition, not the other way around. Even the noblest characters, Hamilton argued, are prone to discouragement. In one of his rare ventures into poetic imagery, Hamilton sketched the possible consequences of term limits by asking whether it would "promote the peace of the community, or the stability of the government," if half a dozen men who had once held the highest position in the land had to spend the rest of their days "wandering among the people like discontented ghosts, and sighing for a place which they were destined never more to possess?"[27] The danger, for Hamilton, wasn't a Caesar but a Caesar's ghost.

By contrast with the millions-to-one odds laid against it by the antifederalist Old Whig and others, Hamilton insisted on the "constant probability of seeing the [presidency] filled by characters pre-eminent for ability and virtue."[28] Two centuries on, we might question whether the supply of ability and virtue has really been "constant." Still, Hamilton/Publius's estimate has proven more realistic than his opponents'. And what these comparisons suggest is that it was also more "realistic" in a technical literary sense: it relied on different, and more modern, styles and conventions of storytelling. Narratives cast in this newer mode had the ring of truth to the extent that they simply "felt" right, had the feel of lived experience. That a first magistrate could set himself up as king, Caesar, or military dictator was not impossible, as Napoleon would demonstrate a few years later (albeit in the much more chaotic conditions of post-Revolutionary France). But in warning of this possibility, the Constitution's critics were not so much describing real characters as invoking an archetype, a stock figure of political argument whose purpose had less to do with explaining the actual dynamics of leadership than with rhetorical heightening. It was a device for increasing the gravity of the critics' objections by emphasizing what was at stake.

Antifederalist narratives, that is, imagined characters of a kind that literary theorists today would describe not as "representational" but as "illustrative": "concepts in anthropoid shape or fragments of the human psyche masquerading as whole human beings." With illustrative characters, "we are not called upon to understand their motivation," as if they were actual people, "but to understand the *principles they illustrate* through their actions in a narrative framework."[29] The presidents-turned-Caesars of the antifederalists were personifications of the classical vices of greed and ambition, projections into narrative of the conventional belief that power corrupts. They did not need a "consciousness" capable of harboring doubts or changes of mind, because their imagined behavior was not the result of any movements of mind. It was predetermined, a playing out of their essential nature—which, in turn, was held to be a projection of human nature, or some crucial facet thereof.

There is obviously nothing wrong with illustrative characterization as such; it was central to Western literature for centuries. By the late eighteenth century, though, it undoubtedly struck some readers as old-fashioned. The novel—a relatively new form, as its name implies (and a term just then coming into use)—was noteworthy for its movement away from the illustrative and toward the representational. Novels featured characters whose significance lay in their particularity, in the details of their inner lives and responses to changing circumstance.[30] Hamilton's imagined president was representational in this sense. If not a character whose psychology was worked out in detail, at least it did possess a psychology. Where the antifederalists drew figures of epic size, large enough to burst the bonds of mere political arrangements and bring down the polity, federalists could respond with a character of such "normal" dimensions that its flaw, if any, was its capacity to be further diminished. It is interesting that Hamilton chose to represent this danger with the disembodied image of ghosts—as if imagining leaders so psychologically sensitive to changing fortunes that they could wind up as nothing *but* their inner discontents.

The Unimaginable President Washington

If the federalists' victory in the ratification debates testified to the power of certain political assumptions and interests, it also testified to the power of new ways of imagining leadership and representing it in language. But the more modern storytelling mode that seemed prefigured in Hamilton's writing was not soon followed up. Well into the nine-teenth century, even as developments in realism and naturalism were furthering what Erich Auerbach has called "the literary conquest of modern reality," the literary conquest of *political* reality lagged, at least with respect to the representation of American leaders. As Auerbach has also noted, "traditional forms" lingered on a relatively long time; in England modern realism emerged only gradually, "without [a] sharp break between 1780 and 1830,"[31] and in America the timetable was sim-ilar: "Augustan neoclassicism," says one historian,

> was a shaping force on American thought, polity, and culture until the political age of Andrew Jackson and the intellectual age of Ralph Waldo Emerson. . . . Most important in determining the shape of the early presidency, the moral and public philosophy articulated by Pope, Swift, Bolinghroke, and their allies in opposition to Walpole became standard opinion among those in power in the new United States and loomed large in American consciousness until well into the nineteenth century.

With his enthusiasm for modern programs of industry and finance, Al-exander Hamilton was among the most "Walpolean" of the framers. It is probably no coincidence, then, that his predictions for the presidency ventured closer than most to the realistic style associated with Wal-poleans like Daniel Defoe. But even for Hamilton, the best leaders would be less like the party-promoted officials we know today and more like Bolingbroke's Patriot King. The creation of the presidency was, in large part, an attempt to institutionalize this neoclassical ideal.[32]

Still, we might expect that once the Constitution was adopted, and once the merely hypothetical presidents of the earlier debates gave way to an actual person, realistic representation would finally become the norm. But what happened with the advent of George Washington, surprisingly, was almost the reverse. Hamilton had argued that presi-dents would, at least, experience rising and falling levels of political confidence—but even this modest degree of inner change and struggle, of what Hamilton called "consciousness," was more than most observ-ers were willing to imagine in Washington's case. The first president was more readily figured as "a secret or semi-supernatural or typological being who is more a projection of the will of God than of an individual personality. Washington's status as sign of Providence frees him from the obligation to be an individual; he need only allow God to work through him and need not worry about developing much of an individual character."[33] That is how one recent critic describes the figure who emerged from the many funeral orations offered on and around February 22, 1800, Washington's first posthumous birthday and a national day of mourning for him. This figure, said his eulogists, had been a man *greater* than Caesar or Alexander, a Moses raised up *in answer to* the (British) Pharaoh. He was, of course—as he himself seems to have fancied—Cincinnatus, the farmer-soldier who, having reluctantly entered service to save the nation, wishes only for an early return to his plow. And in one of the strangest of these images, Washington was cast as a hero out of Celtic or Norse legend, leading his warrior band into battle waving a spear.[34]

Characterizations like these were not offered as fiction, but one could argue that they were more fictitious than most later efforts to depict Washington in novels and films. At least, it is hard for the modern reader to take the traditional strategies of epideictic—the rhetoric of praise—at face value. "Character" in this kind of rhetoric is illustrative by definition: The word refers not to anything complex about the person in question but, on the contrary, to the changeless consistency with which he exemplifies a fixed set of virtues. To the extent that such characterizations were, by 1800, already coming to seem improbable and old-fashioned, they were best reserved for special occasions like eulogies. But the problem then was how to represent Washington the rest of the time while respecting both his prodigious reputation and the emerging new canons of plausibility. Wouldn't placing Washington in a more prosaic or pedestrian story inevitably seem to deflate him or cut him down to size?

In addressing this problem, early nineteenth-century biographers of Washington tried a number of strategies. One was simply to keep Washington at arm's length. To a remarkable degree, Washington's first biographers—even while purporting to narrate the events of his life—contrived to tell us little about the man and even less about the president. In the 239 pages of John Corry's 1800 *Life of George Washington*, for example, Washington is president for just three paragraphs. Corry spends more time on the eight days of Washington's triumphal journey to his inauguration than on the eight years to follow, which are summed up merely as further proof of "the zeal of an honest patriot."[35] David Humphreys, Washington's military aide and close confidant, also ignores the presidency except to suggest, intriguingly, that Washington had resolved to turn down the position until his many conversations with

Humphreys—one of them four hours long—persuaded him otherwise. But nothing either of these conversations or of Washington's doubts and concerns is actually described, since "In all this proceeding . . . there was nothing discoverable but the operation of reason without affectation. Influenced by principles of duty, his private inclination was overcome by a sense of public obligation."[36]

David Ramsay's 1807 biography is likewise notable for the narrative distance it maintains from its subject. Ramsay, a member of the Continental Congress, had known Washington in person, yet in his respectful treatment the first president seldom, if ever, thinks or even acts. He is revealed almost exclusively in policy statements and in actions taken through appointees and intermediaries. Even when some problem in the country "furnishe[s] matter for serious reflection to the President," it does "not affect his conduct," though it might lead him to restate his position.[37] The position itself, however, is not the product of reflection, serious or otherwise. It stems from a simple recognition of necessity or duty, which happens precisely *without* any lapse of time or thought: "About this time war commenced between France and Great-Britain. The correct, sound judgment of Washington instantly decided that a perfect neutrality was the right, the duty, and the interest of the United States."[38] Similarly, when agents of France, including the troublesome envoy Edmond Genêt, tried to mobilize Kentuckians for an assault on Spanish New Orleans, "Washington was officially bound to interpose his authority" to thwart them. "Orders were accordingly given to the civil authority in Kentucky, to use all legal means to prevent this expedition."[39] Here, in two sentences, are three of Ramsay's distancing devices: intermediaries ("the civil authority in Kentucky"), the bow to necessity ("officially bound . . . accordingly"), and passive voice ("orders were . . . given"). This, to modern ears, is an odd way to praise a leader for the brilliance of his command. But a Washington whose decisions were fraught with difficulty would be harder to project as a flawless embodiment of his duty and role.

Most early chroniclers followed these leads. John Marshall gives a more detailed account of Washington's presidency in his five-volume *Life,* treating it perhaps more than any other early biographer in terms of real policy dilemmas and choices that could not be made "instantly." But in discussing these, Marshall neglects Washington for pages at a time, presenting instead what sound like position papers or legal briefs. With the options finally laid to view, Washington "[takes] time to deliberate," much as Marshall himself would have done in his role as Chief Justice.[40] And deliberating, of course, is not the same as feeling. In telling the story of Genêt and the pro-French agitation, Marshall makes frequent mention of "passions," "jealousy," a "restless uneasy temper," and the like, but none of these are qualities of Washington's; they are the problems he faces from the public at large, the demands and upsets of the ill-informed masses that the "prudent" and "pacific" executive branch is continually struggling to contain.[41]

The suppression of affect in prose like Marshall's may be what moved John Adams to compare this massive biography to a mausoleum. But again, it was typical of such early treatments. Jared Sparks, the Harvard historian (and later president) who collected and, apparently, bowdlerized Washington's correspondence, also details events like the Genet affair in more detail but, like David Ramsay, reports the administration's response to them in passive voice ("It was decided," "a declaration was accordingly made," "It was unanimously agreed").[42] And even in the hands of a much more skilled storyteller—like Washington Irving, who had the benefit of fifty years' additional hindsight by the time he finished his own five-volume *Life*—Washington only rarely speaks or acts "feelingly"; most of the story's emotion again lies in the "violent" and "inflammable" mood of the public, the "popular excitement" through which the president makes his "deliberate" way.[43] In Irving's telling as in Marshall's, Washington at times seems almost a minor character in his own later career.

Omissions of this kind are the natural result of illustrative characterization. By the time Washington becomes president in these accounts, his virtues are already well established: The story need not reveal them, nor even necessarily show them in action. It need only affirm that he carried on "with his usual wisdom and firmness, integrity and rectitude," as another eulogist put it, dismissing Washington's presidency in a single sentence.[44] At that point attention pivots to the virtues themselves and away from the man. John Corry's biography concludes by analyzing King Alfred the Great, a supposed Washington prototype, and David Humphreys' ends by cataloguing the traits that Washington kept in perfect balance: "elegance united with simplicity"; "hospitable, without being ostentatious"; modest and reserved, yet "ever communicative, often animated"; "grave & majestic" yet "colloquial" and given to "wit & humour"—none of which humor Humphreys actually reports, since his instrument here is rhetoric, not narrative.[45] But a good story depends on tension, and perfectly balanced virtues don't supply tension, they resolve it.

One might conclude from all this that Americans of the early Republic simply did not want to know more, that they preferred portraits of a great general and flawless public hero to anything more human, intimate, or nuanced. Yet to varying degrees, writers of the time insisted they were taking pains to make Washington real. Such was the claim of Mason Locke ("Parson") Weems, author of the most popular of the early biographies: *A History of the Life and Death, Virtues and Exploits of General George Washington* (or *George Washington the Great*, in a later edition). Weems's "seminal work of historical fiction," as one critic has called it, is the source of the deathless tale of young George chopping down a cherry tree, a story that would come to loom large in Washington legend thanks to its reprinting in generations of schoolbooks.[46] Whether the tale is fiction or not is unclear; Weems did claim to have good sources. At any rate, his biography went further than others in using novelistic techniques to "character-ize" Washington, even if the character that resulted seemed not so much a person as America's answer to Moses and Christ.

In some obvious ways, Weems's portrayal resembles those common at the time. Like Ramsay's biography, for instance, it shows Washington "inflexibly" acting on duty and making decisions as president "instantly," even on such a hotly contested topic as America's refusal to side with France against Britain.[47] But Weems's purpose, as he made clear at the outset, was to go beyond the public man:·

> It is not then in the glare of *public*, but in the shade of *private life*, that we are to look for the man. Private life, is always real life. Behind the curtain, where the eyes of the million are not upon him, and where a man can have no motive but *inclination*, no incitement but *honest nature*, there he will always be sure to act *himself*; consequently, if he act greatly, he must be great indeed. Hence it has been justly said, that, "our *private deeds*, if *noble*, are noblest of our lives."
>
> Of these private deeds of Washington very little has been said. In most of the elegant orations pronounced to his praise, you see nothing of Washington below *the clouds*. . . . No! this is not the Washington you see; 'tis only Washington, the HERO, and the Demigod—Washington the *sun beam* in council, or *the storm* in war.[48]

Offering to correct these portrayals, Weems gives Washington what looks at first glance like a measure of inner life and development. The hero is tracked from his cherry-tree childhood to his deathbed, and some effort is made to depict his emotions—not least in a strange, prolonged death scene in which, "by himself, like Moses . . . he seeks the face of God":

> He sees that, through the rich mercies of God, [his "beloved children," i.e., Americans] have now the precious opportunity to continue their country the GLORY of the earth, and a refuge for the poor and for the persecuted of all lands! The transporting sight of such a cloud of blessings, trembling close over the heads of his countrymen, together with the distressing uncertainty whether they will put forth their hands and enjoy them, shakes the *parent soul* of Washington with feelings *too strong* for his *dying frame*! The last tear that he is ever to shed now steals into his eye.

And so on. This passage, of course, truly *is* fiction. Since Washington is alone in the scene, each of the seven paragraphs that narrate his death—or rather his assumption and transfiguration, complete with angels' voices "(*in Fancy's ear*) warbling through the happy regions, and hymning the great procession towards the gates of heaven"—could only have come from Weems's own imagination.[49] But for Weems, that does not make the story untrue. The question of truth is decided not by what was witnessed or known for a fact, but by what surely *must* have happened given Washington's preternatural patriotism and virtue.

Put another way, in Weems's hands Washington's thoughts and feelings are projections of judgments already made about his character, not the other way around. The same is true of his childhood. It is not as if Weems's Washington really changes as he grows, as we would expect in most modern biographies (and realistic novels). The child, rather, is a projection backward of an already settled view of the man. In giving us "private life, [which] is always real life," Weems makes quite clear that he means to prove that Washington's virtues were, in essence, all present from the beginning. Compared to John Marshall and other early biographers, Weems was a lively writer and crowd-pleasing storyteller, and no one ever called his book a mausoleum. But while purporting to deal with Washington's early years and non-public acts, what it actually did was extend to these the already familiar aura of saintliness.

"The Fear of *George*": Washington in Early Fictions

If realistic conflicts could not be found *within* Washington, in his inner life or changes over time, then perhaps they could be created *around* Washington, in circumstances testing his virtues against others of comparable weight. This was a strategy that writers turned to as soon as Washington began appearing in fiction and drama. In *André*, a play written during Washington's presidency and first staged while he was still alive, William Dunlap used the story of Benedict Arnold and his captured British confederate, Major John André, to explore conflicts among such values as honor, duty, courage, honesty, and loyalty. The play's Washington ("The General") is faced with a tragic dilemma: the need to assert "power," "rigour," and even "vindictive[ness]," as he puts it, by way of promoting "mercy" and "humanity" in the long run.[50] Waxing poetic over a decision for which the real Washington was widely criticized, he refuses to treat the gallant young André as a prisoner of war and instead orders him hanged as a spy.

The situation was exceptionally complex and certainly lent itself, if any ever had, to a depiction of Washington's inner struggle—especially at the hands of an artist like Dunlap, who himself had once been on familiar terms with Washington.[51] And indeed, Dunlap's Washington seemingly does confess to such conflicts:

> O, what keen struggles must I undergo!
> Unbless'd estate! to have the power to pardon;
> The court's stern sentence to remit;—give life;—
> Feel the strong wish to use such blessed power;
> Yet know that circumstances strong as fate
> Forbid to obey the impulse.

He further confesses that he is "tortur'd" by the pleas of others on André's behalf, which seem to bring him to tears: "my heart is torn in twain."[52] But if the point of revealing a character's emotions is to throw light on why he acts as he does—if it's normally assumed that his actions are the *results* of his inner states—then what we have here are feelings of some other sort: not "ruling passions" but "polite sentiments," to borrow terms from one analyst of the period's rhetoric.[53] The tragedy's real emotions don't flow through Washington but around him. Far from moving him to act, they leave him "All *un*mov'd," since he is bound however unhappily by "circumstances strong as fate." Even the characters he turns away in "desperate sorrow" can't help but see this. "Fain would I blame his conduct—but I cannot," says one. "My scrutiny but ends in admiration."[54]

There is, then, ultimately no real conflict of values in the play, only temporary disagreements arising from the passions and self-interest that lead lesser men and women to lose sight of what must be done. And there is certainly no conflict within the General himself. Bound just as rigidly by duty as the Washington in David Ramsay's biography, Dunlap's Washington is defined precisely by his "invaluable temperance"— the ability to feel emotions and even, to a point, express them, *without* letting them influence anything he thinks or does. It is this quality that makes him "first among men," as one of his associates explains in the play.[55] Washington may have an inner life, but it counts to his credit only insofar as it makes no difference.

Still another way of accommodating a figure who was so difficult to represent realistically was, in effect, to give up and recast his story in a style of writing that deliberately went the opposite way—a style whose very qualities not only allowed for but *demanded* reverential treatment. Two works of the early nineteenth century not only exemplified this strategy but also would seem to have taken it as far as it could go. One was Richard Snowden's *The American Revolution: Written in Scriptural, or, Ancient Historical Style,* which appeared in multiple editions between 1802 and at least 1823. This peculiar book set out to retell the famous victories in the antique language of the King James Bible:

> V. 12. And the great Sanhedrim of the people, consulted together where they should find a man that would be able to go out before the host of Columbia, and order the battle for them.
>
> 13. And they chose *George*, whose surname was *Washington*, he was from the south country, and had a goodly inheritance on Mount Vernon, and flocks and herds in abundance.
>
> 14. He was a man of war from his youth, was beloved of the people, and his bowels yearned towards them in the day of their calamity! he was also one of the princes of the provinces, and sat in the Sanhedrim of the people, who bore the burthen in the heat of the day.
>
> 15. And there were captains appointed under him. . . . These were all mighty men of valour, but *George* was chief captain.[56]

The biblical conceit continues with Snowden giving, literally, chapter and verse on the War of Independence. The great captain George, though the choice of the "Sanhedrim" (Congress) as one whose bowels yearned toward the people, faces dissension within the ranks:

> X. 1. Now the host, of the king of Britain, lay encamped in the town of Boston, in the province of the East: and the army of the people of the provinces, environed the town round about. . . .
>
> 4. Now there were certain men in the host of Columbia, who were like the heathen in the desert, they knew not whence good came.

These men spake versus the chief captain, inasmuch as he did not force his way into the town where the army of the men of Britain were encamped.

5. Nevertheless, he bore with these men, and answered them now again; he trode in the footsteps of *Fabius,* who went out against the Carthaginians, and by his wisdom saved the Roman people from falling a prey to their enemies.

6. His wants were many, but he kept the door of his lips, lest peradventure, the enemies of Columbia should hear thereof: the cogitations of his heart were deep and ponderous.

Advised by his officers that it would be better to occupy Dorchester Heights ("the high places") than to attack the British "host" in Boston, the great captain orders his army's "destroying engines" to "discharge . . . their thunders upon the town." The high places are taken, and a great storm brings rains and floods to "beat upon" the British host, inflicting "the fear of *George*" upon them and causing them to flee:

21. And it came to pass, that the chief captain of the host of the people of the provinces, entered into the town that had been occupied by the army of the king of Britain, and the people came out to do him honor: and the fame of *George,* the chief captain, went out into all lands!

And so the great captain's exploits continue. As the story unscrolls, "the cogitations of his heart" are not the only thing that proves ponderous.

It is easy to see why this book, like so much else in the Washington literature, was offered up for illustrative purposes—as a tale meant to furnish edifying examples of "fidelity" and "virtue," in the words of the 1823 publisher's foreword. What seems harder to believe, from today's perspective, is the publisher's claim that its pseudo-Jacobean argot— the most intrusive kind of literary embellishment—actually serves the values of "simplicity" and, indeed, factual truth:

Being written in the manner of an *ancient history,* facts alone are noticed, divested of everything of a speculative nature.—This renders it both impartial and intelligible, and enables the author, to give an ample delineation of the most minute events in a very concise manner.[57]

Nothing about the book seems impartial or especially intelligible, and whatever qualities the constant repetition of faux Old Testament formulas might lend a work, conciseness is not one of them. The same foreword, however, also promises that Snowden's book will "gratify every class of readers"; it will make the events it describes "perfectly familiar to every capacity."[58] This, then, may be the point: To people of a certain class (or "capacity"), a Washington who combined the best qualities of Cicero and Caesar wasn't just unapproachable but rather obscure. What stood to make him "familiar" to such readers was biblical language, however artificial and mannered. As one modern editor has put it, there was "a strain of patriotic religiosity" that early nineteenth-century writers could tap into, one that "had helped make the American Revolution broadly appealing to common folk." Where Washington's own "self-consciously neoclassical concerns with character and reputation" might be lost on the average citizen, the ostentatious display of Christian piety—like the kind found in Parson Weems's more famous book—could translate those concerns "into a popular, democratic idiom."[59]

So a charitable view of Snowden would see him as trying to do Weems one better: If, in this period, the language of Christian piety is the language of the people, then what could be more democratic than making Washington's story literally sound like the Bible? Moreover, it may well have been Weems's tales that Snowden's publisher had in mind in criticizing material "of a speculative nature." Weems, as we have seen, was partial to childhood legends and was perfectly happy to describe things that neither he nor any living person could possibly have witnessed. In that respect, even though Weems's writing style was (marginally) the plainer one, it was actually Snowden's made-up Old Testament that stuck more simply to the facts.

Another effort to recast Washington's story in a suitably elevated style was Francis Glass's *Georgii Washingtonii, Americae Septentrionalis Civitatum Foederatum Praesidis Primi, Vita*, a "Life of George Washington in Latin Prose" modeled on Plutarch's first-century *Lives* of Greek and Roman heroes. Here the revered model wasn't the Bible but the ancient classics, and the mimicry extended beyond idiom and phrasing to the actual language in which the text was written. The idea seemed to be that the soaring encomiums, the hero-worshipping depictions of Washington, would be more at home in Latin than in English. If Washington was to be a monument, not a living, breathing person, then the story might as well be written in a dead language too. Glass's book, composed in 1822 and published in 1835, was the verbal equivalent of dressing Washington in a toga and sandals—a mode of depiction that also was tried: Horatio Greenough's statue for the Capitol Rotunda, carved in 1832–41, modeled Washington on an ancient statue of Zeus. In his lifetime

Horatio Greenough's neoclassical statue of George Washington for the Capitol Rotunda, modeled on an ancient monument to Zeus and now in the Smithsonian's National Museum of American History.

Washington himself had had the sense to veto this sort of portrayal, and the hyper-classicism proved to be more than even his cult could bear. Widely mocked as "offensive, even comical"—to one observer, it looked like Washington was getting ready for a bath—the statue was soon moved out of the Rotunda, where in any case its twelve tons were causing the floor to crack.[60]

If one could, as it were, hope to "naturalize" an abstractly ideal figure like Washington by choosing an equally idealized language or style, one final and somewhat parallel strategy was to choose a story to tell about him in which the failure to reveal an inner being is itself part of the point. Given the right such choice, the plaster-saint treatment of Washington might be exactly what the narrative required. James Fenimore Cooper's *The Spy: A Tale of the Neutral Ground*, a novel loosely inspired by the same events as Dunlap's play *André*, presents us with a story of this kind. The novel is all about keeping secrets: The spy of the title is in the Revolutionary general's employ, and it is crucial to the story's events that no one knows this but Washington himself. Hence a premium is placed on Washington's ability to keep his own counsel, to reveal nothing to others of his true thoughts. He may be moving about among normal, realistically drawn people, but his surreptitious efforts can succeed only if he continues to exemplify the classical virtues—especially the stoic virtue of *enkrateia*, or self-mastery.

In Cooper's hands this strategy yields a Washington who is just as opaque as any nonrepresentational, purely illustrative character.[61] In fact he spends most of the novel incognito, operating under the pseudonym "Mr. Harper." While this at least allows him to interact with others *as if* he were just one of them, it also emphasizes the impenetrability of his real self. When he first turns up in this disguise at the home of the Whartons, the family whose divided loyalties during the Revolution are the backdrop for the novel's events, the other characters do their best to draw him out on such great questions of the day as the likelihood of a British victory:

> The brow of Harper contracted; and a deeper shade of melancholy crossed his features—his eye kindled with a transient beam of fire, that spoke a latent source of deep feeling. The admiring gaze of the younger of the sisters had barely time to read its expression, before it passed away, leaving in its room the acquired composure which marked the countenance of the stranger, and that impressive dignity which so conspicuously denotes the empire of reason.

The Whartons persist in trying to overthrow reason's empire and make Harper's latent deep feeling patent, but these attempts also fail—as, "making no reply, he turned to the fire, and continued for some time gazing on its embers in silence":

> Mr. Wharton had in vain endeavoured to pierce the disguise of his guest's political feelings; but, while there was nothing forbidding in his countenance, there was nothing communicative—it was strikingly reserved; and the master of the house rose, in profound ignorance of what, in those days, was the most material point in the character of his guest.[62]

Even in a later, more impassioned scene, the only gauge others are given of Harper/Washington's interiority is "a lighting of his thoughtful eye, and a slight unbending of his muscles." Thoughtful or not, Washington gives nothing away, and neither does his narrator: "It was at all times difficult to probe the thoughts of one who held his passions in such disciplined subjection as Harper."[63] Here, yet again, we have a Washington who is supremely self-mastered and unrevealing. But that, Cooper could argue, is—realistically—just what spies and spymasters *have* to be.

"To Keep Him First": Particularism and Republican Politics

A 1939 painting by Grant Wood, best known for the immensely famous "American Gothic," satirizes the treatment of Washington to which generations of Americans had by then grown accustomed. *Parson Weems' Fable* poses Weems in the foreground, pulling back a curtain to reveal his book's most famous scene: young George and the cherry tree. But the face on the hatchet-bearing six-year-old isn't a child's; it's the famous Gilbert Stuart portrait of the aged, unsmiling Washington, the Washington who hung on the walls of so many classrooms where the cherry-tree tale was retailed to America's schoolchildren over the decades. An iconic image from early times, the Stuart portrait had so thoroughly cornered the market on Washington imagery that, already in 1823, it was said that if the man himself were to reappear on earth he would be treated as an imposter. Stuart's painting, for most Americans, *was* the real Washington—which in essence is to say that a "real" Washington was unimaginable. As Nathaniel Hawthorne put it, the first president was hard to visualize as a child because he was difficult to picture even as human. The public man was all: Washington "was born with his clothes on, and his hair powdered, and made a stately bow on his first appearance in the world."[64] Early writers and artists who went looking for a character named George Washington soon found themselves in an eighteenth-century formal garden, where every path seemed to lead to the same bronze figure on horseback.

But all this leaves us with several paradoxes. Why would old-fashioned, neoclassical portrayals come *later* than more realistic accounts like Alexander Hamilton's, when literary developments on the whole were moving the opposite way? If, in the constitutional framing debates, the nonrealist conventions of neoclassicism served those who *opposed* a strong executive and its elevating of one man, why were they invoked in support of Washington, thus serving to elevate him that much more? And why, if presidents who did *not* yet exist could be described with some measure of realism, was it apparently so much harder to describe realistically one who did?

To account for these seeming contradictions, we must return to James Madison's twofold definition of republicanism. A republican leader's power, said Madison, had to come from the people; this was what distinguished him from a tyrant. But it also had to come from *all* the people, "the great body of the society, not from an inconsiderable portion or a favored class of it." That second requirement, Madison said, was "essential," and his famous condemnation of "faction" elsewhere in the *Federalist* was a reminder not to overlook that requirement in pursuit of the first: "It is of great importance in a republic not only to guard the society against the oppression of its rulers, but to guard one part of the society against the injustice of the other part." The danger of oppression was familiar enough—it had prompted the Revolution—but the other danger was too easily forgotten.[65]

Warnings like this, echoing Lord Bolingbroke, came from other quarters as well. In a sermon preached to the state legislators of Connecticut, Elizur Goodrich urged officials to conduct their business with "no narrow or private interests at heart." To surrender to the spirit of "party-attachment," he warned, would create "scenes of confusion" like those at the Tower of Babel.[66] Samuel Langdon told citizens of New Hampshire to beware of legislators "whose judgment is partial" and, in choosing a governor, to "be always on your guard against parties."[67] And the Constitution's opponents warned that an ill-designed executive office would not just have too much power but, crucially, would not belong to the people. It would become a "court" party like those familiar in Europe. "The language and the manners of this court," said the antifederalist "Cato" (George Clinton), "will be what distinguishes them from the rest of the community, not what assimilates them to it."[68] Parties, partiality, the rule of one part over others—as much as tyranny, the threat that many saw in the turmoil of the 1780s was *particularism*, the funneling of loyalties and influence toward a favored region or class.

But realistic representation cannot occur *without* particularism. What makes realism different from neoclassical and other illustrative modes is precisely its interest in particularity, in "individual experience . . . which is always unique."[69] At its most extreme, this interest gives us a character like Defoe's Robinson Crusoe. If that famous tale of a castaway was a breakthrough in depicting the inner life, this is also because it's nearly as vivid a parable of apartness from "the great body of the society" as one could imagine. Defoe, as a staunch Walpolean, was friendly to the new politics of party and class. He makes Crusoe a trader, and one so phenomenally enterprising that he can make even a desert island prosper. Thus did Crusoe brilliantly embody the individualistic values of Walpole's rising merchant class. But by the same token, he is just the opposite of the kind of figure that Madison and his colleagues thought was needed to lead a republic. Crusoe is the most "inconsiderable portion" of society there is, a man with the narrowest and most private interests it's possible to have. He is a reductio ad absurdum, a ruler whose particularity does not stop him from embodying the people's values only because he is also, himself, the people, or most of it.

In most realistic stories, as in life, characters don't live on desert islands. They live in societies, which means *with*in them—in some particular social stratum or class. The same distinctive traits that make a character realistic also disclose this positioning, identifying the character with some elements of society as opposed to others. All of this made realism a dangerous mode in which to represent early presidents. A president who was simply another person, a member of some part of the community, would be just that: a *part*-isan, not the patriot leader of the whole. His "language and manners"—that is, the very traits on which novelists rely to define and distinguish characters—would ally him with those of the same station or regional origin, thereby opening a breach between him and the *common*wealth. A George Washington with language and manners identifiable as those of the South, the rural gentry, or the plantation class—precisely the kind of Washington most likely to interest today's novelists and biographers—would fail a key test of republican legitimacy.

So in clothing him in neoclassical decorum, Washington's chroniclers were safeguarding the claims on him of Americans in general. For Parson Weems, Washington's goodness was not just an example for others, it was proof against any lingering particularism—a set of attributes available to *all* classes and, therefore, not specific to any one. Weems demanded that writers "give us his *private virtues!*" precisely because "[i]n *these,* every youth is interested, because in these every youth may become a Washington." Virtue and piety, Weems held, were what substituted in Washington's case for the glory, high birth, and (especially) wealth that would otherwise have placed Washington at a distance from his admirers. "Happily for America, George Washington was not born with '*a silver spoon in his mouth*'" and, to his credit, did not even know Latin.[70]

Similarly, in comparing him with revered figures of the past, Washington's eulogists were partly supplying what neoclassical depictions otherwise lacked. If neoclassicism could not probe a character's inwardness directly, it could nonetheless draw canonical parallels designed to remind listeners that great men, too, had flaws and inner struggles, that they too were in some sense ordinary. Thus, David Humphreys' comparison of Washington to King Alfred the Great was not entirely to Washington's advantage. And in referencing Moses, writers were invoking a figure known to have triumphed in a divinely appointed mission despite his human failings, or perhaps even with their help.[71] As Samuel Langdon explained with deliberate anachronism, Moses was not just a flawed but also a modest figure, one who insisted on making the Israelites a "federal republic" of which he was merely president, not king.[72]

Despite their high-flown rhetoric, in other words, neoclassical encomiums often tried in their own way to ground a character like Washington in life on the human plane. It was not necessary to reveal the president's inner self—to make him, in the manner of realistic representation, socially or psychologically palpable to readers—in order to make him one of the people or associate him closely with those he was to lead. In fact it was hazardous to try. A president who was fully represent*ed* in the literary sense would be less represent*ative* in the way a republic needed him to be.

For those promoting a new and stronger executive, then, the preferred narrative strategy changed as events proceeded. A presidency that existed only in the abstract was subject to limitless enlargement in the minds and writings of its opponents. It tended, that is, toward imagined absolutism, and the need was to contain it, to give it a reassuringly human scale. For this the newer techniques of realism were best suited. But once an actual man held the office, the danger ran the other way. What was needed then was assurance not against a leader too large for the polity, one who would seize and own it, but against a leader who would *be* owned, who would belong to some parts of the country more than to others, who would be too small—too bourgeois, we might say—to encompass the whole.[73] Assurance like that was better provided by abstraction, by projecting the first president as the "union of virtues" that Washington Irving later called the man for whom he had been named. Since no one objects to virtue in the abstract, this neoclassical style of praise made him "*national* property, where all sympathies throughout our widely-extended and diversified empire meet in unison."[74]

But it should be noted that George Washington has paid a price for this ever since. The problem has been well stated in a critical comment on another famous life story, the *Confessions* of St. Augustine. Augustine's account of his spiritual transformation was "realistic" in its insistence on recording emotion, and yet it ultimately presents Augustine as a Christ-figure "type." The story it tells, therefore, "cannot be fairly labeled 'psychological' in anything like the modern sense of the word":

> We do not have a strong sense of the character Augustine's "personality" at the various stages of his development, and we see little of the social influences on it that we expect in modern psychological novels. Above all, Augustine's psychological detail is not offered as an end in itself. Unlike Rousseau [whose own *Confessions* appeared in the 1780s], he has no desire to set forth the intimate record of his emotional and intellectual life for the sake of its intensity and uniqueness.[75]

In likewise draining Washington's story of uniqueness, his early chroniclers, too, robbed that story of intensity. (As we will see in later chapters, that quality did not fully reappear in stories of presidents until Abraham Lincoln.) To this day Washington has remained the unsmiling icon, so much so that when, for instance, a clothier wants to retail splashy Hawaiian shirts, it dresses the Gilbert Stuart portrait in one, promising that "*Anyone* can look cool in the right shirt"—Washington being about as uncool as they come.[76]

Aware of the problem, image-makers for Washington have been redoubling efforts to re-inject intensity by other means. In 2002 the custodians of Mount Vernon hired filmmaker Steven Spielberg, along with experts in forensics, age regression, and computer modeling, to produce films and high-tech physical reconstructions that would "dispel the elder statesman icon" and re-establish the young Washington as an "adventurous, athletic, risk-taking, courageous kind of action hero," as Mount Vernon's executive director put it. A few years later the results were in. "Despite what he looks like on the dollar bill, it turns out George Washington may have been kind of hot," said one admiring appraiser. Presenting the new exhibits as a "multi-dimensional" and "vital representation," Mount Vernon called its plan "George Washington: To Keep Him First."[77] For a modern audience, being first is a matter of dimension, not perfection, of vitality and not just virtue. These projects were reminders that such qualities have been hard to come by for a man who, at a crucial point in his reputation making, seemed to resist being represented at all.

2

Seeing Double

Clowns, Carnival, and Satire in the Antebellum Years

❖

I should not forget to mention, that these popular meetings were always held at a noted tavern; for houses of that description, have always been found the most congenial nurseries of politicks; abounding with those genial streams which give strength and sustenance to faction—We are told that the ancient Germans, had an admirable mode of treating any question of importance; they first deliberated upon it when drunk, and afterwards reconsidered it, when sober. The shrewder mobs of America, who dislike having two minds upon a subject, both determine and act upon it drunk; by which means a world of cold and tedious speculation is dispensed with—and as it is universally allowed that when a man is drunk he sees *double*, it follows most conclusively that he sees twice as well as his sober neighbours.

"Diedrich Knickerbocker," *A History of New York*, 1809

❖

The American founders were regularly denounced in their own lifetimes, not least by each other. Those of a conservative bent were British agents and closet monarchists, while those more inclined toward

45

popular rule were "Democrats, Mobocrats, and all other kinds of Rats" whose aim was "the total destruction of all religion and civil order."[1] Not even George Washington was beyond ridicule. The French noble-man and tourist Chateaubriand, arriving in America in 1791, saw the president riding along in his coach and thought it "somewhat de-ranged" to imagine him as Cincinnatus—the selfless farmer/general who had saved the ancient Roman republic. "Could Washington, the dictator, be any other than a clown," he wondered, "urging his oxen with the goad, and holding the handle of the plough?" In person, as it turned out, Washington genuinely had "the simplicity of the old Roman," though this had not been obvious at first glance.[2]

But the simple old Roman once became "much inflamed" at a cabi-net meeting, according to Thomas Jefferson, and "got into one of those passions when he cannot command himself," over a satirical print that imagined his royal funeral.[3] And after Washington left office, other clowns would come spilling out of the presidential coach. The vitupera-tive political struggles of the early national period were in part a war of caricatures—which is to say, of quasi-fictionalizations. One such image that was often invoked was the cabal, that perennial band of conspira-tors that has been stalking Anglo-American government for nearly three hundred years now.[4] Both sides in the battle between the Federalist Party and the "Jeffersonian Republicans" could imagine the other side as a cabal: the Federalists because they represented bankers and financial interests, and the Jeffersonians because they worked through an early model political machine. Jefferson and his fellow Bavarian Illuminati, moreover, were diabolically scheming to make the entire planet "a sink of impurities, a theater of violence and murder, and a hell of miseries."[5] The fictionalizing went as far as dramatic enactments: in 1805 the Mas-sachusetts legislature staged a mock impeachment trial, giving Federal-ist lawmakers a chance to convict and remove President Jefferson—at least in their imaginations.

Even more imaginative was the thinly disguised Jefferson who ap-peared in "Diedrich Knickerbocker's" 1809 *History of New York*. Knick-erbocker was the fictional and absurdly credulous amateur historian through whom Washington Irving narrated his satirical portraits of the early Dutch governors of New Netherlands, characters who just hap-pened to bear striking resemblances to the political leaders of Irving's own time. Jefferson appears in the *History* in the guise of Wilhelmus Kieft, an actual director of the colony in the 1640s. "William the Testy," as Knickerbocker calls him, was a thoroughly impractical man who governed by hoping that harsh realities would yield to fine words and the abstractions of intellect. He had "so confused his brain" with his studies of logic and metaphysics "that he could never think clearly on any subject however simple, through the whole course of his life afterwards." Like Jefferson, Testy "was much given to mechanical inventions—constructing patent smoke-jacks—carts that went before the horses, and especially erecting wind-mills," which he mistook for fortifications. He had a dangerous tendency to rely on his "innovations and experiments" in defending New Netherlands against the Swedes and the Yankees, whom he thought could be kept at bay by clever deployments of flags, trumpeters, and that "dreadful engine of warfare," the written proclamation—which, to Knickerbocker's surprise, somehow fails to awe the enemy into submission.[6]

Worse, Testy had a gift for rousing the rabble, specifically by convincing them that they were not as satisfied as they thought:

> There is nothing that more moves my contempt at the stupidity and want of reflection in my fellow men, than to behold them rejoicing, and indulging in security and self confidence, in times of prosperity. . . . [T]he very essence of true wisdom . . . consists in knowing when we ought to be miserable; . . . your wise men have ever been the unhappiest of the human race; esteeming it as an infallible mark of genius to be distressed without reason—since any man may be miserable in time of misfortune, but it is the philosopher alone who can discover cause for grief in the very hour of prosperity.[7]

Naturally, the people's new, philosophically induced unhappiness drove them into politics. Soon "all those idlers and 'squires of low degree,' who like rags, hang loose upon the back of society," were rushing to the new popular assemblies:

> Coblers abandoned their stalls and hastened hither to give lessons on political economy—blacksmiths left their handicraft and suffered their own fires to go out, while they blew the bellows and stirred up the fire of faction; and even taylors, though but the shreds and patches, the ninth parts of humanity, neglected their own measures, to attend to the measures of government.[8]

The satirical target here isn't just rabble-rousers like Testy, but the rabble itself. The fact that these assemblies were held in taverns—on the theory that to see double, as when drunk, is to see twice as well—is a further but redundant joke. It was ludicrous enough that ordinary tradespeople thought themselves competent to participate in governing, an effrontery that was bound to irritate old-school Federalists like Irving. But the early nineteenth century was a period of expanding suffrage and the rising "Democracy," a term that had not yet come to name a universally recognized good but could still be used disparagingly (to mean something like "the riffraff"). Though called "republicans," Jeffersonians would actually turn out to be founding members of a new, "Democratic" Party. And as much as conservatives detested Jefferson, they would soon meet a rabble-rouser they liked even less—a Democratic president with a knack for getting Americans to see double.

"The Laws of the Ladies": Andrew Jackson and the Peggy Eaton Affair

Andrew Jackson came from the frontier state of Tennessee, which made his the first presidency that was not rooted in either the founding generation or the traditional East Coast establishment. And that group, like most displaced elites, was apt to confuse its own loss of influence with the collapse of the social order as such. On the day of Jackson's inauguration, March 4, 1829, polite society was scandalized by the new president's open house, or "levee," which saw the White House overrun by "immense crowds of all sorts of people, from the highest and most polished down to the most vulgar and gross in the nation," as Supreme Court Justice Joseph Story put it. "I never saw such a mixture. The reign of King 'Mob' seemed triumphant." Margaret Bayard Smith, a leading socialite whose letters are an important chronicle of the Jackson years, explained that "ladies and gentlemen only" had been expected for the afternoon reception, "not the people en masse." But in the event, "what a scene did we witness! The *Majesty of the People* had disappeared, and a rabble, a mob, of boys, negros, women, children, scrambling, fighting, romping. What a pity what a pity!" And a third witness, Congressman James Hamilton, reported seeing "a regular Saturnalia":

> The Mob broke in, in thousands—Spirits black yellow & grey, poured in in one uninterrupted stream of mud & filth, among the throng many subjects for the penetentiary and not the fewest among them [were] Mr Mercer's tyros for Liberia.—It would have done Mr Wilberforce's heart good to have seen a stout black wench eating in this free Country a jelley with a gold spoon at the President's House.

Robert Cruikshank, "President's Levee, or all Creation going to the White House," 1841. The carnivalesque scene at Andrew Jackson's 1829 inauguration, as depicted in this lithograph, included "a rabble" of some 20,000 well-wishers "scrambling, fighting, romping."

Smith's and Story's comments emphasize the jumbling of class distinctions; the "rabble" reminded Smith of how another old aristocracy had fallen to "the mobs in the Tuileries and at Versailles." For Hamilton the key index of disorder was race—and, by all-too-common extension, incipient criminality.[9] In any case, the witnesses agreed in seeing the crowd as a collection of "others": Smith's "boys, negros, women, children" is like a little field guide to the non-adult white male.

Yet they also conceded that, as one news report put it, this same crowd was in some sense "the Sovereign People." Hamilton's account went on to speak of "the fierce democracy" and of the trouble that "Demos [=the People] kicked up." The question that Jackson's arrival posed was whether the phrase *Sovereign People*, like *King 'Mob,'* was an oxymoron. Was popular rule really possible, or was it just another term for anarchy? Smith conceded that Jackson was "the People's President" through whom "the People would rule"—unless, she worried, "one day or other, the People . . . put down all rule and rulers."[10]

Hamilton's phrase "a regular Saturnalia" is also revealing. Saturnalia was an ancient forerunner of the medieval "carnival," and it's interesting in that regard that the inauguration happened to fall on Ash Wednesday—the end and counterpoint of carnival, or "Mardi Gras" as it's known in the city where, coincidentally, General Jackson's military exploits had first brought him to prominence. Carnival was more than just a holiday; as Mikhael Bakhtin has explained in his influential studies of "the Saturnalian tradition," it was a temporary inversion of the usual order of things, an abandonment of decorum in which normal social roles were masked—literally and figuratively—and revelers took to making fun of anything official or serious. Carnival was therefore closely tied to parody, which Bakhtin defines as "the creation of a *decrowning double.*" In carnival, he writes, "parodying was employed very widely, in diverse forms and degrees: various images (for example, carnival pairs of various sorts) parodied one another variously and from various points of view; it was like an entire system of crooked mirrors, elongating, diminishing, distorting in various directions and to various degrees."[11] Carnival's cockeyed reflections revealed "a second world and a second life outside officialdom." They played on the "ambivalent" or "double aspect" of life, ensuring that every myth and hero was parodied and that every serious story had its "laughing double":

> As in the Saturnalia the clown was the double of the ruler and the slave the double of the master, so such comic doubles were created in all forms of literature and culture. . . . All the parodic-travestying forms of the Middle Ages, and of the ancient world as well, modeled themselves on folk and holiday merrymaking, which throughout the Middle Ages bore the character of carnival and still retained in itself ineradicable traces of Saturnalia.[12]

In Bakhtin's broad definition, the parodic spirit of carnival is not confined to actual festivals, or even to fully crafted works of art, but can manifest itself in a wide range of actions, practices, and gestures.[13]

In America, "official" carnival emerged in the Jackson era. Spontaneous folk merriment had long been making itself felt against conservative resistance; authorities in New Orleans had fought to suppress the "license and revelry" that kept erupting there, worried at the way that masked revels, in particular, jumbled distinctions of race and class and released uncontrolled energies of the kind later seen in Jackson's inaugural melee. Slowly the city's elite learned to co-opt those energies instead,

and by the late 1820s Mardi Gras was becoming the "regular" (and reg-
ulated) Saturnalia that we know today.[14] But the carnivalesque is apt to
reappear wherever popular enthusiasm overwhelms official control and
propriety. That includes moments of political upheaval. When a movement like Jacksonian Democracy offers to empower the "folk," the result will look to traditionalists like an unwelcome holiday from received
values—a topsy-turvy scene like Jackson's inauguration, in which the
space of officialdom is taken over by a mob claiming to be the sovereign
People. And at the head of the rabble is likely to be a jester-in-chief, the
kind of figure known to historic carnival as the "Saturnalian Prince" or
"Lord of Misrule": a person of lower caste comically promoted to king
of the revels. Andrew Jackson, the first self-made president from the
rugged, brawling, uncultivated "West," could appear as either ruler or
Lord of Misrule, depending on which direction one glimpsed him from
in the system of crooked mirrors.

Apart from the scene at the White House, Inauguration Day 1829
confirmed for Margaret Bayard Smith that the rules of polite society
were still in force. Throughout the day, she was pleased to report, pains
had been taken to snub and isolate one particular woman—Margaret
O'Neale Eaton, the new wife of John Henry Eaton, President Jackson's
incoming secretary of war. At the evening ball this young bride "was left
alone, and kept at a respectful distance from [the] virtuous and distinguished women, with the sole exception of a seat at the supper-table,
where, however, notwithstanding her proximity, she was not spoken to by
them." Thus, even as the new president took power, a coordinated campaign of ostracism, begun several weeks earlier and targeting a member
of Jackson's own circle, was continuing without pause.[15]

This high-society imbroglio had started when, with the president-
elect's encouragement, his longtime friend John Eaton had married the
young widow Margaret "Peggy" O'Neale. The Eatons' marriage gave
Smith and her fellow arbiters of social propriety an occasion to nurse
their powerful dislike for Peggy Eaton, "whose reputation, her previous
connection with [Eaton] both before and after her [first] husband's
death, has totally destroyed." Some of the opprobrium directed against
Peggy—she was said to have been unfaithful to her first husband, perhaps driving him to suicide—was probably so much rumormongering
based on charges "which it would not be proper to commit to writing,"
as Smith darkly hinted. More importantly, Peggy struck her critics as far
too assertive and opinionated for a Washington wife, let alone the

A furious President Andrew Jackson (Lionel Barrymore, *right*) prepares to fire his Cabinet with a speech denouncing the "gossip and malice" directed against Peggy Eaton (Joan Crawford) and her husband, Secretary of War John Eaton (Franchot Tone). From *The Gorgeous Hussy*, a 1936 MGM film dramatization of the Eaton affair.

"daughter of a tavern-keeper," as she was somewhat inaccurately known. Her whole manner was an affront to the class and, even more so, the gender norms of her day. "Oh, woman, woman!" Smith exclaimed, by way of summing up the cause of all the trouble. It was widely assumed that John Eaton's marriage to Peggy had sunk his political career; repeating a joke that was apparently making the rounds, Smith suggested that he might be appointed ambassador to Haiti, "that being the most proper Court for *her* to reside in."[16] In other words, in Smith's view the Eatons belonged in a country best known for the shocks of slave revolt and black rule, a place where the old social hierarchies had recently been turned upside-down.

"The petticoat affair," as Jackson would later call it, or "the Eaton Malaria" in the words of Secretary of State Martin Van Buren, began with the ladies of Washington boycotting the Eatons' wedding and continued as other cabinet wives, led by Vice President John C. Calhoun's wife Floride, refused to accept or return Peggy's visits—a deliberate breach of protocol whose meaning was unmistakable. Peggy Eaton "has never been admitted into good society," and Smith was satisfied that she never would be; in the first months of the anti-Peggy campaign,

> public opinion ever just and impartial, seems to have triumphed over personal feelings and intrigues and finally doomed her to continue in her pristine lowly condition. A stand, a *noble* stand, I may say, since it is a stand taken against power and favoritism, has been made by the ladies of Washington, and not even the President's wishes, in favour of his dearest, personal friend, can influence them to violate the respect due to virtue, by visiting one, who has left her strait and narrow path.

For Smith, this noble stand of the ladies was "greatly to the honor of our sex."[17]

But Smith and her fellow virtuecrats had overestimated their power. Though they kept their crusade going for more than two years, eventually creating serious political headaches for Jackson, the president surprised everyone by stalwartly standing by his old friends. Plainly loath to take incoming shots in a gender war without returning fire, the old general proved that he, too, could treat others "coldly": "to be, or not to be, [Peggy's] friend is the test of Presidential favour," Smith complained.[18]

In part, Jackson was predictably irked at being told who should or should not be in his cabinet. But he was also determined to disprove the slanders against Peggy Eaton—so much so that he became his own private investigator, researching and compiling evidence of her pre- and inter-marital innocence. In the words of one astonished observer, the president was "actually for a whole season busied in procuring affidavits and certificates to prove her a virtuous woman! Not only this, but Jackson went to the trouble of writing out a defence for this woman by way of argument founded upon the certificates and affidavits which he had obtained of ninety-one manuscript pages!" Allegedly, Jackson also "had the baseness" to require government appointees and applicants "to visit Mrs. Eaton and defend her as a virtuous woman" on pain of being shut out of office.[19]

The Petticoat Affair had political consequences and, in the end, a political solution when Jackson purged and reorganized his cabinet in the spring of 1831. But the extraordinary personal interest he took in the matter is hard to explain in political terms alone. It seems clear, to use a modern term, that Jackson "identified" with John Eaton. The younger man's career had paralleled his own, including service in the War of 1812—like Jackson, Eaton was known as "General," if only honorifically—followed by years as Tennessee lawyers and planters and, eventually, senators. Jackson would later appoint Eaton to Jackson's own former position as governor of the Florida territory. Eaton, meanwhile, had immersed himself in Jackson's life, writing his campaign biography, and one point that this biography had made was that Jackson had a way of seeing himself paralleled in others.[20] (The biography itself was also "doubled" in a later parody.[21])

If the Jackson/Eaton parallels were clear, moreover, there were even more striking parallels between Peggy O'Neale Eaton and Jackson's late wife, Rachel Donelson Jackson, who had died shortly before Jackson took office. Both Peggy and Rachel had met their future husbands as boarders at their parents' inns (or "taverns"). Both were already married at the time, and in each case the circumstances of the first marriage stirred up scandal over the second. (Rachel's first husband had not yet legally divorced her when she married Jackson.) Jackson, therefore, had good reason for seeing attacks on the Eatons not only as proxy political attacks on himself, but as grim reminders of the smears that he and Rachel had suffered from political enemies. Indeed he blamed those insults for her untimely death just weeks after his election. And it was only ten days after Rachel died that John and Peggy Eaton married, as if picking up just at the point where the Jacksons' marriage had been cut short.

While he likely did not take kindly to wisecracks about Peggy Eaton as Rachel Jackson's "lady in waiting," Jackson might well have agreed with Margaret Bayard Smith that the two women were "birds of a feather"—not least in their disregard for assigned gender roles. Rachel Jackson's pipe smoking was another joke among the Washington glitterati, while Peggy, "one of the most ambitious, violent, malignant, yet silly women you ever heard of," would simply not stop insisting that "she *must be* received into society." With the cabinet purge, Smith's frustration only increased:

> Mrs. E. can not be forced or persuaded to leave Washington. Her triumph, for so she calls the dissolution of the cabinet, her triumph she says is not yet complete. All her adversaries are not yet turned out of office, to be sure, three secretaries and a foreign minister are dismissed, but Mr. and Mr. and Mr. remain, they too must go.[22]

It was said, when she first arrived in Washington, that Peggy Eaton was "irresistible and carries whatever point she sets her mind on," and so she proved to be in the crisis. "Mrs. Eaton's affair, at the beginning, was but a spark, but what a conflagration did it cause," and by helping shift Jackson's personal support from Peggy's critic John C. Calhoun to the Eaton-friendly Martin Van Buren, it did its part to change the course of American history.[23]

But Smith's remarks suggest one other striking instance of doubling: Peggy Eaton, it seems, was a proxy not just for Rachel Jackson but also for Andrew himself. He too was ambitious, willful, and, when crossed, insistent on complete vindication (as vividly demonstrated in his fierce resistance to two Senate censure efforts fifteen years apart). Smith describes both Jackson and Peggy Eaton as "violent," a term she freely applies to anyone she deems a "disturber of the peace" of established rank and social order. In both characters the violence arose from the dominance of will and passion; the "despotism of the President's will" was such that even his political mastermind, "the Little Magician" Van Buren, was "unable to govern or direct judgment so weak and passions so strong."[24] Smith and others were convinced that Peggy was now wielding actual power, that "the U.S. are governed by the President—the President by the Secretary of War—& the latter by his Wife," as another observer put it.[25]

Surveying the Petticoat Affair, Smith and Vice President Calhoun both saw it as a sign of the power of women. Calhoun made the point with a southern gentleman's condescension. Jackson, he said, was discrediting himself and the country by interfering in a "ladies' quarrel." It was useless to try "to regulate the intercourse of female society," since government by women is, and always has been, absolute: "the laws of the ladies were like the laws of the Medes and Persians, and admitted neither of argument nor of amendment." For Calhoun, "this important censorship" was "too high and too pure" to yield to political power or influence, and Peggy Eaton's ostracism was a victory "in favor of the morals of the country."[26] Smith, while agreeing that the struggle was one of virtue against vice, was much less sure which of the two was winning. The only timeless lesson was the "impotency of honor and grandeur," as she put it with characteristic gloom. The affair did reveal the power of women, but not in the sense of proving that things never changed. To the contrary, the ancient laws of the ladies were crumbling in the face of recalcitrant women like Peggy Eaton. Power was shifting to those who violated those laws; the high and pure were giving way under the pressure of social and political changes that affected gender roles along with everything else. "Our government," Smith wrote, "is becoming every day more and more democratic, the rulers of the people are truly their servants and among those rulers women are gaining more than their share of power."[27]

To contemporaries who considered "virtue" a matter of policing class boundaries, Andrew Jackson's defense of Peggy Eaton was an act of power and violence, another instance of the new disorder that had made Inauguration Day so upsetting. But from the other side, or from our perspective today, it could just as easily look like an act of chivalry so old-fashioned that it seems quaint. Put another way, the affair was a "scandal" in the truest sense. Analyzing the role of scandal in comedy, Frank McConnell defines the term to mean "a shocking and challenging inversion of our 'normal' expectations about the order of things, a reestablishment of that order on new *and more generous* grounds" whereby people are recalled to their "civilized responsibilities."[28] What participants in the Petticoat Affair saw as virtue challenging vice was really a struggle over those grounds, a contest pitting supposedly "polite society" against the truly civilized. It reflected the inversion of high and low and the new dignity accorded the latter—the new moral standards and claims that accompanied the rise of new political claimants. Smith's appeals to "public opinion" had the plaintive quality we might expect from someone who had witnessed the scene at the White House on Inauguration Day, and who knew that her "public" and the People were no longer the same thing.

Jackson's Comic Foil: The Jack Downing Stories

Frank McConnell's definition of scandal is part of his extended discussion of satire, which in turn—echoing Bakhtin—he links to carnival. In "the ceremonies of carnival, Saturnalia, and public riot" we find "parallels to the satirist's function," he writes. "Satire as a narrative mode generalizes and intellectualizes the atmosphere of carnival." Among other things, satire's carnivalesque intermingling of the frivolous and the serious produces the figure of the "wise fool," an ancient character type—"a king and not a king, a fool whose foolishness fills the vacuum left by the departure of order, and an agent of order whose clowning holds up a funhouse glass to our own distortions of humanity."[29]

A leading wise fool of the Jackson years was Major (originally Captain) Jack Downing, the fictional creation of newspaperman Seba Smith. Destined to become an important, much-imitated figure in the history of American humor, Jack was a plain-spoken Yankee from the imaginary Downingville, "away down east in the State of Maine," a political adventurer who narrated his experiences in letters back home written in the regional dialect. Republished in many newspapers, these letters became a popular running commentary on the political "duins" of the day.[30] Originally a dealer in cheese and ax handles, Jack had wandered by accident onto the local political stage, and he first travels to Washington in response to the Eaton blowup: The president must need a new "secretary," he figures, since so many secretaries had recently been leaving the cabinet. On arriving he encounters John Eaton himself, who is about to fight a duel with the ex-Treasury secretary over Peggy (this, in fact, almost happened) until Jack heroically intervenes. His bravado wins Jack a special military commission and, very soon, a place as President Jackson's closest confidant and all-purpose troubleshooter.

The letters Jack went on to write from this vantage in his distinctive argot became a funhouse glass held up to "the great consarns of the nashon."[31] Their running joke was that in his naiveté, Jack—like Swift's Gulliver, or like Diedrich Knickerbocker but less heavy-handedly—reveals more of the truth of events than he himself understands. Jack's letters were so popular that other writers and newspapers were soon producing imitations ("counterfeits," the original Jack calls them), and the character sometimes appeared at Jackson's side in political cartoons. And even before all this acclaim persuades Jack that he might run for president himself, it is clear that he and Jackson, the rustic Major and "the old Gineral," are in many ways each other's doubles—two unpolished provincials thrust forward to run the country. Like Jack, Andrew Jackson is just a plain fellow, a man who understands backwoods arts like "raccoonin and skunkin" as well as Jack does and can swap stories on these subjects all night long.[32] (Of course, since Jack narrates all this, Jackson is always heard speaking in Jack's own dialect.) True, Jackson's followers may be a rabble willing to "tare the country to pieces." But Jackson himself "isn't a Jacksonite, you know," insists Jack. "He's a true republican as there is in Downingville."[33]

Jack's first assignment for the president is to lead a militia back to his home state of Maine, where a border dispute over timberlands had recently flared up with Canada. Like Jackson himself in his younger days, Jack is all set to defend the frontiers against a British invasion—until the matter is peaceably settled, seemingly in Britain's favor (a disappointing development for Jack and his troops, as he complains in a letter headed "Madawaska, State of Maine, or else Great Britain, I dont know

Major Jack Downing's handshake doubles for an exhausted President Jackson's. Wood engraving by J. W. Orr, 1859.

which").[34] Later, Jack accompanies the president on a tour, or "progress," of the eastern cities. During one of his appearances on this tour,
Jackson "shook hands with all his might an hour or two, till he got so
tired he couldn't hardly stand it" and had to lie down on a bench. The
crowd kept coming, and "when he couldn't shake he'd nod to 'em as
they come along. And at last he got so beat out, he couldn't only wrinkle
his forehead and wink. Then," says Jack, "I kind of stood behind him
and reached my arm round under his, and shook for him for about a
half an hour as tight as I could spring."[35] Already his sometime stand-in,
Jack becomes the president's "hand"-in, a comically literal extension of
him. It is clear where all this is leading: Jack is soon grooming himself to
be Jackson's successor. After all, he is already the "second best man in
the Government (I and the Gineral bein pretty much the hull on't)."[36]

The presidency should logically follow, and Martin Van Buren would just have to step aside.[37]

As a court jester whose function is to "lampoon the royalty of the court itself," Jack Downing is, in McConnell's terms, a character who combines elements of both the *aladzon* and the *eiron*: "the braggart and the ironist," twinned types that Aristotle identified as basic to comedy.[38] There were plenty of unreliable narrators and even some Yankee bumpkins in earlier literature, but using one to double the president made possible a remarkable range and subtlety of effects. This, presumably, is why Jack could be taken up by different writers: they could use him to modulate their presentations of Jackson, adjusting degrees of sympathy and silliness as their own politics and the situation demanded. In the Downing stories, the joke is not always on Jackson. At times he seems to share his ingenuous aide's cracker-barrel shrewdness; when, for instance, he travels to Harvard to become an honorary Doctor of Laws, the president explains the proceedings to Jack by observing that "there's a pesky many of them are laws passed by Congress, that are rickety things. Some of 'em have very poor constitutions, and some of 'em haven't no constitutions at all. So that it is necessary to have somebody there to Doctor 'em up a little."[39] A misunderstanding like this is classic wise foolishness, an accidental insight that is truer than fact. Jack is to Jackson as the Fool is to King Lear (as at least one cartoonist sketched him). The Downing stories illustrate McConnell's point that "the figures of *aladzon* and *eiron* form a symbiosis," that the two are "mirror twins," and that "In many of the richest and most compelling satires . . . that twinship collapses into a more complicated unity. The braggart and the ironist, the fool as loudmouth and the fool as victim can become a single, heroic and antiheroic, figure."[40] Jack is such a dual figure, and because he doubles Jackson, a similarly complicated unity informs the image of Jackson he conveys. For all their foibles, both characters have a measure of our rooting interest.

This was important in terms of placing Jackson within the churning social energies of the time, energies of which he was the symbol and leading champion but could also become the victim himself. A newly assertive population of crude, blunt, and politically excitable Americans— or so they seemed to some, especially visitors from abroad—was not very deferential even to generals and presidents. With "the decent dignity of a private conveyance not being deemed necessary for the President of the United States," Jackson traveled by riverboat like anyone else, and one foreign tourist who saw him aboard one while he was mourning Rachel was aghast that any "greasy fellow" was free to walk right up to him and ask:

> "General Jackson, I guess?"
> The General bowed assent.
> "Why they told me you was dead."
> "No! Providence has hitherto preserved my life."
> "And is your wife alive too?"
> The General, apparently much hurt, signified the contrary, upon which the courtier concluded his harangue, by saying, "Aye, I thought it was the one or the t'other of ye."

To European observers, loutishness like this proved that "however meritorious the American character may be, it is not amiable."[41]

Even so, a people's president had to move among the people, and some of these did not hesitate to take their grievances straight to the top. In a later, more famous riverboat encounter, a young stranger approached Jackson with the apparent intention of shaking his hand. As Jack Downing fancifully recalled the real-life event, Jackson reached out to oblige—and then

> dab went one of the fellow's hands slap into the president's face.
> In a moment I levelled my umbrella at the villain's head, and came pesky near fetching him to the floor. . . . But, my stars, I wish you could have seen the President jest at that minute. If you ever see a lion lying down asleep and a man come along with a great club and hit him a polt with all his might, and then see that lion spring on his feet, and see the fire flash in his eyes, and hear him roar and gnash his teeth, you might give some sort of a guess what kind of a harrycane we had of it.
> The old Gineral no sooner felt the fellow's paw in his face than he sprung like a steel-trap, and catched his cane and went at him. . . . I dont think but he would have kicked the feller through the side of the steam-boat in two minutes.[42]

As it turned out, the assailant in this case was a victim of the Eaton Malaria—a young Navy officer who believed that Jackson's role in the affair had cost him his commission. His real aim had been to pull Jackson's nose, a ritual act of degradation that the low ranking could inflict on their social superiors.[43] (Jack Downing, of course, was not really present, but among those said to have joined in chasing the miscreant was Washington Irving.)

Incidents like these sparked debate on the place of the presidency in American life. Alexis de Tocqueville had marveled at finding the White

Wielding an umbrella, Major Jack Downing and others defend President Jackson (*left*) against a riverboat assailant who tried to pull his nose. Wood engraving by J. W. Orr, 1859.

House unguarded, and there were those who held such facts to be "the glory of the Republic." No doubt, some who asserted this were Jackson critics who did not mind seeing a bit of mob disorder turned back on the man they blamed for stirring it up. If the great "Democracy" was now to be celebrated, well, so much the worse for the leading Democrat. For purposes of getting his nose pulled, wrote one editorialist, Jackson, his assailant, and for that matter the White House doorman were all on the same footing, legally no different than any of "the humblest private inhabitants." Perhaps in England, "such an assault upon the person of the KING would be HIGH TREASON—but there is no king in the U. States!"[44]

Or, rather, there was a king who was not a king, a figure who by turns could be both agent of order and the clown who filled the vacuum left when order departed. In the same weeks that Jackson was traveling east and fending off nose pullers, this point would be made with considerably more artistry by another and quite different *eiron*—a real-life satirical foil whom Jackson himself unwittingly contrived to give the public.

"The Gallant Mr. Hawk": Jackson's Indian Alter-Ego

Andrew Jackson would have been remembered as a scourge of American Indians even without the help of Makataimeshekiakiak, the Sauk warrior who was known to whites as "Black Hawk" and whose brief and futile 1832 rebellion came to be called the Black Hawk War. By contrast with a huge forced migration like the infamous Trail of Tears, the removal of the Fox and Sauk tribes (or Sac or Asakiwaki) from western Illinois and Wisconsin was straightforward, a simple matter of enforcing the terms of the usual dubiously obtained treaty. Black Hawk's resistance to this, as he explained it, was driven by his paternal responsibility for his tribe's women and children. To white officials, though, it was the Indians who were "children," as they were customarily called, and who depended on the largesse of "the Great Father" in Washington.[45] Indians, that is, ranked alongside Margaret Bayard Smith's "boys, negros, women, children" in the conventional anthropology of the day.

But of course they were also a special case, members of their own societies that in some respects doubled the white man's. Some Indians tried to turn this to their advantage. In 1831, when the Cherokees sought the U.S. Supreme Court's protection against the encroaching states, they declared themselves eager to match their society against that of their "white brethren." Chief Justice John Marshall conceded the point, writing in *Cherokee Nation v. Georgia* that the Cherokees were rapidly achieving a "greater degree of civilization" by mimicking white institutions, including a three-branch government on the U.S. model.[46] Nonetheless he rejected their plea for relief; the Indians' "state of pupilage," he declared, was that of "a ward to his guardian."

Marshall's landmark opinion rested on a narrow parsing of language, even though (or, because) the Cherokees' basic claims were correct. Such rhetorical maneuvers—asserting legal technicalities in lieu of what is obviously right—are a common way of safeguarding an oppressive policy. But they do nothing to extinguish the claims or lessen the moral stature of the victims, which may, in fact, actually be enhanced. Indians had a right to their dignity that became that much more apparent the more ignominiously they were treated. Driving the "red children" off their lands only drove them further onto the moral high ground.

This was the point that the Great Father seems to have missed when, in one of the odder moves in the history of presidential scheduling, he agreed to go head-to-head with Black Hawk in a test of popular approval. The defeated Indian warrior, now in U.S. Army custody, was to be sent on a progress through the eastern cities in the summer of 1833, and this grand tour would parallel one that Jackson himself was about to make. Bringing recalcitrant Indians east had long been a way of subduing and intimidating them. The idea was to "conduct [them] through the principal cities, with a view to exhibit to them the extent of the population and of the country, its wealth, resources, and means of defence, and to impress them with a conviction of its strength and power." Urging that this approach be applied to Black Hawk, one newspaper predicted "lasting good consequences," while another approved of the president's determination to let Black Hawk "see, with his own eyes, that it is vain to war with the *pale faces*."[47]

With some Indians this method worked to a fault. George Catlin, who was inspired to travel the territories painting his famous Indian portraits when he came across one such tour, tells the story of the Assiniboine warrior Wijunjon, "Pigeon's Egg Head," who was so taken with polite society in the East—including his entrée to presidential receptions—that he made himself over completely in the white man's image, winding up as an overdressed fop:

> On his hands he had drawn a pair of white kid gloves, and in them held, a blue umbrella in one, and a large fan in the other. In this fashion was poor Wi-jun-jon metamorphosed, on his return [home] from Washington; and, in this plight was he strutting and whistling Yankee Doodle. . . . I could never look upon him for a moment without excessive laughter, at the ridiculous figure he cut—the strides, the angles, the stiffness of this travelling beau!

Striking poses and belaboring his tales of the wondrous East, Wijunjon gradually wore out his fancy frock coat, his U.S. military dress uniform— a typical presidential gift—and his tribespeople's patience. He wound up a tattered figure, a living example of the blustering *aladzon* whose effort to grasp white prestige literally by the coattails comically devoured itself: "He sank rapidly into disgrace in his tribe; his high claims to Political eminence all vanished; he was reputed worthless—the greatest liar of his nation."[48]

In Black Hawk's case, too, the eastern tour misfired with comic results. But this time the joke was not on the Indian. President Jackson had apparently miscalculated how "irresistibly attractive" Indians could be, in Margaret Bayard Smith's words. As "nature's own nobility" they were "majestic in their appearance, dignified, graceful and lofty in their demeanour." Smith recalled another group of Indians that had visited the White House years earlier; their "*democratic popularity*" had easily out-shone that of fancy-dress ambassadors from the courts of Europe.[49] And popular enthusiasm was even higher for Black Hawk, whose little war had passed almost instantly into romantic legend.[50] The "distin-guished" warrior and his compatriots, said various observers, "behaved themselves with much decorum and propriety" and seemed at least as "enlightened and civilized" as whites. In appearance they were "rather like statues from some master hand, than like beings of a race whom we had heard characterised as degenerate and debased." Black Hawk him-self had "a high forehead, a Roman nose [and] a very fine eye" and as-sumed "the aspect of command" even in defeat.[51]

In short, Black Hawk compared very favorably with Jackson. They were fellow soldiers and "two great men" of remarkably similar charac-ter. Even in "civilized and refined society" one rarely found such "native magnanimity and greatness," wrote one phrenologist whose analysis of the bumps on Black Hawk's head revealed very high quotients of "firm-ness," "self-esteem," "combativeness," and "individuality"—every trait, in fact, that one might expect in a great white leader too. (With one ex-ception: Black Hawk was low on "hope.")[52]

Whether or not Jackson saw these parallels, they were not lost on Black Hawk. Arriving in Washington under guard, he and his compa-triots called on Jackson at the White House. The Great Father gave his errant Indian children the official scolding that was customary on such occasions, then presented Black Hawk with a military uniform, received the gift of an Indian war bonnet, and smoked the Indians' ritual peace pipe. The president, Black Hawk noted, was "a *great brave!*" of precisely his own age. This fact seemed to cast Jackson's career in the same vale-dictory twilight as his own. "He is old and I am old. We shall soon go to the Great Spirit, where we shall rest."[53]

From Washington, Black Hawk and company went on parade through the East. Jackson's parallel tour not only stopped in the same cities but, at times, put the two great braves at the same events. In Balti-more they attended the same theater, and the problem quickly became clear: "Black Hawk is said to have attracted as much attention as the President." Similar scenes recurred in Philadelphia and New York.[54]

"The Grand National Caravan, Moving East." This July 1833 lithograph from Endicott & Swett of New York was evidently meant to satirize President Jackson's eastern "progress." The pseudonymous artist puts Jackson at the head of a burlesque parade that includes Black Hawk and a band of caged Indians under the banner of the "Rights of Man."

Another lithograph drawn by the same artist later that year mockingly praises Jackson as leader of a motley crowd of clowns and carnival figures in a "Grand Fantastical Parade."

Andrew Jackson portrait by Asher Brown Durand, 1835.

One foreign tourist said the two figures "divided public attention. . . . The chief of the white men, and the chief of the red, were alike objects of curiosity, the President holding a levee by day, the Hawk by night." But, he wryly added, "The ladies declared in favor of Black Hawk, some of them actually kissing him, which, it is said, affected the *President's* health."[55]

Black Hawk portrait by Robert M. Sully, painted at the time of Black Hawk's 1833 "progress" or eastern tour. Dressed "*a la mode de* President," the recently captured Indian warrior was widely seen as upstaging and possibly lampooning Jackson. (Black Hawk, Wisconsin Historical Society, Image ID 11706)

Newspapers, too, were full of "Blackhawkiana." With hundreds of thousands of people clamoring to see the Indians, the public's rising "Black Hawk-ism" was making for uncomfortable comparisons between his popularity and Jackson's. At a time when Jackson was getting his nose pulled, Black Hawk was encountering crowds so large that they prevented his boat from landing and made the streets impassable, forcing him to be smuggled ashore (in a move reminiscent of Jackson's own escape from his chaotic inaugural). The president's tour was quickly turning "rude" and "supremely ridiculous."[56]

Worse, the Indians' upstaging (or "Black Hawking") of Jackson was beginning to look deliberate.[57] Black Hawk seemed resolved "not to be out done even by the General," one critic charged, and Jack Downing was sure that the "little, old, dried up Indian king" wasn't just getting as much attention as the president's party but was also "taking the shine off us a little."[58] Like Wijunjon, Black Hawk began to dress the part of a white gentleman. But this time the frock coat and top hat seemed to fit. Carrying himself "*a la mode de* President," he greeted crowds from balconies, doffed his hat, and "bow[ed] to the multitude with un[ex]ceptionable grace."[59] In at least one case, Jackson himself is said to have seen a news report claiming that the crowd's adulation was "a satire on that shown to the President. It was the same as saying, we look at both pretty much in the same light."[60] Apparently concluding that "Twin stars keep not their orbits in one sphere," as one newspaper put it, the president finally parted company with Black Hawk and had him sent back west by a different route.[61] Thus Jackson "admitted spiritual defeat at the hands of an Indian whom he had doomed, he thought, to public chastisement."[62]

Cynics believed that the "the gallant Mr. Hawk" they were seeing was an act, a crafty effort to take advantage of whites' confusion over social rank.[63] One complained that Black Hawk "has rather too much of the gentleman about him, and comes in for too large a share of that flattery, which belongs solely to the greatest and best."[64] Another sneered that his was merely an "*assumed* dignity." All the attention, said this critic, could tempt the Indians to make more wars just so they would get more tours.[65] We cannot, of course, be sure what Black Hawk intended. But given his honor-based view of leadership and status, the anxieties of the white elite on these points would have been no mystery to him.[66] He also seems to have had a sardonic wit. There's a possible *double entendre* in his words of gratitude after the tour: "We saw many of the white men, who treated us with kindness, and we thank them. . . . We never saw so many white men before."[67] Yes, many more than his guides had intended. They had hoped, as Jackson himself had put it, to overawe the Indians with the sheer number of whites while putting the two groups on friendlier terms, but no one had ordered revival-style throngs or white women queuing for Indian kisses.[68] The admiring gaze was not supposed to be quite that mutual.

And there is evidence that Black Hawk and his fellows were well aware of the importance of appearances. "The time and great care bestowed by them at their toilette," said one report, "would put the foppery of a civilized beau completely to the blush."[69] Yet the result, in their case, was nothing like the tragic ridiculousness of a Wijunjon with his umbrella and kid gloves. Black Hawk's doubling of white leaders and their public style was a work of performance art. In the one case the actor's authority was undermined, in the other it was under*scored*. Pigeon's Egg Head had been foolish, but Black Hawk had played the fool, which is quite a different thing: "the satiric mode, the moment of the fool, is somehow always the moment of mockery, of *imitation* of the nobility whose absence it celebrates," in Frank McConnell's words.[70] As a military leader, Black Hawk had no success whatsoever—and yet, today, there are U.S. Army helicopters called Black Hawks, not Pigeons or Egg Heads. (Or even Atkinsons: The general whose troops defeated Black Hawk is all but forgotten.) War and its chaos were not Black Hawk's true métier. He and his fellows were models of self-possession; it was the whites crowding around them who were reduced to a mob.

The Double Aspect of the World

One witness to Black Hawk's progress was moved to put his analysis into verse:

> *He* fought for *Independence* too—
> *He* struck for *Freedom*—with a few
> Unconquered souls. . . .
> But fought in vain—for 'tis decreed,
> His race must fail, and yours succeed.[71]

This comparison puts Black Hawk on a par with George Washington, albeit with a fatalism meant to assure whites that there was not going to be a successful Indian War of Independence. But in the same weeks that the old Indian warrior was playing parody-king in the Jackson administration's inadvertent traveling carnival, a similar analogy was being offered to quite different effect. Jackson's Indian policies had provoked another small uprising in Massachusetts, where a dwindling band of Christianized Mashpee Indians was resisting efforts to drive them off Cape Cod. The leader and spokesman for those Indians, William Apess, relied in making their case on a rhetoric of wholesale doubling—a comparison like the Cherokees' between Indian and white societies, but this time extended to include the whites' own myths of origin. Indians were a "Looking-Glass for the White Man," as Apess put it in the title of one of his polemics. Apess himself, a Pequot who was also a Methodist minister, presumably felt the doubleness acutely. Speaking "with an energy that alarmed some of the whites present considerably," rather as Peggy Eaton had done in the parlors of Washington, Apess seized and refashioned the values of white society into a broad defense of Indian history and conduct.[72]

Thus, Apess argued, the event that signaled the start of the Mashpee revolt—a tussle over hay wagons that white authorities condemned as a "riot"—was merely an Indian counterpart to the Boston Tea Party.[73] Even more boldly, Apess lectured white audiences on the virtues of Metacomet, the "King Philip" of the Wampanoags, whose war against Puritan settlers in the late seventeenth century was remembered in white Massachusetts with horror. In his "Eulogy on King Philip" he drew parallels between this much-feared chief and George Washington, to the point of challenging the Washington cult directly by calling Philip "the greatest man that was ever in America." According to Apess, Washington himself had borrowed military tactics from Philip, one of whose maneuvers was "equal, if not superior, to that of Washington crossing the Delaware." And when seen in this looking glass, the white settlers whom Philip fought were "worse than heathens": it was they, not the Indians, who rained down barbarism and chaos on peaceful, civilized communities.[74]

Here again is the claim that seeming disruptiveness is really the higher order. The excluded minority that so-called civilization has defined itself against, and that happens to be causing trouble or stirring things up, is the true vehicle of civilization's values. We might say that what Black Hawk was doing to the current president, Apess tried to do to white America as a whole. The dialectic of civility and disruptiveness—the ironic notion that the most unpolished and uncouth character may, *thanks to those very qualities*, be the true gallant, the "worthy," the "politest" in the sense of being most attuned to what a *polity* needs—is in Apess's hands both generalized and racialized, put to work to explain the experience of entire peoples. And though Indians won few such arguments, the idea itself has indeed become part of popular myth. The triumph of the underdog, the vindication of hidden virtues in the ostracized or disdained, are not uniquely American tales but are certainly among those that Americans love to retell.[75] In their American form they include the basic question that Apess posed, a question that resonates through U.S. history especially in matters of civil rights: Is the founding just a museum exhibit, or is it an unfinished, ongoing project that the nation intends to continue? Will its promises be extended to those originally left out, and if so, why not now?

In yet another interesting coincidence, Black Hawk's 1833 tour included a Philadelphia theater where he "managed to sleep through the play until the applauses of the audience at the song 'Jim Crow' waked him up." The weary Indian "endured the first repetition with tolerable resignation; but on its being encored for the fourth time louder than ever, cried out, *'Peccabogo agankitchigamink pitchilazo,'*—'When these barbarians come to visit me I shall treat them to a concert of wild cats.'"[76] This remarkable report is a reminder that the musical act "Jump Jim Crow" had also gone on tour, just a year ahead of Black Hawk, thereby touching off the long-lived fad of blackface minstrelsy—that strange and (supposedly) comic instance of white counter-masking whose name has echoed through generations of American racial struggle. The writer who recorded Black Hawk's irritation saw the irony of an Indian whose tastes were more refined than the whites'. But that writer could not have known just how barbaric the performance, and how apt the Indian's critique, would eventually come to seem. What "Jump Jim Crow" proved was that carnivalesque tricks, like the masking and associated race-mingling that had once made carnival a threat to officialdom, can also be seized back and used to reinforce official roles. In a familiar theatrical metaphor, Margaret Bayard Smith described her "disappointed, exhausted, worn out" Washington friends, the elite whose long "drama" had ended with Andrew Jackson's arrival, as leaving the stage and throwing off their masks. In the new drama it was the Jacksonians who would be the "eager, animated actors"—who would play the fool, as it were—until they in turn, "silent and forgotten," surrendered the stage to someone else.[77]

Ash Wednesday, the day of Jackson's inauguration, is not the day of carnival; it's one day later, the moment *after* the moment of the fool. To borrow a later president's phrase, it's the return to normalcy: the (literally) sobering moment at which order resumes. Though it's the endpoint toward which carnivals like Mardi Gras aim, and though anticipation of it is what brings on the frivolity, in itself it's about being responsible for things. And so it was for Jackson. The carnivalesque folk energies that briefly made him Lord of Misrule also made him the actual chief magistrate, and if anything they increased the cross-pressures on him as he struggled for the next eight years to make national policy:

> Well then, Jackson did change. He was *for* the single term—he was *against* it: I confess the fact. He was *for* the Protective system—he was *against* it: I agree to it. He was *for* a National Bank—he was *against* it: what of that? He was *for* the distribution of the surplus, and again he was *against* it: I know it. He was *for* Internal Improvements;—he changed his mind—he was *against* them. Then again, sirs, he was *against* the interference of officers in the elections;—he was sorry for it, and took the other tack. He was *against* the appointment of members of congress—in theory;—in practice he was *for* it. . . . Sirs, it is the glory of his character that he has been *for* and *against* every thing; . . . How else can we be with the majority?

This passage is from John Pendleton Kennedy's 1840 satire *Quodlibet*. It states a complaint often lodged against politicians, but here it is both made specific to Jackson and generalized to democracy as such. To Kennedy, an anti-Jackson congressman, Jackson's doubleness was just what majority rule is all about: It's like "the divine rainbow spanning the earth with its arch, and changing with the sun, now in the East, now in the West."[78]

Even to a more admiring commentator, Jackson was the oxymoronic man:

> Andrew Jackson . . . was a patriot and a traitor. He was one of the greatest of generals, and wholly ignorant of the art of war. A writer brilliant, elegant, eloquent, and without being able to compose a correct sentence, or spell words of four syllables. The first of statesmen, he never devised, he never framed a measure. He was the most candid of men, and was capable of the profoundest dissimulation. A most law-defying, law-obeying citizen. A stickler for discipline, he never hesitated to disobey his superior. A democratic aristocrat. An urbane savage. An atrocious saint.[79]

To commentators of his time, Jackson was simultaneously "King Andrew the First" and "the majority's slave."[80] The "double aspect of the world" glimpsed in carnival and satire was something he carried in his person.

And it was not just his contemporaries who turned to doubles as a way of making sense of Jackson. Modern historians, too, have described Jacksonianism as a matter of dualities, or even of contradictions in terms. The "Jacksonian Persuasion," as Marvin Meyers calls it, reflected the paradoxes of the developing national culture, including an oxymoronic quality that Meyers labels "venturous conservatism."[81] John William Ward argues that Jackson spoke for an ideal of "cultivated nature" whereby Americans defined themselves over against barbaric Indians, on the one hand, and the overcivilized British on the other—the two forces that Jackson had militarily vanquished.[82] Jackson represented "a rejection of two extremes," although what we have seen here is that the phenomenon might also be described as a dialect of doubling: a codependence in which each extreme begets the other.[83] The reason that Jackson could become the "symbol for an age," as Ward calls him, was that his own doubleness made him the right man to double his constituents. One British visitor at the time noted Americans' "ludicrous" taste for militia titles, like that of the local worthy who called himself "General" because he had once been surveyor-general of his district. Like "Major" Jack Downing, any nondescript provincial could project himself onto "the old Gineral"—could receive a commission from him, as it were—and thereby stake a claim to political and social status. He could even imagine himself taking the great man's place. Questioning whether any citizen was really qualified to be president once got this visitor "so heartily scolded," she wrote, "that I shall never again venture to doubt it."[84]

And while ordinary citizens were projecting themselves onto Jackson, Jackson in turn could be projected back onto them, tracking his image into their worlds as his followers had tracked mud into the White House. They could find themselves "bear[ing] his impress," one complained, to the point that "a man can't get shaved without feeling his presence" on the razor box:

> We have Jackson hats, and Jackson coats and Jackson jackets, and Jackson trousers, and Jackson boots, and Jackson slippers. From our public squares to the country taverns,—from the Hall of State to our modest homes, all is Jackson, Jackson, Jackson.—Why, sir, a man can't enter into the retirement of his bed-chamber, but he may see [Jackson's] head, his services, and maybe now, sir, his wounds displayed upon the curtains of his windows, or his couch.[85]

Jacksonianism made itself felt in everyday life because it was the political expression of a social revolution, the moment when "the Democracy" claimed to be the People and not just an unruly mob. This claim was not simply a matter of following rules already established, nor of overthrowing one set of rules for another. It was more like a new vision of what being "ruly" really meant. As revealed in these instances of scandal, satire, and unintended comedy, a society's ordering values can make a mess of the actually existing social order. Jackson's gallantry toward his friends, the Eatons, required waving aside protocol and turning "polite" society upside-down; a navy officer's attempt to vindicate his honor yielded a scene of indignity bordering on slapstick; and the public reflexes developed in part for presidents on tour produced crowds clamoring for glimpses of an Indian warrior tipping his top hat. In each case the mob scene, the surface appearance of turmoil, could be taken as the higher realization of order. And it was higher because it was lower, an irruption of the rabble-roused, which, in the ongoing carnival of Andrew Jackson's America, could no longer be fully contained.

Duplicity and the Divided Nation:
Fictions of Racial and Sectional Conflict

In one of his occasional ventures into literary criticism, Sigmund Freud wrote an essay attempting to explain, psychologically, why "the double" appears as often as it does as a figure in literature and art. According to Freud, doubling evokes "a very early mental stage, long since surmounted . . . a regression to a time when the ego had not yet marked itself off sharply from the external world and from other people." Human consciousness depends on "self-observation," the splitting off of one part of the self to monitor the rest. The various ghosts and doppelgängers met with in fantasy and horror stories are frightening because they make visible this repressed feature of our minds, "which ought to have remained hidden but has come to light."[86]

Freudian theory, in short, makes doubling a prerequisite for psychological depth, and it uses this hypothesis to explain the popularity of certain kinds of characters in fiction. And whether we accept Freud's view or not, it does stand to reason that doubleness of a kind is bound to figure in characters of any complexity. What makes characters psychologically interesting are inner conflicts, hidden urges, and present behavior that bears traces of past traumas. At their most subtle, realistic characters are not just collections of traits; they are systems in motion, products of ongoing negotiations between opposed possibilities: intention and impulse, feeling and thought, desire and scruple, the conscious and the unconscious.

With that in mind, it is worth comparing two literary portraits of statesmen from the period at hand. The first is Daniel Webster's eulogy for John Adams and Thomas Jefferson, written shortly after the two ex-presidents' remarkably timed deaths on July 4, 1826, the fiftieth anniversary of independence. Webster asks his listeners to cast their minds back over those five decades and imagine themselves at the Continental Congress:

> Let us, then, bring before us the assembly, which was about to decide a question thus big with the fate of empire. Let us open their doors and look upon their deliberations. Let us survey the anxious and care-worn countenances, let us hear the firm-toned voices, of this band of patriots.

The eulogy goes on to recall, almost to re-enact, the assembly's great deliberations and the patriotic roles that Webster's two subjects played in them.

Needless to say, "care-worn countenances" and "firm-toned voices" are not literal descriptions. They are more like the character epithets in Homer's epics: The revolutionary Congress's *task* was wearing, yet its members were firm in meeting it, so these facts must have registered in their faces and voices. By projecting the political situation onto the characters' bodies, Webster is performing the literary equivalent of chiseling them in marble—a prerequisite for standing Adams and Jefferson side-by-side in the same national pantheon as the beatified Washington.[87]

Although it starts with the same formula, "Let us," and likewise lingers on facial expressions, a passage like the following—from just ten years later—seems written in a different style altogether:

> Let us again intrude into the sanctuary of majesty. The President is alone, as before. He has the same air of somewhat impatient expectation. A shade of anxious thought is on his brow, and his cheek is flushed with some little excitement. Yet these elements are all so mixed as to be scarcely perceptible; and were he conscious that we are looking at him, they would be completely concealed.

Here the writer, judge, and Southern advocate Nathaniel Beverley Tucker is describing President Martin Van Buren, a Northerner, in an 1836 novel, *The Partisan Leader*—a fiction written in response to and in hopes of fanning the flames of the growing sectional conflict.[88]

Compared to the stereotyped, care-worn faces of Webster's patriots, Van Buren's face is seen in this passage in close, vivid focus: a brow, a flushed cheek, a "shade" of anxiety. And as we surveil this secluded figure, the details accumulate. He displays "a mixture of thought and carelessness," glances at his watch and the door, acts disengaged while "throwing himself against the arm of his sofa," and

> seemed, too, not wholly unconscious of something worthy of admiration in a foot, the beauty of which was displayed to the best advantage by the tight fit and high finish of his delicate slipper. As he lay back on the sofa, his eye rested complacently on this member, which was stretched out before him, its position shifting, as if unconsciously, into every variety of grace. Returning from thence, his glance rested on his hand, fair, delicate, small, and richly jewelled. It hung carelessly on the arm of the sofa, and the fingers of this, too, as if rather from instinct than volition, performed sundry evolutions on which the eye of majesty dwelt with gentle complacency.[89]

Unlike Webster, with his neoclassical orating, Tucker gives us realistic details—an apparently private moment featuring actions that seem to emanate from the depths of the character. The details might or might not be *accurate*: While he was said to be evasive in a way that came to be called "Van Buren-ish," we do not know precisely how the real Martin Van Buren mixed thought and carelessness, let alone how much he admired his own foot.[90] Regardless, such details are "realistic" in the technical sense of the term. Realism does not necessarily mean faithful copying; it refers to an artist's agenda and a mode of representation. Tucker's writing evokes a real place, time, and social milieu; it focuses attention on the thoughts, emotions, and behavior of individuals; and it gives that behavior plausible motives and consequences. The cynicism and deviousness of the novel's Van Buren suggest hidden depths, a more complex inner life than, for instance, that of the blankly inscrutable George Washington of James Fenimore Cooper's *The Spy*. Cooper's Washington was two people, himself and the undercover "Mr. Harper," but the second of those was a literal disguise.[91] Tucker's Van Buren, by contrast, does not need a disguise—or rather, disguising himself is his normal behavior, a reflection of who he is. "Were he conscious that we are looking at him," says Tucker's narrator, Van Buren's emotions "would be completely concealed." If anything, details like these are all the *more* realistic for being inherently fictive: The illusion of close focus that makes them seem present to us depends on novelistic omniscience—on a narrator who knows what the character would do even in situations that haven't occurred, and what emotions or mental states he has even when they cannot be seen.

Of course, Webster and Tucker were writing with different aims and in different genres. Webster is looking back to celebrate the moment when Adams's Massachusetts and Jefferson's Virginia could come together and form the Union. Instructing us in their greatness while supposedly reminding us of it, he asks us to survey his subjects' "care-worn" faces by way of cementing a public legend that was not yet firmly fixed. (Many in his audience would undoubtedly have remembered their one-time hatred of Adams or, especially, Jefferson.) Tucker, a Virginian, believed the Union had failed, and his "Tale of the Future" looks ahead to the coming moment when it would break apart. He purports to chip *away* the public facade, to uncover the secrets that public men cynically construct legends in order to hide. Tucker foresaw Van Buren not only succeeding Jackson but becoming the Cromwellian "usurper" of the Northern states—a dictator whose rule would split the faltering Union, thus obliging the noble *South* to make war in hopes of saving it.[92] The reason to enter the sanctuary and gaze on *this* subject's face is to see past his deviousness, to glimpse emotions we would not otherwise know he had. Even then, Tucker's Van Buren is such a master of deception that those emotions are "scarcely perceptible," which is why the facial changes that register them are so realistically tiny. Van Buren, Tucker suggests, is a man who cannot be understood without doing as he himself does: *ignoring* outward shows of honor or virtue and cynically probing for the self-interested truth.

In the end, though, the apparent differences are misleading. Webster's weary but firm patriots and Tucker's traitorous usurper are fictive constructions of essentially the same kind. The Van Buren in Tucker's novel is a simpler character than he seems. He's a symbolic figure, like one of the Vices in a medieval morality play. Tucker's ultimate purpose is not truly to parse the personality of his real-life subject. Rather, his Van Buren feels and thinks the way he does because he embodies the calculating, remorseless Northern tyranny that Tucker and his compatriots believed was seeking to annihilate the South. In his own way he's as much an embodiment of the nation as George Washington had once been. The difference is that the nation he embodies *is itself divided,* and this dividedness manifests itself in the person. Outwardly the leader of the whole Republic, Tucker's Van Buren is actually the "partisan" leader, a conniving agent of the North. His inner depth and complexity, the qualities that make him seem realistic, are therefore not actually his. Deviousness and malice are qualities of Northern rule, traits that actually belong to another "character" altogether: the (increasingly dis-)United States.

In the years between Jackson's administration and Lincoln's, that character was disintegrating: literally, losing its oneness. It was not yet two things—the Union was intact, for the moment—but it had no one clear meaning or purpose any more than does a complex character like Hamlet or Lear. In struggling through image and language to present it as a singularity, a text like Webster's is arguably fictionalizing to a greater degree, even while recounting things that really happened, than is Tucker's frankly fantasized vision of the future. *All* these early portrayals are finally static and at most two-dimensional, the presidents in them like caricatures in editorial cartoons—which also can be (and often were, in this period) drawn in realistic detail even when their true content was crude, one-sided polemic. What really distinguishes the Van Buren of *The Partisan Leader* from the characters in Webster's eulogy, or from early fictionalizations of George Washington, or even from the Andrew Jackson of the Jack Downing stories, is not actual character depth—although it's presented as this—but the political assumptions that the characters are used to personify. American Union was achieved partly through legends of the founders, particularly Washington, a character of *such* complete integrity (= singleness) that his virtues were all present in childhood and he could not tell a lie. The President Van Buren that we find in Tucker's novel is a living lie, a character of near-total duplicity (= doubleness). He lives and breathes the forces leading to disunion, as Tucker saw them. And if the political upshot of this was eventually war, the literary upshot was realism, or some first efforts toward it—fictional leaders who seemed to have inner battlefields and redoubts of their own.

Other works in the years leading up to the Civil War likewise made characters and stories out of the nation's great racial and regional divisions. Their purpose was often to stoke passions and intensify the divisions but, sometimes, to satirize them. John Beauchamp Jones, a writer who would later work in and chronicle the Confederacy's War Department, tried at different times to do both. The title character of his 1852 *Adventures of Col. Gracchus Vanderbomb, of Sloughcreek, in Pursuit of the Presidency* is a comic antihero, a provincial political naïf modeled on both Jack Downing and Don Quixote. Son of a cross-border marriage,

Vanderbomb spends one-third of his time in the North, one-third in the South, and one-third in a literal house divided: his estate and its mansion, "Halfway House," precisely straddle the line, with rooms in the North tended by white servants and rooms in the South by slaves. As a man of neither region he decides he is the perfect candidate for president, ready to champion both slaveholding and abolition with equal vigor depending on the audience he happens to be speaking to. So Vanderbomb and his Sancho Panza, a Latin tutor named Plutarch, set off on a quest for votes, and the result is a series of misadventures as they antagonize Northerners and Southerners alike.

A few years later, with war looming, Jones offered a more serious fictional treatment of presidential leadership in the crisis. *Border War: A Tale of Disunion*, published in 1859, described the coming conflict in photo-negative reverse: determined to preserve the Union, the wise and virtuous President Randolph leads forces of the South against savage Northern rebels in league with the British.[93] Randolph's daughter Alice, a Southern partisan, appears in a subplot as best friend to the daughter of a Northern senator, whose wedding to the son of a Southern senator is postponed by the war. When Washington, D.C., is at last liberated from the Northern "Despot" and the wedding goes forward, Alice's role in uniting the senators' children parallels her father's in reuniting their states.

"The President's Daughter" was also the original subject (and subtitle) of William Wells Brown's *Clotel*, which appeared in various editions in the 1850s and 1860s and is, by some accounts, the first African American novel. This sentimental tragedy imagines the travels and travails of a runaway slave whom Thomas Jefferson was said to have fathered. Although Jefferson never actually appears in the novel, he is by inference a character who harbored at least that one secret, and therefore—as Brown is at pains to point out—was not worthy of the legend he achieved as author of a famous declaration of rights. Brown himself had been a runaway slave, and his use of Jefferson resembled William Apess's use of George Washington: Both writers rhetorically enlisted a founder in defense of groups that the actual founding had excluded. But where Apess had suggested that the Revolution was unfinished and had to continue, *Clotel* questions whether it ever really occurred. "They boast that America is the 'cradle of liberty,'" Brown writes, but "if it is, I fear they have rocked the child to death." Jefferson's indifference to Clotel is set in stark contrast to Clotel's infinite care for her own daughter, for whom she finally sacrifices herself by leaping into the Potomac—"within plain sight of the President's house and the capitol of the Union," and close to where Washington himself lies buried. The ironies are obvious and angry, but in the end the founders are not really what matter to Brown. In later editions Jefferson was written out, replaced by an ordinary white Southern slaveholder, and the subtitle "The President's Daughter" gave way to "A Tale of the Southern States."[94]

During the war *Clotel* was circulated to Union troops, and so were the stories of "Petroleum V. Nasby," the provincial bumpkin and political amateur created by David Ross Locke. Nasby's resemblance to Jack Downing—who was also revived for wartime service—is even more apparent than Col. Vanderbomb's. He writes in a regional dialect even thicker than Downing's, and although he's on less intimate terms with Presidents "Linkin" and "Androo Johnson" than Downing was with President Jackson, he is equally determined to give them, and us, his own skewed perspective on real day-to-day political events.

In their intense partisanship and lack of subtlety, however, the Nasby papers are closer in spirit to *Clotel* and other propagandistic fiction than they are to their comic predecessors. Nasby, a backwoods preacher, is a racist idiot of questionable loyalty, as cynical as Tucker's Martin Van Buren but without even that much depth. He is the classic unreliable narrator who is wrong about everything, which means his running critique of the war and Reconstruction invariably reflects well on both efforts. When he tells "Linkin" to repudiate the Emancipation Proclamation, for instance, it's expected that the reader will share the president's bemused reaction.[95] Nasby isn't a double for Lincoln, a Downingesque wise fool, but just a fool plain and simple, and this comes across all the more clearly to the extent that he demonstrates no insight whatsoever. Instead, "knoin also that you er a goriller, a feendish ape, a thirster after blud, I speek," he tells Lincoln, as if the most hostile caricatures were the obvious truth.

In light of what was soon to come, it is interesting to see this deliberate reduction of Lincoln to a stick figure. In the years ahead the Great Emancipator's legend would rival even George Washington's. But that legend, as we will see, would take shape in a very different way. The virtues celebrated in Lincoln were sometimes like those of the founders, but not always. They did not always contrast with realistic portrayals; to the contrary, with Lincoln we have a figure whose iconic treatment was itself closely tied to a recognition of inner depths. And since Lincoln, it has been easier to imagine other presidents in that same way—as lifelike individuals whose interest for us lies not in the abstract forces they represent but in their idiosyncratic humanity.

Of course, the old possibilities also remain. Like editorial cartoons, any number of novels, movies, and other fictions even today caricature presidents and candidates, polemically deploying them as stand-ins for some political fear, hope, or other idea. Presidents are represented in all kinds of ways and used to represent all kinds of things. But in the period we have been examining—the early years of what has variously been called "the middle Republic" or "the Party and Progressive Eras"—the range of possible representations began to widen, and it has continued to ever since.[96] Caricature itself points the way. Treating leaders as fools involves mechanisms of doubling, creating the dualities that, once they're internalized into a character's inner being, make for psychological depth. And it is no coincidence that these new possibilities appear above the historical horizon as the founding era is sinking below it, receding from living memory and becoming the stuff of legend. As that happens, official mythographers like Daniel Webster set to work codifying a national self-image, re-crafting onetime bitter disputes like those of the founders into the canon of heroic tales that would thereafter appear in schoolbooks. But no sooner is this done than the reverse becomes possible too. Some other orator, speaking for those whom the community defines itself by excluding—someone like the Indian spokesman William Apess—can reach into the new pantheon and draft even Washington for use in the political disputes of the moment. Whatever the official pieties may do for the cause of national unity, they also invite revisionism and give irreverent writers something to be irreverent about. Legends are never settled but always contested, and every myth lays the basis for counter-myths. Americans eventually went to war over the question of whether they would be two nations or one. That the answer was "one" ensured that the sharpest dualities would remain *within*—that the character "America" and its fictions would thereafter be more complex, not less.

3

Deep, Yet Transparent

Myth, Mystery, and "Common Sense" in Post–Civil War Presidential Fictions

❖

You should not forget there is a skeleton in every house. The finest character dug out thoroughly, photographed honestly, and judged by that standard of morality or excellence which we exact for other men is never perfect. Some men are cold, some lewd, some dishonest, some cruel, and many a combination of all. . . . Don't let any thing deter you from digging to the bottom. . . . In drawing the portrait tell the world what the skeleton was with Lincoln. What gave him that peculiar melancholy? What cancer had he inside?

William H. Herndon and Jesse W. Weik,
Herndon's Lincoln: The True Story of a Great Life, 1888

❖

The presidency was a new kind of office, and, if it wasn't built entirely from the ground up, much of it nonetheless had to be imagined. As we have seen, the acts of imagining that this involved were explicitly those needed in writing fiction: creating characters, developing scenes, and telling stories. Since they were aimed at winning arguments, the stories in question had to be persuasive, which obliged their authors to make them credible and their characters believable. And the best strategy for doing that depended on the circumstances. By cutting characters down to human scale, and by giving the feel of reality to something that did not yet exist, realism was the mode better suited for reassuring Americans that this proposed new type of national leader was plausible and would pose no outsize threat. But realism's emphasis on particularizing characters ran counter to the new nation's need for unifying figures—public icons, like George Washington, whose inner complexities were best left out of account. Moreover, the "politics of deference" of the early Republic demanded that leaders *not* be brought entirely onto the same plane as everyone else.[1]

It is not that early presidents were thought to have no inner lives. To the contrary, they were often accused of harboring dark and secret motives: Washington wanted to bring back the monarchy, Adams was conspiring with the British, Jefferson was a Jacobin who yearned for an American Reign of Terror. But these accusations were not attempts to understand them as people. They were dehumanizing caricatures, arrived at not from the inside out—by considering the person's inner being and how it might project itself into policy—but from the outside in, by projecting onto the person some political specter already stalking the land. That's how they could be so obviously wrong. Political opponents, in any case, do not have much incentive to understand each other psychologically. Understanding is a step toward sympathy and a shared perspective, which are not helpful when the goal is to bring about someone's defeat.

Caricatures, though, can also become satirical doubles that point the way ahead. With Andrew Jackson, the founding succession ran out and the politics of deference came to an end. Jackson's dualities, as the previous chapter noted, were not merely his opponents' libels but an essential consequence of his persona, and the doubles that seemed to proliferate around him included not just the scathing but also the sympathetic— the pre-psychological, we might say. In the years after Jackson, with the strains between North and South increasing, fictions appeared that gave presidents a semblance of realistic depth. But seemingly complex characters can be caricatures too, projections of the fractured state of a nation into individuals. Fictional presidents deployed for symbolic or polemical reasons can range from crude shadow puppets to intricate marionettes, yet in each case be playing merely stereotyped roles in some puppeteer's political dumb show. As the century went on, imagined presidents would be conjured for such purposes any number of times. They would prove especially useful, as we will see, for satirizing Gilded Age corruption, and for managing the perfected politics of Progressive Era utopias.

But meanwhile a turning point was approaching, a moment when the political fractures would be reconciled (or not) within a single national polity. And the moment was also at hand when the stereotyped dualities of earlier fictional presidents would be drawn together in a single character of profound psychological depth. It's not coincidental that these were the same moment, and that the real president who towered over it also towers over America's history of imagined presidents.

"The Heart and Secret Acts": Making Sense of Lincoln in the Late Nineteenth Century

The world would have little noted nor long remembered Abraham Lincoln if he had never reached the presidency. In this he was unlike Washington, Jefferson, and even the provincial Jackson, all of whom already had heroic reputations before and, largely, by virtue of which they held the office. Washington and Jackson were successful generals; Jefferson was a revolutionary founder and draftsman of the Declaration of Independence; and Jefferson and Jackson entered the White House at the head of large and rising political movements that were identified with them personally ("Jeffersonian Republicanism" and "Jacksonian Democracy"). President-elect Lincoln's view of himself as a man "without a name, perhaps without a reason why I should have a name," was a bit overstated: he was already widely known for his debates with Stephen Douglas and his "House Divided" speech.[2] But those were recent events, and, although impressive, they had not made Lincoln a favorite for his party's nomination, nor had he managed to win even 40 percent of the vote in the four-way contest of 1860. Unlike the original "log cabin" candidate, William Henry Harrison, whose aim had been to play down his aristocratic descent, Lincoln truly was the product of a log cabin. In another typically self-deprecating assessment, he called himself "the humblest of all individuals that have ever been elected to the Presidency."[3]

This made the problem for storytellers essentially the opposite of the problem posed by Washington or Jefferson. For them the presidency was one further step in a long career of national leadership; for Lincoln it was the *telos*, the focal point of all other stories and the whole reason for trying to understand him in the first place. Where Parson Weems had to take the greatness of Washington and somehow connect it back to common humanity, Lincoln's chroniclers had to do almost the reverse: explain how the all-too-common humanity could have led to the later greatness.[4] In the words of one recent documentary,

> How did this man who wrote the Gettysburg Address, the Second Inaugural, come out of Indiana? He grew up in Indiana, he grew up in the wilderness, he grew up in the frontier, he grew up in a log cabin. And yet he produced these noble documents, among the most noble in all of the English language. That's a mystery. That's fascinating to contemplate.[5]

For Lincoln's story to make sense, the great public achievements somehow had to be rooted in the humble origins themselves. It had to be shown that the "Indiana" or boyhood Lincoln "is the essence of Lincoln. It's the part that formed him later," that "gave Abraham Lincoln his future."[6] Other presidents offered materials for heroic narrative ready to hand in stories of military prowess and world-shaping events, but Lincoln's mythographers would have to try to dig these out of the prairie soil. It's not just that Lincoln became a figure of myth; that's true of many leaders. It's that without these operations of mythmaking he could scarcely be understood at all.

The success of those operations makes it hard to recall the difficulties that the original mythmakers faced. Today it seems natural to equate a frontier upbringing with hardy common sense and compassion for the common man. But until the myth was fully formed, that equation was not so clear. Even in polite company, for instance, Lincoln loved telling "impure" jokes and stories, and some observers believed that his many years among the unrefined "lower orders" was one source of this "grossness."[7] (Another source: he was a lawyer.) After observing the president closely for six months while working on a painting of him, the artist Francis Bicknell Carpenter mildly disputed reports like these—but he in turn noted that Lincoln, beset as he was by endless requests for military pardons and other favors, often treated supplicants with irritation and indifference, not the pity and mercy of later legend.[8]

This kind of hedged admiration is harder to square with that legend than the fact that Lincoln was deeply hated in some quarters. That he inspired great passions is easy to grasp; what's surprising is how little he impressed even many who wished him well. Having touched off a grave secession crisis, Lincoln's presidency had begun as inauspiciously as one could imagine. In sharp contrast to Washington and Jackson parading into the capital in triumph, Lincoln arrived in secret, having been smuggled through Baltimore at three in the morning to avoid possible assassins. Critics were appalled, and even political allies looked on apprehensively.[9] Charles Francis Adams, who would serve Lincoln as ambassador to Britain and was a son and grandson of presidents himself, took Lincoln's measure and saw "nothing but incompetency. . . . The man is not equal to the hour."[10]

Similar anxieties are a major theme of *The Diary of a Public Man*, an account of the beginning of the Lincoln administration from the viewpoint of someone with ready access to Lincoln and other leading figures in Washington. This short book appeared in 1879, and because the author has never been identified, there are doubts about its authenticity: It could be, in effect, a later novella using the diary form as a literary device.[11] Regardless, the *Diary* is a vivid reminder of how frightfully weak Lincoln was once thought to be. His inaugural address "disappointed every one," and his sentimentality and visible agitation were "not calculated to reassure."[12] The inauguration itself was "shockingly and stupidly" organized: "Mr. Lincoln was pale and very nervous. . . . His spectacles troubled him, his position was crowded and uncomfortable, and, in short, nothing had been done" to make the occasion suitably dignified. Later, confronted with the growing crisis over Fort Sumter—site of an embattled federal garrison and the eventual flashpoint of the war—the new president seemed as unsure what to do as anyone. He waited passively on public opinion, about which he confessed he was baffled: "What I want is to get done what the people desire to have done, and the question for me is how to find that out exactly."[13] He expressed fears that others were controlling events and that he could find himself run out of office, and he left the Public Man, after one interview, feeling "more anxious and disturbed" than before.[14]

The Public Man's accounts of his conversations with the likes of Senator Stephen Douglas and the members of Lincoln's cabinet are plausible enough that some historians have treated them as primary sources. But most intriguing—and tending to point to the *Diary's* authenticity—is the Public Man's relative lack of interest in Lincoln. A story composed fifteen or twenty years later, with full knowledge of how events would unfold, would almost surely be "Lincolncentric" in a way the *Diary* isn't.

In the Public Man's telling, Lincoln's actions are scarcely more likely to make history than those of any other official the book mentions. The hero who overcomes initial weakness and who triumphs in spite of it is, of course, a very old literary type—but the *Diary* does not tell such a story. It ends in mid-March 1861, before the war has even started. At that point, Lincoln looks no better than he did when the book began.

As the years went by and the 1864 election approached, leading Republicans were still saying of Lincoln "that he lacked the essential qualities of a leader."[15] Edward Dicey, a British correspondent who was friendly to the Union cause, reported after meeting with Lincoln and others in Washington that no one would regret it when Lincoln failed to be renominated, let alone re-elected. He would go down in history as "a first-rate second-rate man," a man lacking "instinctive genius." He was, in sum,

> not the noblest product of humanity, and when you have called the President "honest Abe Lincoln," according to the favorite phrase of the American press, you have said a great deal, doubtless, but you have also said *all* that can be said in his favor. He works hard, and does little; and unites a painful sense of responsibility to a still more painful sense, perhaps, that his work is too great for him to grapple with.[16]

If not for the turn that things took in the final six months or so of his life, comments like these might have been the last word on Lincoln. Instead, events as large and fateful as any in American history, all happening in rapid succession, would do more than merely raise his political stature. They would recast politics as theology, demanding an apotheosis even grander than that which had followed George Washington's much quieter passing. A man of sorrows and acquainted with woe; a man literally hailed as a messiah by those whose chains he had recently loosed; a man who sought "to bind up the nation's wounds," who bore the burdens of a war that he himself spoke of as God's "mighty scourge," as the judgment due a nation that owed debts in blood for its sins—this man was bound over for death at his enemies' hands *on Good Friday*, a day that could not have been better (mis)calculated to recall another martyred Redeemer to whom pious Americans looked for the same array of saving graces. There was little doubt what direction the mythologizing would take. The delays and frustrations that had once been blamed on Lincoln's limited competence now appeared in a new light: they were tokens of "the deliberateness of destiny," said one early biography, proof that Lincoln had worked in slow and mysterious ways, just as God had done in creation. This biography closed with a paragraph that can only be described as a prayer to the sainted leader, thanking him for "thy life and its immeasurably great results, as the choicest gifts that a mortal has ever bestowed upon us."[17]

Early post-assassination paintings and prints were also thick with Christian and classical symbols. Lincoln was seen rising through clouds, surrounded by angels, and mourned by typological figures representing "Columbia" and "Liberty" as well as Diogenes, the legendary ancient seeker after one honest man.[18] This strain of Lincolnography would continue, with variations, into the twentieth century, with Savior and man-of-destiny motifs foregrounded and the Lincoln myth all but visible as the moving finger writing the story. Such mythmaking did not just revere Lincoln but treated him as a typological figure himself, an embodiment of the nation or of the forces at work in history. In extreme cases the larger meanings all but obliterated the actual man. Rufus Blanchard's 1882 "historical romance" *Abraham Lincoln: The Type of American Genius,* for instance, is a throwback to a genre popular in the early years of the republic, the long neoclassical poem of the "Rising Glory of America" kind in which conventional figures like Columbia were made to move, act, and speak.[19] In Blanchard's opus, the mythic figures representing America's "genius" are so busy speechifying on whatever Olympian plane they inhabit that Lincoln himself, the poem's purported subject, is not even born until two-thirds of the way through—much as Jesus, the fulcrum of Christian history, isn't born until two-thirds of the way through the Christian Bible. But, as the title says, "Lincoln" in this piece is not really a person but a type: a symbol, in this case, of America's European heritage crossed with its pioneer spirit.[20]

Neoclassical abstractions like these would soon cease to be intelligible at all, and in the late nineteenth century they were already antiques. (Blanchard's work appears to have been self-published.) Even Francis Bicknell Carpenter, who saw the great events in his mind's eye as the Archangel Michael slaying the "'beast' of Secession, offspring of the 'dragon' Slavery," ultimately chose to paint his immensely popular portrait of Lincoln and his cabinet, *The First Reading of the Emancipation Proclamation,* without "allegorical statue" or other old-fashioned "appliances and tricks of picture-making." Lincoln, Carpenter decided, had to be seen amid "the strife of a living humanity."[21] As another early

D. T. Weist, "In Memory of Abraham Lincoln: The Reward of the Just," 1865. Lincoln's head and epitaph replace George Washington's on an older lithograph originally depicting Washington's "apotheosis." Bearing Lincoln heavenward are allegorical figures representing Time and Immortality, while his mourners include Faith, Hope, and Charity (*background*) and Liberty and an Indian, representing America (*foreground*). So little has the picture been altered that it still includes medals representing the Freemasons and the Society of the Cincinnati, which Washington belonged to but not Lincoln.

biographer put it, people loved Lincoln—unlike Washington, whom they merely venerated—because he seemed to be of the same "order of being" as themselves.[22]

For those who sought to represent him, though, this meant that Lincoln posed a different and more complicated problem. Removing Washington from the strife of a living humanity had helped safeguard Americans' ability to claim him without regard to region, party, or class.[23] But putting Lincoln on the same high pedestal would make him *harder* for them to claim. If what they loved was a figure of their own order of being, then it was hazardous to raise him to a higher order. Yet it was only in some such higher order that Lincoln's life and death found their great meaning. It seemed, then, that love and meaning were at odds. And there was also the problem of believability. A person as grand and dignified in life as the great General Washington had been easy to cast as a neoclassical man of marble, but Lincoln was more like the kind of rude character who might be found in one of his own backwoods folktales. Without projecting him full of abstractions, how was such a figure supposed to be made grand?

One helpful but incomplete answer lay in the analogy to Christ. Here a similar conundrum had already been addressed, and in a book that pious Americans knew better than any other. Representing a figure who was true God yet true man, intersecting the two planes of being in stories of ordinary people at the very center of history and God's plan, had made the Gospels one of the great achievements in the history of literature.[24] Early writers on Lincoln borrowed from and tried to mimic that achievement, looking for a similarly singular duality in the story of America's own homegrown savior. Lincoln's "painful sense of responsibility," as Edward Dicey had seen it, now became his dutiful willingness to suffer the burdens of his great mission, while his unassuming and at times undignified manner was now reinterpreted as Christlike humility. Lincoln was a man who "knew no distinction," who had worn the same "garb" in both private and public, and who had "brought to every question—the loftiest and most imposing—the same . . . working-day, plodding, laborious devotion, which characterized his management of a client's case at his law office in Springfield." He felt "warm charity toward his foes" and "a tender, brotherly regard for every human being," especially the poor and oppressed. True, his were not exploits of "mighty genius"—they were something greater: "the work of the heart, [rather] than the head." Lincoln had "[t]he power of a true-hearted

Christian man, in perfect sympathy with a true-hearted Christian people." He was, therefore, another great mediator between God and humankind, "[o]pen on one side of his nature to all descending influences from Him to whom he prayed, and open on the other to all ascending influences from the people whom he served."[25]

This image of Lincoln has been a durable one, but making him a Christ figure was, finally, another way of recasting him as a type. For all their proto-realism, the New Testament stories are sketchy when it comes to the backgrounds and private thoughts of their characters, and their central character remains not only superhumanly flawless but, for the most part, opaque. Framing Lincoln as that kind of character was a way of expressing what was great about him, but it was a dead end in terms of explaining what *made* him great. It did not fulfill even the early chroniclers' own stated aim: "to portray *the man* as he was revealed to me, without any attempt at idealization," as Carpenter put it with his own emphasis.[26] Already by 1867 Carpenter's memoir of his *Six Months at the White House* had been retitled *The Inner Life of Abraham Lincoln*, apparently in the belief that an "inner" Lincoln was what Americans of the time were still seeking.

But in terms of what we now understand as inner life, the book did not justify its new title. What it provided was what we would now call "inside knowledge" — things like what Lincoln said in private about the timing of the Emancipation Proclamation. These were political insights, not Freudian-style revelations of Lincoln's subconscious. A less attractive side of Lincoln is glimpsed in some of Carpenter's anecdotes, but the book's promise to avoid idealization is quickly negated: Almost in the same breath, Carpenter calls Lincoln "the best product and exemplar which the world has yet seen of American soil and institutions." It was a foregone conclusion what would be learned from studying his character, "illustrating as it did the highest form of statesmanship, founded upon truth, justice, and solid integrity, combining the deepest wisdom with a child-like freshness and simplicity."[27] The supposedly childlike was part of the idealization, not a buried layer to be uncovered when the idealizations were torn away.

The real pioneers of Lincoln's terra incognita were Ward Hill Lamon and especially William Herndon, the two influential biographers who had both been Lincoln's law partners. Herndon's lectures, which he began giving soon after the assassination, along with his wide-ranging research and the books that Lamon and then Herndon both based on it, are the sources of much of what has since become standard Lincoln lore. Yet their portraits of Lincoln are, at times, sharply and surprisingly critical. Besides suggesting that Lincoln was not a Christian, an extremely sensitive question at the time and one that caught both Lamon and Herndon in a great deal of controversy, Lamon described Lincoln as largely self-seeking, "a man apart from the rest of his kind, unsocial, cold, impassive," and given to "extravagant visions of personal grandeur and power." There was depth to him, but not of a good kind: Knowing that "no qualities of a public man are so charming to the people as simplicity and candor, he made simplicity and candor the mask of deep feelings carefully concealed, and [of] subtle plans studiously veiled from all eyes but one."[28]

Herndon took a more charitable view, but he too presented his work as a response to the prevailing idealization of Lincoln. Although Lincoln himself admired and may even have tried to model himself on the iconic George Washington of Parson Weems, Herndon sought to rescue him from the Weems-ification that had quickly followed his death.[29] Like Carpenter, Herndon promised not to shrink from "the whole truth—the inner life," but for him this meant "the heart and secret acts" that, if "faithfully photographed," would allow the reader to "live with [Lincoln] and be moved to think and act with him."[30] The goal of his research, said Herndon, was "an analysis of the man and a portrayal of his attributes and characteristics," with special attention to Lincoln's youth and early manhood, and with "nothing colored or suppressed."

Of particular interest to Lamon and Herndon was Lincoln's famous melancholy, which "never failed to impress any man who ever saw or knew him." Lamon called the reason that Lincoln was "the saddest and gloomiest man of his time" a "mystery" that probably had multiple causes. Herndon likewise concluded that the cause of "this morbid condition" was "occult, and could not be explained by any course of observation and reasoning."[31] But both writers also linked it with the story of his near-suicidal reaction to the death of Ann Rutledge. This tale of doomed love, involving Lincoln and a young woman he had supposedly wooed when he was twenty-six, would become one of the best-known episodes of Lincoln's early life. Developed from fragmentary reports of old Lincoln acquaintances, it was first floated in one of Herndon's early lectures—and in elaborating it years later, he made clear that he understood its novelistic potential:

Lincoln began to court Miss Rutledge in dead earnest. Like David Cop-
perfield, he soon realized that he was in danger of becoming deeply in
love, and as he approached the brink of the pit he trembled lest he
should indeed fall in. . . . In a half-hearted way she turned to Lincoln,
and her looks told him that he had won. She accepted his proposal.[32]

Meanwhile, "the ghost of another love," a fiancé who was away for
an extended period, "would often rise unbidden before her. Within her
bosom raged the conflict which finally undermined her health." Stricken
with typhoid—or, as Lamon and Herndon would have it, with that familiar malady of Victorian fiction, the "brain-fever" brought on by inner
turmoil—Rutledge died, plunging Lincoln into "no little mental agony." His inconsolable grief, which raged for the next several weeks, so
alarmed his friends that they put him under guard to make sure he
didn't kill himself:

> He had fits of great mental depression, and wandered up and down the
> river and into the woods woefully abstracted—at times in the deepest
> distress. If, when we read what the many credible persons who knew
> him at the time tell us, we do not conclude that he was deranged, we
> must admit that he walked on that sharp and narrow line which divides
> sanity from insanity. . . . There is no question that from this time for-
> ward Mr. Lincoln's spells of melancholy became more intense than
> ever. . . . The little acre of ground in Concord cemetery contained the
> form of his first love, rudely torn from him, and the great world, throb-
> bing with life but cold and heartless, lay spread before him.[33]

And with that, in Herndon's telling, Lincoln's political career begins.

The Rutledge tale is a remarkable vignette, one that answers to both
ancient and modern biographical assumptions about great men and
women. It has Lincoln enduring a time of trial like the saints of centuries past, complete with his own wanderings in the wilderness and re-
emergence to undertake his life's mission. But it's also a story of early
trauma, depression, and "coping," a case study that lends itself to these
terms from the modern clinic. Herndon's project was an important step
in the shift from one mode to the other.

At the same time, Herndon never quite reconciled the different aims
of understanding and mythologizing. In introducing his work on Lincoln, he defended it against "over-sensitive souls" who might object to
its "ghastly exposures." To comprehend Lincoln, "we must have all the
facts—we must be prepared to take him as he was":

Many of our great men and our statesmen, it is true, have been self-
made, rising gradually through struggles to the topmost round of the
ladder; but Lincoln rose from a lower depth than any of them—from a
stagnant, putrid pool, like the gas which, set on fire by its own energy
and self-combustible nature, rises in jets, blazing, clear, and bright. I
should be remiss in my duty if I did not throw the light on this part of
the picture, so that the world may realize what marvelous contrast one
phase of his life presents to another.[34]

Ghastly exposures are nothing to shrink from if the goal is psychological
truth, and the contrast in Lincoln that Herndon speaks of could well
suggest a complex interiority that developed in interesting ways over
time. Although Herndon himself associated the word *psychology* with
"metaphysics" and "abstruse mental phenomena"—matters at odds
with Lincoln's own practical-mindedness—one later editor credits him
with the kinds of insights that "would now be called psychoanalytical."[35] But Herndon's own reason for highlighting the lower end of the
marvelous contrast was to establish a background against which the
"exalted" Lincoln would stand out that much more sharply. Like conventional mythmakers, he was ultimately "determining Lincoln's title to
greatness." If ghastly exposures help to do this, then they are not really
all that ghastly.

Herndon's work, in other words, still has an old-fashioned feel. It is
psychological because it is sentimental, which is to say, concerned with
emotion. Herndon was a storyteller, and whether or not he solved the
riddle of Lincoln's melancholy, he taught other storytellers that violent
emotion could animate young Lincoln's story just as youthful derring-do
enlivened Washington's and Jackson's. But in teaching this lesson, Herndon pointed a way forward. Perhaps the best tribute to his incipient
modernity is the outrage his book provoked in some critics, like the one
who charged that it "vilely distorts the image of an ideal statesman, patriot and martyr":

> It clothes him in vulgarity and grossness. Its indecencies are spread like
> a curtain to hide the collossal proportions and the splendid purity of his
> character. . . . It brings out all that should have been hidden . . . it mag-
> nifies the idle and thoughtless antics of youth as main features of the
> man in his life and accomplishments. . . .
>
> The obscenity of the work is surprising and shocking. . . . It is not fit
> for family reading.

For this same critic, the Ann Rutledge episode was "indelicate, in every way in bad taste." Judged according to "the proportions" of literature and life, "this book is so bad that it could hardly have been worse."[36] Imprecations like these nicely capture what was bound to seem outrageous about psychological analysis from the standpoint of a Victorian (and older) sensibility, an ethic and aesthetic of decency, purity, proportion, and discretion. From that standpoint, grossness is gratuitous, and equating the idle youth with the honored man is just incoherent. For writers of the old school, the "indecencies" are a curtain that hides the true person; for modern practitioners they are the truths that the curtain of decency hides.

Over the years, Abraham Lincoln has continued to be sentimentalized at least as much as any other president. But he has also been the source and subject of a whole modern industry of close analysis. He marks the point at which the presidency became a matter of psychohistory and psychobiography, as they came to be called: efforts to explain the complex achievements of prominent people in terms of a few elemental emotions and drives, of forces that generate inner conflicts and of personal histories reaching back into childhood. Today it seems normal for a book to analyze *Lincoln's Melancholy: How Depression Challenged a President and Fueled His Greatness,* to take one recent title.[37] Psychobiography acknowledges the depth and doubleness, the layered quality, that people harbor within, and that literary treatments are now expected to disclose if their characters are to seem full and believable. Older modes praised characters for their perfectly balanced virtues (or damned them for their conniving duplicity). When dealing with someone responsible for great things, they sought to construct a character to match—a portrait that found its unity and coherence, and a model worth emulating, by painting greatness in every brushstroke. Modern psychology seeks integration of a different kind. It construes a person as a unified whole by treating the flaws and the virtues, the private and the public, hidden feelings and well-formed beliefs, the traumatized child and the accomplished adult, as aspects of a single, dynamic system. It assumes that even a character's duplicities are integral to him or her at some subconscious level, that all can be understood—that, as Frederick Douglass said of Lincoln, "though deep, he was transparent."[38]

It is hard to be sure how much of that transparency is an illusion in Lincoln's case (or any other). The Ann Rutledge tale, for instance, is a literary construction—at best, a representation of things that Lincoln *might* have felt and been influenced by in the ways Herndon and others have supposed. Careful historians have noted the shortage of evidence for it, and one declared that "the story should be left for the fiction writers."[39] Yet to the extent that the Rutledge story is fiction, it illustrates all the better how important the devices of literary realism were in the making of the Lincoln myth. Even today, when the notion that some things "should have been hidden" seems quaint, when virtually nothing in a president's life is kept behind the curtain of decency, one rarely sees a national leader in such extreme close-up: pausing from a White House meeting to negotiate his son's allowance; staring in shock at a ghost-image of himself in a mirror; delivering one of the great speeches of American history, the Cooper Union Address, while fretting about the awkward cut of his coat collar.[40] To a psychological realist, the speech and the coat collar are both aspects of the same reality. Lincoln's political ideals and commitments, his humor, his anxieties, his legendary honesty, even his interest in spiritualism and his fondness for egg-and-coffee breakfasts, are all projections from the same source. No detail is too trivial, because the portrait they make is like a three-dimensional hologram in which each tiny piece includes the whole picture.[41] To explain Lincoln meant making him a *character*, meant treating everything about him, including his public acts, as character notes. Lincoln's was a "storied" presidency in more ways than one.

"The Great American Mystery": Fictional Presidents in the Gilded Age

Tales of Lincoln aside, the first significant fictional president to appear after the war—and therefore in the shadow of the Great Emancipator—was the "Hoosier Quarryman," the character whose new administration is the backdrop to Henry Adams's 1880 *Democracy: An American Novel.* Adams was a distinguished historian from a distinguished family: great-grandson of John, grandson of John Quincy and son of Charles Francis Adams, whom he served as private secretary during the latter's Civil War ambassadorship to Great Britain. He was also close friends with President Lincoln's own private secretary, John Hay, who later became secretary of state, and the two were prominent in Washington high society. The houses they built together eventually gave way to the Hay-Adams luxury hotel, which today claims to be "as close as anyone can get to staying at the White House, short of being invited by the President."[42]

And in addition to *Democracy* and another novel, *Esther,* Adams's work in the 1880s included the nine-volume *History of the United States during the Administrations of Thomas Jefferson and James Madison.* In all, Adams—who later said of himself that "as far as he had a function in life, it was as stable-companion to statesmen, whether they liked it or not"[43]—was exceptionally well informed about the presidency and well positioned to capture it in fiction.

Moreover, in a period of what historians today call "congressional government," Adams seemed open to something like the modern view of presidents as culturally defining figures whose importance extends well beyond the duties of their office.[44] In his *History,* for instance, he wrote that "Jefferson's personality during these eight years [of his presidency] appeared to be the government, and impressed itself, like that of Bonaparte, although by a different process, on the mind of the nation."[45] Yet, like other historians of his time, Adams does not delve deeply into that personality. Though he reconstructs events sometimes in hour-by-hour detail, what interests him are official acts and the conscious, political intentions that make themselves apparent in policy. If there were hidden depths to either Jefferson or Madison, Adams is not the writer to reveal them to us.

Democracy is nonetheless classed today as "American realism," a term that implies a narrative based on some degree of psychological insight, and to the novel's first readers it apparently felt quite real. Published anonymously on April Fools' Day, the book was a sensation in both Washington and London, and speculation continued for years both about who had written it and about which members of the capital's political and social elite had been the models for its characters.[46] The story's heroine is a thirty-year-old New York society woman, Madeleine Lightfoot Lee, a widow who "in growing older . . . began to show symptoms of dangerous unconventionality." Much like Adams himself, she had traveled in Europe and "had read philosophy in the original German, and the more she read, the more she was disheartened that so much culture should lead to nothing—nothing." To relieve her "*ennui*" she leaves New York, "this great million-armed monster," and moves to Washington, "bent upon getting to the heart of the great American mystery of democracy and government. . . . She wanted to learn how the machinery of government worked, and what was the quality of the men who controlled it."[47]

In Washington Madeleine frequents the Senate gallery and reads the *Congressional Record* each morning until it finally gets too dull even for her.

But her attention is soon drawn to the powerful Senator Silas P. Ratcliffe of Illinois, "the Prairie Giant, the bully of the Senate," a man known to "watch you as though you were a young rattlesnake, to be killed when convenient. . . . His eyes only seem to ask the possible uses you might be put to." Ratcliffe "loved power, and he meant to be President." But he embodies the "robust Americanism" that Madeleine had come to Washington looking for, and his drive for power includes a "practical sense and cool will" she finds appealing. Since the president's wife is arguably more important than the president himself, and since "there was a very general impression in Washington that Mrs. Lee would like nothing better than to be in the White House," the upshot is clear: "Mrs. Lee was properly assumed to be a candidate for office. To the Washingtonians it was a matter of course that Mrs. Lee should marry Silas P. Ratcliffe."

On first getting a good look at the president at a White House reception, though, what Madeleine encounters is "a horrid warning to ambition":

> Madeleine found herself before two seemingly mechanical figures, which might be wood or wax, for any sign they showed of life. These two figures were the President and his wife; they stood stiff and awkward by the door, both their faces stripped of every sign of intelligence, while the right hands of both extended themselves to the column of visitors with the mechanical action of toy dolls. Mrs. Lee for a moment began to laugh, but the laugh died on her lips. To the President and his wife this was clearly no laughing matter. . . . To [Madeleine] it had the effect of a nightmare, or of an opium-eater's vision. She felt a sudden conviction that this was to be the end of American society; its realisation and dream at once. She groaned in spirit.
>
> "Yes! at last I have reached the end! We shall grow to be wax images, and our talk will be like the squeaking of toy dolls. We shall all wander round and round the earth and shake hands. No one will have any object in this world, and there will be no other. It is worse than anything in the 'Inferno.' What an awful vision of eternity!"

To Madeleine, "The sight of those two suffering images at the door is too mournful to be borne. . . . I don't believe they're real. I wish the house would take fire. I want an earthquake. I wish some one would pinch the President, or pull his wife's hair." If she were the president's wife she would "put an end to this folly" and, she jokes, dare Congress to impeach her for it.

Much of Madeleine's and Ratcliffe's courtship consists of conversations about politics, in the course of which he defends his belief in power and party loyalty over what he calls "abstract morality." When Madeleine and her group go on an outing to Mount Vernon, the repartee becomes an extended, skeptical postmortem on George Washington, whose supposed virtues Ratcliffe dismisses as "old clothes." Contemporary politicians look foolish dressing in them, he says, and "only fools and theorists imagine" that they could be a basis for practical governing. "If virtue won't answer our purpose, we must use vice," he declares—a credo he has already confessed to acting on when, in 1864, he had falsified election returns from Illinois to ensure Lincoln's re-election and save the Union from defeat. Madeleine had brushed that revelation aside: "Women cannot be expected to go behind the motives of that patriot who saves his country and his election in times of revolution." But others in her circle, including her younger sister and a rival suitor, anxiously set about to turn her away from "that coarse, horrid" politician, "that great oaf," as Ratcliffe is variously called.

And while this is happening the president-elect is choosing his cabinet—a major event in the life of elite Washington, especially as it struggles to get to know this former one-term governor of Indiana whose obscurity until now makes him a "new political Buddha." The new president is "a hard-featured man of sixty, with a hooked nose and thin, straight, iron-gray hair" and a voice "rougher than his features":

He had begun his career as a stone-cutter in a quarry, and was, not unreasonably, proud of the fact. During the campaign this incident had, of course, filled a large space in the public mind, or, more exactly, in the public eye. "The Stone-cutter of the Wabash," he was sometimes called; at others "the Hoosier Quarryman," but his favourite appellation was "Old Granite," although this last endearing name, owing to an unfortunate similarity of sound, was seized upon by his opponents, and distorted into "Old Granny." . . .

That he was honest, all admitted; that is to say, all who voted for him. This is a general characteristic of all new presidents. He himself took great pride in his home-spun honesty, which is a quality peculiar to nature's noblemen. Owing nothing, as he conceived, to politicians, but sympathising through every fibre of his unselfish nature with the impulses and aspirations of the people, he affirmed it to be his first duty to protect the people from those vultures, as he called them, those wolves in sheep's clothing, those harpies, those hyenas, the politicians; epithets which, as generally interpreted, meant Ratcliff and Ratcliffe's friends.

But having come to Washington "determined to be the Father of his country; to gain a proud immortality and a re-election," the old stone-cutter "had suffered since his departure from Indiana" and was now "like a brown bear undergoing the process of taming; very ill-tempered, very rough, and at the same time very much bewildered and a little frightened":

> The Hoosier Quarryman had not been a week in Washington before he was heartily home-sick for Indiana. No maid-of-all-work in a cheap boarding-house was ever more harassed. Everyone conspired against him. His enemies gave him no peace. All Washington was laughing at his blunders, and ribald sheets, published on a Sunday, took delight in printing the new Chief Magistrate's sayings and doings, chronicled with outrageous humour, and placed by malicious hands where the President could not but see them. He was sensitive to ridicule, and it mortified him to the heart to find that remarks and acts, which to him seemed sensible enough, should be capable of such perversion.

In very short order, the neophyte president is

> overwhelmed with public business. It came upon him in a deluge, and he now, in his despair, no longer tried to control it. He let it pass over him like a wave. His mind was muddied by the innumerable visitors to whom he had to listen. But his greatest anxiety was the Inaugural Address which, distracted as he was, he could not finish, although in another week it must be delivered.

The Hoosier Quarryman is also nervous about his cabinet appointments, and is especially preoccupied with Senator Ratcliffe. Like real-life presidents of the time, he is under pressure to maintain party unity by surrounding himself with his rivals. Ratcliffe is the biggest of these, a prominent party leader who expected to win the presidential nomination that the lesser-known governor narrowly stole away. And everyone now knows that the president "is to be allowed no peace unless he makes terms with Ratcliffe."[48]

The Ratcliffe "stumbling-block" has the president-elect stymied. "His cardinal principle in politics was hostility to Ratcliffe," but he also needs Ratcliffe and is panicked at the thought that the senator might refuse a cabinet post. That's the dilemma on his mind as he waits for Ratcliffe to arrive for an interview:

> He was pacing his room impatiently on Monday morning, an hour before the time fixed for Ratcliffe's visit. His feelings still fluctuated violently, and if he recognized the necessity of using Ratcliffe, he was not the less determined to tie Ratcliffe's hands. He must be made to come into a Cabinet where every other voice would be against him.

The Quarryman "thought himself a profound statesman, and that his hand was guiding the destinies of America to his own re-election." But his fretful scheming "was needless, if the President had only known it," because he stands little chance of out-scheming the bully of the Senate. The moment Ratcliffe arrives, he seizes on the president's "nervous eagerness" and puts himself fully in charge; soon the government is staffed with Ratcliffe's cronies, the president's reform principles lie forgotten, and Ratcliffe has even made the president his mouthpiece by dictating his inaugural address—all while getting the president to thank him for the favors.

Thus politically neutered, the Hoosier Quarryman largely exits the story. We do, though, get a glimpse of his inauguration from Madeleine's point of view. Again she finds fault: "it was of the earth, earthy, she said. An elderly western farmer, with silver spectacles, new and glossy evening clothes, bony features, and stiff, thin, gray hair, trying to address a large crowd of people, under the drawbacks of a piercing wind and a cold in his head, was not a hero," and in fact looks like he might die of pneumonia, as had been known to happen. Madeleine also pays a visit to the president's "insane" wife, who receives her with a hostility reserved for those associated with Ratcliffe. Madeleine decides "that an equally good President and President's wife could be picked up in any corner-grocery between the Lakes and the Ohio; and that no inducement should ever make her go near that coarse washerwoman again."

Yet by the end of the novel it is less clear how far we should trust Madeleine's judgments of character, or whether she even trusts them herself. Just as she is about to accept the anticipated marriage proposal from Ratcliffe, now the Treasury secretary and a good bet to be the next president, Madeleine learns that he once got his party a large kickback from a steamship company in return for a federal subsidy. For reasons neither of them fully understands, this revelation shocks her more than the unprincipled conduct to which he has already freely admitted. Suddenly she sees Ratcliffe as a "moral lunatic" who "talked about virtue and vice as a man who is colour-blind talks about red and green." She angrily banishes him, but she also recognizes her own folly:

> Had she not come to Washington in search of men who cast a shadow, and was not Ratcliffe's shadow strong enough to satisfy her? Had she not penetrated the deepest recesses of politics, and learned how easily the mere possession of power could convert the shadow of a hobby-horse existing only in the brain of a foolish country farmer, into a lurid nightmare that convulsed the sleep of nations? The antics of Presidents and Senators had been amusing—so amusing that she had nearly been persuaded to take part in them. She had saved herself in time.

Abandoning Washington, "she was glad to quit the masquerade. . . . Let Mr. Ratcliffe, and his brother giants, wander on their own political prairie, and hunt for offices, or other profitable game, as they would." Madeleine would return to philanthropic work, "the true democracy of life."

Focused as it is on Madeleine and her circle, *Democracy* is not mainly about the presidency. In fact, the president's comparatively minor role would seem to be part of the point: presidents who arrived in post–Civil War Washington nominally bearing the people's mandate were easily overshadowed and made the playthings of slick patronage politicians like Ratcliffe. Apart from his wife's one reference to him as "Jacob," the president is known throughout the novel by either his title or his political nickname. Thus he becomes just another figure in Adams's gallery of political types. We do see a bit of the Quarryman's inner life, of his anxiety, homesickness, and sensitivity to ridicule. But mostly his emotions are political: they exist in connection with public events. The reason they are shown to us is not to make him a more interesting character, more distinctive and idiosyncratic, but almost the opposite—to illustrate, by way of a character, the daunting position in which presidents generally were placed by the politics of the day.

But similar points could be made about Ratcliffe, and even Madeleine. Ratcliffe's duplicity and Madeleine's self-delusion about it drive the story, but the hidden depths that matter most to Adams do not lie within the characters. They lie within the political culture as a whole, that "mystery of American democracy" that gives the novel its title and to which Madeleine had hoped to get to the bottom. Democracy, political America, is the true central character whose inner life cries to be understood. As Madeleine recognizes when she first sees a president in person, individual political actors are more like wind-up dolls, mechanically playing out the roles they have been assigned in a tragicomedy that just seems to keep recurring. If Madeleine finds this "horrid," it is apparently because she had hoped to encounter political figures whose movements were more authentically inner-directed, who would be *governed* in their conduct by something apart from, and if need be at odds with, the machinery of government and politics to which the people she meets are clearly so well adapted. Such an inner governing force is what she seems to mean by "principle." Ratcliffe is not unusual in lacking principle, and because he takes no pains to hide this he is not psychologically interesting in the way that unscrupulous characters often can be. To the contrary, what makes him noteworthy is simply his frank admission that he is, in the end, a toy doll himself. Not only does he let political roles and imperatives control his actions, he openly argues for the virtue of doing so. For him, political expediency is itself a personal ethic. Ratcliffe is the vehicle through which Madeleine, and the reader, discover a secret that has been hidden in plain sight: the mystery of American democracy, and the corruption of Gilded Age government, are more or less the same thing.

Inspired in part by *Democracy*, other fictions of Washington society explored similar themes in the years following.[49] The most notable writer to tap into this vein was Henry James, who included a newly inaugurated president in "Pandora," his 1884 story of a "self-made girl" and the "new type" of woman she represents. It was a type that impressed the observers in James's stories as both distinctively American and utterly confounding. In sketching the new woman, James is following up his own more famous "Daisy Miller," but with a shift of scene. As if wondering how Daisy would fare on her home ground, James begins "Pandora" just as the title character returns from Europe. He then proceeds to study her, as he had studied Daisy, from the standpoint of a mystified male acquaintance—in this case, the German diplomat Count Otto Vogelstein.

The unnamed president appears when Count Otto attends a Washington social function and finds him "comfortably unbending" in a private tête-à-tête with Pandora. Most of the story concerns the efforts of Count Otto, who "had never seen any girl like her," to make sense of Pandora's remarkably free spirit. That she commands the attention even of presidents surprises him; since he finds Pandora "very significant, very representative" as Americans go, he had assumed her to be lower class (which, of course, in a James story does not mean poor). What Count Otto cannot understand is how a daughter of "complete little burghers" could qualify as a member of the elite, let alone convince a president to return her to Europe in the distinguished role of wife to a newly appointed ambassador. She seems indifferent to traditional social rules, and this nonchalance is, for Count Otto, what Ratcliffe's indifference to political principle is for Madeleine Lightfoot Lee: a negligence that should be disqualifying, yet seems no bar to power or social status.[50] It is that puzzle that, in both these novels, is the mystery of America—the potential for social chaos that makes America Pandora's box, and that preoccupied both these writers throughout their careers. In neither *Democracy* nor "Pandora" is the president a main character, but in both he is important insofar as he leads a society and government that, quite aside from any ill intent on his part, is "democratic" to the point of making no sense at all.

In his cryptic autobiography, *The Education of Henry Adams*, Adams would develop perplexed observations like these into a self-mocking story of personal failure. There were many quests underway in the nineteenth century to find the fundamental laws of history and social evolution, elaborate attempts to explain the past and point the way to the political future on the basis of some single grand theory. Indeed, two of the most influential of these theories, Marxism and Social Darwinism, both eventually became bywords for the dangers of such a project. Adams presents himself as a lifelong seeker after the basic laws of society and politics, but one who, to his dismay, can never find any that work. His benighted view of the effort, his pose of genteel bafflement at the way modern society seemed to be *de*volving or falling to pieces, can seem strikingly contemporary and old-fashioned at the same time. On the one hand, it anticipates today's widespread skepticism toward grand theories—the exhausted retreat from simple, monocausal views of society like those that helped make the twentieth century an epoch of genocide and world war. But it can also come across as haughty and cynical, a Victorian aristocrat's failure to credit the possibilities for democratic reform that were already taking shape in a number of movements: labor, socialist, women's suffrage, Populism, Progressivism, the movement for racial "advancement," and others.[51] *Pace* Henry Adams, principled politics had not disappeared by the 1880s. The Gilded Age was not going to last forever, even if some of its problems have proven stubbornly persistent.

"The Rule of Common Sense":
Administration and Apocalypse in Fictions
of the Progressive Era

The reformers who made the years around the turn of the twentieth century "the Progressive Era" had motives for writing political fiction that were not solely artistic. Depending on how generous we are, much of their large literary output might be called either "novels of ideas" or unsubtle propaganda—political pamphleteering by another name. The best-remembered of these novels today is Edward Bellamy's 1888 *Looking Backward: 2000 to 1887*. This book, an enormous popular success, helped inspire a boom in similarly speculative fiction—novels that, to borrow from some of their titles, promised looks not just *Backward* but *Further Backward, Forward, Further Forward, Ahead, Further Ahead, Far Ahead, Within,* and *Beyond*; at *The World of Tomorrow, the Future,* or the *Twentieth, Twenty-first, Twenty-second, Twenty-fourth, Twenty-eighth, Forty-ninth,* or *Ninety-sixth Century*; at *New Eras, New Commonwealths, Utopias, Edens, Hidden Cities, Ideal Cities,* and *Ideal Worlds* with no cities; and at people waking up from a very long sleep, which is what the young Julian West does in *Looking Backward* with the help of one Dr. Leete and his daughter, Edith.

Having accidentally spent the entire twentieth century in a hypnotic trance, Julian West wakes to discover a perfected American society in which inequalities, interest groups, money, and the other irritants that make for political conflict are things of a dimly remembered past. At the heart of the new order is a system for managing the production and distribution of goods, an "industrial army" that puts the whole messy business of running a modern economy on a rational basis. Coming as he does from a squalid era whose social arrangements are one big "hideous ghastly mistake, a colossal world-darkening blunder," Julian finds the new system endlessly surprising. Much of the book consists of his—and the reader's—tutelage in its principles, a task that mostly falls to the Leetes:

> "You have told me in general how your industrial army is levied and organized, but who directs its efforts? What supreme authority determines what shall be done in every department, so that enough of everything is produced and yet no labor wasted? It seems to me that this must be a wonderfully complex and difficult function, requiring very unusual endowments."

"Does it indeed seem so to you?" responded Dr. Leete. "I assure you that it is nothing of the kind, but on the other hand so simple, and depending on principles so obvious and easily applied, that the functionaries at Washington to whom it is trusted require to be nothing more than men of fair abilities to discharge it to the entire satisfaction of the nation. The machine which they direct is indeed a vast one, but so logical in its principles and direct and simple in its workings, that it all but runs itself; and nobody but a fool could derange it, as I think you will agree after a few words of explanation."[52]

Several hundred words of explanation later, we learn that the president of the United States in 2000 is the "general-in-chief" of the industrial army—a vast and highly regimented apparatus through which all material goods are produced with virtually no waste or scarcity. Most workers under the universal retirement age of forty-five are members of the industrial army, which has no say in choosing the president ("That would be ruinous to its discipline") but which needs none thanks to an alert and powerful "inspectorate" that keeps the system working smoothly. The president is elected from among the retired "generals" who had risen through the ranks to head industrial departments, and who themselves were chosen by alumni of the industrial guilds. These mechanisms ensure that he will be both knowledgeable and impartial—a perfect technocrat, to use a term that another Bellamy-like enthusiast would coin in 1919. Moreover, an "exclusively feminine regime" handles matters pertaining to women, which are submitted to a separate female general-in-chief who is chosen like the male president and who can veto "measures respecting women's work." Harmony therefore prevails between the sexes, as Julian personally demonstrates by marrying Edith Leete and living happily ever after.[53]

Julian slept while society's problems were being solved, and the purely managerial presidency he awakens to is so uncontroversial as to merit only the paragraph or so that the novel gives it. By contrast, *President John Smith* is the main character of Frederick Upham Adams's 1897 novel of that name, and his presidency is the key to this "Story of a Peaceful Revolution" through which the more rational social order is achieved. This work, which sold an impressive 125,000 copies, takes the Panic of 1893 and other social and economic turmoil of the decade as occasions to picture the upheaval that might follow if a radical Populist were elected president. John Smith is a retired judge "in the full prime of a magnificent manhood," a quiet figure who "looks like a banker and writes like a labor agitator" and who has "none of the personal magnetism of the successful politician." Nonetheless, having written articles in favor of nationalizing key industries, he rouses his fellow Populists at the People's Party national convention with a "bold appeal for radical action" that gets him drafted to lead the party's ticket. Rejecting piecemeal reform in favor of Smith's proposals, the novel's imagined Populist campaign of 1900 affirms an inalienable right to employment while denouncing both the U.S. Constitution and representative government in general. The Constitution, Smith and the novel both argue, was a conspiracy of monarchist diehards against majority rule; in effect it nullified the Declaration of Independence, paved the way for plutocracy, and became a stick to wield against reformers—"something to venerate, to worship, to scare little children with."[54]

Taking advantage of the Constitution's byzantine electoral procedures, and supplementing them with bribery and vote fraud, a conspiracy of old-line Democrats and Republicans tries to rob Smith of his rightful victory in the election. But enraged mobs shut down business and storm the U.S. Capitol, and the crisis is not resolved until a constitutional convention is called, Smith is chosen to head it, and the voters "almost unanimously" elect him their first president under a new, streamlined constitution. Smith finally takes office "amid scenes of popular rejoicing unparalleled in the history of the United States," and he and his elected cabinet set about to reconstruct industry under the close government supervision that the new constitution makes possible.[55] Meanwhile the traditional parties go into eclipse, pushed aside by "Majority Rule Clubs" that mobilize citizens in support of the new system of legislating by plebiscite. (Frederick Adams tried to set up such clubs in real life, apparently without great success.)

President Smith's reforms are not as far-reaching as the utterly new society to which Julian West would awaken in 2000. They are presented as a rejection of habit and superstition in favor of "the rule of common sense": currency reform, nationalized railroads, an end to corrupt city governments, and—most importantly—a new system in which the national government conducts its own manufacturing and retailing, thus forcing honest competition on the great monopolistic trusts. Unlike the Progressive "trust-busters" or the small-business advocates of the day, Adams argues through this novel that huge, integrated industrial enterprises are the inevitable result of "scientific economy," and that government power should check and balance them rather than break them up.

Pretending to write from the perspective of twenty years later, he reports that the new system has been an unqualified success. Like Bellamy's, it has accomplished a goal much sought at the time but less often heard of thereafter: a new, more rational and efficient division of labor that literally "economizes" production and distribution, eliminating wasteful overlap and returning a greater share of the economy's wealth to the average workers who are credited with creating it.[56]

In some ways, *President John Smith* is realistic to a fault. Most of the story is told in documentary fashion—through speeches, news clippings, government reports, and innumerable statistics. Adams, a Chicago newspaperman, was well informed and in some ways prescient.[57] Better than the agitated partisans of either the gold standard or "free silver," those hotly competing nostrums of the time, he saw that the monetary future lay with dollars backed by government fiat, and that the U.S. dollar in turn would anchor the whole system of global finance. His "peaceful revolution" is both too revolutionary and too peaceful to believe, but unlike Bellamy's wish-fulfillment fantasy it appeals repeatedly to real or plausible fact. That's the problem: it is hard to get compelling fiction out of industrial-output numbers or long discussions of the currency question. The book's very specificity makes character, and therefore *psychological* realism, almost irrelevant. As his very common name suggests, John Smith is hardly a person at all; he is political "common sense" personified, and *President John Smith* is only barely a novel—as opposed to a political tract touched up with some novelistic devices.

Although long, verbatim speeches were a common feature of the era's political novels, there are others whose aesthetic weaknesses run to the opposite extreme: not too many facts and figures, but too much melodrama and bathos. Sutton E. Griggs's 1899 *Imperium in Imperio*, for instance, resembles William Wells Brown's *Clotel* in the way it marshals such devices as family secrets, hidden crimes, concealed paternity, doomed love, and suicide for the sake of honor.[58] The story's main feature is itself a deep secret—that black America has developed a vast underground, a parallel nation complete with a hidden government whose courts and Congress operate in synch with their visible counterparts in Washington, D.C. The leader of the underground Congress, Belton Piedmont, is a childhood friend of Bernard Belgrave, a rising politician who grew up not knowing that his father was a white senator who had kept his marriage to Bernard's black mother a secret. "Born of distinguished parents, reared in luxury, gratified as to every whim, successful in every undertaking, idolized by the people, proud, brilliant, aspiring, deeming nothing impossible of achievement," Bernard learns of the Imperium's existence when Belton recruits him to serve as its president. Accepting the post, he "steps out to battle for the freedom of his race."

But after a vicious racist attack on a black family moves the Imperium to respond, Bernard and Belton fall out over what purpose, ultimately, the secret government exists to fulfill. Its Congress debates this question while the U.S. Congress is considering war with Spain; thus, "These two congresses on this same day had under consideration questions of vital import to civilization." Bernard's plan is to take over Texas and declare it an independent black homeland, but Belton rejects this "treason" and insists on working for justice within "Anglo-Saxon" civilization. "Soaked as Old Glory is with my people's tears," he says in the novel's typically fustian style, "and stained as it is with their warm blood, I could die as my forefathers did, fighting for its honor and asking no greater boon than Old Glory for my shroud and native soil for my grave." That is indeed how he dies, condemned by the Imperium itself. From then on President Belgrave is "a man to be feared." One of those who fear him is the book's narrator, an official of the Imperium who ultimately betrays it to the white authorities in hopes of heading off a race war. While the Imperium is an early and extreme form of what would later be called black nationalism, it has to be destroyed, says the narrator, "in the interest of the whole human family—of which my race is but a part."[59]

Similarly arch in its style, but also aiming like *President John Smith* to lay out a detailed reform program, is the undramatically titled *Philip Dru, Administrator.* Set in the 1920s and 1930s, this "Story of Tomorrow" was published anonymously in 1912, the year of Woodrow Wilson's election. Its special claim to importance is that it was written by "Colonel" Edward Mandell House, the advisor and confidant whom President Wilson once called "my second personality. He is my independent self. His thoughts and mine are one."[60] The title character is a young West Point graduate, a prodigy with a brilliant strategic mind who gives up his military career after getting lost in the desert and temporarily losing his eyesight. Recovering from this affliction, whose symbolism is hard to miss, he becomes alert to the plight of the downtrodden and resolves to give over his "supernormal intellect, tireless energy, and splendid constructive ability" to a life of social work. Meanwhile, though, the U.S. government is falling under the control of a sinister conspiracy fronted by the newly elected President Rockland. Senator Selwyn, the mastermind of this political-industrial cabal, is a strategic genius himself, though his skill is all devoted to forging "a subtle chain with which to hold in subjection the natural impulses of the people." His black arts include organizing leagues of big-money donors, targeting undecided voters, and sending out direct mail—in other words, the standard methods of American political campaigns today. House was correct in seeing such techniques as the wave of the future.

But there the novel's resemblance to real history ends. When a mislaid phono-recording exposes the nefarious scheme, Americans rise in revolt under the generalship of Philip Dru:

> Selwyn, great man that he was, did not know, could not know, that when his power was greatest it was most insecure. He did not know, could not know, what force was working to his ruin and to the ruin of his system.
>
> Take heart, therefore, you who had lost faith in the ultimate destiny of the Republic, for a greater than Selwyn is here to espouse your cause. He comes panoplied in justice and with the light of reason in his eyes. He comes as the advocate of equal opportunity and he comes with the power to enforce his will.

Commanding a popular insurgency against the plutocrats, General Philip Dru wins a brief but horrible civil war and agrees to rule as "Administrator" with dictatorial powers. With the help of his fiancé-apparent—a wealthy but socially conscious woman with a high tolerance for his political lectures—and of a chastened Selwyn, who puts his insider's knowledge to work for the new order, he undertakes a broad program that intertwines political reconstruction with national spiritual renewal. This program ranges widely, from the writing of a new constitution with a greatly weakened executive to such everyday concerns as "burial reform." Like other reformers both fictional and real, Philip is incensed at capitalist inequality not just on moral grounds, but because it seems mindlessly inefficient. His domestic program aims to put the economy on a rational footing, and his foreign policy secures the homeland by pacifying the continent under benign American "protection." In a final act of disinterested service, he decides he must free the new republic "from the shadow of my presence and my name. I shall go to some obscure portion of the world where I cannot be found and importuned to return." And with that, Philip and his new wife sail off literally into the sunset.[61]

House calls this final departure "The Effacement of Philip Dru," and "effacement" is an apt term for what happens to the protagonists of these novels in general. As literary creations they tend to fade to irrelevance; the story's real central character is the plan it offers for a better society. Since articulating that plan is the point, it makes a kind of sense that the dialogue reads like an elocution lesson. But the creaky didacticism is nonetheless a literary weakness, as are heroes who are one-dimensional epitomes of virtue. It's no coincidence that *Philip Dru's* most interesting character is not Philip but Selwyn, the corrupt boss of the old system. Philip himself does not mean to be interesting. He means to be scientific and spiritual—impulses that might seem at odds, but that had fused in some strains of late nineteenth-century thought and that both represent a flight from the messily human.

The reformers' literature is conventionally classed as "utopian," and some of it does describe ideal societies.[62] But not all; President John Smith's America is greatly reformed, but not ideal. It's a utopia in one sense of the word—the good society—but not in the other sense of a never-never land. It is, however, no longer in the hands of politicians. That's the key, and indeed a better generic term for these imagined societies might be *upolian:* that is, societies whose idealized unreality lies in their absence of politics. What happens most predictably in the stories in question is that once the new order is in place, everyone sees that it's the better way. Opposition and political conflict essentially cease, not because they're suppressed but because the unassailable logic of the new arrangements leaves nothing to disagree about: "the interest of each and that of all were identical," as Bellamy puts it.[63] Precarious compromises, temporary expedients, unceasing pressures from all sides on leaders—the familiar features of real political life—are consigned to the "hideous ghastly mistake" that is the (then) present.

Unwilling to tolerate that mistake, and assuming that no John Smith or Philip Dru is at hand, the enlightened have limited options. One is separatism of some kind: a parallel or underground *polis,* as in *Imperium in Imperio,* or removal to a distant enclave or "lost world." The *Herland* described in Charlotte Perkins Gilman's 1915 novel of that title is an all-female society that has been cut off from the rest of civilization for two thousand years. The problems of uniting people in a single purpose and maintaining a single set of values have been greatly simplified by just eliminating the male half of the population. Political conflict and even the concept of evil have disappeared, and the tribal order that remains is so naturally cohesive that it needs little in the way of government—only a chief, the "Land Mother," who rules by simply being wise.[64]

The problem with such a scenario, of course, is the cleansing required to create such conditions. Where that has not yet occurred, the remaining option is a fight to the death. In stories where half the species hasn't conveniently died out, or where the plutocracy is slow to surrender, the ensuing struggles could be apocalyptic. Ignatius Donnelly's 1890 *Caesar's Column: A Story of the Twentieth Century* predicts the collapse of global civilization by 1988; only after this do the survivors settle into their enclave. Jack London's 1908 *The Iron Heel* foresees a civil war lasting centuries and growing ever more horrifically violent, although the faceless, fascist oligarchy is ultimately vanquished and "the world-movement of labor [comes] into its own." *Dystopian* is the term typically used for novels like these, but that term is no more exact than "early science fiction," which is also sometimes applied. Actually they are stories of utopias hard-won. The obstacle to progress is a version of that familiar old cabal, but one that has grown in size and reach from a few cigar-chomping bosses to a world-crushing colossus—not a political agency anymore, really, but a secularized nightmare of Satan's dominion over the earth.[65] Presidents usually do not even appear, because the forces in play are far larger than that.

At any rate, when the old order is beaten at last and "the people" have triumphed, injustice and inequality are looked back on as more than just evil. They're also baffling: Why would anyone have ever put up with such things? Philip Dru surmises that in the future, "our civilization of to-day [will] seem as crude, as selfish and illogical as that of the dark ages seem[s] now to us." This, in a sentence, is the recurring theme in upolian works, whether they see the glorious future arriving in years, decades, or centuries. Politics is not a contest of legitimately competing visions; it's a failure of logic, and political societies are dark ages awaiting the onset of science, reason, or "common sense." Eventually the New Deal and the welfare state would vindicate many of the reformers' specific proposals. But if their grander dreams of upolia are largely forgotten, it may be for some of the same reasons that most of their novels have been too. The most interesting characters and stories are driven by the same thing that drives politics: people's stubborn refusal to be reasonable, or even to agree what that is.

The Search for Secret Doors:
Lincoln in Early Twentieth-Century Fictions

While utopian reformers were imagining the political struggle for the future, the literary struggle over the Lincoln legend also continued into the new century. "The man of history [had] already become a man of fable" by then, said one writer, who noted that "[p]eople read about Lincoln with a weird sense of the supernatural, of something apart from human affairs."[66] The evidence William Herndon and others had offered of a psychologically more complex Lincoln did little to undercut the Christ-figure Lincoln of the early apotheoses. As we have seen, that figure had itself been a way of grappling with the "marvelous contrast" in Lincoln, as Herndon had called it. It was a way of acknowledging Lincoln's rude origins and private miseries while assimilating them to the fable, making everything about him so many steps on the eventual road to Mount Rushmore. Apotheosis had once been a bar to analysis, but with Lincoln it could call on analysis for help.

Thus, the problem of squaring Lincoln's statesmanship with his folkish origins could be solved simply by recasting even the statesman as a character in a frontier tall tale. In Joel Chandler Harris's short story "The Kidnapping of President Lincoln," Lincoln charms the Confederate agents sent to kidnap him, telling them stories and enlisting their help with a practical joke while also becoming the heart's desire of a female Southern spy.[67] And in the fiction of Ida Tarbell, the well-known muckraking journalist and "goddess of Lincolniana,"[68] an old Illinois crony named "Billy Brown" reminisces about Lincoln in the native prairie dialect they presumably shared. Tarbell has Billy traveling to Washington in the summer of 1864, hoping to cheer up a politically beleaguered Lincoln with stories of Illinois and a reminder of how "we set such store on his comin' home if they didn't want him for president." Though warned that "[f]olks don't visit the President of the United States without an invitation, and he's too busy to see anybody but the very biggest people in this administration," Billy quickly gets an audience with Lincoln, who admits he is "plumb homesick" and is moved to tears at encountering someone whose only claim on him was that "we loved him and . . . he loved us."[69] The two talk for hours and swap stories like old pals, and Billy finds that the presidency has changed Lincoln "not a mite." And it falls to Billy, of all people, to reassure him about the course of the war and his own re-election:

There was a bench there and we set down and after a while Mr. Lincoln he begun to talk. Well, sir, you or nobody ever heard anything like it. Blamed if he didn't tell me the whole thing—all about the war and the generals and Seward and Sumner and Congress and Greeley and the whole blamed lot. He just opened up his heart if I do say it. Seemed as if he'd come to a p'int where he must let out. I dunno how long we set there—must have been nigh morning, fer the stars begun to go out before he got up to go. "Good-by, Billy," he says. "[Y]ou're the first person I ever unloaded onto, and I hope you won't think I'm a baby."[70]

This scene suggests that the mature president's emotional well-being was nearly as precarious—and just as dependent on careful hometown nurturing—as Herndon believed the young law student's had been back in the days of Ann Rutledge. Yet the message is also that Lincoln was still his old self even at the highest circles of power. When this deeply sensitive friend of the common people dies, Billy can't bear to see him "havin' all that fuss made over him. He always hated fussin' so."[71]

If "psychologizing" Lincoln was originally a way of explaining his improbable rise to grandeur, Tarbell's writing illustrates another use it could have as well. The term can mean both inner complexity of one's own and insight into that of others, and Lincoln was credited with both; indeed, the one was seen as making the other possible. In denying Lincoln's interest in "the intricacies of psychology," William Herndon had meant that he didn't think like a scientist. Though Lincoln did have an ability to change the mood and thinking of others, especially with the help of his "infectious" sense of humor, Herndon believed that his grasp of others was largely abstract: "Although a profound analyzer of the laws of human nature he could form no just construction of the motives of the particular individual." Lincoln dealt in the rational above all; in reading people's emotions or expressions, "he was pitiably weak."[72] Ignoring that judgment, Tarbell and other writers insisted on Lincoln's superior insight, which Tarbell frames as a general principle. Lincoln's own inner state—the fact that he was "in many ways starved, starved for love and hope and gaiety," that he felt old even when young—was, she said, of a piece with his ability to go

unerringly and unconsciously for the most part, to the meeting place that awaited him in each man's nature. There might be a wall, often there was; but he knew, no one better, that there is always a secret door in human walls. Sooner or later he discovered it, put his finger on its spring, passed through and settled into the place behind that was his.

Lincoln's indifference to "social veneering" made him equally at home with "the bully, the scholarly, the cunning, the pious, the ambitious, the selfish, the great, the weak, the boy, the man." And this, in turn, made his political achievement possible. Because his saving acts—freeing the slaves and preserving the Union—depended on being politically effective, Tarbell believed he "could not have done what he did had he been less understanding of men," or "less experienced in passing behind human walls" and entering human hearts.[73]

So if psychological understanding had once threatened "ghastly exposures" difficult to square with the image of Lincoln as Christ, Tarbell's formula suggested that readers could have it both ways. Christianity's Redeemer was one who walked among us, who "humbled himself to become a man," who sympathized and communed with lepers and publicans. His saving sacrifice had been possible because he "felt for" us, meaning both that he cared about us and that he substituted his pain for ours: Surely he hath borne our griefs and carried our sorrows.[74] Finding depth in Lincoln made it easier to analogize these qualities to him. In fact, the more Lincoln's humility was emphasized, the more grandiose his myth became. Like some kind of prairie Pantocrator, it expanded until it filled the entire universe. Even the modest little Ann Rutledge episode grew to literally epic dimensions, in one case becoming a whole volume in a tetralogy of book-length epic poems about Lincoln. The author of these, Denton J. Snider, had also written books on psychology, but when treating Lincoln he envisioned him as a "mediator and harmonizer between the nation's Folk-Soul and a kind of Hegelian World-Spirit," in one critic's words.[75]

Grand literary gestures of that kind were popular in the early twentieth century, and not just in Lincoln's case. S. Weir Mitchell's 1904 *The Youth of Washington: Told in the Form of an Autobiography,* for instance, is part of a multivolume story cycle on Washington that Mitchell published over a twelve-year period. One might expect such a novel to have some psychological depth: it concerns Washington's developmental years, Washington himself narrates it, and Mitchell was a pathbreaking neurologist with a particular interest in nervous disorders and traumas. But instead it's a tale of war and adventure, a standard example of the historical romance genre then in vogue.[76] Dealing as they did with great events and larger-than-life heroes, the nonrealistic, belles lettres styles of epic and romance were, in their way, natural vehicles for stories about presidents. They were the literary equivalents of the period's other grand, neoclassical acts of solemn remembrance, like the Lincoln Memorial and Mount Rushmore. And, as one might expect, they revealed the inner person about as well as a block of granite.

The same years, though, also saw a vogue for works that went the opposite way: toward the microscopic analysis of inner states, the springing of "secret doors in human walls" in political leaders along with everyone else. The advent of Freudian psychology encouraged the hope that those springs could be found. Freud himself collaborated on a study of Woodrow Wilson that was rife with characteristically Freudian terms and concepts (including extended analysis of Wilson's dependence on Col. House, the *Philip Dru* author). Explicitly disclaiming interest in Wilson's conscious mind, Freud and his co-author had "no apology to offer for our concentration on his deeper mental mechanisms":

> The more important portion of the mind, like the more important portion of an iceberg, lies below the surface. The unconscious of a neurotic employs the conscious portion of the mind to achieve its wishes. The convictions of a neurotic are excuses invented by reason to justify desires of the libido. The principles of a neurotic are costumes employed to embellish and conceal the nakedness of the unconscious desires.

Given assumptions like these, no greatness is required. In fact Wilson fares very badly on the Freudian couch; by the end of the session he has been diagnosed as a delusional psychotic with a world-threatening messiah complex.[77] And even in better-regarded figures, terms like *greatness* no longer really operate once the focus shifts to Oedipal conflicts, primary narcissism, object-cathexis, and other such mechanisms of psychobiography (a term first used in this period). Under a microscope, everyone looks about the same. In fact, another president who was closely scrutinized in the years before 1930 was Warren G. Harding. When historians today are asked in surveys to rate the presidents, Lincoln is invariably first or second on the list while Harding is usually last or near last. But Harding's conspicuous weaknesses and quirks, including his alleged affair with a woman more than thirty years his junior, make him—from a purely clinical standpoint—just as interesting a specimen as Lincoln.[78]

If there was something unique about Lincoln, it's that he was of equal interest to the romancers and the psychobiographers alike. The "unprecedented abundance of books" about him that appeared in this period included everything from melodramatic novels and long poems to biographies describing his alleged neuroses, weak ego, and mother-fixation—which, incidentally, was claimed to have caused his attachment to Ann Rutledge.[79] In one celebrated case, fictional love letters between Abe and Ann were published as a real discovery after several historians were duped into authenticating the forgeries.[80] What the hoax pointed up was the Rutledge tale's tremendous literary value, its exquisite fit with both approaches: it was very romantic and *also* of great psychoanalytical interest. Understanding it could mean understanding Lincoln, and understanding Lincoln could mean understanding what made an American president great—and therefore, perhaps, what made America great.

And so the old ways of seeing Lincoln lived and thrived alongside the new. With the rise of motion pictures they even received a new lease on life. Early films featuring Lincoln offered an iconic figure at least a generation or two out of date. D. W. Griffith's *The Birth of a Nation* (1915), John Ford's *The Iron Horse* (1924), and Griffith's later "biopic" *Abraham Lincoln* (1930) all seemed to pick up where Francis Bicknell Carpenter's lithographs left off. Although Lincoln "moved," he often seemed as stiffly posed in Griffith's frame as in any print of Carpenter's or studio portrait of Matthew Brady's. The ad campaign for *Abraham Lincoln* declared him "the most romantic figure who ever lived," and the film-makers who treated him seemed especially drawn to old-fashioned "appliances and tricks of picture-making," as Carpenter had called them in Lincoln's own time. Thus *Abraham Lincoln* and even John Ford's livelier *Young Mr. Lincoln*, which are discussed in the next chapter, dissolved in the end to images of the Lincoln Memorial, visually equating the movie character with a statue—and assuring us that the events just witnessed all fit within the Lincoln canon.[81]

In *The Fall of Public Man*, Richard Sennett describes a broad cultural change that, he argues, helped create the set of assumptions implicit in the literature we have just been examining. A general withdrawal from "public culture" since the early nineteenth century has created "the intimate society," a narcissistic world in which "the psyche is treated as though it has an inner life of its own" and in which "we seek out not a principle [like religious transcendence] but a reflection, that of what our psyches are, what is authentic in our feelings." Authenticity is therefore sought in private, in families and intimate relationships, while public life suffers a number of deformities—one of which is the cult of charisma in political leaders, "a politics of personality [that] consists of the revelation of intentions unrelated to the world of action."[82] It is somehow imagined that politicians' motives are more important than what they actually *do*, what measures they take in defense of citizens and their concrete interests.

Sennett's hypothesis is complex and would be hard to prove in all its particulars.[83] But it does sit well with the Lincoln myths familiar to Americans of the twentieth century. Widely sneered at in his own time, Lincoln would eventually become the quintessence of the authentic political leader—a president seen as living and dying for policies whose rightness is somehow inseparable from the greatness and depth of his person. A "fall" from an older understanding of public life and responsibilities would account for characters like *The Unknown Lincoln*, the figure whom bestselling author and super-salesman Dale Carnegie peddled in a book of that title as basically a font of self-help techniques. It would also explain the most striking feature of Mark Van Doren's stage play *The Last Days of Lincoln*, in which all the characters *except* Lincoln speak in Shakespearean-style blank verse. Other public men around Lincoln, Van Doren seems to suggest, were still living in an older era of artfully constructed personas; only Lincoln was a natural, authentic person like ourselves.[84]

And again, while Lincoln may be the paradigm case, it is all but routine today to see political leaders' actions explained less in political or public terms than as symptoms, products of deep-seated motives that originally arose outside politics—in difficult family circumstances and the like—and that then for good or ill guided their decision making decades later. There was a time when explanations like that were not of nearly as much interest—just as there was a time when a joke like the following, from a 1922 parody of etiquette manuals, would probably have made no sense:

A Correct Letter from a Mother to Her Son Congratulating Him on His Election to the Presidency of the United States

DEAR FREDERICK:

I am very glad that you have been elected President of the United States, Frederick, and I hope that now you will have sense enough to see Dr. Kincaid about your teeth. . . . [85]

The spoof of maternal advice continues for a long paragraph in which Frederick's mother never expresses the slightest interest in the presidency as such. Frederick's public role means nothing to her apart from the fact that he might have to give speeches outdoors, and if it's raining he had better be sure to wear his galoshes. A related joke is that becoming president is just another event in everyday life, an occasion hardly to be noticed except for these pesky questions of etiquette. (Don't we *all* sometimes need help with correct ways of addressing the presidents-elect in our personal circles?) Etiquette manuals were widely read in the eighteenth century; George Washington even composed one for his own use. But he did this precisely as part of his preparation for a career as a public man. The joke here lies in imagining how such manuals might read if public man were to disappear altogether. A grown-up president with such a relationship to his mother would be hard to see as anything *but* a subject for psychoanalysis.

In the Progressive Era, as noted earlier, reformers craved presidents with "common sense" and hoped to rebuild the whole social order on that principle. Common sense is the stock in trade of advice manuals, and in its facetious way this parody of one also raises a crucial and troubling question: What *is* common sense in an age when conventions of public decorum are "falling," when it is widely assumed that the real truth always lies in the personal and private? The term itself suggests that which is simple and shareable (common) and coherent (sense), as opposed to the subtle, strange, irrational, or idiosyncratic. It would seem to connote the steady, calm, and anti-ideological, the effortless clarity that allows some people to see the obvious ahead of everyone else. For that reason it was often associated with Lincoln, who was credited with preserving America whole against those overwrought passions that will otherwise tear a society apart.

But what makes the notion of common sense inoffensive also makes it dangerous. Plainspokenness is a rhetorical style and humility a performance. A common "man of the people" with these qualities can be politically manufactured. If authenticity is the test, his words will be compelling as long as they're simple and seem to come from the heart: He's not lying, so he must not be wrong. And he's saying what others have not, so he must be onto the real truth. He must, therefore, see things plainly while the rest of us are confused. Thus is common sense turned against itself, becoming, in the worst cases, a cloak for the strangest and most senseless politics of all. By the 1930s there was apparently a widely shared wish for leaders who could touch the feelings of the people, who could reach into and change their everyday lives. And soon there was serious worry about what might happen when one of them did.

4

A Simple, Honest Man

Presidential Character in the Fictions
of the 1930s and 1940s

❖

Who will make your taxes light?
Mr. No-body!
Who'll protect the voters' rights?
Mr. NO-body!
Who fills up your flour keg?
Who cares if you have to beg?
Who cares if you break a leg?
Mr. *NOOO*-body!

Betty Boop for President, 1932

❖

With her campaign promises of a chocolate ice-cream utopia, free cabarets, and her trademark "boop-oop-a-doop," the Jazz Age cartoon temptress Betty Boop had little trouble winning the White House in 1932, easily defeating "Mr. Nobody," a headless stick figure whose platform included the cynical lines just quoted.[1] And sure enough, within a few years of this imaginary contest the New Deal would solidify a view of the presidency as the dispenser, if not of chocolate ice cream, then of other necessities and comforts of everyday life. Under the New Deal's new "regime," says Theodore J. Lowi,

> ultimately the national government would be responsible for every injurious act sustained by any individual citizen, and also for providing the conditions for every individual citizen's well-being. No matter that government has fallen short on both fronts. The establishment of those obligations solemnized the new social contract by putting the national government at the very center of American society. . . .
>
> This change is of fundamental importance to the continuing legitimacy and stability of modern government. And its importance has intensified as it comes more and more narrowly to focus on the presidency.[2]

The advent of "the personal president," says Lowi, was a revolution in itself—a change not just in administrations but in America's whole system of government.[3]

Lowi and most other commentators rightly count this among the legacies of FDR. "Before Roosevelt's time," according to Bruce Kuklick, "Washington rarely intruded into the life of the ordinary citizen. After Roosevelt, the presidency became part of the daily world of the populace."[4] But even before Roosevelt was elected, the new promises and aspirations that would be channeled through government were already animating, as it were, the administration of President Boop, particularly by contrast with her unpopular opposite. First appearing in the songs and routines of the breakthrough black vaudevillian Bert Williams, Mr. Nobody was a sardonic expression of sympathy for the put-upon common man. Someone does care about your troubles, Williams had sung. Unfortunately that person is "Nobody," so no one cares about your troubles. But Williams's early-century laments did not suggest any political solution. In reviving Mr. Nobody and running him for president, Betty Boop's creators not only enlisted him in the cause of political satire but changed what he stood for. The point was that by 1932, a viable presidential candidate would *have* to care about things that affected people's everyday lives. If Herbert Hoover was a Mr. Nobody, his opponent was going to waltz right past him, despite not having legs like Betty Boop's.

There are other pre-Roosevelt fictions of the time that likewise point toward a new kind of presidency. Indeed the years around 1930 were a kind of "big bang" of fictional presidents, the point at which presidents as wholly literary creations began to appear in large and increasing

"Mr. Nobody" makes his musical pitch to a crowd of booing voters in the film *Betty Boop for President.*

numbers. This was not a coincidence. If the personal president was one who connected with citizens in their personal lives, he was by the same token one whom citizens could imagine they knew as a person. By slow degrees, real presidents had by the 1920s come to be imagined with inner lives like those of characters in realistic fiction. But the flip side of this, a fully realized imaginary character as president, was still rare — until, all of a sudden, it wasn't.

Court Jesters and Thinking Machines:
Of Thee I Sing, The Phantom President, and
Gabriel over the White House

As noted in chapter 1, party politics and political administration as we know them today have a continuous history reaching back to the so-called Augustan Age of the early eighteenth century. That was when Robert Walpole became the first British leader to live at 10 Downing Street and, by most reckonings, the first prime minister. Walpole guided his Whig party — and dragged his Tory opponents kicking and screaming—into a new era, one whose financial and mercantile brand of national governance has mostly ruled the West ever since. To horrified adversaries like Jonathan Swift and John Gay, Walpole and his colleagues looked like a bunch of crooks—a "cabal" of bankers, brokers, and their political minions, openly committed to "the money power" and determined to turn politics into a sordid contest of class interests. Whether personally corrupt or not, they embodied a new political order that Augustan writers viewed as corrupt by definition. It was by way of making this point that Gay wrote *The Beggar's Opera* in 1728. If Walpole and his cronies were forerunners of our modern style of politics, Gay's hugely popular satire of them was the forerunner of the modern musical comedy.[5]

Two hundred years later the cabal was not only still scandalizing critics, it also had recently seemed to come to life in the corrupt "Teapot Dome" cabinet of Warren G. Harding. The typical fictional president of the 1930s came accompanied by a Hardingesque group of shady powerbrokers and kingmakers—cigar-chomping cynics for whom politics and pocket-lining seemed to be one and the same pursuit. And the very first of these presidents, John P. Wintergreen, had something else in common with Peachum, the pseudo-Walpole of *The Beggar's Opera*: Both helped to usher in a new style of musical theater. *Of Thee I Sing*, the Broadway hit in which Wintergreen presided, was a landmark, the first musical whose "book" was published as a piece of literature and the first to win a Pulitzer Prize.[6]

Personal and political life are brought together in *Of Thee I Sing* in just about the simplest way possible: Wintergreen makes his personal affairs the subject of his presidential campaign. Like most candidates chosen in the proverbial smoke-filled room (a term coined in reference to Harding), he is a party hack, a man whose nomination is engineered by the cabal—a group of press and political bosses who make up the party's "National Committee." Politically, the party stands for nothing—the committeemen can't even remember if they're Republicans or Democrats—and the chief qualification they see in Wintergreen is that he has pledged "to do any dirty work" they suggest.

But the voters, they fear, may be starting to get wise. So the group decides it needs to find a "good live issue," meaning "something that everybody is interested in, and that doesn't matter a damn." The solution is "a one-word platform: 'Love!'" Wintergreen will turn his campaign into a courtship, a quest to marry a woman chosen for him in a nationwide beauty contest. Since "everybody loves a lover . . . a hundred million hearts will beat as one," and Wintergreen will be "swept into the White House on a tidal wave of love!"

The contest is held, and Wintergreen's cronies pick a "thorough-bred" of a winner. But Wintergreen rejects her in favor of the secretary who happens to be managing the event. Mary Turner, "the loveliest example of typical American womanhood," impresses Wintergreen with her talent for baking corn muffins, and his winning campaign consists of proposing to her in each of the forty-eight states. Their wedding is combined with Wintergreen's inauguration—his oath of office and wedding vows are pronounced in the same sentence—and the couple takes up joint residence in the Oval Office, which is divided in half: one side of the desk is "piled high with various state papers," and the other is "lined with perfumes, powders and other perquisites of femininity." In the Wintergreen administration, the presidency's political and personal sides are made literal even in the White House décor.

Scandal erupts, though, when the French ambassador lodges a protest on behalf of the jilted contest winner, Diana Devereaux—"the illegitimate daughter of an illegitimate son of an illegitimate nephew of Napoleon." This further comic mixing of state and family matters leads to Wintergreen's impeachment, which he survives only because Mary suddenly announces that she's pregnant. When she delivers twins, the Supreme Court is convened to rule on their gender (one of each), whereupon France threatens war if they are not placed in French custody. But all is happily settled when Wintergreen, invoking Article 12 of the Constitution, devolves his duty of marrying Diana and having children with her onto his nondescript vice president.

At a time when the indifference of political leaders was becoming a major issue, *Of Thee I Sing* turned it into one long joke. Wintergreen is no FDR; with campaign slogans like "The Full Dinner Jacket," "Turn the Reformers Out," and "Vote for Prosperity and See What You Get," he gives not the slightest hint of concern for citizens and their everyday struggles. His politics therefore have no content, which is precisely what makes it possible to fill them up with everyday concerns—a personal pursuit of happiness essentially the same as any other eligible bachelor's. At one point Wintergreen briefs the vice president, Throttlebottom, on his duties should he succeed to the office:

THROTTLEBOTTOM. Isn't there some book I could read?
WINTERGREEN. Sure—I'm writing one. *"What Every Young President*

Ought to Know." . . . Tells you just what to do. Of course the first four years are easy. You don't do anything except try to get re-elected. . . . The next four years you wonder why the hell you wanted to be re-elected. Then you go fishing.

THROTTLEBOTTOM. Well, couldn't I save a lot of time and go fishing right now?

WINTERGREEN. No, you got to wait until an important matter comes up and then you go fishing.

Popular manuals of personal advice in the 1920s had carried titles like *What Every Young Man and Woman Ought to Know.* Wintergreen's riff on such titles imagines the presidency as just another set of common social situations and problems that anyone might need help to navigate.

The kicker is that if getting elected (Act 1) and governing (Act 2) both depend on getting the president's personal life in order, then personal crises are also political: When your quest for office is a search for a bride, your romantic misadventures are, literally, affairs of state. That's the upshot of the bosses' decision to set aside issues and "appeal to your hearts; not your intelligence." But it's all in good fun; the cynicism is essentially benign. As light comedy, *Of Thee I Sing* invites us to laugh at the notion of a brainless politics, to recognize it as all too true. There is no real harm done when intelligence is set aside.

Things are different in the darker comedy of *The Phantom President,* the 1932 novel by George F. Worts that became a movie musical starring George M. Cohan in a rare film appearance. This story starts from the same premise as *The Prince and the Pauper* and *The Prisoner of Zenda*: a commoner temporarily doubles for the monarch.[7] Theodore "T. K." Blair is a young, good-looking and brilliant tycoon, America's preeminent business leader, and "the one man in America with the brains to put the country on its feet." Selfless and patriotic, he has "thoroughly, scientifically, made himself fit for the Presidency," and the bosses of the Prosperity Party, "the oligarchy which ruled American politics . . . because the people were too busy to do it," are thinking of making him their candidate. If elected, he would be just about the most capable and knowledgeable president ever.

But, the bosses realize, there is one little problem:

What the country needed was a man who could carry in his brain a thousand streams of consciousness. What the country needed was a thinking-machine.

But what the country needed was not, alas, what the country wanted. The country would elect, not a thinking-machine, but a warm and pleasing personality; a President it could call Bill or Jim or Hank; who shook hands, loved small children, gave apples to horses, and pointed with pride to the tenement or humble farmhouse where he had been born. On its sickbed, the country called, not for a doctor, but a court jester.[8]

T. K. Blair, though, is no court jester. To most people he seems to be nothing *but* intellect, "a cold, nerveless machine, as impervious as chromium." As Lorenz Hart succinctly put it in lyrics he wrote for the film: "Blair has no flair for savoir-faire."[9] His personal side is so stunted that he has never wooed anyone other than a woman he grew up with, Felicia, and then only clumsily and without any luck. Felicia flatly rejects the party bosses' idea of a campaign romance designed to help humanize Blair. She refuses even to call him by the nickname "Teddy," which she says "would be worse than calling God 'Goddie.'" Felicia could be speaking for all of America when she tells Blair, "I admire and respect you more than any man alive. But I'm not in love with you." Since his genius for dispassionate problem solving also makes him "as emotional as an oyster," the bosses are stumped: Blair is "the one man in the country we want in the White House. And we can't put him there."[10]

But then, as luck would have it, they discover a man who is Blair's exact look-alike. Peter Varney is a charming rogue with a colorful past, a fugitive and con artist not above impersonating Blair to pull off the occasional stock swindle. (In the movie he's "Doc" Varney, a medicine-show huckster whose salesmanship skills are another of his assets.) Varney has "an air about him, an indefinable magnetism, which he would never lose, and which, no matter how long the association continued, Blair would never acquire." Or, as Hart's lyrics for the movie put it:

> What a smooth talker,
> What charming rascality.
> There's just one word for it—
> Personality!

In Varney, the party cabal sees a desperate solution: Blair, hidden away, can do all the thinking while Varney delivers the speeches and makes the public appearances. By relieving Blair of "a thousand irksome details," like laying cornerstones and pinning medals on Boy Scouts, the scheme will enable him to focus on solving the nation's problems.

At first this arrangement works. Varney kisses babies, gives apples to horses, and wins a landslide for "Teddy" Blair, who works his magic on policy as Varney works his on the public. But over time Varney becomes more and more demanding; the role of acting president goes to his head, especially when he discovers that it fools even Felicia and makes "Blair," at last, irresistible to her. Before long he and Blair are plotting each other's murder. "I'm the man the people elected," says Varney. "I'm President of the United States morally. I'm going to be President actually!"[11]

As Varney stops taking direction, the scheme becomes increasingly hard to manage. A police detective who had been tailing Varney starts to get wise to it. Complicated comings and goings and mistakes of identity mount. Varney finally escapes the bosses' control altogether—he "regained the Presidency of the United States by climbing out of a bedroom window"—and just when it seems the ruse is about to be exposed, Varney is shot to death by an assassin who thinks he's killing Blair. Having suffered through a thankless presidency that stuck him with all its burdens while another man soaked up the praise, the newly "dead" Blair is only too happy to seize this chance to escape. Succeeded by his vice president, a reasonably able party boss who had never liked the scheme to begin with, he runs off with Felicia, whose shocked discovery of the substitution has finally convinced her of her true feelings for Blair.

In the same way that earlier stories of substitute monarchs took the ancient division of "the king's two bodies" and made it literal, *The Phantom President* brings to life the newly divided roles implied in the term *personal president*. As Varney explains them, "People have known for years that the country needs two Presidents: one to do the concentrating, the other to have his hands mashed by visiting westerners." What motivates the story is the fact that the two get along uneasily, if at all. Charisma by its nature is hard to control; the same personal magnetism that attracts the public to Varney also attracts him to the public, and the megalomania this induces cannot be contained. Inevitably, the two roles—and therefore, in this story, the two men—clash. In such conflicts, the Varneys have a natural advantage over the Blairs. You can elect a man who isn't brilliant (to say the least), but "What, Blair bitterly asked himself, is a brain without a personality?"[12] One is optional but the other essential: personality is the one thing that modern politics can't do without.

If we cannot assign the president's two functions to body doubles, then what will ensure that we have brilliance like T. K. Blair's at hand—that there will be someone "to do the concentrating"—when it's most badly needed? Another fiction soon suggested one possible answer:

divine intervention. That's the premise of *Gabriel Over the White House,* both the novel by Thomas F. Tweed and the popular film version that quickly followed. Neither of these works is a masterpiece of its genre; many of the aptly named Tweed's sentences have the stuffy syntax of an Oxbridge don at a queen's garden party, and the book made an igno-minious later appearance as pulp science fiction in a 1950s paperback reissue (a "fantastic adventure of the future," albeit a future that had somehow skipped World War II).[13] But it's a remarkable story nonethe-less. A new president, scion of a wealthy family, takes office in the depths of the Great Depression. Soon he surprises everyone by launching a sweeping series of federal relief measures, including a massive public works program that enlists the growing legions of the unemployed into a military-style civilian corps. His unprecedented use of federal author-ity threatens old-style vested interests and raises cries of "dictatorship," but the president wins public support for his program through an inno-vative series of appeals directly to citizens via the new electronic media.

Later, as his economic recovery gradually takes hold, the presi-dent turns his attention to the rising troubles of Europe and the Far East. When Japan strikes, he takes the country to war at the head of an Anglo-American alliance that, after early setbacks, finally prevails with assist-ance from the Soviet Union. To enforce the postwar order, he lays down blueprints for a new, more effective world body that would replace the moribund League of Nations. But he never lives to see it: At the moment of triumph, the president collapses and dies.

All this, of course, could be a thumbnail account of Franklin D. Roosevelt's administration. What's remarkable is that *Gabriel Over the White House* appeared in early 1933, *before* FDR took office and events like these proceeded to happen for real.[14] To be sure, life did not per-fectly imitate art; the fictional war, for instance, is confined to the Far East. But the biggest difference is the one suggested in the story's title: President Judson Hammond is not just politically but also divinely in-spired. At the outset he's another backslapping lightweight, a party hack known for his fine speeches and his careless indifference to public af-fairs. Chosen as a compromise candidate in the same way as Warren G. Harding, he seems intent on governing in the same lackadaisical style. But one of his irresponsible pastimes is racing around in his car, and after the inevitable crash puts him in a coma, he wakes up completely changed—serious, focused and fanatically determined to save the world.

President Judson Hammond before his injury, laughing off the idea that he could do great things with Lincoln's quill pen, in *Gabriel Over the White House*.

A changed man after awakening from a coma, Hammond describes his emergency reform program in a radio speech to the nation.

What follows is a nonstop series of initiatives that astonish even his closest aides. Dismissing Congress and welcoming the label *dictator*, Hammond rules by executive decree. He replaces Prohibition with a socialized system for selling liquor from government-run stores. This puts him at odds with gangster bosses who try to kill him (in the movie, by tommy-gunning the White House). The international peace pact he forces on reluctant world leaders abolishes armies, navies, and national currencies in favor of a single currency and a global peacekeeping force under the command of a "World Council." And everything he tries works just as planned. Though he never says so himself, his aides believe him to be getting policy advice from the archangel Gabriel.

To readers and viewers resigned to long years of hands-off governing under Harding, Coolidge, and Hoover, an energetic president may well have seemed an otherworldly hope. Certainly the movie struck a chord. Directed by Gregory La Cava and starring Walter Huston as the crusading president, it was made for MGM by Cosmopolitan Pictures, a William Randolph Hearst company. Legend has it that when the picture was screened for Louis B. Mayer, a Republican who had been friendly with Harding and Hoover, he recognized it as pro-FDR propaganda and ordered it "put back in the can." Hearst's involvement, though, made that impossible, and so the film appeared, as scheduled, in the spring of FDR's first inauguration. It was a hit not just with the public but also reportedly with Roosevelt himself, who is said to have screened it several times at the White House.

It's not impossible that the novel, too, found its way to FDR or his advisors, and thereby encouraged if not actually contributed to the famous burst of policymaking that launched the New Deal. The novel is very concerned with policy. Like the Progressive/utopian novels of a generation earlier, its interest lies less in story or character than in political ideas, and its suggestion that the ideas are God's own could be seen as a more extreme version of *President John Smith's* claim that progressive politics are just inarguable common sense.[15] The difference here, though, is that they are not the product of any Progressive movement. Like T. K. Blair in *The Phantom President,* Jud Hammond is a lone genius living in terrible isolation. But this is not, like Blair's, the isolation of a prisoner—it's that of a prophet or holy man for whom the upper floor of the White House is the proverbial mountaintop. Having ascended there, Hammond returns bearing the laws that will deliver his people from their afflictions.

As unreal as it was for *The Phantom President* to imagine two very different men with identical bodies somehow becoming the same president, it's obviously even more unreal to hope that two very different presidents might somehow inhabit the same body. And in the end, Tweed's novel questions whether it would even be a good thing. No matter what their political content, messianic fantasies are not a political solution. Thus the convoluted fate of the novel's President Hammond. During a gangster's attempt on his life, he suffers a second head injury, improbably wiping out the results of the first. Restored to his former self, and confronted in Rip Van Winkle fashion with the new world he has made, Hammond is appalled. What has he done to the Constitution? Why has he sacrificed a self-sufficient America to radical schemes of global governance? He plans to resign after giving a final radio/TV address, repudiating his own handiwork and urging that it be undone. But his cabinet won't let him; they cut off the broadcast just as he starts to speak, at which point his weakened heart fails and he dies.[16]

The people therefore never learn of Hammond's re-conversion, and the reader is left to choose which of the two Hammonds is more devoutly to be wished. One is a lot like *The Phantom President*'s Peter Varney: Cynical and careless but personally magnetic, he's got that charming rascality they call personality. The other, a "super-genius" whose "negative virtues and monastic seclusion" set him apart from ordinary mortals, is more like T. K. Blair. But again, there is a difference. To attract voters and tend to a suffering nation, Blair needed be made more human—by hook or (literally) by crook. Hammond needed to be made *less* human, more otherworldly. His personal magnetism exerts its pull only when he ceases to be "a definite personality, or even an ordinary human being." His story is a reminder that "charisma" was originally a religious concept—not an aspect of personality, but a way of transcending it.

"The Magic of the Amplifying Circuit"

President Hammond's unearthly power over the millions may or may not have come from the sky. But there's no question that it came in large part over the air. Conventional wisdom credits FDR with discovering the political possibilities of radio. But even before he took office and launched his famous "Fireside Chats," there were worries about this new mass medium and its impact on politics.

Expressions of these worries include the novels just discussed. In *The Phantom President*, the political cabal behind T. K. Blair decides to make the announcement of his candidacy a big event. So they pay to have it carried worldwide by radio. But the bosses don't know how their man will sound on radio, "whether or not Blair's voice had sufficient warmth and color to be satisfactory for broadcasting purposes. If not, Varney would have to double for him on the mike." A microphone test is set up and both men are auditioned. Blair, of course, is a disaster—as warm and friendly on radio "as a couple of icebergs grinding together." Dials are twiddled, but nothing helps; the mike even picks up a previously un-noticed rasp in his voice. Peter Varney, by contrast, has "undeniably, richness and warmth and color in his deep voice. The magic of the am-plifying circuit intensified it, as the circuit had intensified Blair's cold-ness and his faint rasp." So, despite the added risks, Varney becomes Blair's public voice as well as his face.[17]

As much as this irritates Blair, his problem is relatively simple. Rely-ing on radio does not put him at odds with his party—in fact, it's the party bosses' idea—and *The Phantom President* implies that once Blair is in office, his brilliant policies speak for themselves. Governing is one thing, appealing to the public is something else, and it's awkward but not im-possible to divide these functions between two different men. Coming across passably well on radio is just one more challenge that has to be met if the party's product, Blair, is to reach its market.

Gabriel Over the White House presents a different and, again, more om-inous picture. President Judson Hammond uses broadcasting as FDR soon would: as a key element of his politics, a means of overcoming resistance and mobilizing people behind a vigorous, controversial pro-gram of reform. This raises the stakes considerably. Hammond's elec-tronic persona cannot be merely acceptable, he has to be—and is—mesmerizing. In fact the novel suggests that radio alone would not be adequate to the purpose:

> For two decades presidents had used the obsolete radio with variable success. Now for the first time, however, one was to carry himself by sight as well as sound directly into millions of homes.
>   . . . . Department of Education agents set up huge televisor screens in the parks of over five hundred cities where thousands of citizens could congregate to look and listen. Empty theatres were hired and thrown open to the public for the same purpose. Schools receiving Fed-eral aid were likewise used.

When the first of the televised talks takes places, it's "an amazing performance":

Crowds in the parks stood breathless and spellbound for a solid hour as they beheld their President ten times larger than life talking in heart-to-heart fashion to them from the White House. Even the bookcases and mantel in the Lincoln Study were plainly visible as a background. Countless citizens got the impression that they had been individually invited into the White House to receive from the President a private report on the state of the nation.

At the end of his first talk, President Hammond had captured the country's imagination; by the end of the week he was a popular hero, a national leader who had established himself in the people's homes and hearts.

The effect of the talks on Americans is "staggering," and later the president gains a similar hold on world opinion by insisting that his global disarmament summit be carried live over radio.[18]

This passage is notable both for what it predicted and for what it didn't. For novelist Tweed, the power of the president's broadcasts depends partly on "the simplicity of his language and explanations," and partly on the impression made on citizens when they hear the president in their own homes—factors in FDR's later radio success as well. But for Tweed the staggering effect also came from *seeing* the president on the huge screens. In real life television would indeed have tremendous impact, but the Fireside Chats proved that radio, in the meantime, was far from "obsolete." The amplifying circuit would work its magic for the right president even if he was not seen, and his words might even have *more* of the personal touch if he was not projected ten times larger than life.

Mistaken predictions like Tweed's point up how hard it was to imagine the Fireside Chats until they occurred.[19] Both *Gabriel* and *The Phantom President* were written when the example at hand was Herbert Hoover, a man who "regarded public speaking as an unfortunate duty to be undertaken only to educate the electorate. When he did use the radio," says Bruce Kuklick, "his voice, which many citizens now heard, was harsh and monotonous."[20] In this respect Hoover was the obvious model for T. K. Blair. Before 1933, a president with a radio presence less like Blair's and more like Peter Varney's may have seemed almost as unlikely as a president with a body double.

But *The Phantom President* did correctly foresee that such a presence would be needed for a president to succeed. And the novel *Gabriel*, if not the movie, brilliantly guessed at what such success might look like—how citizens would react to a president's "simple straightforward phrases" delivered "heart-to-heart." When they heard Hammond, "their leader, their President, talking to them in their homes as man-to-man,"

> popular excitement ran like a prairie fire throughout the length and breadth of the land. . . . People poured turbulently out of their houses to join friends, neighbours, even strangers on the streets, to gather at every corner, to talk and to argue what the President meant.[21]

That, apparently, is just what FDR's listeners heard. Americans who flooded the White House with letters after the first of Roosevelt's chats included many like Chester E. Bruns of Chicago, "[o]ne of the average citizens," who thanked him for his "directness and also the 100% American language you used." The letter writers described scenes very similar to those in *Gabriel*: groups of spellbound listeners sitting in amazed silence, then joining excitedly in the conversations that followed. Bruns informed the president that "our country is united again" as Chicago's "lawyers, brokers elevator men doctors janitors" all chimed in their approval. Likewise in suburbs and small towns; in Bellevue, Kentucky, a "grateful fellow-citizen" named B. A. Bonte reported any number of "conversations of the great, common people assembled in groups and knots at every fireside and street corner."[22]

Certainly part of what people responded to in the chats was that "heart-to-heart" feeling that came from hearing Roosevelt's own voice "clear as a bell," in the words of Mrs. Anna Koulevard of Pawtucket, Rhode Island. Here was a leader whom people could imagine in unusually intimate terms. "The broadcast brought you so close to us," wrote Virginia Miller of Sierra Madre, California, who praised Roosevelt's radio voice but was alarmed to hear that he had been eating from a tray in his office. She beseeched him to "please, Oh please give your body the rest and care it needs." (Her further advice: Get "an easy reclining chair with a head rest.") Mrs. Koulevard had similar thoughts: "When you coughed a little, I wanted to run and get you some water, yes we all love you, and pray for your good health."[23]

But intimacy alone was not the source of the chats' power. It also mattered that they were broadcast live. That's the significance of those little coughs—they are reminders that the speaker is real and the speech natural (not "orated"), but also that it's happening in real time: The man needs water because he's coughing *at this very moment*. And because live broadcasts are received by all listeners simultaneously, Americans tuning in to the chats knew that millions of other Americans were doing exactly the same. Each knew, therefore, that countless others were on similarly personal terms with the president. Each was aware of being part of a larger community of listeners, and each little group of neighbors talking it over the next day knew it was joining a conversation in progress from coast to coast. If not literally identical to the nation, FDR's radio audience was a good proxy for it. Listeners were made to feel, according to Newton C. Fetter of Cambridge, Massachusetts, "that we are a part of the government and that we have some responsibility." Or as Mabel L. Morrissey, a Brooklyn schoolteacher, told the president: "I am forty-three years old and during the past week is really the first time that I have felt that I am an active part of the U.S.A."[24]

Precisely by having such effects, however, the broadcast media usurp a previously key function of political parties—and, worse, open the way to the audience/nation becoming a single "party" into which normal politics is in danger of disappearing. These problems, too, were foreseen in *Gabriel Over the White House*. Before his coma, President Hammond had no program and, he claimed, no power to carry out his campaign promises even if he wanted to. "The *party* has a plan," he says in the movie. "I'm just a member of the party." Addressing Congress after his change, he declares not just himself but everyone in government "answerable directly to the public conscience." When a congressman calls him a "traitor to [his] party," he responds that he's a "representative of the American people." Parties, he implies, are not a vehicle of representation but an obstacle to it. The logical consequence is not hard to predict: Before the scene is over, Hammond has assumed total power.

And what makes his power effective is one other feature of broadcasting, perhaps the most important one, to be seen in the fictions of the time: its complex ability to convey emotion. *The Phantom President*'s phony president, Peter Varney, is all the better on radio when he's upset, for then "[h]is voice shook with feeling. It lent to Blair's brilliant views on national and international issues a fervor, an emotional quality, which gave them the sincerity of opinions thundered from a pulpit." On-air emotion, that is, conveys sincerity even when the speaker cares nothing for what he's saying. Likewise, *Gabriel*'s President Hammond relies on the magic circuit to amplify his "humor, criticism and great dignity." Frighteningly unstable in private meetings, he radiates "warmth and affection" on air.

All this is extremely dangerous. A "heart-to-heart" relationship between citizens and leaders trades off wisdom for (supposed) virtue, elevating intention and feeling at the expense of policy. It becomes less important whether the president does well than whether he *means* well, or seems to, and less important whether he does good than whether he *sounds* good. In *The President Vanishes,* a 1934 Rex Stout mystery novel directed on film by William Wellman, a national crisis ensues when the fictional President Stanley disappears, possibly kidnapped by right-wing "Gray Shirts." Though the nation is just then precariously balanced between isolationism and war, the problem this poses is not so much that Stanley is missing; that might even be for the best, since he's a weak man who would as·likely as not decide things wrong. The problem is that Americans feel affection for him, and they want *whatever* decisions are made to come from someone they like.[25]

Judgments about whom one likes are necessarily intuitive, and in that sense are not really "judgments" at all. You either feel "connected" with someone or you don't. Since the heart cannot be read directly, its contents have to be inferred from expressions, gestures, body language, and vocal inflections: subtle markers that most Americans previously had no way of gauging in presidents. For most of history, the subtleties of the human voice had been inaudible at distances of more than a few feet. Suddenly they could be carried anywhere. Radio put the president right there in the parlor, delivering his words not through cold and time-delayed newsprint but with all the shadings he himself meant to give them. Hearing the inflections, the listener could suppose he was tuned directly into the president's heart.

But when the power to convey emotion is increased by orders of magnitude, so is the power to manufacture it. Combining this with the power to dissolve traditional politics could do a lot worse than produce a Franklin D. Roosevelt. If a leader's sympathy for average citizens was something to be read in his face and voice, then mimicking the needed expressions and inflections could allow the most appalling character to become the people's tribune. There need not be any T. K. Blair in the back room, diligently applying his wisdom to the nation's actual problems; the charismatic phantom might be all there is. In fact, it might even be worse if the magnetic persona belongs to the policy genius himself. *Genius* didn't originally refer to the very smart; like *charisma* it's a term with ancient and mystical roots, a name for spirits that were sometimes demonic. A genius like *Gabriel's* Jud Hammond *might* be benevolent in his dictatorial power, but there's no way we can ensure this once he has us in his mysterious grip. If we're lucky, his mystique will have limits. It will stop short of making us *ein Volk,* our united nation *ein Reich,* and our beloved chief *ein Führer*. But, as some storytellers recognized, there is no guarantee that we'll be that lucky.

Chambers of American Horrors: *Let 'em Eat Cake,* *A Cool Million,* and *It Can't Happen Here*

There were fictional American dictators before the 1930s. But the works in which they appeared usually had the earnest, humorless quality of political tracts—which is basically what they were—and some were even pro-dictator.[26] The notion of playing a native despotism for laughs apparently had to wait until October 1933, when George S. Kaufman and the Gershwins returned to Broadway with the further adventures of John P. Wintergreen.

Lately rescued from impeachment in *Of Thee I Sing*, Wintergreen does not fare as well when he runs for re-election after one disastrous term. Nor is radio his friend; in fact, on election night it's how he learns the bad news. His victorious opponent, John P. Tweedledee (America's unfortunate choice is between two indistinguishable John P.'s), "will enter the White House on January 20 with the greatest popular vote ever accorded a Presidential candidate," says the announcer. "This program has come to you through the courtesy of the Little Gem Exterminator Company, which positively and permanently eliminates cockroaches and white ants from your home." Commercial broadcasting's gift for comic juxtapositions is not lost on Wintergreen:

> WINTERGREEN. White ants! I'm on a program with white ants.
> LIPPMAN. Say! Cockroaches ain't so good either.
> WINTERGREEN. Yes, that was a fine program. Cockroaches, white ants, and Wintergreen.

Wintergreen's political extermination is the opening scene and setup for *Let 'em Eat Cake,* the musical sequel to *Of Thee I Sing.* Thrown out of office, the former president and his cabinet cronies suddenly need jobs just like everyone else. Wintergreen is sure that "there must be some racket we can go into," but at first they can't think of one. Then, in the same way her superior corn muffins got things going in *Of Thee I Sing,* Mary Wintergreen's sewing skills provide a solution here: Wintergreen and company will go into business selling Mary's finely made blue shirts.

Of course, in the country that Wintergreen's presidency has helped bankrupt, no one can afford to buy shirts; the traffic outside the new shirt shop in Union Square isn't customers, it's all soapbox orators and would-be revolutionaries. But this parade of "shirtless and unshaven radicals" gives Wintergreen another idea:

> WINTERGREEN. Shirts! Blue shirts! You can't have a revolution without shirts!. . . . Italy—black shirts! Germany—brown shirts! America—blue shirts! By God, if the American people want a revolution we can give it to them! We've got the shirts for it! . . . We'll put a Maryblue shirt on every man in the country! "And we'll guarantee a revolution or your money back!"

That does the trick. With the help of Kruger, a professional agitator whose theme song is "Down With Everything That's Up," shirt sales sky-rocket. Wintergreen and his newly outfitted Blue Shirts march on Washington, and the revolution is launched on July 4 with a plan to depose President Tweedledee in the middle of his Independence Day speech.

The farrago of nonsense that follows includes Wintergreen as a Napoleonic dictator headquartered in the "the Blue House"; a game of exhibition baseball pitting the nine former Supreme Court justices against nine ambassadors from nations with unpaid war debts; a show trial in which Vice-President Throttlebottom is accused of umpiring the game fairly, thus allowing the foreigners to win (the revolutionary tribunal ponders the musical question, "Shall we throttle Throttlebottom / Shall we throttle him or not?"); two or three further coups; and a long sequence in which the characters crack wise around a gaily decorated but malfunctioning guillotine. What it all amounts to is a catalogue of jokes on the topic of revolution. *Let 'em Eat Cake* stirs together revolutions of all kinds—American, French, Bolshevik, and, most importantly, fascist—with careless comic abandon, riffing on just about every image popularly associated with the word. It seems almost insistent on making no serious point. As a revolutionary leader, Wintergreen is no more interested in actually achieving something than he was as president in *Of Thee I Sing*. Mostly he just wants to sell more shirts, although he'll happily seize any business opportunity that comes along. "Look at this!" he crows. "A hundred thousand dollars! Just sold the movie rights to the revolution!" Like so much else in an America given over to the arts of the hard sell, this revolution is nothing but hucksterism and showmanship— another chance to make a quick buck off of all those suckers who are born every minute. The musical's title captures the attitude nicely. "Let them eat cake" is the classic expression of aristocratic indifference to the plight of the common people. It's the one sentence that best sums up why those people might revolt and why the revolt might be justified. Turning *them* to *'em* makes it colloquial and distinctly American, the language of a salesman who disdains the people because he knows he can sell 'em anything. And here it's the slogan of the revolutionaries themselves—the credo not of the old regime, but the new.

Unlike *Of Thee I Sing, Let 'em Eat Cake* was a commercial flop. Perhaps this merely reflects the fact that one was a love story and the other wasn't. But the Marx Brothers' political send-up *Duck Soup*, which today tops some lists of all-time greatest film comedies, also flopped when it was released one month later. For whatever reason, farcical despots like Chaplin in *The Great Dictator* and the Three Stooges in *You Nazty Spy!* got bigger laughs *after* Hitler, Stalin, and Mussolini had been wreaking havoc for several more years. It may be that Americans failed to see the humor in totalitarian rule as long as it still seemed like one possible direction their own country might soon take. In the grim circumstances of the early 1930s, it was too easy to imagine the United States falling to some home-grown dictator who, in all likelihood, would be neither a clown like Wintergreen nor a prophet like Judson Hammond. The appropriate response to this possibility was anger and fear; any humor the situation might offer was most likely going to be black.

And so it is in Nathanael West's 1934 *A Cool Million.* This short novel is not as well remembered as West's acclaimed *Miss Lonelyhearts* and *The Day of the Locust,* and critics typically discuss if not dismiss it as a satirical assault on the old Horatio Alger myth—that archetypal American story of the plucky youth from the provinces who comes to the big city to make good.[27] But in West's mordant version of the tale, an important secondary role is assigned to a fictional ex-president. This new element gives West opportunities for sly comment on the Alger myth's political importance. At the same time, the story's focus on an Alger-type naïf and his misadventures gives us something we have not yet seen in the fictions we've been discussing: a "bottom-up" view of the era's political dangers from the standpoint not of the kings, but the pawns.

The pawns in this case are Lemuel Pitkin of Ottsville, Vermont, and his small-town sweetheart, Betty Prail. The story begins with young Lem in search of $1,500 to prevent foreclosure on the house he lives in with his poor widowed mother. Looking for help, he approaches Nathan "Shagpoke" Whipple, Ottsville's leading citizen and a former U.S. president whose own house doubles as the Rat River National Bank. Shagpoke refuses to take over the mortgage, but, with the widow Pitkin's only cow as collateral, he offers Lem a few dollars and a pompous lecture—the first of many through which, in another intentional literary parallel, Shagpoke will become the Pangloss to Lem's incurably credulous Candide.[28] America, Shagpoke explains, is "the land of opportunity":

> She takes care of the honest and industrious and never fails them as long as they are both. . . . Let me warn you that you will find in the world a few scoffers who will laugh at you and attempt to do you injury. They will tell you that John D. Rockefeller was a thief and that Henry Ford and other great men are also thieves. Do not believe them. The story of Rockefeller and of Ford is the story of every great American, and you should strive to make it your story. Like them, you were born poor and on a farm. Like them, by honesty and industry, you cannot fail to succeed.

Encouraged, Lem takes Shagpoke's advice to "Do as I did, when I was your age. Go out into the world and win your way."[29]

What he finds is more than a few scoffers. Nearly everyone Lem crosses paths with does him some kind of injury. As he ventures to New York and, later, Chicago and California, he is repeatedly robbed, beaten, kidnapped, framed, imprisoned, frozen until he catches pneumonia, and tricked into fronting for various hucksters and scam artists. In one typical incident, he performs the Algeresque feat of heroically stopping a runaway horse wagon from flattening a rich old man and his daughter. In an Alger novel the rich man would reward this act by giving the lad a job that starts him on the path to his "cool million." But all Lem gets for his efforts is a stern scolding. A poet who purports to extol his deed to the gathered crowd is actually a shill for pickpockets, and the autograph someone asks him for is really his signature on an insurance form releasing the wagon's owner from liability.

At various points Lem also meets up again with Betty Prail, who had been carried off and forced into prostitution, and Shagpoke Whipple, who has been spending a brief spell in prison—a result, he says, of a conspiracy among Communists, "Wall Street," and "the Jewish international bankers" to spread "rumors" about his management of the Rat River National Bank. Undaunted, the penniless Shagpoke—ever the long-winded believer in "the American Spirit"—is already planning a political comeback. But he has no use anymore for the Democratic Party, whose socialistic leanings threaten "to take from American citizens their inalienable birthright; the right to sell their labor and their children's labor without restrictions as to price or hours." So he has quit conventional politics in favor of street-corner speechmaking among the miserable patrons of Salvation Army canteens:

> The time for a new party with the old American principles was, I realized, overripe. I decided to form it; and so the National Revolutionary Party, popularly known as the "Leather Shirts," was born. The uniform of our "Storm Troops" is a coonskin cap like the one I am wearing, a deerskin shirt and a pair of moccasins. Our weapon is the squirrel rifle.[30]

As an errand boy useful for fetching his soapbox, Lem is appointed "Commander Pitkin" on Shagpoke's "general staff."

The Leather Shirts are a clever twist on *Let 'em Eat Cake*'s point that "You can't have a revolution without shirts," as well as its corollary: same-color shirts are a pretty good sign of incipient fascism. (Likewise, in *Gabriel Over the White House*, it is held to be at least a bit worrying that one of President Hammond's programs, a new federal strike force, is known as the "Green Jackets.") But Shagpoke takes the idea a step further. The shirts needn't be just some arbitrary color but can become the revolution's billboard, advertising in coonskin and deerskin its attachment to the myth of the great American frontier. If it's hard to say which is phonier, the attachment or the myth itself, that's because phoniness is everywhere in *A Cool Million*. In the world Lem traverses, everything seems to be fake—or, more precisely, everything seems to be an effort to trade on something authentic while draining its authenticity away. The house that Lem was trying to save from foreclosure winds up as a department-store window display. The brothel where Lem finds Betty Prail is a "House of All Nations," its food, clothes, and furnishings chosen to mimic various foreign climes (with Betty as the "real American girl"). At one point Lem and Shagpoke join a traveling show called the "Chamber of American Horrors/Animate and Inanimate Hideosities." The animate hideosity is a crude propaganda pageant, and the inanimate include—besides a giant blinking hemorrhoid—"collections of objects whose distinction lay in the great skill with which their materials had been disguised":

> Paper had been made to look like wood, wood like rubber, rubber like steel, steel like cheese, cheese like glass, and, finally, glass like paper.
>
> Other [display] tables carried instruments whose purposes were dual and sometimes triple or even sextuple. Among the most ingenious were pencil sharpeners that could also be used as earpicks, can openers as hair brushes. Then, too, there was a large variety of objects whose

real uses had been cleverly camouflaged. The viewer saw flower pots
that were really victrolas, revolvers that held candy, candy that held collar buttons and so forth.[31]

In the end the most hideous of the hideosities is Lem himself. "The
Dismantling of Lemuel Pitkin" was the novel's original subtitle; as he
follows Shagpoke's disastrous lead from one calamity to the next, Lem
loses his teeth, an eye, a thumb, a leg, and—when yet another attempt to
rescue Betty triggers an Indian attack—his scalp. The transformation
these injuries work on him recalls that of the Tin Woodman in *The
Wizard of Oz*: as he surrenders real body parts for prosthetics, Lem himself becomes a collection of materials artificially contrived to resemble
something else. In the last and most dismal of his efforts to make his
way, he takes a job as the stooge to a pair of slapstick comedians who
play his dismantling for "Belly Laffs Galore." Lem's part in the act is to
get beaten on until his false teeth, hair, eye, and leg are all knocked
loose. He dutifully takes these lumps until, one night, the Leather Shirts
persuade him to take the stage as Commander Pitkin and incite the
crowd to join their revolt. Agreeable as always, Lem is reciting the
speech he's been given when he is shot and killed by a Communist assassin. But death, ironically, finally gives him his big break. He becomes the
National Revolutionary Party's counterpart to the Nazis' Horst Wessel,
the celebrated young martyr whose legend helps a racist demagogue
seize total power.

And so the simple believer in a nation's myths becomes a new myth
himself, his birthday a national holiday and his life and death a story to
be remembered "a thousand years hence," as dictator Shagpoke puts it
in his closing eulogy. Shagpoke would have his listeners believe that ven-
erating Lem somehow redeems the evils he suffered, but in fact it's the
last of those many assaults. From beginning to end, Lem and Betty have
been objects for others to use and abuse. In a country where nothing is
valued except as a spectacle or something to sell, their all-American innocence is just another commodity—attractive merchandise for an endless supply of cynics. Buffeted by forces they could never understand,
they look to Shagpoke for guidance; and the man who would make himself everyone's guide—*guide* in German is *Führer*—happily obliges, rolling out America's received wisdom like a red carpet.

As custodian and expositor of the nation's myths, Shagpoke is the
perfect front man for this cold-hearted order. He's a master of the art on

which a rapaciously commercial society depends: convincing people that getting snookered is some kind of lucky break. What gives him political power is his ability to practice that art on a grander scale. Having sold Lemuel Pitkin on America's myths, he turns around and uses the sorry results to sell America on poor Lemuel Pitkin. No one's misfortunes are better proof that honesty and industry don't pay, so naturally no one serves Shagpoke's new regime better as proof that they do. And this, the novel suggests, is how fascism takes hold. It exploits people at least as cruelly as capitalism and even borrows some of the same rhetoric. But where capitalism's outrages are freewheeling, entrepreneurial, and purely materialistic, fascism's are regimented, leader-focused, and pseudo-spiritual—brutality repackaged and peddled like snake oil for the nation's soul.[32]

A Cool Million concludes with the onset of the fascist regime; fascist dictatorship is an effect of the story's events, not their cause. Sinclair Lewis's *It Can't Happen Here* also describes an American dystopia as seen mostly from the standpoint of its victims, but the focus of this 1935 novel is on fascism as process: how it rises, spreads, consolidates its power and, through a phony promise of unity, proceeds to tear a society to pieces.

It Can't Happen Here, like *A Cool Million*, begins in small-town Vermont, a state that writers of the period seemed to gravitate to as a symbol of common sense and old-fashioned Yankee rectitude.[33] The novel's embodiment of those virtues is its main character, Doremus Jessup, the seventy-year-old editor and publisher of the Fort Beulah *Daily Informer*. Although his newspaper is "the Bible of the conservative Vermont farmers up and down the Beulah Valley," and he himself is a third cousin of Vermont's favorite-son President Calvin Coolidge, Doremus's own politics are liberal and cosmopolitan. In this he has a natural ally, Lorinda Pike, a young widow and boardinghouse keeper who "was constantly poking into things that were none of her business, and at town meetings she criticized every substantial interest in the whole county: the electric company's rates, the salaries of the schoolteachers, the Ministerial Association's high-minded censorship of books for the public library." The "brassy" Lorinda is "the village scold, the village crank," while Doremus, though "a competent business man and a writer of editorials not without wit and good New England earthiness . . . was yet considered the prime eccentric of Fort Beulah"—an image he cultivates by wearing a beard, "just to be 'highbrow' and 'different,' to try to appear 'artistic,'" according to his more conventional neighbors. Together,

Doremus and Lorinda represent just about all the political and cultural dissidence one is likely to find in a small town like Fort Beulah.

Unfortunately the same is true for the rest of Lewis's nation of Babbits. This, the novel suggests, is one reason why "it" can indeed happen here. Such a nation is primed for what Doremus calls "funny therapeutics": "Cure the evils of Democracy by the evils of Fascism!" And so America does, or tries to. Over the course of three years beginning in 1936, the novel follows the lives of Fort Beulah's citizens as the country slides toward totalitarian dictatorship. Elbowing aside a one-term FDR, the demagogic Senator Berzelius "Buzz" Windrip seizes the Democratic nomination and goes on to win the presidency with the help of a familiar fascist apparatus: antisemitic conspiracy theories, paramilitary marching clubs (Windrip's are known as the "Minute Men"), a bombastic radio preacher even more effective than the real-life Father Coughlin, and a brilliant chief aide and strategist who has mastered the dark arts of "Modern Advertising." Before long, power is consolidated around Windrip, and an American *Reich* begins to emerge. Jews are harassed and killed, intellectuals are persecuted ("Albert Einstein, who had been exiled from Germany for his guilty devotion to mathematics, world peace, and the violin, was now exiled from America for the same crimes"), the most loathsome characters join the regime as local "commissioners," and schools are converted to concentration camps for anyone thought insufficiently enthusiastic toward the rule of Windrip and his fellow Corporatists, or "Corpos."

As detailed in the novel, this process closely resembles the *Gleichschaltung* then underway in Germany. Even more than strongman rule, *Gleichschaltung*—"synchronization" or, literally, "same-switching"—is the essence of totalitarianism, the thing that makes it "total." It's a radical policy of state-sponsored cultural change in which all the diverse, organic institutions of civil society, including churches, clubs, universities, and trade unions, are replaced with the manufactured, monolithic culture of the ruling party. Old sites of private life and affiliation, "all vastly different one from another but alike in not yet having entirely become machines," are systematically closed or absorbed. And in trying to destroy everything culturally distinctive in America, the Corpo regime destroys the things that make America culturally distinctive. Like others who failed to see the true scale of the Windrip threat, Doremus had relied on the widespread assumption that "If there ever is a Fascist dictatorship here, American humor and pioneer independence are so marked that it will be absolutely different from anything in Europe." And, in the first year of Windrip's rule,

> this seemed true. The Chief was photographed playing poker, in shirt-sleeves and with a derby on the back of his head, with a newspaper-man, a chauffeur, and a pair of rugged steel-workers. [Windrip lieutenant] Dr. Macgoblin in person led an Elks' brass band and dived in competition with the Atlantic City bathing-beauties. It was reputably reported that M.M.'s [Minute Men] apologized to political prisoners for having to arrest them, and that the prisoners joked amiably with the guards . . . at first.

But this interlude does not last, and soon "surprised scientists discovered that whips and handcuffs hurt just as sorely in the clear American air as in the miasmic fogs of Prussia." Before long, "in the humorous, friendly, happy-go-lucky land of Mark Twain, Doremus saw the homicidal maniacs having just as good a time as they had had in central Europe."

Much of the novel's second half is concerned with Doremus's dangerous work as a member of the "New Underground," a resistance movement that Windrip's onetime Republican presidential opponent supervises from Canada. Resistance work also finally brings Doremus and Lorinda together romantically. Anticipating the more famous analysis of totalitarianism in George Orwell's *1984*, *It Can't Happen Here* sees totalitarian regimes as most threatened by love, the ultimate private affiliation. The greatest danger to the regime is the continued existence of distinct human personalities, which not only make for diversity in the culture—and therefore competing centers of power—but also bind people to each other, making one individual of potentially infinite value to another. Romantic love expresses that value with special vividness, creating tenacious loyalties outside the state's control. In loyalties like these lie an ongoing and self-intensifying potential for opposition: People's love for each other affirms their existing identities, which reinforces their distinctiveness and maintains them as objects of love, which continues to give them something to live for other than the party, its *Führer*, or some abstract "folk."[34]

For a totalitarian state to succeed, therefore, *Gleichschaltung* is just the beginning. Individual identity and the capacity for love itself must be pulled up by the roots. The Inner Party of *1984* would come close to perfecting the means for doing this, but Windrip's Corpos are still a bit clumsy at it. However miserable they manage to make things for the likes of Doremus, they cannot touch the core of his identity—the eccentricity and plain cussedness that will always make him a nuisance to whomever tries to wield power. (The novel closes by declaring that "a Doremus Jessup can never die.") Even Windrip himself, unlike the characterless "Big Brother" of *1984*, is a bit too human for his own good. His faltering morale—he finds it lonely at the top—makes him a ready target for palace intrigue, and by the end of the novel the regime seems to be coming undone in a series of coups. But a return to normalcy is far from assured, and in the final pages Doremus is still in business as "a spy and professional hero" for the spreading resistance.

It Can't Happen Here anticipates *1984* in one other important way. Orwell's novel is famous for its recognition of the central importance of language. Political regimes of all kinds depend on euphemisms and propaganda, but in *1984* this technology, too, is in the process of being perfected: the Party has invented an entirely new language, Newspeak, and has criminalized any thoughts beyond those that this official language permits. Here we have *Gleichschaltung* carried to its logical conclusion. To eliminate the diversity among people, one must finally eliminate the diversity *within* people—their capacity for formulating new or independent ideas, choosing their loyalties or changing their minds. As practiced on Winston Smith, *1984*'s wretched hero-victim, enforced changes in language and logic are steps toward regimenting emotions. They are what finally destroy the last vestiges of individuality and recalcitrance, eliminating all other attachments and wholly assimilating the shell of a person's former self to the state's structure of total power. As long as Winston can think, he can remember—and choose—what and whom he loves. Obliterating his mind, therefore, is the key to the novel's conclusion, with its chilling final sentence: "He loved Big Brother."

The Corporatist regime of *It Can't Happen Here* struggles toward a similar goal, but again, luckily for America, with less success. Its manipulation of populist rhetoric and the nation's traditions and symbols fools people for a while, but it's transparent enough to fail with independent-minded citizens like Doremus. Yet even he feels its pull. And the point at which he feels it most keenly is also the one point at which he actually sees and hears Buzz Windrip in person, addressing a giant election-eve rally in Madison Square Garden:

> He slid into a rhapsody of general ideas—a mishmash of polite regards to Justice, Freedom, Equality, Order, Prosperity, Patriotism, and any number of other noble but slippery abstractions.

Doremus thought he was being bored, until he discovered that, at some moment which he had not noticed, he had become absorbed and excited.

Something in the intensity with which Windrip looked at his audience, looked at all of them, his glance slowly taking them in from the highest-perched seat to the nearest, convinced them that he was talking to each individual, directly and solely; that he wanted to take each of them into his heart; that he was telling them the truths, the imperious and dangerous facts, that had been hidden from them.

To Doremus, "It sounded almost reasonable, for a while":

The supreme actor, Buzz Windrip, was passionate yet never grotesquely wild. He did not gesture too extravagantly; only, like [socialist leader] Gene Debs of old, he reached out a bony forefinger which seemed to jab into each of them and hook out each heart. It was his mad eyes, big staring tragic eyes, that startled them, and his voice, now thundering, now humbly pleading, that soothed them.

He was so obviously an honest and merciful leader; a man of sorrows and acquaint[ed] with woe.

Doremus marveled, "I'll be hanged! Why, he's a darn good sort when you come to meet him! And warm-hearted. . . . Seeing Buzz and then listening to what he actually says does kind of surprise you—kind of make you think!"

The passage concludes, "But what Mr. Windrip actually *had* said, Doremus could not remember an hour later, when he had come out of the trance." What had absorbed him emotionally, though not finally absorbed him into the movement, was exactly the thing that a Buzz Windrip exists to provide: not the fascist ideology's inane content but its very compelling performance. Or we might say that fascism's content *is* performance, a rhetorical "hooking out of each heart" that depends not just on deploying emotive language but on *enacting* it—reinvigorating it with the deep feeling that the stereotyped rhetoric of politics otherwise lacks.

The great leader who delivers this kind of performance is an artist, or really a medium: he succeeds by mining the emotions of his individual hearers, refining these into a grand (if absurd) collective vision, then funneling the new, manufactured emotion that this vision inspires back into the waiting heart. In other words, skillfully performed rhetoric is a means by which people's communication with *themselves,* with their own fears and desires, can be managed and transformed. It can thus generate

Newspeak-like effects even within traditional language. Berzelius Windrip manages this best the old-fashioned way, by orating before a live audience. But he also has help from rudimentary efforts in other media, including radio and "Modern Advertising." What Doremus succumbs to only temporarily and in Windrip's presence, other Americans are swayed by en masse or, in the case of right-wing radio preachers, by proxy. Further developments, especially television—which allows such performances to be seen as well as heard, and which, as Orwell recognized, could also be used the other way, for surveillance—would only increase the demagogue's reach. As any number of later writers would attest, both with and without reference to presidents, it might not even be necessary to develop a Newspeak. The mass media themselves are the ultimate "rhetoric." By using those media to leverage the power of their appeals, evil but clever leaders might, like other Modern Advertisers, have little trouble stealing a nation's souls.

Judging from *Let 'em Eat Cake*, *A Cool Million*, and *It Can't Happen Here*, the specter of 1930s fascism loomed larger with each passing year. These three works, appearing in quick succession, treated this anxiety first with light humor, then with dark humor, then with a grim if sardonic earnestness. And a striking number of other well-remembered works from the years immediately following also dealt with civic or political breakdown and a closely related issue, mob violence.[35] Mobs are crude, temporary pseudo-polities, their violence a parody of democratic decision-making. Their leaders are not public servants who can be held to account—in many cases, they cannot even be identified—but are more likely chosen according to who shouts the loudest or is willing to throw the first brick. Fascist and totalitarian dictators take advantage of mob-like conditions on a national scale. Such conditions primarily result from the tremendous stresses on modern societies, the depressions, migrations, and rapid industrialization that upend old communities and ways of life. But modern media also play a key enabling role. They bypass traditional institutions and give the demagogue direct access to the shattered masses, the angry but aimless grievants who were once a civil society of free citizens. Through radio and TV, and to some extent through newsreels and "the talkies," millions of people who never meet in person—and certainly never deliberate—can be incited to act as unthinkingly and impulsively as a vast crowd, their emotions triggered by the voice and gestures of a leader who can give the illusion of speaking to each of them personally. Or, on the model of the Nuremberg rally and Leni Riefenstahl's *Triumph of the Will*, they can be mobilized to "join" and share the emotions of an actual crowd somewhere else. According to Susan Sontag, the Nuremberg rally "was from the start conceived as the set of a film spectacle."[36]

What all these media innovations had in common was their ability to expand the range and power of the human voice. With that in mind, it's interesting to note that developments on Broadway in the same years also involved putting the voice to new uses. *Of Thee I Sing*—like *Showboat* and the many subsequent shows these two influenced—was not the first musical, let alone the first use of song to express emotion. But in weaving songs more tightly with plot, the new style of musical introduced a new way of using emotive voices to advance a story. This in turn affected what kinds of stories would likely be told. If the sunniest of the works that imagine an American dictatorship is *Let 'em Eat Cake*, that's not just because musicals as a rule are upbeat. It's also because choreographed movements are the opposite of mob chaos. (The "mob" in *Let 'em Eat Cake* is a chorus.) And it reflects the prevalence in American musicals of an optimistic theme: the power of song and dance to burst through stuffy conventionality. Again and again, Broadway shows pit the personal energy and dynamism of the singers and dancers against the rigid forms and formalities of "high" or officially approved culture. And the singers and dancers always win.[37]

In *Of Thee I Sing* and *Let 'em Eat Cake*, that official culture includes, literally, the world of officialdom—America's institutions of government and the patriotic pieties that sustain them. Any solemnity toward those institutions goes by the wayside as soon as "Love is Sweeping the Country." The same theme is made even more explicit in *I'd Rather Be Right*, a 1937 George Kaufman/Moss Hart musical with songs by Richard Rodgers and Lorenz Hart. Here, President Roosevelt himself—played by George M. Cohan, who had earlier sung and danced on film as *The Phantom President*—materializes onstage, promising to bend national policy to the needs of a young couple who can't get married until the federal budget is balanced. It's hard to imagine a more emphatic parable of public affairs intersecting with the private lives of citizens.[38]

Since *The Beggar's Opera*, musical comedy has lent itself to depictions of political leaders as "low" figures—if not crooks, like *Beggar's* Peachum and company, or clowns like John P. Wintergreen, then ordinary family men and women with the usual range of everyday worries.[39] (To the extent that great matters of state are treated as such, musical theater tends toward opera—the best illustration being John Adams's 1987 *Nixon in China*.) If radio domesticates great issues and leaders by bringing them right into the family parlor, the musical does it by translating them into the vernacular of popular music. But like the Franklin Roosevelt, the Buzz Windrip, or, for that matter, the Adolph Hitler who uses radio to reach directly into citizens' homes, the political leader who tap-dances his way into their lives might be either the problem or the solution. As we've noted, John P. Wintergreen and his crew are classic instances of the ruling cabal that has been appearing in political storytelling ever since *The Beggar's Opera*. So are Buzz Windrip and the shadowy characters who put him in power in *It Can't Happen Here*. To the deluded masses, though, Windrip does not come across as the leader of a cabal. Instead he is the *answer* to it, the plain man of the people who will expose the scoundrels and put them to rout. This, of course, is also how Hitler and other demagogues have presented themselves. Fascist dictatorships claim to be final solutions to the problem of cabals. Coming to power on the promise to overthrow them, the dictator and his cronies instead become the worst cabal of all. As Lord Bolingbroke wrote of another ruler at the time of *The Beggar's Opera*: "Because he had governed ill, it was put in his power to govern worse; and liberty was undermined, for fear it should be overthrown."[40]

"Sincerity Is Everything": *Young Mr. Lincoln,* *Mr. Smith Goes to Washington,* and *State of the Union*

Corruption, mob rule, dictatorship, and the totalitarian cult of the charismatic leader are all substitutes for the rule of law, all various kinds of failure to secure "a government of laws, and not of men," in Chief Justice Marshall's famous phrase.[41] At least since the American Founding, there have been lengthy debates about how such failures are best avoided. "If men were angels, no government would be necessary," wrote James Madison in an often-quoted *Federalist* paper. Is there some way, then, of constructing a government so that it does not depend on angels—a government that will safeguard liberty even in the hands of lesser beings, with baser motives? Can ambition "be made to counteract ambition" if the system is cleverly enough designed?[42] Can liberty and democracy, once set in motion, be made regular and self-perpetuating like the clockwork universe of the eighteenth-century Deists? Or will they always have to depend on the goodness and self-restraint of the powerful—on what the founders called "virtue," and what analysts today refer to as a healthy, robust "political culture"? The founders themselves famously split the difference. With considerable thought and debate they designed a governing machine of daunting complexity, not least in its procedures for choosing the president. But they also defended this system on the grounds that it would identify the virtuous and put them in power. And as their first chief executive they chose the man whose personal virtue they trusted most and whose ambition they feared the least.

To the authors of the cautionary tales of the 1930s, it was clear what kinds of qualities Americans needed their leaders *not* to have. The trickier question was how, positively, to channel the rule of law through personal leadership, since the two are really different principles. Was it possible to have, not a government of laws instead of men, but a government of men who would stand up for the laws against other men? Were there leaders who would not be mere creatures of the system—hence unwilling or too weak to deliver the policies the people needed—yet who were also not dictators or demagogues, as even the virtuous Jud Hammond essentially became in *Gabriel Over the White House*? Against the threats of corruption and mob violence, to whom could Americans turn as the *human* face of the rule of law? These are the questions taken up in two movies of 1939, John Ford's *Young Mr. Lincoln* and Frank Capra's *Mr. Smith Goes to Washington*.

Ford explores the questions through the vehicle of Lincoln, whom he presents as having already faced them some fourscore years earlier. In doing this, Ford and screenwriter Lamar Trotti make a particular choice. As we saw in the last chapter, the mythic Lincoln had long been established as a character in whom greatness was somehow the product of ordinariness. The two traits were inseparable, but the question facing any popular teller of Lincoln stories was which was figure and which was ground. Lincoln could be presented as a monumental man with whom ordinary people should feel comfortable because he had been ordinary too. Or, he could be viewed as great *even in* his ordinariness—a man of towering character even while moving among mere mortals, even before being called to do his great work. His folksy qualities could either be a prologue and contrast to greatness or the qualities through which greatness was acted out. By the 1930s both approaches had firm roots in Lincoln tradition, but choosing one over the other made for a significantly different kind of story.

Ford's choice of the second approach therefore contrasts his Lincoln with, for example, the title character of D. W. Griffith's 1930 film

Abraham Lincoln. With help from Stephen Vincent Benet, the novelist and poet who wrote the screenplay, Griffith had presented Lincoln (Walter Huston, the same actor who played Jud Hammond) as a young man given over to nature's impulses, a roughneck whose main interests seemed to be drinkin' and rasslin'. That made Ann Rutledge, his soon-to-be lost love, the civilizing force in his life—a time-honored role for the frontier woman. In a long courtship scene, Ann (Una Merkel) struggles to get Abe to stick to his lessons, turning aside his impish, Huck Finn–like protests. The scene begins as he's pounding rails, a muscular but apparently unwelcome task, while Ann tries to take him through a recitation:

> ANN. [*reading from a book*] "In this sense, the term 'law' includes any
>   edict, decree, order, ordinance, statute, resolution, rule, etcetera."
> ABE. Whew! "Etcetera." Well, my ol' daddy taught me how to work,
>   but he never taught me how to like it.[43]

Pausing from his labors, Abe lounges next to Ann and, for the rest of the scene, stares dreamily into her eyes while trying to get her to put the book down:

> ANN. Reckon I'd better keep on with the lesson.
> ABE. I'd rather keep on with somethin' else.
> ANN. [*weakly resisting*] You made a bad bargain, makin' me the
>   professor.
> ABE. Well, he told me about that too—he said, if you make a bad
>   bargain, hug it all the tighter. . . .
> ANN. [*getting up*] Now Abe, your professor needs a seat where there's
>   more law and less temptation.

Thanks to Ann, the temptation is turned to a civil purpose: soon the young buck is dressing better and proposing marriage. But then, in a deathbed scene well worthy of Griffith's reputation for melodrama, Ann is tragically carried away. Like the psychologically scarred young Abe of William Herndon's original Rutledge story, Griffith's Lincoln carries the melancholia of that event on into his public career.[44]

If the Lincoln of *Abraham Lincoln* brings an earthy, emotional element to the White House, a bit of the frontier amid all the stateliness, Ford's lanky future statesman does almost the reverse. As played by the soft-spoken Henry Fonda, this ambitious but humble young frontiersman is already *Mr.* Lincoln, a more polished and self-controlled figure than most others in his rustic surroundings. For him studying law *is* the

Abe Lincoln (Henry Fonda) communes with his law book in *Young Mr. Lincoln*.

temptation, not a chore from which other temptations might lure him away. When he's caught staring dreamily, it's not at Ann but at his law book: "*Law*," he whispers with obvious reverence when he first holds the book in his hands. The courtship scene begins with a kind of soliloquy; Abe, alone and sprawled under a tree, is reading the book to himself and pondering its profound lessons:

> ABE. Law—"it's the rights of persons and the rights of things." "The right to life, reputation, and liberty." "The rights to acquire and hold property." [*reading further*] "Wrongs are violations of those rights." By jing, that's all there is to it—right an' wrong. Maybe I oughtta be gettin' to take this stuff serious.

Ann (Pauline Moore) interrupts his musings, not to encourage his studies but to tease him away from them: "Aren't you afraid you'll put your eyes out, reading like that upside down?" Only with her arrival does Abe's attention turn to nature—the flowers she's been picking, the picturesque riverbank they stroll along. Ann takes note of Abe's intellectual pursuits, but as one who has no idea what they are: "You think a lot about things, don't you?" But the thinking that interests her is his opinion of the color of her hair.

Unlike Griffith, who wrings Ann's death for maximum emotion, Ford presents it abstractly, as a "time dissolve" turning the lovely landscape to snow and ice—a visual image of the "cold and heartless" world of Herndon's Rutledge legend. But far from being shattered, Abe reacts to Ann's death with calm deliberation. Buried on that riverbank, she literally belongs to the frontier, and young Mr. Lincoln is bound to leave the frontier behind. In another soliloquy, this one delivered at Ann's grave, he pledges to go forward to become the Lincoln of history, a Lincoln whose destiny will lie in the civilized but cruel world of courtrooms and capitals.[45]

This treatment of the Rutledge legend is the template for Ford's whole approach to Lincoln. In Ford's telling, Lincoln not only belongs in civilization but is also the agent who makes civilization possible. The film's only reference to the reputation for youthful brawling that Griffith highlighted comes in Ford's first scene in Lincoln's law office, when Lincoln briefly, but only verbally, invokes it to persuade two litigants to *stop* fighting and settle their pointless but angry dispute in a civil way. Following that scene is a long sequence designed to represent frontier America at its best and worst. A happy, communal July 4th festival—at which the town itself, not Lincoln, is the main character—eventually leads to a brawl in which a man is stabbed to death. When two young brothers are arrested, each having confessed in an effort to protect the other, the festive crowd degenerates into a lynch mob. It is Lincoln who stops the mob at the jailhouse door, calming it with an impromptu speech that weaves together appeals to the rule of law and to Christian mercy.

Law and mercy are two virtues that dramatists often put in conflict, but in that speech—and in *Young Mr. Lincoln* in general—they are civilization's two alternatives to mob violence, and Lincoln is the spokesman for *both*. The scene at the jailhouse door appears to be wholly invented; its obvious purpose is to make Lincoln the local champion of these virtues, as he would later become their national champion.[46] When the boys' mother had first asked Lincoln who he was (the mother of the real defendant they were based on had known Lincoln for decades), his simple answer, "I'm your lawyer, ma'am," captured the truth through deliberate understatement. Thanks to those lazy days of reading under the tree, the Lincoln we see here *is* the law. Without him, this distant outpost of semi-civilization would dissolve into chaos.

The remainder of the film portrays the brothers' trial. In a dramatic flourish, Lincoln wins their acquittal—emancipates them, as it were—by revealing a key prosecution witness as the real killer. Thus the boys and their mother are spared having to choose between them, sacrificing one brother for the other's sake, and the town is saved from forcing them to—which itself would be a tragic choice between family loyalties and the law's demands. For purposes of the drama as Ford has structured it, it's a further, final bonus that Lincoln finds the solution to the case in the motions and phases of the moon. (Waving an almanac, he proves that the witness could not, as claimed, have seen the killing by moonlight.) This detail is based on fact, but it neatly suggests that even in his role as redeemer of civilization and its values, Lincoln is in touch with nature. It is he who brings nature's order and law to bear on a community and its human law, just in time to restore that law to its freeing and civilizing purpose.

Although Griffith's Lincoln is the rougher, less disciplined young man of feeling, and although it's Griffith who actually sticks closer to the historical record (the "Almanac Trial" that Ford dramatizes took place, in reality, when "young" Mr. Lincoln was forty-nine years old), Griffith's depiction is the stiffer, stagier one, while Ford's is the livelier and more real-seeming. As important an innovator as he was in early silent films, Griffith was an older and, by the 1930s, more old-fashioned filmmaker. But more important than this is the two directors' different choices of emphasis within the Lincoln legend. Where Griffith fore-grounded the later statesman who weighed great issues of war and peace, yet who would set those issues aside to join his children in eating soup, Ford emphasizes the plain-folks Lincoln, the judge of a local pie-baking contest who would bring the same serene judgment to the great contest between North and South. Yet Ford's Lincoln would just as surely end up on a slow ascent to Mount Rushmore. In the closing scene of *Young Mr. Lincoln* he parts ways with the riverbank, walking up a hill and into the coming storm before the image dissolves into the statue in the Lincoln Memorial.[47]

When he first arrives in the capital, the title character of *Mr. Smith Goes to Washington* makes a point of visiting that same statue—a gesture, the film suggests, that other Washingtonians don't make because they're too busy subverting the ideals for which Lincoln stood. In fact, what Jefferson ("Jeff") Smith discovers is that lawless mobs come in many guises, one of them being the U.S. Senate. Smith, played by Jimmy Stewart, is the impossibly virtuous Scout leader chosen by Montana's political bosses to fill the state's vacant Senate seat. Those bosses are another classic cabal, a textbook case of that perennial old blight, and in Smith they see the perfect patsy: Naive, guileless, easily awed, he reveres the stories and symbols of American patriotism, has no idea how real politics works, and is clearly unprepared to do anything but vote the way the bosses tell him to. But Smith needs to keep busy and would like to do a little good of his own. So, with a jaded and skeptical secretary-minder (Jean Arthur) guiding him through a system she rightly regards with contempt, he drafts a bill that would realize his one vision: an outdoor camp "for the purpose of bringing together boys of all walks of life from various parts of the country, boys of all creeds, kinds, and positions; to educate them in American ideals; and to promote mutual understanding; and to bring about a healthful life to the growing youth of this great and beautiful land." America itself writ little, in other words.

As it turns out, the piece of land that Smith has in mind for his camp is tied up in the bosses' graft, and when they block his bill he discovers and tries to expose their corrupt dealings. The bosses counterattack, smearing Smith as a grafter himself and, worse, one who steals from the very "Boy Rangers" whose admiration for him first got him noticed and put in office. While the bosses unleash their goons against Smith's young supporters, Smith stands and fights using the best weapon a lone senator has: the filibuster. The effort to stay on his feet and keep talking, hour after hour, in the faint hope that honesty is not "a lost cause" and the truth will somehow prevail, exhausts him to the point that he collapses in utter despair. But it also works, and at the last instant Smith wins the day when the sheer force of his moral example shames one of the reprobates into confessing.

Smith is merely a senator, not president, but the filibuster rule—under which one member could bring the whole Senate to a halt—briefly gives him control of the government, making him the de facto leader of the United States. While he carries on we see citizens massing in rallies both for and against him, incited by news and radio coverage to choose sides as they would in a campaign for the presidency itself. In fact, Smith is another answer to the cynical, unreformed President Hammond of *Gabriel Over the White House*. In one early scene in that film, Hammond—still a member and willing tool of the cynical cabal—had mocked the idea that the quill pen with which Lincoln had signed the Emancipation Proclamation could be used for great things in his hands too. Instead he uses it to sign a bill funding a new sewer. The old Hammond is as impervious to the Lincoln legend as Jefferson Smith is awestruck by it. But unlike Hammond's own later, changed self, the maniacal visionary bent on doing *only* great things, Smith is not looking to accomplish much. He just wants to build a camp. The greatness of his vision is not its size or impact but its purity. Only because such purity is so rare, and the system so thoroughly corrupted, does a little idea for a boys' camp become a great issue on which the fate of the Republic might hinge.

Mr. Smith raises the same questions that Hammond's aides had pondered in *Gabriel*: Is it possible that "a simple, honest man can solve everything"? Or can one be "*so* simple and honest it sounds crazy"? In pursuing his modest, crazy little goal, Smith achieves both less than Hammond and more. He leaves untouched the big problems of depression, disorder, and war for which Hammond found answers through spiritual guidance, yet for one brief moment he redeems the nation in spirit. Naive enough to be capable of shock, he clings in his wounded innocence all the more fiercely to America's ideals. In so doing he reclaims them, transforming them from words carved on marble monuments to something living and real. So resonant is this dream of the common man with the common name that it became part of the country's political myth. A "Mr. Smith going to Washington" is, for contemporary Americans, what Cincinnatus leaving his plow was for Americans of George Washington's time: shorthand for a whole, larger vision of public-spiritedness and what it can do. In the high drama of one simple, honest, stuttering amateur staring down the Senate, the bosses, the cynics, the thugs, and the whole seamy structure of American power, the movie asks us to see that one concerned citizen can carry the hope of the nation, if he's sincere and determined enough.[48]

Of course, the wish for a Mr. Smith poses dangers of its own. The notion that simple, honest men can solve everything, that political choices are ultimately easy because "By jing, that's all there is to it—right an' wrong," is one that even Lincoln himself might have called crazy. *Mr. Smith Goes to Washington* does not even try to picture it working in practice; the last we time we see Jefferson Smith, he's being carried unconscious from the Senate floor. He is never shown going on to become an effective workaday legislator, let alone president, nor does the film even suggest this is possible. And in other films, notably *Meet John Doe*, Frank Capra acknowledged the dark, demagogic side of popular movements founded on simple sincerity. Especially with the help of the new technologies, the cabal could create a Mr. Smith of its own—or, worse, co-opt a real one, turning his sincerity and appeal to its advantage in a much bigger way than even *Mr. Smith*'s bosses had hoped to do. Under the spell of such a manufactured hero, whatever abuse the bosses meant to inflict on the public could become the demand of the people themselves. As the movie mogul Samuel Goldwyn reportedly said, "Sincerity is everything. If you can fake that, you've got it made."

Exactly that danger drives events in *State of the Union*, the Pulitzer Prize–winning 1945 Broadway play that Capra directed on film in 1948. In this film, one of several famous movie pairings of Spencer Tracy and Katharine Hepburn, an idealistic businessman and political outsider is recruited by Republican power brokers to run for the presidency. Grant Matthews (Tracy) is, they think, "a rare combination of sincerity and drive that the common herd will go for." They also believe they can control him, especially since his mistress—a power-mad newspaper heiress—is a key member of their cabal. As the campaign unfolds and Grant submits to their machinations, it looks as if they'll be proven right. Gradually he abandons his plainspokenness and surrenders to the system's corruptions. Worse, the campaign also ensnares his estranged wife, Mary (Hepburn), who reluctantly agrees to act happily married for the sake of Grant's political ambitions.

The climactic scene begins with Grant's handlers having assembled an expensive and elaborate apparatus to broadcast his radio address, a faux-humble fireside chat that happens to fall on his and Mary's wedding anniversary. Grant is set to go along with the scheme, which will probably clinch the Republican nomination for him, until Mary begins to broadcast a testimonial to his integrity that he knows he no longer deserves. Tearing up his speech, he confesses on air that he's been "a phony" and denounces the whole campaign. He had, he says, temporarily lost faith in both himself and the people. Rather than seek office, Grant vows to become a kind of career Mr. Smith, an ombudsman who will fight for citizens against the parties and political bosses. The screeching response to this from the bosses on hand is carried over the open radio mike, so the medium that was about to be misused to fake sincerity instead becomes an instrument for bringing the backroom wheeling and dealing into the open. Best of all, the recovery of Matthews's authentic self also looks to revive his marriage—the other "union" whose state had been imperiled. The health of the private relationship, it seems, is a gauge or even precondition for the health of the other, public Union.[49]

State of the Union bookends the period that began with *Of Thee I Sing*. To get elected president, John P. Wintergreen launched a cynical ploy to find love and marriage; to reignite love and save his marriage, Grant Matthews rejects the cynical ploys that might have gotten him elected president. From here on the merging of personal and political in a president's life would cease to be remarkable. *Personal president* would therefore take on a new meaning. For political scientists, the term refers to a president to whom citizens feel personally connected and who promises to solve problems in their everyday lives. But for storytellers it can mean a president whose *own* life revolves around everyday problems, who experiences the struggles of home, family, and career in the same ways as other citizens. In addition to public figures whose political dealings are complicated by the personal and private, the fictions soon to come would give us presidents whose private concerns are foregrounded as they come under pressure from public events. Howard Lindsay and Russel Crouse, who co-authored *State of the Union*, would collaborate years later with Irving Berlin on such a work, a musical romantic comedy called *Mr. President*. Dominated by songs of love and longing like "It Gets Lonely in the White House" and "Empty Pockets Filled with Love," *Mr. President* did not do well on Broadway, and the more recent *I Love You, Madame President*—the musical tale of a woman who struggles to balance work and family when her work just happens to be running the country—also failed to make an impression.[50] In these works and their many successors and counterparts in other media, some of which are discussed in coming chapters, we have presidents whose *almost* normal lives include dealing with household problems around the kitchen table before they head off to work at the (Oval) office. In 1932 it was startling to imagine a president this way; by 1962 it no longer was, and this as much as anything might explain the commercial failure of *Mr. President*.

Put another way, the writers, filmmakers, and audiences of the 1960s were preoccupied with different issues than those of the 1930s. The rise of the personal presidency—the narrowing of the gap between leader and citizen, and the expectation that the one could solve problems in the life of the other—brought to politics a new question: Is our president enough like us? Many stories would appear suggesting that the answer could be yes. But these in their turn raised another question: Could the president be *too much* like us? What would it mean, in a very dangerous world, if our national leaders shared our weaknesses and vulnerabilities? Starting around 1960, questions like these would spill over from the pages of political science texts to become the preoccupations of novelists, filmmakers, and their audiences.

5

The Human Element

*Presidential Strength, Weakness, and Difference
in the 1960s and 1970s*

❖

Whenever the Monorail ran in these sections [of the New York
World's Fair], there would be a power surge, causing Lincoln
to spasm. Surge suppressers didn't work, so Lincoln's power
line was run under Town Square and linked to another sub station behind City Hall. . . . "Great Moments with Mr. Lincoln"
first opened at Disneyland on July 18th, 1966. Again, problems
arrived with the figure. Sometimes, Mr. Lincoln would start
having spasms or just bow forward and stop in the middle of
the show. . . . Once a mechanical failure during a show caused
Mr. Lincoln to bend sharply at the waist and begin talking to
the floor.

"Great Moments with Mr. Lincoln": The exhibit and its problems

❖

After its glitches were finally worked out, a life-size talking robot
version of Abraham Lincoln did succeed at becoming a long-
running attraction at Disneyland.[1] But the back spasms and other ills
that had plagued the "animatronic" figure, allowing it to perform only

161

with frequent technical help from experts, oddly paralleled the ordeals of another president who was not animatronic:

> During his time in the White House . . . medical attention was a fixed part of [JFK's] routine. He was under the care of an allergist, an endocrinologist, a gastroenterologist, an orthopedist, and a urologist. . . . His physicians administered large doses of so many drugs that [Dr.] Travell kept a "Medicine Administration Record," cataloguing injected and ingested corticosteroids for his adrenal insufficiency; procaine shots and ultrasound treatments and hot packs for his back; Lomotil, Metamucil, paregoric, phenobarbital, testosterone, and trasentine to control his diarrhea, abdominal discomfort, and weight loss; penicillin and other antibiotics for his urinary-tract infections and an abscess; and Tuinal to help him sleep. Before press conferences and nationally televised speeches his doctors increased his cortisone dose to deal with tensions harmful to someone unable to produce his own corticosteroids in response to stress. . . . In 1961 [Dr.] Burkley concluded that the injections, along with back braces and positioning devices that immobilized Kennedy, were doing more harm than good. Burkley and some Secret Service men, who observed the President's difficulties getting up from a sitting position and his reliance on crutches, feared that he would soon be unable to walk and might end up in a wheelchair. Out of sight of the press, Kennedy went up and down helicopter stairs one at a time.[2]

Reports like these suggest an obvious irony. It was not unusual in the 1960s for Americans to be called on to "stand up" for this or that: to stand up to the Russians; to stand up against war; to stand up for freedom, equality, or civil rights; to stand up and proclaim their ethnic pride or "personhood." Having written a book on the theme, *Profiles in Courage,* John F. Kennedy exhorted his listeners to stand up to pressures of all kinds.[3] But for Kennedy, we now know, it was difficult just to stand up, period.

That he shared this problem with a robot Lincoln may seem like just a quirky coincidence, one more to add to the long lists of pointless, parlor-game Lincoln/Kennedy "parallels" that include, for instance, the fact that Lincoln's assassin fled from a theater to a warehouse, Kennedy's from a warehouse to a theater.[4] But this particular parallel points to some real political and cultural concerns of the time. Among questions that had already preoccupied storytellers, as we've seen, was how similar to the rest of us a president could really be—how well he could "relate" to ordinary citizens and vice-versa, to use a term that was popular in the 1960s. In one key respect, of course, we are all the same: We all inhabit human bodies. That almost goes without saying, but suddenly it seemed worth pointing out; Kennedy himself noted that "our most basic common link" is that we are all mortal and breathe the same air. And what prompted that observation was the nuclear threat, which raised two terrifying prospects: "that mankind is doomed"—because human life is so fragile—and "that we are gripped by forces we cannot control," in part because controlling them depended on leaders who themselves could break down like faulty machines.[5]

If the irreducible reality of the body made our leaders resemble us, though, it could also make them different from us—or rather, similar to an "us" that in this period was embracing difference, treating bodily distinctions of race, gender, and age as matters of "identity" (in another of the era's fashionable terms). Machines, after all, can be improved, re-designed, replaced over time with better and more powerful machines. Maybe the same is true of the organic "machines" that make human life what it is. President Kennedy himself rejected hopes for "a sudden revolution in human nature," but others dreamed of precisely that.[6] Transcending nature's limits, expanding and re-engineering "the human," was one of the paramount cultural projects of the era. And if personhood itself could be reimagined, the presidency was bound to be too.

His "Simple Presence": Fears of a Weakened President

It is easy to recall the presidency of the 1960s as a site of unparalleled power. The Cold War had promoted the American president to "Leader of the Free World." He was the commander-in-chief of a global military machine whose every nuclear-armed bomber and submarine was capable of wreaking greater destruction than all earlier armies combined. He could promise, as Kennedy put it, to "bear any burden, meet any hardship" in defense of America and the West. And when he wasn't busy staring down the Soviet menace he could launch grand projects, from wars on poverty to the conquest of the moon. If there was a problem in all this, it would logically have seemed to be not weakness but *hubris*, an exorbitant faith in the power of one man.

Yet the concern that one finds expressed repeatedly in this era is that the president was dangerously weak. The very size of the challenges facing the office threatened to dwarf the individuals who held it. Having recently emerged as a leading critic of America's "power elite," C. Wright Mills noted widespread doubts that even that elite was controlling events. "The omnipotence of evil tyrants abroad," Mills wrote in 1958, "and the prevalence of virtuous but impotent leaders at home are widely assumed."[7] Discussions of the presidency among political scientists were replete with words like *prisoner, paralysis,* and *collapse.* Looking back on the first edition of his widely used textbook, *Presidential Power*—a book said to have "served as John F. Kennedy's primer"[8]—Richard Neustadt noted that despite its title, its real theme had been presidential weakness. The presidency, Neustadt argued, required skill and expertise, and there was nothing in the system to guarantee those qualities. Worse, America's "dangerous dependence" on its presidents was increasing, even as their ability to be "alive and fully useful" was becoming ever more uncertain.[9]

Neustadt's study of presidential power (or lack thereof) originally appeared in 1960, the same year that Rudolph Marx, a medical doctor, published his study *The Health of the Presidents* (or lack thereof).[10] Both authors, that is, were writing at the close of the Eisenhower administration. Eisenhower was the last president to reach the White House as a political amateur—a man with no prior experience of elected office, let alone the kind of presidential expertise that Neustadt called for. He was also not a well man. Neustadt and Marx both analyzed several presidents, but, if not directly inspired by Eisenhower, their conclusions certainly matched up with the Ike who had himself described his duties as "at times . . . very fatiguing." Neustadt's criticism of Eisenhower as not "purposeful" enough and as lacking a "sense of direction" got little argument even from sympathetic firsthand observers.[11] Emmet John Hughes, a presidential speechwriter, thought the Eisenhower years exemplified *The Ordeal of Power,* as he titled his own memoir. Ike's political energies were "The Faltering Force," and in watching him, Hughes confessed to an anxiety centered on "the curse of Sisyphus": a "kind of slow anesthesia" that dissipated the energy behind every bold initiative.[12]

The metaphor of anesthesia is telling. Political critiques of the time were often linked to reflections on the president's physical person. "A historic figure," Hughes noted, "may have enormous force and impact *physically*"; his "simple *presence*" was one important but often ignored way to "weigh the strength of a man."[13] Or again, Hughes feared, his lack of it. For all his world-historical stature, Eisenhower was physically ordinary to an almost frightening degree. While in office he suffered a heart attack, had surgery to relieve a life-threatening bowel obstruction linked to Crohn's disease, and had his speech impaired by a stroke. That his presidency had meanwhile ground to a halt was the implied message of Kennedy's promise to "get the country moving again."

Today we know that the forty-three-year-old Kennedy was perhaps even sicker than Ike, and in fact had already been close to death at least once. But the very lengths to which he went to hide his infirmities were a tribute to the political value of *vigor*, a concept so closely associated with JFK that comedians could get laughs just by pronouncing that word with a Boston accent.[14] And the fears of Kennedy-watchers echoed those of Eisenhower's associates: Even vigorous presidents were too weak. Theodore Sorensen, Kennedy's close aide and reputed author of the promise to "pay any price, bear any burden," contrasted a president's "extraordinary powers" with his "extraordinary limitations," stressing the loneliness, danger, and dependence that had made the president's job "infinitely more difficult" than in any previous era. A few years later, George E. Reedy, a friend and counselor of Lyndon Johnson's, spoke in a similar way of the "misery" of a job that imposed "the burden of Sisyphus."[15] Johnson himself left office lamenting not just the limits of its power but "the agony and cruelty of the American Presidency."[16] Again and again throughout the 1960s and 1970s, analysts fretted that the presidency's demands were simply more than mere mortals could bear. Neustadt, among others, recalled Woodrow Wilson's warning that the office might be too much for a person of "ordinary physique," then added: "The strain is vastly greater now, with no relief in sight."[17]

Nor was the strain merely physical. The new concern that had arisen since Wilson's day focused on the presidency as a "psychological environment" that all but guaranteed pain, vulnerability, and suffering. Serving in it was not merely a large challenge, or even ordeal, but a "torment." Inevitably it was suggested that presidents seek relief through methods borrowed from the so-called Human Potential Movement:

> There are certain measures a president can take in his own behalf. He might employ the self-help and stress reduction techniques currently in vogue in society at large. Meditation, self-hypnosis, mind control and other self-administered nostrums aimed at the cultivation of psychological detachment from life's trials and tribulations are as available to presidents as they are to the rest of us.

Unless something was done, the nation was in danger: presidents might crumble under the mental as well as physical stress. Presidents' "neurotic drives," said George Reedy, would only be reinforced in office, perhaps putting the nation at the mercy of a "highly irrational personality, who under other circumstances might be medically certifiable for treatment."[18] Reedy's fears seemed borne out by events, most dramatically during *The Final Days*—the title that Watergate reporters Bob Woodward and Carl Bernstein gave their novel-like depiction of Richard Nixon going to pieces.[19]

Running through all this like *leitmotifs*, moreover, were the linked themes of assassination and conspiracy. In the 1960s and early 1970s, assassinations or assassination attempts helped shape three consecutive presidential elections. An assassination, perhaps especially by gunshot, is nothing if not proof of the shocking fragility of a political leader's person. One minute he's a civic being, a symbol of larger aspirations and fears, and the next he's a broken creature of flesh and—all too vividly—blood. And where questions linger about why this occurred, the focus on organic detail can become almost literally microscopic. The murder of JFK was picked over second by second, shot by shot and, thanks to the Zapruder film, frame by frame; one book devoted a whole chapter just to "The Throat Wound."[20]

That a presidency, especially one identified with youth and vigor, could be so easily destroyed was too much for many to accept. The Warren Commission may have thought that its failure to find a wider conspiracy would be welcomed as reassuring. But for some it was cause for alarm. A conspiracy theory at least helps right the balance between the political gravity of the event and the almost frivolous ease with which it's made to occur. In the words of another blue-ribbon panel convened to examine the decade's political violence,

> the vast audience which is apparently so willing and anxious to be convinced of a conspiracy exists because the alternative is unbearable. It is unbearable because it makes the entire system of controlled relationships in which they live, and upon which the security and sense of their lives rest, vulnerable to destruction by the vagaries of the totally unpredictable. The most conspicuous and most powerful representative of the principles that shape and guarantee their lives can be destroyed in seconds by the attack of a nonentity. It seems incredible that the man who commands the largest power in the world could be destroyed by a man who commands no one, not even himself. . . . If we must suffer parricide, if our father is to be taken from us, he must be taken by a most powerful, if malignant, counterforce. We cannot lose him to a casual crank.[21]

Just so, ruling out a conspiracy in the Kennedy assassination meant locating its causes somewhere in the troubled mind of Lee Harvey Oswald. The Warren Report duly undertook to psychoanalyze Oswald, but in so doing it merely ratified the larger fear: that great affairs of state could indeed hinge on one man's mental disturbance.[22] And it wasn't even necessary for that man to be a leader himself; any nonentity would do as long as he was a good shot.

On the other hand, if conspiracy theories offered hope of finding causes large enough to match the dramatic effects, they were also cold comfort. Even a conspiracy aimed at some rational purpose was, by definition, dark and inscrutable, submerged beneath events—not much better in that sense than the disordered psyche of some obsessed loner. Worse, a cultural environment hospitable to conspiracy theorizing encouraged the thought that presidents *themselves* might be conspirators. This was an even grimmer variant of the fear that they might be paranoid neurotics. And events, again, made such worries hard to dismiss. LBJ had not ordered the death of JFK, as some suggested, but he did keep secrets of the kind revealed in the Pentagon Papers—and his successor, an "unindicted co-conspirator" in the Watergate scandal, was responsible for terms like *hush money* and *black-bag jobs* becoming part of everyday political speech.

Nightmares and Shadows:
The Manchurian Candidate and *Seven Days in May*

As well aligned as it was with real events, the issue of presidential weakness did not simply migrate from life to art. Like the 1930s image of the personal president, it appeared in stories even before the reality had unfolded.[23] Its new centrality was apparent in *Sunrise at Campobello,* the 1958 Dore Schary play and its 1960 movie adaptation about FDR's midlife struggle with polio. As recently as 1944, the political "biopic" *Wilson* had downplayed the real severity of Woodrow Wilson's stroke-induced impairment. But *Sunrise* underscored Roosevelt's disability, emphasizing the feats of physical exertion and stage management that had previously kept it from public view.[24]

Of course, in this case the happy ending was known in advance: Even from his wheelchair, Roosevelt would guide the nation through not one but *two* world-historical crises, setting the modern standard for presidential longevity and power. Most fictions premised on fears of a weakened president were much darker, their plots driven by irrationality and looming disaster like nightmares from some collective political id. In fact, one bit of good news amid the mounting anxiety was that all this tension could make for a fine story. If only by law of averages, tales of the presidency are rarely premier examples of the art forms in which they're produced. But if any ever were, it would be the cycle of political "suspense thrillers" that appeared in the early 1960s. In a brief period roughly coinciding with the Kennedy administration, this genre produced not only some of its own most celebrated works but a group of films widely seen as classics of cinema in general.

The first of these was *The Manchurian Candidate,* John Frankenheimer's 1962 adaptation of Richard Condon's 1959 novel. As in many political thrillers, the presidency functions in this story as a "maguffin"— an object seen, if at all, in sidelong glimpses, and unimportant except for the frenzied activity it motivates.[25] One could say, in fact, that motivation is the story's theme. A war veteran, Sergeant Raymond Shaw (Laurence Harvey), has come back from Korea a victim of Communist brainwashing, subconsciously programmed to kill on command. Along with his stepfather, the demagogic but weak-willed Senator Iselin, he is also in thrall to his mother (Angela Lansbury), a latter-day Lady Macbeth who is in league with the Communists to install Iselin in the White House and take over the world. The plot requires the robotic Shaw, after killing everyone in his way, to shoot a presidential nominee as the candidate is addressing his party's convention. Iselin, then, will rush forward both literally and figuratively to fill the breach.

Luckily, the sinister Russo-Asian scientists of "The Pavlov Institute" were not content with brainwashing Shaw; they also tested their wicked arts on the other men in his old unit. These include Shaw's former commander, Major Marco (Frank Sinatra), who has been having recurring nightmares in which he begins to remember what really happened. Even as Shaw is setting out on his killing spree, Marco finds and tries to de-program him. In the final scene he races against the clock to stop Shaw from firing the fatal shot. He's too late, but his de-programming has worked: At the last second Shaw aims his rifle away from the candidate and instead kills Iselin and his evil mother, then himself.

Marco's dreams resemble what Freud called "the return of the repressed," and it's impossible to miss the Freudian undertones in Shaw's relationship with his mother. Shaw's drives, indeed, are a parody of the Freudian unconscious. As instances of both conspiracy and individual derangement, they represent the twisting of these two fears into one.

But because they are products of pure compulsion they lack even a "psycho-logic," the loose connection that the unconscious normally has to the self. Shaw is a blankness on which the motives of others have been drawn; in the words of the Pavlov Institute's chief thought-controller, he is "a normally-conditioned American," a "productive, sober, and respected member of the community," who "has been trained to kill and then to have no memory of having killed. Without memory of his deed, he cannot possibly feel guilt. . . . Having been relieved of those uniquely American symptoms, guilt and fear, he cannot possibly give himself away." Brainwashing, that is, literally makes politics of insanity: Shaw becomes a political agent only to the extent that he loses his mind.

As if dissatisfied with *Manchurian*'s complexity and psychotheorizing (as well as the fact that the evil candidate never does make it to office), the ABC Television anthology series *The Outer Limits* reprised *Manchurian*'s theme in an episode called "The Hundred Days of the Dragon" in September 1963. In this version the plot to install a foreign agent as president succeeds, this time through the perennial device of the doppelgänger. Those ever-resourceful scientists "in that part of the world we call the Orient" have developed a technology that permits replacing one person's facial features with another's. Using this, they substitute their man for the candidate favored to win the upcoming election. The result is a president who, until he is finally exposed, surprises everyone with a newly peaceable—that is, weakened—policy toward a rising East Asian power and "its close-packed millions."

Much of the appeal of stories like this is in their "look." Both *Manchurian* and "Hundred Days" rely on the calculated eeriness of white faces becoming Asian and vice-versa. In the latter this is accomplished through another ancient device, the mask; it is when the double removes a face-mold that we see the startling transformation.[26] Masks, doubles, and other such contrivances have long been associated with what Freud called the *Unheimlich*, or "uncanny." The uncanny was not merely the strange, but the strange giving way to shocked recognition. It was the feeling at the heart of horror stories, especially the "B-movie" style of sci-fi horror that viewers of the time knew so well from their local drive-ins. Indeed, "Hundred Days" was directed by Byron Haskin, who had worked in the 1950s with George Pal, the leading impresario of movie science fiction. (It was Haskin who directed Pal's still-impressive *The War of the Worlds*.) And the series in which it appeared, *The Outer Limits*, was ABC's answer to the popular CBS series *The Twilight Zone*, brainchild of the writer/producer Rod Serling. In turn, Serling's follow-up series *Night Gallery* frequently showcased the work of Lionel Lindon, the cinematographer on *The Manchurian Candidate*. Lindon's earlier work had helped create film noir, a visual style heavy on darkness and shadow, and it is not surprising to find his imprint on movies and TV series whose visual effectiveness reflects their origins in the last period when Hollywood studios were still regularly filming in black and white.

A few years later Lindon would also direct photography for *Vanished* (1971), sometimes classed as the first-ever TV miniseries, in which Richard Widmark—"the face of *film noir*"[27]—starred as a fictional president in a story based on a novel by Fletcher Knebel. In another Hollywood roundelay, Knebel had earlier co-authored the novel that Rod Serling adapted for the next film by *The Manchurian Candidate*'s director, John Frankenheimer. This was *Seven Days in May* (1964), the second of the period's great political suspense thrillers and a film whose striking visual impact has two main sources. One was the work of another great cinematographer, Ellsworth Fredericks, who had also photographed *Invasion of the Body Snatchers*—that 1956 landmark in creepy, *unheimliche* stories of body-switching and the annihilated self. Though nominally sci-fi, *Invasion* had been written and directed by veterans of film noir. And the other source of the visual power of *Seven Days* was the screen presence of Burt Lancaster, yet another film noir antihero (who had recently played opposite Richard Widmark in *Judgment at Nuremberg*).

In *Seven Days* Lancaster plays General James Mattoon Scott, chairman of the Joint Chiefs of Staff and leader of a conspiracy to take over the government in a military coup. Scott was reportedly modeled on the real-life "superpatriot" General Edwin Walker, a notorious right-wing agitator whose superiors suspected him of clinical paranoia and who, in April 1963, escaped an assassination attempt by a gunman only later identified as Lee Harvey Oswald. Scott is a cooled-down version of Walker, but therefore, if anything, he seems even more dangerous. His views have put him at odds with President Jordan Lyman, who has just signed a sweeping new disarmament treaty with the Soviet Union. Scott has been leading a movement against the treaty, which he denounces for putting the nation fatally at risk. His indictment of Lyman, bluntly stated—and Lancaster's Scott is terrifically blunt, firing his words like bullets—is that President Lyman is "a criminally weak sister."

In this dispute, the storytellers side with Lyman. But even their sympathy locates him squarely amid the anxieties surrounding the presidency in these years. In the novel by Knebel and Charles W. Bailey II, Lyman is described as an unlikely president, a man who more closely resembles a bookish college professor or "country poet." A Korean War veteran, he has succumbed to "that utter exhaustion of body and spirit known as combat fatigue," and as president he suffers from persistent nightmares. Rather than offering him relief, the cold light of morning brings the nightmares to life, moving him to reflect on the "crushing emotional load" and ultimate feebleness of his high station:

> Through the tall windows overlooking the south lawn Jordan Lyman could see the steady morning rush of cars along Constitution Avenue. It's a funny thing, he thought. The people in those cars work for the government, just as I do. I can tell them what to do. I can make their jobs or wipe them out. But they have the power to undo what I do, by simple error, or by omission, or even by design.
>
> He was president and famous. They were little bureaucrats and obscure. But they were, by and large, secure and befriended in their obscurity, while he stood vulnerable and alone in his fame.[28]

In comparing himself with General Scott, Lyman feels "inadequate and puny," and as the story unfolds he grows even sadder and frailer. Though never quite cracking under the strain, he does seem to age rapidly.[29] This portrait, along with those in other novels by Fletcher Knebel—whose typewriter became a virtual factory of fictional presidents—led LBJ's worried friend George Reedy to credit Knebel, and novelists like him, with having been quicker than most observers to take the problem of presidential breakdown seriously.[30] There are indeed passages in Knebel's fiction that read as if they were ghostwritten by the era's fretful political analysts.[31]

Since the film version of *Seven Days in May* lacks the moody interior monologues of Knebel's book, filmmakers Serling and Frankenheimer capture the president's fragility in a visual image. President Lyman is played by Fredric March, an actor then in his late sixties—about fifteen years older than the novel's Lyman—and when we first see him, he is wearing a blood-pressure cuff and brushing off the warnings of a hovering doctor. "Why in God's name," the doctor grumps, "[do] we elect a man president, and then try and see how fast we can kill him?" Lyman agrees with the doctor that the controversy over his disarmament pact has been taking a physical toll. But, he argues, the real danger to a president's health is the Cold War predicament itself: the power he has to destroy the world, and the responsibility this gives him to protect it.

President Jordan Lyman (Frederic March, *left*) gets his blood pressure checked at the beginning of *Seven Days in May*.

Lyman confronts General James M. Scott (Burt Lancaster) over his secret plans for a military coup. Relying on the constitutional processes and powers of his office, represented here by a desk behind which he seems almost trapped, Lyman looks small, tired, and dangerously weak compared to the charismatic Scott.

"Instead of my blood pressure, I think [the doctor] should worry about my sanity," says Lyman. Despite all the turmoil it's causing, he suggests, disarmament is not the problem; it's the cure.

This physicalizing of the president's political plight is consistent with the film's rhetoric, which pits the haggard March (and his even more broken-down ally, an alcoholic senator played by Edmond O'Brien) against a handsome and frighteningly virile Scott/Lancaster, a character wholly believable as a crowd-pleasing demagogue. Fortunately, President Lyman has the help of Scott's worried adjutant, Colonel Casey (Kirk Douglas), who agrees with Scott in opposing the Soviet treaty but nonetheless hopes to avert a coup. Upon discovering the conspiracy, Casey alerts the president to it, giving Lyman and his confidants the seven days of the title in which to head it off. But it's difficult to see how they can. Lyman scarcely has anything like Scott's sheer political and personal charisma. All he has are the powers of his office. He is merely president, which is to say, weak—seemingly no match for Scott's American Caesar.

The Scott-Lyman confrontation thus boils down to a contest between charismatic authority—the "force and magnetism that men call leadership," as the novel puts it—and the much shakier authority of constitutions and laws.[32] It is this perilously abstract ethic that President Lyman embodies and that he doggedly insists on honoring. In the movie's key scene, facing down Scott (or rather facing him up: we see Lyman seated, in the presidential chair as it were, while Scott towers over him), Lyman puts it this way:

> Why in the name of God don't you have any faith in the system of government you're so hell-bent to protect? . . . You accuse me of having lost [the people's] faith, deliberately and criminally shut my ears to the national voice. Well, where the hell have *you* heard that voice, General? In freight elevators? In dark alleys? In secret places in the dead of night? How did that voice seep into a locked room full of conspirators? That's not where you hear the voice of the people, General, not in this Republic. You want to defend the United States of America, then defend it with the tools it supplies you with—its Constitution. You ask for a mandate, General, from a ballot box. You don't steal it after midnight when the country has its back turned.

Even with his efforts to prevent the coup facing collapse, Lyman declines the easy solution of blackmailing Scott—whose own human weakness, it turns out, involves a secret love affair—and he also spurns advice to break up the conspiracy by force. Instead he stakes the fate of the nation on his belief that constitutional ends must be pursued by constitutional means. At one point he literally clutches a flag stand bearing the flag with the presidential seal, as if leaning for support on that fragile symbol of official authority. Lyman insists on believing that what appears to be his weakness is really his strength.

The story convincingly suggests that he's right, but just barely. If not for Colonel Casey, Scott's machinations would likely have worked. They fail because Scott is so sure of his *personal* authority that he fatally misjudges the other kind. He assumes that the presidency is weakened by the man in it, when in fact it's the other way around: the man is enlarged by the office, which exerts a claim on the loyalty of people like Casey that the individual does not. Casey admires Scott and even agrees with him about the Soviet treaty, yet he still blows the whistle on Scott's conspiracy because his allegiance, in the end, is not personal but attaches to the system and its assigned roles—"the uniform," as he puts it in his final facedown with Scott. Whatever his doubts about President Lyman's policies, he shares Lyman's faith in a government of laws, not men. The constitutional order survives thanks to a handful of people like Casey, genuine patriots for whom that order looms larger than any issue—even the threat of nuclear war—and larger than any man, even the very imposing General Scott.

Seven Days, then, turns on this question: What combination of Cold War pressures and popular demands for strongman rule would it take to overthrow a pedestrian system like ours, a checked-and-balanced regime of limited powers whose intricate network of mutual dependency makes even the president, as Lyman muses, just another government worker? The force with which this question comes across onscreen is crucially a function of these actors and this style of filmmaking artistry. Without the brooding shadow world conjured by Serling, Frankenheimer, and Fredericks, and peopled by Lancaster, Douglas, and March, the question loses much of its urgency. This becomes clear if we compare *Seven Days* with similar but less effective works. In *Twilight's Last Gleaming* (1977), another film noir reunion (the director was veteran noirmaker Robert Aldrich), Burt Lancaster is again cast as a rogue general, this time threatening to launch World War III from a nuclear missile silo unless the president—Charles Durning, whom we first see bleeding from a shaving nick—admits that the public was lied to about the Vietnam

War. It's an odd demand; government lies about Vietnam were already old news, and it makes Lancaster's character seem strangely desperate and overwrought. Having aged fifteen years since *Seven Days in May,* Lancaster himself has begun to look broken down. His character is now the victim, a prison escapee whose superiors framed him in order to keep him silent. Chief among those superiors is a senior general played by Richard Widmark. Widmark, not Lancaster, is the movie's "heavy," and while he may be politically in the wrong, it's hard not to agree that he is right to order his forces to seize back the missile silo. Worse, Lancaster's character is required to spend the whole movie stuck in that silo. Unlike General Scott he has no power in his own person, nothing that would pose a threat to anyone once he re-emerges aboveground. This denies us a real confrontation between opponents. The president even claims to share the general's righteous indignation about government lies. So when he consents to become the general's hostage and the two of them finally meet in the missile silo, there is no spark to the scene—nothing like the high voltage of the parallel scene in *Seven Days.*

The virtues of *Seven Days* have also been highlighted by later but less successful borrowings and remakes. For instance, *The Enemy Within,* a made-for-cable effort to update the story for the 1990s, made two large mistakes: it unconvincingly cast Jason Robards as the scheming general, and it replaced the threat of Soviet nuclear attack with an economic threat from Japanese imports. Not only are trade disputes a poor substitute for the Cold War, but the septuagenarian and somewhat frail Robards hardly seemed a frightening figure. Likewise as regards a later radio adaptation. Scott's commanding presence and Lyman's haggardness are invisible on radio, which makes their confrontation a question of voices—and there, a character actor like Edward Asner, playing Lyman, has a natural advantage (more "character") over just about anyone chosen to play Scott.[33] More importantly, it is harder in this medium to perceive Lyman as the agent and champion of a whole, complex, precarious political order. As FDR recognized, radio collapses political distance, turning even the commander-in-chief into just a friendly fellow with whom you're having a "chat." The radio playwright may have been correct to play up this persona (making Lyman a family man who is awaiting the birth of his first grandchild), and it well suits the gruff-but-lovable Ed Asner. But the idea that this man stands for a threatened *state* is thereby obscured.[34]

"The Machines Are Winning": *Dr. Strangelove* and *Fail-Safe*

Along with *The Manchurian Candidate* and *Seven Days in May*, the third of the great early 1960s political films set in the shadow world is *Dr. Strangelove: Or, How I Learned to Stop Worrying and Love the Bomb*. Stanley Kubrick's satirical comedy about accidental nuclear war is so full of unforgettable images and characters that it's typically cited as a career highlight for any actor who appeared in it. Peter Sellers alone played three of those characters, and each of them is a study in disability or inability of some kind.[35] One is Group Captain Mandrake, a Royal Air Force officer temporarily posted to America's "Burpelson" Air Force Base. There Mandrake finds himself playing nursemaid and confessor to the demented base commander, General Jack D. Ripper (Sterling Hayden), a fanatical anticommunist who has become convinced that fluoridated water is an evil Soviet plot to pollute "our precious bodily fluids." (This was an actual concern of some on the far right at the time.) To prevent this, Ripper decides to force a U.S.-Soviet showdown. Using a war plan meant for the ultimate crisis, when all higher authority is gone—as well as machine-coded orders fatally well designed to prevent anyone from interfering—he launches a fleet of nuclear-armed bombers toward the Soviet Union. As he explains to Mandrake, the president will soon realize that he cannot recall the bombers, and will have no choice but to fight an all-out nuclear war. Mandrake's responses to this are a model of British politeness and by-the-book propriety, a very funny send-up of the officer-and-gentleman type well known from traditional war films—and, of course, exactly the wrong instruments to wield against a raving madman like Ripper.

Sellers also plays that beleaguered president, Merkin Muffley, whose anxious crisis conference with advisors in the Pentagon's War Room is a large part of the subsequent action. President Muffley is a bald man with big glasses and a widely noted resemblance to the twice-defeated Adlai Stevenson. He is ineffectual in every way: he can't stop the B-52 flown by a cowboy airman, Major "King" Kong (Slim Pickens); he has trouble reaching the drunken Soviet Premier "Kissof" on the hotline and has to get a number for Kissof's high command from directory assistance; and he can't even keep control of his own advisors, particularly the blustering General "Buck" Turgidson (George C. Scott). When Turgidson almost comes to blows with the visiting Soviet ambassador, Muffley is reduced to scolding them like an exasperated grade school principal: "Gentlemen! You can't fight in here—this is the War Room!"

The third of Sellers's characters is Dr. Strangelove himself, the German émigré scientist to whom the president must finally turn for answers. Strangelove appears to be the most disabled character of all: he is confined to a wheelchair and seems to have lost control of his arm, which springs upward in involuntary Nazi salutes. Entering the story only near the end, he also spends relatively little time onscreen. Yet, as the movie's title suggests, he is in a sense the shadowy presence behind the whole situation—and indeed, his first entrance is a slow, dramatic emergence out of the War Room's heavy shadows. If anyone could be said to have created the system that is now (literally) flying out of control, it is Strangelove, a man whose mind has far outrun his body and who views the nuclear standoff as a kind of intellectual puzzle. For Strangelove, the ultimate weapon isn't the nuclear bomb but the slide rule.

It is worth pausing here to consider other works closely related to *Strangelove*, as well as the matrix of ideas out of which they all emerged. In *Fail-Safe*, which followed *Strangelove* by a few months, director Sidney Lumet offered essentially the same plot as serious drama, casting Henry Fonda as a president grimly facing a very similar crisis and trying similarly frantic means to contain it. (This movie, like *Seven Days*, aged its worried chief executive by some fifteen years: The unnamed president in the novel *Fail-Safe* was obviously JFK.) Both *Fail-Safe* and *Strangelove* had common sources in the nuclear strategizing of the time, a chilling hyperlogic known to the public through the writings of defense analysts, "game theorists," and foreign-policy "realists" like Drs. Henry Kissinger and Herman Kahn (both reputedly models for the character of Dr. Strangelove, as well as his *Fail-Safe* counterpart Dr. Groteschele). Kahn's 1962 book *Thinking About the Unthinkable* had tried to explain strategic thought to the public, breezily musing on such engaging brain-teasers as which city should be traded for which in case of an accidental nuclear strike. To many at the time, a disaster on that scale seemed not only thinkable, but likely. Nuclear "defense" relied on postures of deterrence and "MAD," mutually assured destruction, which had led both the United States and the USSR to put their faith in enormously complex, hair-trigger mechanisms designed to make World War III possible at the push of a button—a frequently used metaphor that suggested both instantaneousness and impersonal mechanization. These mechanisms, in

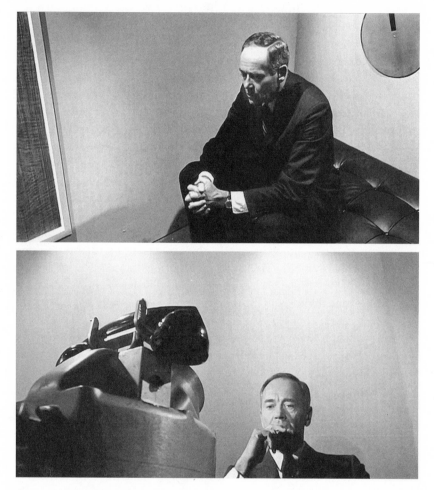

Cornered in a tiny, windowless bunker, *Fail-Safe*'s president (Henry Fonda) waits helplessly as an accidental nuclear confrontation spins out of control. In this and related stories the intentions of human leaders are overwhelmed by the perverse logic and machinery of the Cold War, represented here by the "hotline" phone to the Soviet premier.

turn, increased the chance that the wrong button might be pushed or the wrong person might push it. *Fail-Safe* and *Dr. Strangelove* respectively play out these two "scenarios," to use another of the nuclear strategists' favorite words. Both begin with the United States attacking the Soviet Union against the president's wishes, and both depict him as helpless to shut down a system that seems to have developed rules and purposes of its own.

In the novel from which both stories indirectly derive, Peter Bryant's 1958 *Red Alert*, the rogue general who launches the attack is not insane in the least. The real insanity, in all these works, lies in the system itself, and it's precisely because he sees its logic so lucidly that the general can use that system to wreak havoc.[36] To assure destruction, the system must be rigged to leave as little room as possible for human decision-making. It must, one might say, mechanically (dis)embody the cold logic of deterrence, which requires that retaliation be guaranteed no matter who is left in charge—that the war machine can still "act" even if it loses all political direction, which after all must come from fragile beings like presidents who could be lost if the enemy strikes first. This logic has taken "the button" out of the president's hands, while also, the rogue general calculates, forcing war on the president once the button is pushed. But the Soviets also understand the MAD logic, and they too have developed a way of assuring destruction if all else fails: a secret "doomsday machine." The two equally logical emergency systems are mutually exclusive, and by provoking an emergency the general has unwittingly put them on a collision course. This leaves the president—in Bryant's novel, a "stooped, scholarly man" whose ailing predecessor could not bear the pressures of the office—with a choice between *two* appalling logics: MAD, or an "eye for an eye" scenario straight out of Herman Kahn.[37] It appears that his only rational, yet absurd, course will be to OK Soviet retaliation against an American city.

In *Red Alert* this outcome is averted, partly through good luck—the U.S. bomber misses—and partly because the president turns out to be tougher than he looks and is able to stare the Soviet leader back from the brink. It is left to *Fail-Safe* and *Dr. Strangelove*, then, to take the two logics to their respective conclusions. Forced to trade an eye for an eye, the president in *Fail-Safe* averts a general war by blowing up New York City himself in exchange for a nuclear-flattened Moscow. In *Dr. Strangelove* the luck is bad, and the doomsday machine actually goes off; obeying the same logic that had led them to build it, the Russians had set it on automatic. Mutual destruction is thus assured after all—although the film closes with the feckless officials at the American end already plotting their comeback, after the hundred years or so they will now have to spend living in mine shafts.

In an interview, Sidney Lumet summarized *Fail-Safe*'s message as "the machines are winning."[38] The automating of things, following nuclear-age logic, has finally put them truly beyond people's control—or worse, in the accidental control of the wrong people. "I admit, the human element seems to have failed us here," *Strangelove*'s General Turgidson drily observes. Apart from its final absurdity and the fact that it plays the whole crisis for laughs, what makes *Dr. Strangelove* a classic of political satire is its generalizing of this fundamental problem. Whereas *Fail-Safe* has the war machine literally short-circuiting, *Dr. Strangelove* is finally more interested in that human element. What would lead people to build such machines in the first place? Kubrick seems to insist that for all the protestations of rationality on the part of the system's masters, their real motive is emotional and bodily—the instinct-driven strange love that men, in particular, harbor for weapons and war. This implicit claim is the source of innumerable jokes: the "mating" of two military aircraft in the title sequence; General Ripper's rants about "bodily fluids" as he fondles his big cigar; the famous image of Major Kong whooping it up like a rodeo rider atop a huge phallic warhead; Strangelove's mathematical calculation of the optimum women-to-men ratio in mine shafts once these are the only habitable places left on Earth. Clearly aware of his debt to Jonathan Swift (at least one joke name, "Laputa," is borrowed from *Gulliver's Travels*), Kubrick seems to say that the modern, automated military's elaborate bureaucratizing and intellectualizing are just a thin veneer over basically animal urges toward sex and violence.[39]

Thus it's not just the government or military that is out of control; it's our human nature—and the surest expressions of this are the mechanisms of control themselves. In the "novelization" of *Dr. Strangelove*, which includes bits probably salvaged from earlier drafts of the screenplay, this point is highlighted even as President Muffley is first introduced. Suffering from a runny nose and bad headache, Muffley almost doesn't make it to the War Room at all: an elevator chair malfunctions, leaving him suspended in midair, and a hyper-vigilant sentry demands that he produce the correct ID (pursuant to "Security Regulation 134B section 7 subsection D item 6").[40] When even the smallest components of our overdeveloped machines and security systems fail—or, rather, work too well—the problem is not just in the grand design; it's a pervasive feature of our whole condition.

In the same way that film noir techniques came to be widely imitated, the shadow world of the political thriller also devolved onto lesser, B-movie talents and mass-audience TV.[41] But that itself was testimony to how important this distinctive look is to the genre. For an April 2000 "CBS television event," actor/producer George Clooney remade *Fail-Safe* as a live broadcast in black and white, with Stephen Frears directing and a graying Richard Dreyfuss as the president. Advertised as a tribute to the live dramas of television's "Golden Age," and aimed in part at capturing the urgency of a story that unfolds in approximately real time, the anachronistic staging also fit the story's theme: The look of 1950s TV lends itself to Cold War atmospherics, and a live telecast—with theater-style lighting on high-contrast monochrome video—makes for a vivid play of shadows: the "black" is literally just a few steps away.[42] In this case that encroaching void might represent nuclear oblivion, but of course the link between darkness and threat is one of the oldest story elements of all. Shadows have long been a way of visualizing the id, the realm of secrets, hidden purposes, unacknowledged desires, insanity and mindlessness. What these classic thrillers did was give that image political meaning. As if literalizing JFK's "long, twilight struggle," they painted the presidency in chiaroscuro, transposing a rhetoric of strength and weakness into visual schemas of light and shade. *Seven Days in May* states the connection in so many words. The real enemy he's fighting, President Lyman says, is not the conspirators who prowl the dark alleys in the dead of night. It's "a sickness, a frustration—a feeling of impotence, helplessness, weakness" that has gripped the nation in the nuclear age. In the closing speech of this shadow-saturated film, Lyman both calls on Americans to remember their strength and promises a future in "the bright sunshine of freedom."

"To Perform as a Man": Race and Gender in *The Man* and *Kisses for My President*

The political thrillers of the early 1960s have another, even more obvious feature in common: Virtually all the main characters in them are men. And the weaknesses those characters suffer are all, in some way, question marks over their masculinity—insinuations that what they lack is potency of a specifically male kind. It is this manhood gap that President Lyman must close in his struggle with General Scott, and which seems to drive the madness of the military men in *Dr. Strangelove.* (Least preoccupied with it is President Merkin Muffley, whose name suggests that he's a hopeless case: the rude puns mark him as effeminate born and bred.) The most important female character, Mrs. Iselin in *The Manchurian Candidate,* is the exception that proves the rule. Her function is plainly to emasculate both her husband and son, and it's significant that the antidote to this, the last-second restoration of sanity, comes from the brainwashed son's old army commander—a timely bit of male bonding that winds up saving the day.

Looking to presidents for traditionally masculine virtues has a long history. It gave us Teddy Roosevelt with his big stick and, long before that, an Andrew Jackson whose "virulent hypermasculinity" helped him push his cerebral predecessor aside.[43] The Kennedy image of the early 1960s was assembled from old materials: sports, seamanship, wartime exploits, "profiles in courage," and even a suggestion of knights in shining armor (conveniently supplied via the popular musical *Camelot*). It's intriguing that when the administrator of NASA went to brief the new president on the space program's need for more money—far from pledging to put Americans on the moon, Kennedy at first resisted funding Project Apollo—the talking points he spoke from warned against leaving the program "emasculated." Similar language figured in later debates over Vietnam and even the Great Society.[44]

But whatever their continued salience for policymakers, the assumptions behind this kind of imagery were soon giving way in the wider culture. Some groups were seeking to re-appropriate the masculine ethos while others questioned its value altogether. The new "interlopers" were blacks, gays, and women—historically marginalized groups that "irreversibly transformed the landscape on which American men have sought to test and prove their manhood," as Michael S. Kimmel puts it. According to Kimmel, "the social movements of those two decades [the 1960s and 1970s]—the women's movement, the civil rights movement, and the gay liberation movement—all offered scathing critiques of traditional masculinity and demanded inclusion and equality in the public arena. . . . The very groups that had been so long excluded from American life were making their own claims for identity. And for manhood." It's obvious why movements for sexual equality and liberation would challenge traditional notions of masculinity, but, as Kimmel observes, even the civil rights movement was notable for its "gendered" appeals. Especially as "enlarged to include movements for black power and black pride," it revealed an oppressed people "reclaiming a manhood stolen from them." [45]

Presidents, naturally, were expected to respond to this new politics of "identity," and there were the usual fears that they would not be up to the task. George Reedy worried that America's executive-centered system, which needed presidential leadership "to withstand the stresses of the modern world," was fatally ill-suited to the "revolutionary forces" then at work. "Can our political system cope with these strains? The answer is probably not," he wrote. "It is a form of government which basically centers on one man and therefore does not allow adequate outlets for the aspirations of minorities."[46] More recently, the historian Eli Zaretsky has offered a different verdict. The "overall rejection of (paternal) authority that had erupted during the 1960s," leading as it did to "an irreversible cultural revolution in such areas as women's rights, homosexuality, and sexual permissiveness," produced "enormous and deeply positive changes in family life and sexuality." Given its modern mission, the presidency was bound to be caught up in these changes:

> In [Franklin] Roosevelt's time, the president led the way against a set of sacred shibboleths: the "free" market, the Social Darwinian "laws of nature," the right of the rich to their riches. . . . The results were the almost revolutionary changes brought about by the New Deal. In the 1960s, the executive branch of government became the focal point for a new series of struggles—against racism, sexism, and homophobia— which both continued and diverged from the economic struggles of the previous epoch. A new leadership had to preserve the gains made in the New Deal era as well as repudiate additional shibboleths, for example the naturalness of a particular family norm.

These struggles continue into the present. For more than a generation now, says Zaretsky, the presidency has stood at "the convergence of two intense and opposed currents in the American psyche, one aimed at resurrecting patriarchal authority, the other aimed at destroying it."[47]

But this position in the crosscurrents affected more than just what presidents were expected to *do*. More profoundly, it affected what they might *be*—what range of *personae* could be imagined as bearing the authority of leadership (or faulted for not bearing it). If a leader's physical condition was an index of political health and strength, what might follow from assigning the president a different kind of physicality altogether? The masculine ethos demanded that the president "be a man." But what if she wasn't?

Variants of this question inspired a number of popular works, each involving characters marked by some nontraditional cultural identity—presidents or candidates who were black, female, or young (at a time when youth was widely seen as a distinct movement or "subculture"),[48] or whose sexual orientation was in question. The latter motif was the natural result of an early Cold War rhetoric that linked "communists and queers" or "pinks, pansies, and punks," in Senator Joe McCarthy's memorable phrases. On the color spectrum of political invective, the "pink" of covert Communist sympathy easily shaded into the "lavender" of homosexuality, which in turn, until the mid-1970s, was officially listed as a mental disease. Both, then, were linked with illness and contagion, as complementary varieties of "softness" capable of sapping the national will.[49]

Easily hidden, such conditions smacked of conspiracy and scandal: they were the dark secrets most effective in discrediting political opponents. This fact supplied the key conflicts in Allen Drury's novel *Advise and Consent* (1959), a record-breaking bestseller, and Gore Vidal's play *The Best Man* (1960), both of which were made into movies starring Henry Fonda. Fonda's character in each case is a rising politician with a career-threatening secret; the plots turn on McCarthyesque smears and counter-smears, as the politician and his accusers variously threaten to expose each other as onetime Communists, homosexuals, or mental patients. And as if to prove that physical health is inversely related to Machiavellian ruthlessness, both stories feature a sick and dying president who goads all this on (prompting *The Best Man*'s hero to protest that he "just want[s] to be *human*").[50] As Vidal, who called himself a "same-sexualist," implies in his punning title, the issue in each case isn't just who is the *best* man, but who is the best *man*.

A similar anxiety drives events in Irving Wallace's 1964 novel *The Man*. This bestseller had a long shelf life; ABC-TV aired a movie version in 1972, with a script by Rod Serling and starring James Earl Jones as President Douglass Dilman. At a time when African Americans were still struggling for basic voting rights, a black man seriously vying for the presidency was hard to imagine—although a 1968 biography recalled rumors that America had already had one ancestrally "black" president, Warren G. Harding.[51] Color aside, Douglass Dilman is something of a Harding-like figure, a passive naïf who finds himself, to his own and everyone else's surprise, thrust into the Oval Office through a strange accident of succession. Like Frank Capra's Mr. Smith and other such political novices, Dilman openly frets that he's not ready for the job, and before he can get his bearings he's subjected to a number of excruciating pressures: from the Soviets, from the rising black nationalist movement, and from a familiar cabal of scheming machine politicians and power brokers.[52] In this story, though, the old-boy cynics are not merely corrupt, but racist; Dilman is a threat to them because he's an honest man, but also because he's "The Man," period. The well-established slang use of that term to refer to the white powers-that-be makes this book's title, too, a double entendre.

The title also names what Dilman sees as his problem: to whites, he is "a black man, meaning a half man," as he tells his lawyer and confidant Nat Abrahams. Dilman's worries are registered bodily; he takes office feeling "almost physically ill" and wakes up on his first morning as president with a headache. And his first outing on the presidential yacht makes him seasick, a condition he tells Abrahams is symbolic of his inborn inadequacy. His white aides and colleagues topside, he fears, "know I'm as out of place here as in the White House":

> I've devoted every minute to not throwing up. I guess I wanted to uphold my position of authority. Tell me, how can you be Commander in Chief of the Navy and have your head in the toilet bowl the whole lousy voyage? They're born to it, up there, their stomachs trained for it. How can I let them know . . . that all the President accomplished today was that he didn't vomit?[53]

As he nonetheless begins, tentatively, to assert himself, Dilman makes enemies on all sides. The radicals target him for assassination, and the old guard accuses him of imposing on America "the tyranny of the weak." Driven to the point of resigning, he seeks advice from a retired ex-president—a Trumanesque plain-speaker whose talk is all down-on-the-farm common sense. This crusty old stock character is the story's oracle, and his way of framing Dilman's challenge puts it in explicitly masculinist terms. Dilman, he says, must not let the United States be a country "where a Negro is afraid to perform as a man, act as a man, live as a man, because he's scared we won't let him do it. . . . Hell and tarnations, fellow, stop crawling. Stand up on your two hind legs like a man. . . . Don't let any man force you to walk out because you think he is a man and you know he thinks you're not." Dilman's job, he adds, is to "make [emancipation] a fact, and to make it a fact not as a Negro who is President but as an American man who is President."[54]

So Dilman stays and fights, and before long this gets him impeached. Determined to wrest the presidency back for one of its own, the ruling cabal concocts a number of viciously false charges—among them the old racist canard of preying on white women like a "beast." Presenting Dilman's defense, Abrahams attacks this characterization directly. "The President is not a four-legged brute, but a man, as you are men, no more, no less," he indignantly tells the Senate. "You are here to sit in judgment on the future of a human being who is the President of the United States." The appeal works, and Dilman is dramatically acquitted by a single vote. Only then does he finally relax and begin to settle into his role: "I wake up, I work, I go to sleep. I'm trying to handle life a day at a time. That's a big job, a big, strange new job for a person who only recently found out he has a right to perform as a man and not just a colored man. It's like starting afresh, with a new mind, new limbs, new nerve apparatus, new outlook. You have to get used to it before you can use all that health and strength."[55] This new normalcy, Dilman suggests, goes hand in hand with both physical vigor and what we might call a "remasculated" sense of himself.

Remasculation is also the theme of *Kisses for My President,* the 1964 film comedy starring Polly Bergen as the first female president and Fred MacMurray as her husband, Thad, a successful business executive haplessly trying to manage the new role of "First Gentleman." The joke throughout this film is the upending of gender expectations, starting with an opening sequence in which we are invited to mistake MacMurray for the "Leslie McCloud" who is being sworn into office. The actual President McCloud has a challenge of her own—to prove that a woman need not be "soft" or averse to "showdowns," as her leading opponent charges, with "those who would destroy our way of life." But this is a subplot; the movie's focus is on Thad. It is a role well suited to the ambiguity in MacMurray's screen persona: By the 1960s he had moved from tough-guy westerns and film noir (notably the classic *Double Indemnity*) to family-friendly Disney films and the long-running *My Three Sons,* which put him in the pantheon of "TV sitcom dads."

Sure enough, from the moment he moves into his White House quarters with their gender-inappropriate décor, Thad McCloud suffers all manner of bodily indignities and comic assaults on his manhood. Like Dilman in *The Man,* he gets seasick aboard the presidential yacht. While having his makeup applied before a Jacqueline Kennedy–style televised tour of the White House, he calms his nerves by taking one too many tranquilizers—that favorite nostrum of the era's stereotypical overstressed housewife. Indeed a recurring gag is that Thad competes for the president's attention in the same way that a pre-feminist wife would compete for her busy husband's. Each time they steal a private moment, the business of state interrupts.

Inevitably Thad blunders into that business himself. While he manages the little indignities with aplomb—even modeling the gift of a ladies' hat decorated with fruit—he rebels against the biggest indignity: the lack of anything serious to do. A hard-charging former company president who had been forced to step down (by ethics rules, since his company was a government contractor), Thad cannot accept that his new position is so vapid. Since he refuses to settle for the First Spouse's historic function as mere ornament, the plot mostly consists of his search for some useful role.

A couple of possibilities present themselves. First, Thad is assigned to look after a visiting South American dictator, Valdez (Eli Wallach). Valdez is a masculine caricature, a macho blusterer whose idea of diplomacy is wooing the female president like a Latin lover. He needs a man to accompany him around town because the activities he prefers—and on which he drags a reluctant Thad—are parodies of manly pursuits. They include exotic dancers, daredevil antics in speedboats and a souped-up sports car, and finally a barroom scuffle that winds up with Thad throwing the headline-grabbing punch.

This annoys the president but delights Thad's ex-girlfriend, Doris, an old rival of Leslie's who now runs her own perfume company. Having already eyed Thad and judged him "as virile as ever," Doris offers him a second chance to make himself useful: he'll become vice president of Doris's company, lending his image to her line of men's products. Thad takes to the project with more than expected enthusiasm. He decides to launch a new line of men's toiletries, "the most rugged products in the history of the business. We're gonna have colognes that smell of campfires, and giant redwoods, and, and the open sea—with names like 'Huntsman' and 'Forest Ranger' and 'Ship Ahoy.' And we're going to have an after-shave lotion that when a man slaps it on his face, it's guaranteed to slap him back!" For a man in Thad's predicament it's the perfect solution. In a kind of gender-role jiujitsu, he dreams of doing for an overly feminized industry what Leslie, in reverse, has done for national leadership.

But meanwhile the First Family's troubles continue to mount. Leslie and Thad's young son is picking fights at school, their teenage daughter is dating a wild boy nicknamed "Sneaker," and the president's political opponent, Senator Walsh, is hoping to use Thad to discredit the president's program. Summoning him before a Senate committee, Walsh accuses Thad of incompetence, fatherly unfitness, and willing service as a "dupe" in the president's plot "to sabotage our foreign relations." It does not take Thad long to turn the tables, exposing Walsh as a foreign agent secretly working on behalf of Valdez. Suddenly Thad is a hero, and Leslie's political success seems assured. But the sheer force of conventionality proves too much for them both. Thad can no longer work with Doris once her romantic intentions become clear. And President McCloud, already juggling job and family like any harried working mom, suddenly faints from what turns out to be an unplanned pregnancy. Warned that the pressures of office could put her baby at risk, she resigns. As they depart and the movie ends, she and Thad joke that it took forty million women to get Leslie into the White House—but "just one man to get me out."

Cybernetics, Hallucinogenics, and Superheroics: The Search for the Transcendent

Both *The Man* and *Kisses for My President* allude to a fear that may be endemic to democracy: that the disempowered masses actually will, at some point, rise up and take control. President Dilman's accidental promotion is anxiously seen as emboldening angry blacks, and President McCloud is accused of giving those forty million women funny ideas— making them a "pain in the neck," as one character says of his own wife. In both cases it's assumed that ethnography could be destiny, that the new regime will represent not the People but "those" people, the kind the president physically resembles. And both works answer these fears in the voice of traditional liberalism, assuring us that this will not happen: Such differences are only skin deep. Dilman and McCloud are conventional politicians and only incidentally non-white males. Both downplay their differences from the presidential norm, insisting that race and gender are merely their attributes, not their agendas.

A few years and several irruptions of radical politics later, American International Pictures—a smaller studio best known for B-movies, drive-in fare, and films made for teenagers—dealt with the same fears in a very different way. *Wild in the Streets* (1968) is often classed as a "cult" film, an apparent reference to its mix of counterculture motifs with low-budget campiness. Its main character, twenty-four-year-old Max Frost (Christopher Jones), is a pop-rock singer and teen idol who becomes a

Addressing Congress on the state of the Union, twenty-four-year-old President Max Frost (Christopher Jones) of *Wild in the Streets* blames the country's troubles on those who are "stiff with age" and announces a plan to send everyone over thirty-five to "groovy" rehabilitation camps.

leader and spokesman for rebellious youth. As the price for lending his mass following to Johnny Fergus (Hal Holbrook), an ambitious Democratic Senate candidate, Frost demands reductions in the voting age— eventually to fourteen, which Congress approves after Frost and his friends send it on an "acid trip" by spiking the D.C. water supply. With his supporters enfranchised and massed in the streets, Frost is handed the Republican nomination and wins the presidency in a landslide. From there he launches a program of generational cleansing, ordering everyone over thirty-five rounded up and sent to "groovy" rehabilitation camps. ("Some of them are really gonna dig it," he promises.)

These events are played in a spirit of grim humor: not frightening, exactly, but not all that funny either. *Wild*'s premise is the full, absurdist realization of the anxiety only alluded to in *The Man* and *Kisses for My President*. Though white and male, Max Frost is even further from the mainstream than Douglass Dilman or Leslie McCloud. He is dangerous in a way that they aren't precisely because his "difference" is not mere physiology; it's a carefully constructed cultural style. (Among other things, he is the avatar of an ambiguous sexuality—the kind of androgyny known at the time as "unisex.") More importantly, that difference is the essence of his politics. Where Dilman and McCloud hope to show how reassuringly conventional they are, race and gender notwithstanding, Frost sets out to seize power for those of his own demographic, and his radical platform is to remake America in their image.

In Johnny Fergus, *Wild in the Streets* has its own Thad McCloud—the bystander whose problem is positioning his conventional persona in relation to the disconcerting new order. And here, too, conservative opposition is represented by an old-school senator, Albright, who warns Fergus against the monster he is helping create. "Youth is a disease!" Albright thunders. If not quite the movie's thesis, this is the point it means to test. Just as the biological reality of pregnancy caught up with Leslie McCloud—thus proving, as Thad jokes, "the superiority of man"—so the final scene of *Wild* reveals the grim joke that biology is already playing on Max Frost. "You're *old*," declares a group of children who find him contemplating his own reflection in a pond. Like an anti-Narcissus, Frost appears to see this too. Youth is always relative, and power derived from it is weakness in disguise, ineluctably leading to its own overthrow. The "disease" that is the human condition does not yield to politics.

If suspense thrillers projected the presidency in black-and-white shadows, *Wild in the Streets* splashes it with the swirling colors of counterculture Day-Glo. The results are absurd for the nation and tragic for Max Frost, who ends the story poised to become his generation's Johnny Fergus. In a film that both plays to and looks askance at the youth movement, this would seem to be Frost's comeuppance. But it also reflects a tension inherent in the story's premise. Countercultures cannot lay claim to mainstream institutions because the mainstream is what they are defined against. If they take over the culture, then they cease to be "counter." A counterculture presidency, therefore, is probably a contradiction in terms. "Turning on, tuning in and dropping out" is hopelessly at odds with presiding, which anyway is something only "squares" would want to do. The nation's most powerful political office can borrow only so much from a movement that claims to reject politics and power.

But how much? The inexhaustible Fletcher Knebel took up that question in yet another novel, *Trespass*, his 1969 story of a president facing his greatest crisis just after he's been turned on and tuned in. President Philip Randall, a "sunny, swinging, forty-seven-year-old," had resisted the usual role of "national father." Having launched his administration by growing long sideburns, he now cuts a figure more like "the young swinger next door." An "emotional man" and an amateur in the view of the political old guard, he is planning to shake things up even further, to bring about "a revolution in attitudes that could make America over." It's a hope that comes from his recent introduction to encounter groups. Tutored by a guru psychologist, along with "five young Negroes" and his college-age daughter, Randall had hosted such a group in the White House, exploring his deepest feelings about sex and race and exuberantly discovering that "We are all just human." Now he wants to send "encounter ambassadors" around the country, spreading this good news under the slogan "Know Thy Neighbor." He plans, that is, to use the power of the presidency to spread the counterculture's anti-power gospel.

Alas, just then black militants revolt, seizing the homes of rich white families and taking them hostage. Randall is called upon to respond. Unlike Douglass Dilman, whose fear was that he would never be accepted as "the man," Randall is thrust back into that role whether he wants to be or not. Still, he is a different man than he was, less triggerhappy than his advisors who have not yet had their minds blown. And though he is now "a great, lovin', crazy cat," he also knows when to send in the troops. Modeling an ideal frequently found in fictional presidents, the newly enlightened "Mr. President Phil" succeeds at resolving the crisis with a wise balance of conciliation and force.[56]

While more conventional than Max Frost, a crazy cat like President Phil was still only barely believable even in 1969. And neither of the two characters was a genuine counterculture product. When the real counterculture bothered with anything as square as the presidency, the results were outlandish enough to make *Wild in the Streets* look like *Advise and Consent*. In an act of "guerrilla street theater," for instance, the Youth International Party or "Yippies," a political arm of the counterculture, had staged a mock campaign to nominate a pig for president during protests at the 1968 Democratic National Convention. (Chicago police busted the pig along with its political handlers.) Praise for this gesture, characteristically, ignored its political usefulness to rhapsodize that it was "transcendentally lucid."[57] And after the Yippies' lucid protests had helped elect Richard Nixon, a 1971 cult film called *Tricia's Wedding* burlesqued the event of the title with male "drag queens" in the roles of the Nixon women. Even granting that it came from San Francisco's gay club scene, not Hollywood, the contrast between underground work like this and mainstream political fare would be hard to overstate. Here, just a few years after *Advise and Consent* and *The Best Man*, the scandalous secrets that had dared not speak their name in those straitlaced dramas had become tickets of admission to a White House party, one where the punchbowl was (again) spiked with LSD.

As these examples suggest, the counterculture's concerns were not political in the usual sense of the word. In some ways they were antipolitical. Peopling one's imagined presidency with women or nonwhites is still thinking in the political system's own terms; recasting it with pigs or drag queens is thumbing one's nose at the whole enterprise. Yet those gestures, too, rely on re-envisioning the body. If anything, they put the physical person (or porcine) even more centrally at issue. But their point is that physical criteria are nonsense, as are limits or definitions of any kind. No gender, no type, not even a particular species has any special claim to occupy the circles of power, because "circles of power" should not even exist.

In an odd but logical way, this critique of the mainstream as too fixated with power dovetailed with the period's fixation on presidents' weakness. In both cases, the ultimate if wildly impractical solution was a total rethinking of received images of the body. If the solution to bodily frailty is strength, then the ideal solution is super-strength—and the ideal president would be a *Super President.* That, in fact, was the title of a Saturday morning cartoon series that ran on NBC-TV in 1967 and 1968. The Kennedyesque President James Norcross had the impressive ability to change his own molecular structure, thus becoming whatever substance was needed—steel, granite, even ozone—while battling a range of colorful villains. Such superpower overcame bodily limitations altogether; not only did Super President not have to be human, he did not even have to be animate.[58]

Super President was a children's cartoon, but other superhero presidents were explicitly created to champion the causes of the counterculture and protest movements. Updating an image from a 1943 comic book, the feminist magazine *Ms.* premiered in 1972 with a first-issue cover touting "Wonder Woman for President." And in 1973–74, Wonder Woman's creator DC Comics published *Prez*, "the world's first genuinely political comic book, and a 'right on' one at that."[59] This peculiar nod to the fading counterculture chronicled the exploits of "Prez" Rickard, the turtleneck-wearing "FIRST TEEN PRESIDENT OF THE U.S.A." Partly modeled on Max Frost of *Wild in the Streets,* Prez was more wholesome than Max as well as an action hero. With the help of his sidekick, a Native American FBI director who declared himself "one with nature" and refused to live indoors, he repeatedly found himself forced to put aside normal duties (like meeting with the king of "Fredonia," a nod to the Marx Brothers) to engage in hand-to-hand combat with vampires, right-wing revolutionaries, giant robot chessmen, and other such threats to the Republic.

Superheroism makes a virtue of extreme differences from the bodily norm—and clearly, when the issues before the nation are not crime or civil rights but Giant Vegetable Disintegrators or Space Ghost attacks, the traditional white male molecular structure cannot be expected to meet the need. But the real issues raised by bodily difference were serious and far-reaching. And the different forms those issues (and bodies) took matched the difference between the liberal critique of the prevailing order and the counterculture's more radical critique. Liberalism was a politics of inclusion, an effort to see that blacks, women, and, ultimately, gays advanced to full citizenship—that they were not left out of the "anyone" in the proverbial saying about who could grow up to be president. The liberal goal was to ensure that categories of race, gender, and sexual identity did not become a trap or a rationale for inequality. The counterculture, by contrast, attacked those categories as such. Its attempt to imagine alternatives to established roles was more than just political or sociological; it was *ontological,* part of a still broader questioning of received ideas about reality itself. Are *masculine* and *feminine,* even *white* and *black,* simply facts of nature? Or are they unstable, contingent, and "socially constructed," to use a term just starting its lively career?[60]

We might say that writers and filmmakers of a liberal bent were asking: Why do presidents have to be white and male? In reality, can't anybody be president? To this the counterculture posed two alternative questions. Why does anybody have to be president—can't we do without those structures of hierarchy and power? And, why does anybody have to be white or male? In reality . . . well, *is* there any "reality," apart from the ones we choose to make?

Like counterculture protest, questions of this kind spilled over into the mainstream. It was this period that gave us books and movies recounting both *The Christine Jorgensen Story,* about the first American

sex-change recipient, and John Howard Griffin's experiment in temporarily changing from white to *Black Like Me*. Griffin would also write a
book titled *A Time to Be Human*, and it's interesting that this same phrase
sums up President Phil Randall's encounter-group experience in *Trespass*. The point of the encounter is to make Randall and his fellow great,
lovin', crazy cats newly and more profoundly aware of their bodies, thus
exposing the social roles and identities they came in with as mere dead
weights on true human *being*. The fact that "President of the United
States" is lumped in with the other discarded identities is a bonus, a tribute to the audacity of such a consciousness-raising project.

Moreover, once the weights are removed, the way should be open to
new depths of experience and new heights of perception. Such was the
hope animating the counterculture's search for transcendence, a quest
that involved not just encounter groups and acid trips but performance
art, "freaky" music, vegetarianism, Eastern religion, meditation (including "transcendental"), and experiments in natural, communal, and
"whole earth" styles of living and working. On its face, the counterculture's reliance on devices like these was a thoroughgoing rejection of the
technocratic ethos—the enthrallment with machines and engineering
that was driving everything from nuclear strategy and theories of
"counterinsurgency" to robot Lincolns and the crew-cut men of Mission
Control. What the counterculture countered, after all, was "the Establishment," that alliance of political and cultural authorities that, says
one recent account, had been seduced by an "enthusiasm for the power
of technology to replace politics." By the Kennedy era this enthusiasm
had reached a peak. Encouraged by academic talk of an "end of ideology," it had become "the quasi-official doctrine of the administration."[61]

Against this dream of some final perfection of "systems analysis"
and "the administrative state," the counterculture—"technocracy's children," as they were called at the time—rebelled in the name of the mystical and organic.[62] Promising to reconnect with both earth and cosmos,
the hippies and encounter-groupies and others who sought to "follow
their bliss" were self-consciously the opposite of the squares with slide
rules, the colorless mandarins, and the powers-that-be to whom the
squares lent their expertise. Hence our two contrasting visions of leadership. In the one we have just traced, presidents are imagined for
whom the political is personal—who literally em-*body* the heated political struggles of race, class, gender, and generation. And in the other
they are coolly apolitical specialists, individuals "trained to design and

run our socio-politico-economic systems, as readily as an electronics engineer plus a mathematician can whip up a computer," as one cheerleader for the "managerial revolution" enthused in 1966.[63]

But for all these contrasts, the technocratic impulse was aligned with the countercultural in one crucial respect. It too drew energy from visions of transcendence, from the dream of more fully realizing what the gurus liked to call "human potential." As one manifesto of the time put it, "Science has proven that there's no such thing as 'human nature,'" no fixed limits on what people could be. Existing realities were mere illusions and would soon give way to a "metamorphosis in the nature of life on earth." And this was no idle wish brought on by meditating or dropping acid; art, science, and "metaphysics" all pointed the same way.[64] Counterculturalists mostly hated the hugely expensive space program, yet their goal and NASA's had some things in common: both grew from a restlessness with the familiar constraints of life on Earth, and both sought access to the boundless and unexplored realms beyond.

The difference was that technocracy's machines for achieving transcendence were not Zen mysticism or sex, drugs, and rock 'n' roll. They were actual machines. For the first time in history, it seemed, technological progress was not just helping people do things more easily or powerfully. It was promising improvement into infinity, new powers so vast that to wield them would be to reach some higher plane of existence. As the science-fiction writer Arthur C. Clarke was often quoted saying, a sufficiently advanced technology would be indistinguishable from magic. At its furthest advance, Clarke's fiction suggested, the body would be left behind as human beings evolved first into machines and, finally, into beings of pure, unconstrained cosmic energy—in essence, gods. These were mystical visions of another kind, yet no one would have mistaken Clarke for a hippie.

Clarke was thinking in terms of thousands or millions of years, but other writers believed a transformed human condition was already at hand. As the calendar promised, a new millennium was in the offing; it was the "dawning of the age of Aquarius" (a notion based on an astrological scheme of 2000-year-long eras); a new and final "Consciousness III" was already beginning to appear. Some spoke of an "Apollonian" cultural style giving way to a "Dionysian," naming these two contrasting principles for the ancient gods of rational intellect and rapturous intoxication. Again, though, the contrast was not as absolute as such a schema suggests. Insofar as they both expressed hopes for transcendent change, technocracy and the counterculture were, in 1960s vernacular, "cy-bernetic" and "hallucinogenic" versions of the same great quest.[65] It is not surprising, then, to find works in which the two overlapped—like Clarke's and Stanley Kubrick's *2001: A Space Odyssey*, the blockbuster 1968 epic whose punning lobby cards touted a space voyage as "the ulti-mate trip."

Among other things, *2001* was an attempt to answer the question that Kubrick's *Dr. Strangelove*, his previous film, had raised but left hang-ing: What, if any, hope is there for a race of creatures as twisted as these? Can anything stop them from destroying themselves? National leaders clearly couldn't; in the final crisis, President Muffley and Soviet Premier Kissof were as crippled in their own ways as Dr. Strangelove, and they controlled the greatest powers on earth, if anyone did. So where can we look to find an even greater power? In *2001* the answer lies deep in space and time, in a quest for the godlike presence—visually represented by a large black monolith—that had sparked humankind's struggling primate ancestors with the two intertwined traits that let them survive: intelligence and murderous violence. The irony is that our envoys on that higher quest are themselves listless technocrats, human beings who seem to operate like clockwork (an impression memorably conveyed as one astronaut jogs around his spacecraft in huge circles). The only creature who seems to feel anything is a piece of machinery, the sentient computer HAL. And in acquiring our intelligence, HAL has also taken on our narcissism and morbid anxiety, as he soon demon-strates by trying to kill the spacecraft's whole crew. The commander and the mission survive, but the film seems to say that machines and systems can get us only so far: In the end, someone has to go ahead and spike the punchbowl. The cybernetic quest for transcendence has to give way to hallucinogenics—as it does in *2001*'s wordless, dreamlike final sequence, a visual fable of cosmic rebirth that the counterculture happily em-braced as its own.[66]

Whether or not *2001* was the ultimate trip, it was probably the ulti-mate effort to marry a vision of high technology with mystical rumina-tions and counterculture psychedelia. And as a popular work that bor-rowed freely from experimental filmmaking, it was hailed as a sign that basic human experience was already expanding thanks to at least one class of machines. In countercultural circles there was a new, giddy optimism about the media, a televisual techno-optimism fanned in no small part by the teachings of Marshall McLuhan. McLuhan called the media "extensions of man"; as technologies that act directly on the mind and senses, they were going to free us, McLuhan's acolytes promised, from the "limited range of ordinary consciousness." Amid a breathless rush of scientific-sounding neologisms—"videotronics," "synaesthetics," "technoanarchy," "negentropic," "the noosphere"—the McLuhanite dream of transcendence came to rest on the "intermedia network of cinema and television," which would soon become nothing less than a new nervous system for the planet itself.[67]

Large claims like these smack of the enthusiasms of the time; it is not clear that the medium really *is* the message, as McLuhan so influentially preached.[68] But it no doubt *affects* the message. As was true of radio and stage musicals in the 1930s, certain facts about film and television and how they function do seem implicated in the period's characteristic narrative styles and themes. One such feature is the *You Are There* quality, to borrow the title of a 1950s TV series. Restaging historical events in the style of news reports, *You Are There* had been an early attempt at "docudrama" (a word that apparently originated with television). As photographs that move and talk, film and TV create the illusion of actual presence at times and places that would otherwise be inaccessible: the past, outer space, or, say, the White House and its inner sanctums. Television, moreover, could carry images live, was delivered directly to the viewer's home—no special, "theatrical" occasion was needed to view it—and very soon took on a central role in news and visual reportage. Its generally lower production values could even enhance the "hyperreal" effect, giving the impression of events that could not wait to be artfully staged and that had to be shot on the fly. From the start, critics praised television for giving audiences the feeling that whatever they were seeing was happening in the present, and for "unit[ing] the individual at home with the event afar. The viewer has a chance to be in two places at once. Physically, he may be at his own hearthside but intellectually, and above all, emotionally, he is at the cameraman's side."[69]

Docudramas and "biopics" were not new in the 1960s, of course, and real presidents had been captured on film for decades. But audiences of the television era soon came to expect a position at the cameraman's side. President Eisenhower tried to give them one on October 25, 1954, when he arranged for the first telecast of a cabinet meeting. This event, it seems, had about as much revealing spontaneity as a primitive, stiff, stagey silent film like *President McKinley and Cabinet at Camp Alger, May 28, 1898*. But it did help establish what was possible. If one could stand at the cameraman's side, one could also look over the president's shoulder. An audience could sit with him, as it were, at the desk or conference table and see the problems facing him from his own point of view. Indeed that is almost exactly the perspective we're given in *Seven Days in May,* both book and movie, when we first encounter President Jordan Lyman. In the book we gaze with him out the Oval Office window as he reflects on being "vulnerable and alone." In the movie we are right beside him when he first sits down at his desk. The viewer is positioned like one of his closest aides, as if summoned to counsel and commiserate with him while he is warned of his rising blood pressure and sinking popularity. In both cases, the perspective lends itself to picturing the president as limited and possibly weak. It's a modified first-person viewpoint from which things look as bad to us as they do to him. Not surprisingly, *Seven Days, The Manchurian Candidate,* and *Fail-Safe* were all directed by veterans of *You Are There.*[70]

Film and television have one other such feature worth mentioning: they allow for close-ups. This gives them an unusual vantage on the human body. As Jonathan Swift's Gulliver noticed almost three centuries ago, the body looks very different "through a Magnifying Glass, where we find by Experiment that the smoothest and whitest Skins look rough and coarse, and ill coloured . . . so varified with Spots, Pimples and Freckles, that nothing could appear more nauseous."[71] TV and cinema are modern magnifying glasses, devices through which poor health, fatigue, injury, or old age can expand to fill the whole field of vision. Thus, even without the example of Abraham Zapruder's shocking footage, the televisual media that McLuhan proclaimed "dominant" in "the electronic age" could be seen as creating a particular "media environment," as he put it. It was an environment in which physical defects loomed large—in which viewers were easily reminded that presidents are hostage to the human body and its precarious well-being. As one woebegone fictional president asks himself, "How much might the future depend on the simple fact that an elderly man—himself—had had a long and tiring day?"[72]

From Tragedy to Farce: *Being There* and *First Family*

In the 1960s the image of a president under a doctor's care was iconic, instantly recognizable for its symbolic meaning: that "the patient is the nation," in the words of one such fictional doctor. It was also common enough to undergo a number of different inflections, furnishing material not just for political dramas and thrillers but also for mystery and adventure stories.[73] By 1967 it could even be played for laughs. James Coburn, as *The President's Analyst*, attends a patient/president whose mental state is conveyed through a visual gag: The analyst leaves each of his (White) house calls more and more discombobulated, as if the president's nuttiness were contagious.

Further expansions of the motif produced stories in which fictional presidents fell into the hands of mad scientists—characters who combined some part Faust or Frankenstein with some part Svengali or Rasputin. By succumbing to those with unnatural powers to create or control, these stories suggested, presidents could wind up not just needing treatment but in danger from it.[74] In fact, while the sick president was the paradigm case, one of its analogues was the president as captive.[75] In this variant, the president's imprisonment in human finiteness is visualized by way of some actual prison. Confined to bodies, presidents are vulnerable to having their bodies confined, and that is just what we see happen in a number of works of the 1970s. In *The Kidnapping of the President,* a president (played by Hal Holbrook in the film) spends most of the story shackled inside a booby-trapped armored car.[76] In *Twilight's Last Gleaming,* mentioned earlier, the president is compelled to let extortionists take him hostage inside the missile silo they've hijacked. Like other presidents in nuclear-crisis thrillers, this one finds his options foreclosed by the Cold War system and its mad logic; here, though, his political entrapment is made literal. And in *Escape from New York,* the president in the distant future dystopia of 1997 is held hostage by inmates of a prison colony that was once New York City. Several scenes feature this president tied down or handcuffed, and for a while he is tracked via radio transmissions of his vital signs.[77] As the years went on, captive presidents became even more of a stock image than sick presidents.[78] Constraint, like illness, was an obvious political metaphor; in real life, President Johnson reportedly said that he "was constantly plagued by dreams of being bound to a chair, powerless to release himself."[79]

Still another change rung on the main theme was the *absent* president. What if we had a president adequate to the crisis at hand, but, for some reason, no one knew where he was? That is the premise of *The President's Plane Is Missing,* the 1967 bestseller by Rod Serling's brother Robert. Here the character with the glaring deficiencies is not the president, Jeremy Haines, a brilliant and inspiring figure of "wise, firm kindness," but the vice president, "Kermit," a "hack politician with all the intellectual depth of a shyster used-car salesman." (In the film he is played by Buddy Ebsen, best known at the time as the bumpkinesque patriarch of *The Beverly Hillbillies*). The problem is that Haines disappears en route to a stress-relieving holiday, an attempt undertaken on doctor's orders to combat the "reduced life expectancy" of presidents. This leaves Kermit to manage world affairs just as they seem to be spiraling toward disaster.[80]

Though published the same year, *The President's Plane Is Missing* is not to be confused with *The President Is Missing*, the lesser-known tale of a president who mysteriously disappears from a Camp David–like retreat. The president's frantic aides worry that he may have cracked under his job's pressures; perhaps he has run off to see a mistress ("THE PRESIDENT WAS HUMAN," says the book's back cover), or perhaps he has even lost his mind ("THE PRESIDENT WAS . . . INSANE?"). When he's eventually found, he's in the clutches of kidnappers.[81] Thus the story turns on several variants of the weakened-president theme. Indeed, years later these durable motifs—bodily frailty, absence, insanity, and loss of control—would come together at least once in a single work. *By Dawn's Early Light*, a made-for-cable nuclear-crisis thriller based on William Prochnau's novel *Trinity's Child*, has a lost and badly injured president struggling after a nuclear attack to seize back power from the secretary of the interior—his highest-ranking survivor and another dangerously poor, possibly mad substitute.[82]

We see, in short, various kinds or manifestations of weakness, as well as various levels of threat: to the president's own person, to the political system, to the nation or even the world. On this point, as we have noted, storytellers shared an interest with the era's political scientists. At a time when technology was (literally) promising the moon, it was not unusual to see political analysis cast in terms of engineering. Presidents were "made" things, as Theodore H. White's bestselling series of *Making of the President* campaign chronicles pointed out.[83] Perhaps, then, they could be made better, some analysts proposed. Perhaps the presidency itself could be retooled or a new kind of president created: the president as technocratic expert, managing the government like a problem-solving machine. But not everyone who saluted such goals in principle believed they would likely be reached. And there were those who just rejected the premise. "Somehow," George Reedy said, bluntly, "this thing must be made human again."[84]

Perhaps because storytelling is humanistic, not scientific, most fiction writers and filmmakers seemed inclined to side with Reedy. More often than not their work implied that machines are not to be trusted, that engineering is more problem than solution. It overlooks the human element. In *The President's Plane Is Missing,* the pilot of Air Force One reflects on his "vague uneasiness" with the aircraft's state-of-the-art perfection. It may have been well designed, but still "he inherently mistrusted the plane. It handled almost too easily . . . like power steering on a heavy automobile. Power steering, [he] worried, that seemed to lack the feel of the road."[85] Sure enough, the plane crashes just as World War III is about to erupt. And while the day is eventually saved (the president was somewhere else, on a secret mission to salvage the peace), it might not always be. The greater the machine's size and sophistication, the greater the danger to those who do trust it. Like the homicidal computer HAL in *2001,* machines can turn out to be Frankenstein's monsters: human creations that rage uncontrolled, threatening to destroy their creators.

By the 1960s there was already a long line of such monsters in fiction. The new additions were stories that took this theme "global," locating versions of it in the lofty realm of politics and presidents. *Fail-Safe* and *Dr. Strangelove* were two of these. Both posit that the ultimate Frankenstein's monster is the system itself, the grand convergence of automation with technocratic management. The presidents in such stories learn too late that the system and its machines are actually managing *them.* In the most extreme case, that could even be the intent. The title character of *Colossus: The Forbin Project* (1970) is a supercomputer designed specifically to take nuclear decisions out of the president's hands. The story's main character, Dr. Charles Forbin, is also its latter-day Frankenstein, the brilliant inventor who failed to foresee the death struggle he would wind up in with his misbegotten brainchild.[86] Or, perhaps, Forbin and his technoscience are the modern Oracle at Delphi, the font of Apollonian wisdom—and the luckless president who approves the project, unwittingly sacrificing the nation to it, is the nuclear era's King Oedipus: the ruler who discovers that his faith in the oracle has put his people under a curse. Technocratic faith may be a meager substitute for the classic tragic flaw of *hubris,* since by ceding human agency to machines it denies its victims even the personal greatness of tragic heroes. Yet they find themselves no less stupefied by fate and mischance. In *By Dawn's Early*

Light, the president who is desperately trying to "turn it off" (as if the whole crisis were one big, malfunctioning machine) even suffers in the same way as Oedipus. He is driven out of the city and blinded, albeit in the flash of a nuclear explosion—a different kind of self-inflicted wound.

Late entries like *Trinity's Child, By Dawn's Early Light,* and *World War III*—a novel and TV miniseries in which the overwhelmed president was played by Rock Hudson—suggest that the power of images like these lasted at least until the end of the Cold War. But at the same time, they gradually gave rise to exaggerations, parodies, and comic inversions. The title character in *The President's Analyst,* for instance, winds up discovering that his First Patient's illness merely reflects the broader lunacy to be found in high-level global intrigue. In 1971, Philip Roth's comic novella *Our Gang* spun a (pre-Watergate) send-up of the Nixon administration around a medical crisis: While President "Trick E. Dixon" is undergoing secret surgery to have the troublesome sweat glands removed from his upper lip, he is assassinated by anti-abortion activists. To make their point, the assassins leave him stuffed like a fetus inside a giant Baggie.[87] In 1975–76, Chevy Chase of NBC's *Saturday Night Live* famously played a stumblebum President Gerald Ford for slapstick, making a "standing" joke of his falling down. Presidents have been criticized and lampooned for any number of failings over the years, but Ford—ironically, a onetime athlete—was possibly the first to be arraigned for sheer physical clumsiness.[88] And a few years after that, the very low-budget *Blood Suckers from Outer Space* cast as president another comic, Pat Paulsen, known to TV viewers for his joke presidential campaign of the late 1960s. Heralding his first appearance with a patriotic anthem played on kazoos, this horror-film spoof has the president too busy canoodling with a comely assistant to bother saving the nation from rampaging zombies.[89]

At some point, then, ineffectual presidents came to be figures of fun rather than fright, and the strength/weakness issue migrated from tragedy to farce. So it usually goes; any cycle of thematically similar stories is prone to what some critics call "exhaustion of the genre," and any scary or solemn subject eventually begs to be satirized. But the end of one cycle is often the beginning of another. As tales of presidential weakness reached their *reductio ad absurdum,* they also hinted at what would come next. Two movies at the close of the 1970s charted the alternative paths ahead. One was *Being There,* adapted by Jerzy Kosinski from his own novel and starring Peter Sellers in his final role. The other was *First Family*, written, directed by, and featuring several *Saturday Night Live* regulars, and starring comedian Bob Newhart as the president.

In *Being There* Sellers plays Chance, an illiterate gardener and a childlike man who talks "gobbledygook" and whose mental abilities amount to having been "stuffed with rice puddin between the ears," as his childhood nurse puts it. Addicted to television, he incarnates the passivity and vacancy often charged to TV-age culture in general. The names are obvious clues. Chance neither acts nor chooses his own course but blithely submits to whatever fortune may bring. He contents himself with just being there, if it can even be said that he really is "all there." One day, literally by accident (he is knocked down by a limousine), Chance is taken in by the Washington elite, a circle of powerbrokers who greet his banalities about gardening as the oracles of a political sage. Soon he has become a celebrity and trusted advisor to the president and his cronies, a group plainly modeled on the age-old cabal.[90] By the end, this crew is scheming to put Chance himself in the White House. The point, presumably, is that presidents don't need to be competent, not even in the minimal legal sense of the term.

In addition to Chance, *Being There* gives us a number of weak, absent, or inadequate men: his lifelong guardian, who has recently died; his new patron, who is terminally ill and needs constant medical help; and the current president, who is virtually an employee of that same powerful patron and who, in office, has become both politically and literally impotent. *First Family* goes a step further by rolling all these weaknesses into a single figure. President Manfred Link is a classic buffoon, a ludicrous excuse for a leader who squeaked into office only because his opponent died on election eve. Bob Newhart's portrayal recalls the balding, buffaloed President Muffley that Peter Sellers played in *Dr. Strangelove*. But where Muffley spluttered, Link's characteristic reaction to the zaniness around him is a slow, puzzled blankness more reminiscent of Chance. Newhart had long since made quiet befuddlement his comic trademark, and his characters also resemble Chance in their mystifying banality: even Link's recurring nightmare is bafflingly dull.

From start to finish, *First Family* looks for humor in once-fearsome threats—insanity, injury, disability, and death. "Of *course* he's having a nervous breakdown," says an aide. "All presidents have nervous breakdowns. That's why they all look like that." And if he does not break down he might just break, period. A decoy mannequin that substitutes for Link in motorcades has its head knocked off, and in one slapstick segment a badly injured First Family hobbles around in bandages and casts. After an exchange of state visits with the tribal African nation of "Upper Gorm," Link signs a secret agreement to import Gormian manure into the United States. Taking this as proof that he's lost his mind, the Supreme Court decides that the best thing for the country is to keep Link and his family in hiding and declare them legally dead.

In the end, though, Link returns in triumph. His successor dies of a heart attack "brought on by the burdens of his high office" even before he has finished taking the oath, and Link's imported manure turns out to be a miraculous fertilizer—a source of "giant purple figs like domes of Muslim temples, and potatoes as large as Volkswagens." With this wacky achievement Link fulfills his pledge: to "give [America] back our 'bigness.'"

As all this suggests, *First Family*'s satire is as lowbrow as *Being There*'s is high. Most of its jokes about race, death, bodily functions, and gender bending are none too funny, and its commercial failure was no doubt deserved.[91] But the point is that it tried to make such jokes at all. Issues that previously gave rise to suspense and foreboding were now available for clowning around. And in one crucial respect, *First Family*'s toilet humor converged with the high-toned irony of *Being There*. Not only did both films spotlight idiocy at the top; they both went on to suggest that it might be a positive virtue. The inane, insane, or simply pathetic might be just what America needs.

That was the message that emerged as the narrative cycle made its final turn. For those who had worried about inadequate presidents, and whose worries had generated some twenty years' worth of both fiction and political analysis, it was not a message of comfort. And as noted, it did not rule out additional "straight" treatments of the theme. Any number of thrillers and spy stories continued to appear in which the nation or world faced imminent disaster that the president seemed helpless to stop. Alarming weakness in the White House became a standard device, familiar to the point of cliché.

But it was the silly, not the serious, that previewed what would come next. Or rather it was the collision of the two. In *First Family*'s best scene, President Link is forced to convene his National Security Council in the middle of a state dinner whose guests are costumed in honor of American holidays. The officials involved don't have time to change, so they report to the Oval Office in various ridiculous getups: a giant pumpkin, a turkey, the Easter Bunny, a leprechaun, a Cupid in a pink leotard. Link himself presides in a George Washington outfit, complete with knee breeches and powdered wig. The costume is a sight gag that extends the satire from presidents to patriotic symbolism in general, yet it also gives Link an odd, cartoonish dignity, a kind of goofball gravitas. This tension—between dignity and disgrace, between the noble and the nonsensical—would soon become a major source of storytelling possibilities. As the frailties of presidents had been the leading theme of one era, their foibles would be the theme of the next.

6

Who Am I?

Presidents and Their "Issues" in Fictions of the 1990s

❖

Jack was holding a copy of his first speech. It was past time for
him to close his eyes and wish everything away. Now he felt like
a boxer, overmatched by his opponent but unable to take a dive,
taking every punch as best he could and trying not to disgrace
himself. . . .

"Jack, get used to it, okay? You're not allowed to be 'just a
person' anymore. Okay, you've had a few days to get used to the
idea. When you walk downstairs, you are the United States of
America, *not* just a person."

Tom Clancy, *Executive Orders*, 1996

❖

Societies are often said to need their myths and illusions. But an illusion requires energy to sustain, and anything that requires energy
is eventually exhausted. In reality, of course, presidents are human beings, so the authority they carry has to be constructed and made to ad-
here to them. Even as this is done, even as they become projections of
the United States and bearers of the "dignities of office," they remain
people. The changes we have been tracing in narrative themes and

conventions—changes that brought the personhood of presidents, and then their sheer physicality, to the fore—have resulted in part from political changes, and in part from the advent of new storytelling media and the rise and fall of particular concerns in the broader culture. But there has also been another factor at work: loss of that sustaining energy, exhaustion of the old myths, the gradual exposure of the hidden workings on which authority depends. Over time, as more citizens become aware of those mechanisms, as they come to recognize that political power is not "just there," God-given, inherent in nature or set for all time, the constructions through which power operates begin to be deconstructed. Authority is "demystified," and the old fictions lose their power to persuade. At some point, no matter which symbols and rituals are deployed, no matter how well the story is told, it just becomes impossible to convince most people that the king is God's anointed and that he is entitled to rule because he's the son of the previous king. Where kings are concerned, people long ago became, literally, *disillusioned*. New constructions, like constitutions and presidents, were then called for; the resources of fiction were put to use to create new myths and illusions—which then began to decay in their turn.

At each step in this long process, new stories are generated, and by surveying some of these we have been able to track it through several phases. One thing that such a survey makes clear is that even though it may be inevitable, the process of disillusionment and deconstruction is not linear. It would more accurately be described as dialectical, or—in plainer terms—as happening in fits and starts. Counter-myth paradoxically reinforces myth, as we saw in the case of Lincoln. Evolving visions of the presidency give rise to their own opposites: the hope for a president invested in citizens' personal lives and loves (and vice-versa) raises fears of totalitarian regimentation; awareness of presidents' immense global power provokes the anxiety that they might be too weak.

By the 1990s the further consequences of these developments were becoming clear. One was the fact that if presidents are just people, then they can be presented on the same terms as any other characters in a story. This expanded the range of possible roles they could play, of possible character types to which they could be assigned. Second, reducing presidents to mere human scale (or lower) raised questions about how such ordinary mortals could maintain the dignities of office, and what would happen when they couldn't. These questions would provide material for new rounds of stories. And third, exposing the mechanisms of authority also meant exposing the operations of storytelling. Fictional genres, like other art forms, eventually reach a point where the search for new subject matter turns attention to the form itself. Like a painting of a painting, stories begin to present reality as itself containing stories; the making of narratives comes to be narrated. At the two-hundredth anniversary of the creation of the presidency, this was the point that the trajectory of fictional presidencies had reached.

Maguffins and Others: The Many Uses of 1990s Presidents

The association—or collision—of reality with storytelling is the running joke of *Tanner '88,* the twelve-episode 1988 miniseries directed for HBO cable television by Robert Altman and co-scripted by *Doonesbury* cartoonist Garry Trudeau. Jack Tanner is a fictional ex-congressman and candidate for the Democratic presidential nomination. He is played by Michael Murphy, one of those supporting actors whom audiences often feel they recognize from previous TV and movies but cannot quite name or place. That is, Murphy occupies roughly the same niche among actors that a real-life Tanner would occupy among politicians. The series was shot in "video vérité" and partly improvised, with Murphy/ Tanner and his entourage moving among, and interacting with, real political candidates, journalists, and other well-known figures, including the Democrats actually running for president in the 1988 primaries. Much later, in 2004, a four-episode sequel called *Tanner on Tanner* purported to chronicle the making of a retrospective documentary about Tanner's 1988 campaign, with the same characters—and, again, real political celebrities—reflecting on the "events" of sixteen years earlier.

Tanner: A Political Fable, as the series was originally called, was one of several satirical replies to the rightist politics (and cultural politics) of the 1980s.[1] To satirists who had grown up or made their mark in the 1960s–'70s protest culture, the Reagan administration in particular was a bizarrely comic mix of illusion and dangerous reality, headed as it was by an aging movie and TV actor who, for all his tough talk and hard-edged ideology, seemed strangely passive and even befuddled at the goings-on in his own administration. In a further variant of that very old motif, the political cabal, Reagan was seen as a kind of reverse Wizard of Oz: his role was to project harmless geniality while the truly frightening operations of power went on behind the curtain. Politics, it was widely if somewhat glibly asserted, had become indistinguishable from showmanship. With Reagan installed as their figurehead, the masters of illusion had moved in and taken it over.[2]

Tanner '88 crossed the blurred line between politics and acting from the other side. If actors could become politicians, real politicians could likewise be cast as actors in a quasi-fictional comedy. The result was a kind of alternate history, a parallel universe featuring well-known people and events but inflecting them in some way—in this case, by shoehorning another candidate into the actual Democratic race. Alternate history is a genre that would become increasingly familiar in the 1990s and thereafter.[3] So would a number of the themes essayed in *Tanner*: family issues, love affairs, scandals, indignity, and the crucial role played by presidential staffers, aides, and campaign "operatives." Indeed one prominent theme would be the humbling dependence of political leaders on those around them. In that respect, Jack Tanner's closest forerunner was Jim Hacker, the hapless government minister played by Paul Eddington on the 1980s British sitcoms *Yes, Minister* and *Yes, Prime Minister*. Well-meaning but dimwitted, Hacker was the pawn of the slick and conniving Sir Humphrey Appleby (Nigel Hawthorne), the civil servant whose brilliantly drawn character became a part of British political folklore. Sir Humphrey's machinations usually worked to stymie whatever Hacker was trying to do, but eventually they also got Hacker promoted to prime minister and Sir Humphrey to chief of the civil service—the position from which he proceeded to do most of the real decision-making for the British government.

That was the recurring joke: the nation's nominal leaders served, in effect, at the pleasure of a permanent class of shadowy power brokers. Every episode of *Yes, Minister* and *Yes, Prime Minister* ended with someone speaking the title phrase—but this and other elaborate shows of deference from the civil "servants" did little to mask their true loyalties, which lay with their own privilege and a more or less dismal status quo. If American political fiction has not produced a Sir Humphrey, that's because American power brokers are usually imagined not as oily civil servants or smooth-talking mandarins but as fat cats and party bosses. But the cruder kinds of power such oligarchs wield is often that much greater than Sir Humphrey's, and the presidents and candidates who do their bidding are, if anything, even more at their mercy.

The treatment of political leaders as pawns or punching bags—hapless, pratfall-prone figures of fun—may be an inevitable step in their demystification, and at any rate follows the path we have traced through earlier periods. Roughly speaking, the theme we saw recur in presidential fictions of the 1930s was the intersection (or clash) of public and private: what it might mean that the president is an ordinary person. The parallel issue in the 1960s was weakness and strength: what it might mean that the president is a physical being with all the frailties of flesh and blood.[4] Jack Tanner appears at the point where those issues converge. A divorcee, he is led into misadventure both by problems in his private life, like difficulties with his ex-wife and teenage daughter, and by the temptations of the body, which land him in a secret love affair with a top aide to his leading opponent. Tanner is not completely ineffectual and passive, but his tendencies that way are an important source of the humor in *Tanner '88*. In the 1960s, as we saw, presidents were often depicted as medical patients; in the 1990s they would frequently be seen as "patients" in the broader sense—characters to whom things happened or were done, as opposed to "agents" capable of making things happen.

In fact, in much of the mass-market or genre fiction and film of recent decades, the president is reduced to a stock (or even stick) figure while the real hero is, literally, an agent—a spy, a military or political operative, a member of the FBI or Secret Service. The president in many such stories hardly acts at all but is simply a *maguffin*, an object or device that exists mainly to motivate the actions of others. He, or more rarely she, is just *Hostage One* or the *First Target*, to name two vividly titled examples. To the extent that there is character development in stories like these, it's someone else's.[5] In Barry Levinson's and David Mamet's 1997 *Wag the Dog*, a satire on the cynicism of political image-making, the president not only scarcely appears but is incidental even to the movie-within-the-movie, the faked war concocted to distract the public from his misdeeds. The whole point of that movie-war is to overshadow the president—to make the tail/tale wag the dog—and it's the tale's makers, the masters of illusion, who are the real political actors and, therefore, the story's main characters.[6]

If the president is not simply a maguffin, an object of others' activity, he or she may still be little more than a traffic cop—the authority who sends the agents off in this direction or that. This often produces characterizations in which presidents are just flat projections of their official duties. Such presidents are common in "airport paperbacks," the mass-market suspense thrillers and other novels that people buy at airports to while away time on long flights. To take one typical example,

Joe Weber's 1989 *Defcon One* features a president confronting the Soviet premier on the brink of World War III (a brink piled high with genre novels of this kind). In this "technothriller," so-called because it combines a politically themed suspense plot with a focus on military hardware, the president registers emotions perfectly synchronized with the public demands of his office. As global tensions escalate we see "his neck becoming rigid"; when the military situation sours, his eyelids sag or "the color drain[s] from his face"; when he resolves to be firm, he clenches his fist. With the president's role in the story and his political role as national leader perfectly superimposed, all character depth collapses. And with a little further thinning the president may disappear altogether: as agency shifts to literal agents, traffic-cop presidents follow maguffins into narrative irrelevance.[7]

In reality, of course, presidents do mostly give orders and act through others. But while relying on that fact may be accurate, it tends to make a story less rather than more realistic in literary terms.[8] Like maguffins, traffic-cop presidents and their inner lives—if any—are usually mere instruments of the story's schematics. This functional similarity is nicely illustrated in *Escape from New York* (1981) and its sequel, *Escape from L.A.* (1996). Both these movies, directed by John Carpenter, envision a broken-down, noirish near future of a kind familiar from many contemporary American thrillers. The main character in both is also a familiar type, the cynical, lone-wolf action hero (Kurt Russell, in this case) who quips, complains, and wisecracks his way through any number of explosions and shootouts en route to "just getting the job done." And in both films that job involves a president. The difference is that in *Escape from New York* the president is a maguffin—a gang leader's hostage—and in *Escape from L.A.* he's the traffic cop who cynically orders the hero around. But in each case the president himself is contemptible, someone the hero serves only because he is forced to. Though the president's purposes are the fixed point around which the action circles, they are not the same as either the hero's or the storyteller's.

One could argue that reducing presidents to mere narrative devices scarcely counts as "imagining" them at all. But in addition to the sheer number of works in which such devices appear, what makes the phenomenon worth studying is the fact that those devices are also gears in a larger mechanism. As they are shifted this way or that they drive the bigger machines—the "story cycles" or subgenres in which presidents figure more prominently and are more fully developed as characters.

A relatively few such cycles account for most of the fictional presidencies of recent years, including nearly all the best known.[9] One of these subgenres involves presidents caught somehow in criminal conspiracies. Movies like *Clear and Present Danger* (1994), *Shadow Conspiracy, Murder at 1600,* and *Absolute Power* (all 1997), and the Fox TV network's suspense-thriller series *24* (2001–) all had presidents embroiled in conspiratorial "plots" in both senses of the term. The hero of such a story is a truth-seeker of some kind, a detective, reporter, agent, aide, or innocent bystander who desperately needs to figure out what's really going on. In a variant of the old "cabal" motif, the presidents in *Shadow Conspiracy* and *Murder at 1600* turn out to be dupes or victims of conspirators operating inside the White House. And where the presidents are themselves conspirators, they're basically traffic cops gone bad, their power to direct and legitimate others' actions having been corrupted by cynical politics (in *Clear and Present Danger* the "war on drugs," in *24* the geopolitical struggle for oil) or by criminality pure and simple (in *Absolute Power,* misogynistic violence).

Obviously this theme bears the imprint of real-life scandals like Watergate and the Iran-Contra affair. But more importantly, it extends and modifies themes we saw foregrounded in earlier eras. The question of presidents' personal character was prominent in fiction of the 1930s, and the shadow world of conspiracy and intrigue was the setting for several important works of the 1960s.[10] What was noteworthy in the 1990s was the way these issues became detached from politics and policy. Where the works of earlier periods tended to highlight threats to the nation, the more recent conspiracies have had a tawdrier quality: Some involve nonpolitical secrets and crimes, or if politically motivated they may be simply palace coups, takeover plots by a scheming vice president or chief of staff. Or they have degenerated into simple cover-ups best dealt with by professionals, characters who are all the more effective for not having any political motives themselves. By contrast with their predecessors, recent presidential fictions have tended to focus on "private" evil and to treat it as an issue in its own right, an occasion to be not so much scared as merely scandalized. *Absolute Power*'s President Allen Richmond is a danger to his mistresses, certainly—the story begins when he attacks one and gets her killed—but as far as we know he is a capable and maybe even superior chief executive. (In the movie he's played by Gene Hackman, an actor who more often plays reassuring good guys than villains.)

Even where crime is not involved, scandalous and career-threatening personal secrets also loom large in many other recent novels, films, and TV movies.[11] Like 1930s fictions that tied the fate of the nation to the president's personal character, these stories, too, work at the intersection of private and public lives, although to narrower effect. In the more recent works the personal secret tends to be a maguffin, a convenient device for raising other issues: the limits of loyalty, the tension between love and politics, the vagaries and idiocies of public opinion. And where the private demons are more central to the story, they often belong not to the president but to someone he or she relies on—for instance, Secret Service agents whose ability to protect some President Maguffin or other is tied up with proving themselves, redeeming past failures, or mending rifts in their own families. "The crisis is global," said the advertising "tag line" for one made-for-cable movie, "but their battle . . . is personal!" By the 1990s, highlighting personal drama had become almost a storytelling reflex. One of the last "accidental nuclear war" thrillers of the Cold War, HBO's 1990 *By Dawn's Early Light*, combined a number of memorable 1960s motifs—including both an absent and injured president and his frighteningly inadequate stand-in—with a 1990s-style romantic subplot: the pilots of the runaway bomber are a male-female couple whose decision for or against war depends on how they settle their relationship issues.[12]

In the better-known political drawing-room dramas of the past, like Henry Adams's *Democracy* or the plays and films *First Lady* and *State of the Union*, the parlor intrigues revolved around public questions like who would hold office. Similarly, in 1960s dramas like *Advise and Consent* and *The Best Man*, the important thing about the scandalous private secrets was the way they motivated political events. Whatever went on upstairs or in the back room, its effects would ultimately be realized on the floor of the Senate or a national party convention. In cases where the private affair became all-important, the result was a farce like *Of Thee I Sing*. Even in *State of the Union*, which—in Frank Capra's film version—highlighted the personal relationship by, in effect, casting a real couple (Tracy and Hepburn) in the leading roles, it's the health of both the smaller *and* the larger "union" that is in question.[13]

In recent fictions the emphasis has shifted. Politics, if not unaffected by private doings, is more often treated as just another set of external pressures on presidents' and candidates' private and, especially, family lives. Frequently we are given no hint at all of the president's public actions or views. These indeed may simply be something to escape, particularly for a *First Daughter*. In two different movies of that title, a 1999 TV thriller (to which *First Target* was a sequel) and a 2004 theatrical film, the fact that dad is president is at best a nuisance, at worst a source of suffocating control. Like the *senex* character in ancient comedy, he is the patriarch who stands in the way of happiness for a vibrant young woman—one whose vibrancy is established, in the second *First Daughter*, precisely by her resistance to public life and its spiritless routines. The same is true in *Chasing Liberty* (also 2004), whose title is a pun: "Liberty" is the first daughter's Secret Service code name, and the plot involves the president's agents chasing her after she eludes them to "chase liberty" herself. (That title, though, was a later choice, replacing the working title: *First Daughter*.)[14]

That a president would ordinarily be a family man or woman—a father, mother, wife, husband, ex-husband, boyfriend, etc.—obviously follows from the recognition that he or she is an ordinary person. But while presidents' family relationships appeared here and there in the fictions of earlier eras, by the 1990s they had ceased to be the exception and had seemingly become the rule. Families came to be depicted as sites of both virtue and danger, the one source of pressure on presidents that cannot be negotiated or politically finessed. Like private secrets, they often appeared as an overlay on other plots. The scoundrel president in *Absolute Power* is done in by old-fashioned family vengeance; his power, finally, is not so absolute that it can stop his murdered mistress's father from killing him.[15] The presidents in *24*, both the virtuous David Palmer and his conspiratorial successor, Charles Logan, have to pause from fending off (or plotting with) terrorists in order to deal with troublesome wives, ex-wives, or girlfriends. Even Richard Nixon, one of the least personable presidents, was situated in Oliver Stone's 1995 *Nixon* in relationship to a long-suffering wife and a mother and brother seen in childhood flashbacks. We might say that in recent years the vector of storytelling has reversed direction. Where the fictions of the 1930s had asked how a president's actions might affect citizens and *their* families, the question now was more likely to be how family relationships affected the president.[16]

And since family situations can also be comic, one obvious further step was to recast the presidency as a TV "sitcom." At various times this has been done by wrapping reimagined real presidents in sitcom formulas, or by grafting the presidency onto the story of a standard sitcom family—putting *The Brady Bunch in the White House,* in the title of one such effort.[17] The old notion that it was women who took care of family matters presumably explains why, in the earliest such comedies, it was mom rather than dad whose job just happened to be running the U.S. government. In any case, the presidency has not yet proven comic enough, as situations go, to sustain a TV sitcom series of any length. Among theatrical films with sitcom-like premises, *My Fellow Americans* (1996) and *Welcome to Mooseport* (2004) both looked for laughs in a slightly different situation, that of ex-presidents reduced in their retirement back to normal human scale. *My Fellow Americans* paired Jack Lemmon and James Garner in a tale that mixed the situation comedy of Neil Simon's Broadway hit *The Odd Couple* with elements of the "road" and "buddy picture." Two cantankerous former presidents of opposing parties are forced to flee from hit men working for their corrupt successor. As they cross the country in each other's unwelcome company, the comic misadventures begin.[18] In *Mooseport* Gene Hackman plays a smug ex-president whose divorce has exiled him to his vacation cottage in small-town Maine. Not long after moving in, he finds himself running in an unexpectedly contentious race for village mayor against a popular local—played by Ray Romano, a comedian best known to audiences as a TV sitcom dad.

In reconnecting with ordinary citizens, the former presidents in these movies rediscover their own ordinariness. President Cole in *Mooseport* learns what kinds of issues really matter in people's everyday lives, and the political differences between Presidents Kramer and Douglas in *My Fellow Americans* re-emerge on the road as bickering and personal dislike—which, in a familiar formula, eventually give way to grudging affection. National politics either fades to irrelevance (the bad-guy incumbent's secret in *My Fellow Americans* is apolitical, garden-variety graft) or is reduced to the comically literal: in an obvious borrowing from the famous role that Lemmon once played in *The Odd Couple,* his character in *My Fellow Americans* is fussy and penny-pinching, traits that made him a budget-cutting Republican while in office.[19]

In movies, the most fully developed character study of a president as family man was Rob Reiner's 1995 *The American President.* Scripted by Aaron Sorkin a few years before he created NBC-TV's *The West Wing,* this film starred Michael Douglas as President Andrew Shepard, a widower and single dad whose presidency is upended when he begins dating a feisty environmental activist and lobbyist, Sydney Ellen Wade

(Annette Bening). As would also be true of *The West Wing*, *The American President* treated politics and policymaking more seriously than did most of the period's well-known fictions. When he first meets Wade, Shepard is working Congress in hopes of passing a crime bill modeled on the real one that President Bill Clinton promoted early in his administration. (Reiner is a friend of Clinton's, and the filmmakers spent time at the White House observing how things there were done.) Vote-trading soon puts that bill in conflict with the environmental measures for which Wade has been lobbying, and when Shepard chooses his crime bill over the environment he puts the couple's relationship at risk. Also threatening that relationship is the criticism it generates from Shepard's political opponents; the same headstrong qualities that make Wade attractive and suitable for Shepard also make her a political target. How Shepard responds to all this, how much he is willing to risk for love, does therefore have implications for the nation as a whole.

But ultimately this movie, too, slights the political to foreground the personal. In one scene, Shepard has to cut short a date with Wade to meet with his generals about a cruise missile strike against Iraq. The point of the scene is not America's foreign or military posture, it's the special difficulties a president has in pursuing romance. Viewers of *The American President* are not expected to care much about this or that policy or pending bill—legislation is this story's maguffin—and in the end it's not clear how much even Shepard really cares about them. Instead, in a denouement that plainly owes something to the closing recognition scene and speech in *State of the Union*, he decides that the real question is not the government's obligations but his own. What is really at stake is his own character: He has allowed political calculation to interfere with his real feelings, which are not just pro–Sydney Wade but pro-environment. But love has now recalled him to the true liberal faith, and he vows to carry his political gospel throughout the land in the most personal way possible—door-to-door, if need be.[20]

"Ich Bin ein Asskicker": Indignity and Action Heroics

For a head of state shielded from the little challenges of day-to-day life, the problems posed by romance are mildly comic. Andrew Shepard learns, for instance, that it's difficult for presidents personally to do something as simple as call a florist and order flowers. (He finally gives up and picks his own from the White House Rose Garden.) A number of Shepard's colleagues among 1990s movie presidents face problems that are a bit more exotic. President Thomas J. Whitmore (Bill Pullman) in the 1996 *Independence Day* has to contend with the destruction of Earth's cities by enormous alien spacecraft, and President James Marshall (Harrison Ford) in the 1997 *Air Force One* is up against terrorists who have hijacked him along with the title plane. As it happens, both presidents are former combat pilots and therefore just the right men for the moment. Marshall outwits the terrorists and eventually defeats them in hand-to-hand struggle, and Whitmore personally leads the ragtag squadron of fighter jets that finds the aliens' Achilles heel and ends the threat from outer space. (In a parody sketch on NBC's *Saturday Night Live* later that year, hapless Republican nominee Bob Dole, already trailing badly in the polls, has a nightmare in which his debate opponent isn't Bill Clinton but President Whitmore, who calmly recounts first-term achievements that include personally saving the Earth.)[21]

As we've seen, action-hero presidents of the 1960s and 1970s counterpointed that era's worries about presidents being vulnerable and weak.[22] In the 1980s the Reagan administration got a superhero makeover that we will consider below. But these were all cartoons and comic books. The more recent, live-action presidential heroics seem to have sprung from a different set of concerns. They were, first, one answer to a problem that storytellers were bound to run into with presidents: their frustrating immobility and dependence on others. Presidents can make all kinds of things happen, especially in their traffic cop roles. But how interesting is it to watch a traffic cop—or, in this case, a guy who is forever stuck in meetings and offices and has to bark his orders into a phone? Action heroics allow presidents to reclaim agency from their agents; at moments of ultimate peril, they get to step in and duke it out with the bad guys themselves.

And while such stories might seem a long way from romantic comedy or sentimental family drama, it is no coincidence that the action hero presidents of the 1990s also tended to be family men. Even while organizing *Independence Day*'s planet-wide counterattack, President Whitmore has to watch out for his young daughter and deal with the death of his wife—a sequence whose sentimentality rivals the death scenes in Victorian novels. President Marshall, likewise, has to worry not just that the terrorist hijackers of *Air Force One* will succeed at destabilizing the former Soviet Union; even more urgently he, too, must protect his wife and young daughter, who happen to be along on the flight. With the Secret Service having been infiltrated, Marshall must become his own Secret

Short on pilots, President Thomas J. Whitmore (Bill Pullman) personally leads a fighter squadron in an *Independence Day* counterattack against invading space aliens.

President James Marshall (Harrison Ford) finds himself in hand-to-hand combat with the terrorist mastermind who hijacked him and his family aboard *Air Force One*.

Service for their protection as well as his own.[23] If anything, action hero presidents are the *ultimate* family men, reacting to dangers that threaten kin and country alike. Politics in such stories is either ignored or reduced to the hand-to-hand struggle from which it primordially arose; policy positions and goals give way to a tribalistic reflex to protect and avenge one's own.[24] In one striking case, this deeply visceral reflex was presented as the solution to a mystery. A 1995 sequel to *Prez,* the 1970s comic book series, introduced an element of family drama, revealing that the teenage, turtlenecked, counterculture action hero "Prez" Rickard had a son he never knew. Now a teenager himself, P.J. ("Prez Junior") wants to learn what became of his father, who mysteriously disappeared after retiring from office. What his quest uncovers is the fact that Prez, a devotee of Native American rites, had eventually died of grief arising from his mystical bond with America. Attuned to the nation as if to his own flesh and blood, Prez had thrived while defending it from physical threats but could not survive its spiritual decline.[25]

Family issues and action heroics are easily linked because they are both formulas for suppressing politics—two different but related consequences of keeping stories focused on the president's person. In the 1990s it often seemed that creators of political fiction were doing their best to steer clear of anything truly political. But something else was at work too, another theme that linked these and other clusters of stories in a still deeper way. Again and again, the problem facing fictional presidents in the 1990s was *indignity* of one kind or another. Much like strength and weakness in the 1960s, dignity and indignity were overarching issues, the two ends of an armature that drove a number of story cycles at once.

Needless to say, indignity has been a comic motif since time out of mind. But the presidency in particular lends itself to indignity precisely because it is, itself, a "dignity" in another and older sense of the term. When the dignities of office are laid aside, or when they fail to shield the person holding them from some humbling experience like those familiar to ordinary mortals, the resulting situation is necessarily problematic in a way that can generate a joke, a story, or an incident within one. Kevin Rafferty and James Ridgeway's *Feed* was one such extended joke, a 1992 docu-comedy assembled from news outtakes. Featuring then President Bush, future President Bill Clinton, and other candidates in footage normally left on the cutting-room floor, this "blooper reel" found comedy in such candid moments as a candidate slicking his hair down or waiting uncomfortably for a camera cue. With the protective stagecraft revealed and removed, running for president looked like nothing but one long string of indignities.

Other instances can be found in the works already mentioned. The messy scrapes and minor humiliations that made for humor in *My Fellow Americans* and *Welcome to Mooseport,* or even in *Tanner '88* and *The American President,* mostly involved losses of dignity. *My Fellow Americans* begins with the consecutive defeats of its two aging protagonists, each expelled from the White House after just one term. Ignominiously deprived of the dignities of office, they have to bumble their way to re-acquaintance with the real America. In *Mooseport,* a frustrated ex-President Cole rapidly tires of slipping on various small-town banana peels. "I had *dignity* once!" he splutters. "Does anybody remember that?"

A similar basic situation can also generate drama. What if the president were stuck somewhere—say, in a tiny, snowbound rural eatery, a space even more confined than Air Force One, and certainly less presidential—just when World War III threatened to break out? Stated that way, the question sounds like the makings of a spoof in the spirit of *Dr. Strangelove.* But in fact this was the premise of *Deterrence,* Rod Lurie's low-budget 1999 theatrical suspense thriller. Trapped by a blizzard while campaigning in a Colorado diner, President Walter Emerson (Kevin Pollack) and a few of his aides have to improvise ways to manage a Cold War–style global crisis without the usual high-tech resources and other trappings of the presidency. An "accidental" president like Gerald Ford, Emerson already lacks such dignity as a democratic leader gains from the people's endorsement. He also lacks "the physical bearing of a president," we are told, and he's disdained by Arab leaders because he's Jewish. Now, at a critical moment, Emerson finds himself just one of several random individuals thrown together by chance, even as an implausibly powerful Iraq (beefed up in order to fill the USSR's old movie role) suddenly goes on the march. Like his comic counterparts, Emerson is reduced to regular human scale—in this case temporarily, not by losing office but by being cut off from his *literal* office, his workspace, as well as the elaborate simulacrum of it that normally surrounds him wherever he goes. The result, among other humiliations, is that he is forced to listen to geostrategic advice from a short-order cook and other plain citizens. And while the movie hints that this might be good for him, it also has him lashing out, deliberately escalating the crisis by throwing down the nuclear gauntlet. It's as if he seeks to offset his humbling personal predicament by flaunting his powers as commander-in-chief that much more shockingly.

These movies are reminders of the dual nature of dignity and, therefore, of its loss. The term can refer either to character or to situation: One can behave in undignified ways, or one can "suffer the indignity" of circumstances beyond one's control. Presidents suffer that indignity more acutely than others. Since their job is to make decisions and wield power, anything that immobilizes or stymies them necessarily makes them less "presidential."[26] And since one way of resisting immobility and retaking control is through action heroics, these can also serve as a means of recovering dignity. It might seem undignified for the president personally to beat up the bad guys; it gets his hair mussed and his suit wrinkled. It might seem less than stately that he's a family man with the usual family worries, especially if terrorists can use his family to hold him hostage. But a story like *Air Force One* suggests just the reverse. The terrorists may have the initiative for the moment, but what allows President Marshall to seize it back is his refusal to follow procedure and make his escape in a parachute pod. He chooses not to immobilize himself in this little cage for two reasons: because it would compound the humiliation, and because he won't leave his wife and daughter to the mercies or protection of others. By handling things himself, by acting like a family man or even just a mad-as-hell everyman, he reacquires the dignities—for himself and the nation—that were lost as long as he was acting like a mere president.[27]

As cartoonish exaggerations of strength, action-hero and superhero presidents first appeared against a cultural backdrop of concerns about presidential weakness. But given the way these issues are linked, they can also be deployed against threats of indignity or humiliating defeat. The very odd comic book *Reagan's Raiders,* which ran for just three issues in 1986–87, chronicled the adventures of the aging then-incumbent after "a process of genetic engineering, and a combination of laser technology and intricate molecular chemical balancing" gave him the physical qualities of Rambo, the reluctant but deadly commando famous from the movies of Sylvester Stallone. With the strength of twenty men, and leading a band of similarly enhanced members of his cabinet, the brawny, bandana-wearing, bazooka-firing Reagan battled terrorists and other threats in traditional comic book superhero style. Among his triumphs was the rescue of American soldiers missing in action and enslaved in the Far East—one of Rambo's missions too, although in

Reagan's Raiders we are told that "Rhombo and Schwartzenheimer" had tried it, failed, and wound up captured themselves.[28]

Obviously this plot, like those of the Rambo movies and to some extent the policies of the real-life Reagan administration, was a cathartic fantasy of revenge for America's undignified, humiliating exit from Vietnam. But it was a fantasy carried to the point of self-parody. Exaggeration can generate either superheroism *or* satire, and it's a fine line that divides the one from the other. In the 1990s other cartoonists deliberately stepped across that line. Scott McCloud's *The New Adventures of Abraham Lincoln,* a 1998 "graphic novel" (or, longer comic book), brought the title character back to life to do battle with a rampaging look-alike who was really the advance man for invading space aliens. The satirical point was that present-day Americans were ready to put an imposter in office, thus surrendering the planet, because they preferred this Dishonest Abe's slick, media-savvy style and prettified clichés about American history over the messier truths represented by the tired, faltering figure who just happens to be the real Lincoln. Because he doesn't come off well on TV, the onetime hero of the Lincoln-Douglas debates is unable to defeat the aliens' Lincoln even in debate, and as the story unfolds the Great Emancipator winds up caged and helpless. But the day is saved when the Lincoln Memorial's Lincoln statue comes to life, tearing away the fake Lincoln's mask and revealing him to be Benedict Arnold.[29]

Even more farcically, Robert Smigel and Adam McKay's *The X-Presidents* has made crime-busting political superheroes of recent, former chief executives—Reagan, Ford, Carter, and the first Bush, occasionally joined by Nixon and later Clinton—who, the series explains, accidentally acquired superpowers when they were "struck by . . . radiation while appearing at a celebrity golf tournament." Presented as occasional cartoon shorts on *Saturday Night Live* since 1997, and as a graphic novel in 2000, *The X-Presidents* parodies "serious" superhero comics like *The X-Men* as well as cheaply produced Saturday morning TV cartoons from the baby boom years. The targets of its many jokes and sight gags include both superhero clichés and various topical political events. Thus, the X-Presidents have a secret lair, the Gerald R. Ford Presidential Library ("a place of solitude where humans never venture"), and they are summoned in response to threats from bad guys ranging from Saddam Hussein and Osama bin Laden to the "United Villains for the Overthrow of America" and "a race of communist aliens from the Telion Galaxy" whose planet's only source of fuel is burning the American flag.

In one segment inspired by the Clinton impeachment, the X-Presidents battle a walking, talking, fighting copy of the U.S. Constitution that has come angrily to life in response to its constant misuse in congressional debates. Another adventure sends them to Disney World's "Hall of Presidents," where they take on a gang of evil animatronic robots who, "freed from thirty-five years of repetitive motions," have gone on the attack while shouting things like "Ich bin ein asskicker!" and "The only thing you have to fear is my foot up your ass!" Fighting back in their own trademark allusive style ("Read my lips—you're *toast*, punk!"), the X-Presidents put down the robot revolt—at which point the animatrons go safely "back to just being disturbing."[30] But such victories have never reflected well on the X-Presidents, who may be able to lift buildings and fly through the air but are as undignified a pack of buffoons as it's possible to imagine. The notion that presidents are mostly idiots is hardly new, but by making superheroes of *former* presidents, *The X-Presidents* gives it a twist. The series' central joke is that it is *only* when they are old, retired, or even dead that our leaders are finally of any use.

The Many Varieties of Mr. Smith

If the theme of dignity and indignity logically extends the theme of strength and weakness that we saw recurring in fictions of the 1960s, it is also an extension of the "authenticity" issue that we tracked through several key works of the 1930s. That issue seemed to reflect a concern that presidents might be too aloof, too dissimilar to the people they govern.[31] Indignity is the related but opposite problem. It's the danger (or, for farceurs, the opportunity) that arises when presidents become *too* ordinary, when the demystifying and disillusioning threaten to go too far. To this problem, action hero presidents are one answer. They are above the ordinary yet right in the thick of things, the most hands-on problem-solvers it is possible to be. They can also be objects of admiration for a citizenry that seldom looks to politics for anything to admire. On the other hand, exaggerated shows of strength are cartoonish, literally the stuff of comic books. Most presidents are not skilled fighter pilots or molecularly rearranged super-strongmen, and if they were we would have trouble identifying with them. And most national problems, while they might call for courage, do not demand and will not yield to a president's physical prowess.

A more plausible answer, therefore, is a "Mr. Smith," a humble, sincere, guileless anti-politician in the mold of Jimmy Stewart's Senator

Jefferson Smith.[32] Beginning in the 1990s we see redoubled efforts to find a Mr. Smith, a character who would demonstrate that ordinariness can itself be a source of moral and political strength. One of these efforts was *Dave*, a 1993 film comedy with Kevin Kline as both a corrupt, cynical president and the ordinary citizen who happens to be his dead ringer. When the real president has a stroke, which happens in typical 1990s fashion in the middle of an adulterous tryst, his comatose form is hidden away like the prisoner of Zenda's, and poor but honest Dave Kovic is drafted to impersonate him. (As the filmmakers no doubt knew, "Kovic" is an eastern European—hence, in America, working-class— variant of Smith.) As he grows more comfortable mimicking a president, Dave winds up not only exposing the administration's corruption but also turning the government on its ear, reforming the way things are done simply by applying a little humility and plain speaking. The federal budget, for instance, is easily brought under control once Dave and his bookkeeper roll up their sleeves and get to work on it. That frees up funds for a new jobs program, thus allowing Dave to do on a national scale what he had previously been doing for individuals as head of a local employment agency. And though he is acting another man's role, Dave can infuse the real president's speeches with emotions the speechwriter himself had hoped only to simulate. These displays of unforced humanity warm the long-frozen heart of the First Lady (Sigourney Weaver), but naturally they also put Dave at odds with the cabal—the handlers and operatives who had co-conspired with the real president and mistakenly thought they could make a patsy of this political naïf. Dave finds a clever way to thwart them while also escaping back into blessed obscurity, and in the end the movie's lesson is an old-fashioned one: a little honest naïveté is exactly what the perverse and ingrown political world needs.

Other recent works have updated the search for a Mr. Smith, adding distinctly contemporary elements. *Bob Roberts*, Tim Robbins's 1992 film satire, charted the rise of a counterfeit Smith—a dangerous demagogue who co-opts the energy and imagery of 1960s-style protest movements and folk revivals, and even finally the mystique of Kennedy-like assassination attempts, to serve a proto-fascist politics. *Mail to the Chief* (2000) featured a non-Smith who wants to become one, a patrician president who turns for lessons in regular-guyhood to a middle school student he meets in an Internet chat room. *Mr. Smith Goes to Obscuristan*, a stage revue that the San Francisco Mime Troupe toured in 2002, used a singing and dancing Smith (closely based on Stewart's original and, like him, named

Jeff Smith) to satirize the Bush administration's post–September 11 foreign policies. And *Commander in Chief,* which ran on ABC-TV in 2005–6, starred Geena Davis as a female Smith. President Mackenzie Allen was not just the first woman president, she was a political independent who was not ambitious, never sought high office but instead had to be drafted to it, and seemed to want only to do what was "right" in some abstract, ad hoc sense—all the hallmarks of a Mr(s). Smith.[33]

In one especially intriguing twist, both Warren Beatty's 1998 *Bulworth* and Chris Rock's 2003 *Head of State* floated the idea that a true Mr. Smith might have to be black. Beatty's Jay Billington Bulworth is a Democratic senator whose suicidal despair drives him to a drastic change of personality. Abandoning conventional politics and its soul-destroying routines, he makes himself over in the anti-establishment, African American style of "hip-hop" and sets out to tell the truth through rap—a lyrical style that still seems uncompromised, the authentic diction of the dispossessed. Rock's character in *Head of State*, Alderman Mays Gilliam, is, like Dave Kovic, a D.C. local unwillingly thrust into presidential politics at the behest of that tireless cabal. Picked to fill in for a dead Democratic nominee, and expected to lose (party leaders don't want him actually taking over their turf), Gilliam has a groundedness and a common touch that come straight out of life in the "hood." His presence in the race blows hip-hop culture through official Washington like a fresh breeze, loosening up the society swells and, of course, putting him on track to the White House after all.

Like Bulworth, candidate Gilliam is defined by his alienation from the system; his charm lies in his unwillingness to play by its rules or put on airs.[34] Unlike Bulworth he comes by this style naturally, not out of life-changing trauma. In that respect he resembles the classic Mr. Smiths. But there is also a key difference: The old, white Smiths were un-hip and not clued in—less sophisticated, to their credit, than the party and establishment regulars. The new Mr. Smiths are hipper and *more* sophisticated, a product of alternative or marginalized cultures whose vitality and disdain for convention have long since escaped the (white) fuddy-duddies' control.

Despite this pedigree, and even though Smith-creators like Tim Robbins and Warren Beatty are two of today's better-known "Hollywood liberals," the left has no monopoly on Mr. Smiths. The title character in Martin L. Gross's 1997 novel *Man of Destiny* is a young, self-made software executive, Charles Palmer, who rises with phenomenal speed from a seat in Congress to the presidency on an independent but basically libertarian platform. "Charlie" aims to cut taxes, shut down large parts of the federal government, and put an end to political parties, which he calls "a refuge of half-baked ideologues." Here we have the very old view that parties are by definition cabals, and that partisan politics is per se corrupt—an idea that reaches back even further than the American nation itself. Charlie, like other Mr. Smiths, is a modern variant of the old Patriot King ideal, a dream whose American form is sustained by the notion that there are "common sense" solutions to problems, obviously correct policies that cannot be located on any ideological spectrum and that the people would readily embrace if only organized politics were not rigged in favor of an elite of self-seeking insiders.[35] Charlie's radical reforms are popular with 80 percent of the public; the only threat to them comes from those scheming elites, some of whom do not even dispute that they're parasites flouting the people's will. As one party elder puts it, Charlie "doesn't give a damn about the party, or you, or me. He's a bomb thrower for the people, and that's exactly what we need. Someone to spit in our faces and rip the place up—to bring it down to people's size, not to the fancy expectations of the bureaucrats and us professional politicians. We're fiddling while Chicago and Kansas City burn." Though it makes for some odd sentence constructions, the dialogue here and throughout *Man of Destiny* avoids referring to the political parties by name. Such is the novel's hostility to parties that it sacrifices natural speech in the interest of tarring them with the same broad brush.[36]

But while a Mr. Smith, or the storyteller who creates one, may disdain politics, parties, and even "the government," he is likely to revere political institutions as civic symbols. Unlike those jaded insiders, he brings a childlike awe to the capital. Here we have another trait typical of Mr. Smiths. While they are sure of their own moral instincts and their feel for the country's needs, they're humbled at the prospect of high office and seriously doubt their readiness for it. We can rest assured that they won't lose touch with ordinary people because they never forget how ordinary they are themselves. In one recurring image, the new president finds the Oval Office intimidating: Dave Kovic tumbles out of his desk chair, and Charlie Palmer makes his first tentative visit during one of several sleepless nights brought on by a sense of his own frailties. Charlie's growing anxiety and "turmoil"—"What was he feeling? He really had no idea. It was all too much to handle at one time"—are tied to his sense that the public that drafted him to run would surely want someone worthier, "If they only knew."

But Charlie did, nonetheless, accept the draft, and he does arrive in the White House with concrete policy goals, albeit goals we are asked to see as apolitical common sense. The perfect Mr. Smith is even further from politics than that. Like Jefferson Smith, he's in office because he is perceived as having no agenda at all apart from doing his patriotic duty. The modest virtue that makes him self-effacing also prevents him from thinking in larger—that is, political—terms. He has no goals that would lead him to relish power, hence he is a seemingly safe choice to fill a temporary vacancy. And then fate intervenes.

That is the story of the most fully developed of the recent Mr. Smiths—John Patrick "Jack" Ryan, the hero of several of Tom Clancy's bestselling technothrillers and of four big-budget movies made from them.[37] A remarkable creation, Jack is family man, action hero, and political Mr. Smith all rolled into one. A former Marine lieutenant and mild-mannered professor of naval history, he becomes a reluctant fighter for truth and justice when terrorists nearly kill his family. Joining the CIA, he rises through its ranks while battling various marquee villains— Soviet agents, drug cartels, more terrorists, and corrupt officials within the U.S. government itself. These successes lead to a series of high-level appointments, culminating in a request from his friend, the president, that he fill the recently vacated vice presidency just until the approaching election. Jack accepts this caretaker role as a final act of public service. But then a disgruntled Japanese pilot crashes a 747 into the Capitol during a presidential address, killing the president and most of the cabinet and Congress.[38] Suddenly Jack's eagerness to retire goes the way of General George Washington's, and at the beginning of Clancy's *Executive Orders* he finds himself, like Washington, presiding over a nation badly in need of a new government.

Besides that huge task, President Ryan has a lot to contend with in the novel's more than 1,350 pages. An aggressive Iranian theocracy takes over Iraq, launches a bioterror attack on several American cities, infiltrates an assassin into the Secret Service, and attempts to kidnap the Ryans' toddler daughter. (The Irish-Catholic Jack Ryan has a young family like Jack Kennedy's, right down to a son named John Jr.) And the crises all come to a head in a brief desert war and a strike against a malevolent Ayatollah, with technothrills provided by an array of amazing U.S. intelligence and combat gadgets.

Most of this keeps Jack deskbound—although he has to be physically stopped from savaging his would-be assassin, a moment when he
hoped he would "actually get to *do* something instead of just sitting here
like a goddamned king." Since he has little interest in making policy,
the president's daily work seems to him like just sitting there. We are
reminded continually of Jack's unhappiness and deep discomfort with
"Executive Orders," both the fact that he is expected to give them and
the unfamiliar "order" in which he struggles to find his place. He has
trouble remembering what is in order and what isn't—at one point he
forgets that the president is not supposed to fetch his aides' coffee—and
before long the job is giving him literal headaches. In the Oval Office he
feels lonely, and in public he feels an "overwhelming sense of not be-
longing": If the people cheering him "only knew what a fraud he was,
Jack thought, what would they do then? *What the hell am I doing here?*" In
one of his first opportunities to act "presidential," Jack shocks the TV
pundits and his fellow heads of state by discarding a prepared eulogy for
the dead president and First Lady. Instead he uses the occasion to comfort their orphaned children, speaking to them like "a real person":

> It was Jack's job to protect a nation. He'd sworn to preserve, protect,
> and defend the Constitution of the United States, and he would do that
> to the best of his ability. But the purpose of the *Constitution* was pretty
> simple—to secure the blessings of liberty for *people,* and that included
> kids. The country he served and the government he was trying to lead
> were nothing more or less than a mechanism to protect individual
> people. *That* duty was not an abstraction.[39]

There, in a word, is the enemy: "abstraction." It's what makes the presidency powerful, but also what makes it odious to any decent human
being.

A member of no party, Jack sees himself as having no positions on
most issues: "I don't have a fucking clue" how to do politics, he insists.
Still, he is soon the target of what is left of the old guard, which consists of overlapping groups of soft-on-defense liberals, career political
insiders—"ticket-punchers who know how to work 'the system,'" Jack
calls them—and a cynical press. Besides their contempt for a political
amateur, this bunch of diehards objects to Jack's instinctive fiscal and
social conservatism and his support for high defense spending. But those
positions, of course, are "common sense," just as the opposite positions
were common sense to the Progressive Era's President John Smith.[40]

Speaking to a prospective cabinet appointee, Jack explains that he needs "somebody who isn't political. You aren't. I need a dispassionate pro. Most of all, George, I need somebody who's going to hate his job as much as I hate mine":

> Ever since I started with the [Central Intelligence] Agency, I've had to watch how things work on the inside, and guess what? I never did like it. I started on the Street, remember, and I did okay then, too, remember? I figured I'd become an academic. . . . History's my first love, and I thought I'd teach and study and write, figure out how things worked and pass my knowledge along. . . .
>
> Look, George, I don't know *how* to be a politician, and I don't have time to learn. I never liked the game. I never liked most of the people in it. I just kept trying to serve my country as best I could. Sometimes it worked, sometimes it didn't. I didn't have a choice. You remember how it started. People tried to kill me and my family. I didn't want to get sucked in, but God damn it, I learned that *somebody* has to try to get the job done.

Jack complains that his original goal, protecting his wife and children, is exactly what he can no longer do. The skills he learned for doing it got him promoted, which means that even more people now want to kill them, which puts their safety in the hands of the Marines and Secret Service because Jack's job now is to safeguard America, the family writ large. For Jack, the question this irony raises is "*Who am I?*"[41] All these Hamlet-like doubts and frustrations probably help explain why *Executive Orders* was never as ripe for the big screen as other Clancy novels. Formerly an action hero, Jack as president is reduced to traffic cop—a boon for the country, we are frequently told, but a quasi-tragedy for Jack himself.

At least since Lincoln, it has been possible to imagine a president suffering inner turmoil. But for Lincoln, at least in fiction and legend, the suffering was usually a consequence of identifying with a horribly wounded nation and people. Jack's "*Who am I?*" is the hand-wringing of a man *resisting* that very identification, a man for whom the horror to be endured lies less in the catastrophes he presides over than in the fact of becoming president itself. His public rhetoric, consequently, is the opposite of Lincoln's. Where Lincoln grieved for the dead at Gettysburg in language that was all abstraction, Jack addresses grieving kids at the cost of setting the abstract nation aside. Jack is a fictional president of a distinctly contemporary kind, the kind we might get if Rambo and Mr. Smith appeared together on *The Oprah Winfrey Show*. Because they are not politicians, true Mr. Smiths often doubt themselves and hate their unasked-for jobs. Letting them *talk* about this, though, risks making them look self-absorbed. Before the 1990s it was hard to imagine story-tellers running that risk, especially in the macho tale of a president who means to be a no-nonsense man of action.

But if a thick book like *Executive Orders* at times reads like Jack's therapy journal and at other times serves as a soapbox for Clancy's libertarian views, its heart—like Jack's—lies in foreign and military affairs. That's where the action is. Only with the outbreak of war does Jack seem to perk up, since war finally puts him back in his element. It allows him, at last, to "*do* something." War is also where the upshot of Jack's "common sense" becomes clearest. The U.S. posture in the world is, it seems, just a given. It would never occur to Jack to rethink, for instance, America's vexed relations with Saudi Arabia, because that would be to snub the Saudi operatives he has personally been pals with since his CIA days. Here we arrive at the core of Clancy's fiction, if not of the whole technothriller genre: Even more than children and families, its focus of value is military and intelligence professionals. The safety of the first group, finally, depends on the second—on technical experts, engineers, streetwise agents, and "dispassionate pros," of just about any nation, whose training, tactics, equipment, and steely resolve allow them to do whatever is needed to get "the job" done. The job itself is just there; it is not the result of political decisions or choices that could, legitimately, have been made differently. In fact national leaders and policymakers are mostly more trouble than they're worth. Their professionalism is the wrong kind, self-interested yet, at the same time, abstractly ideological—seemingly opposed attitudes, but joined by the fact that they are both part of "the game." To professionals of the *right* kind, the game is "unreal." That is how the presidency seems to Jack Ryan, and that is why, old pro though he is, he's still "the first President in one hell of a long time who really *is*" just one of the citizens.[42]

From "Darling Sweetheart" to "The Big Creep": Mistress Memoirs and the Lewinsky Affair

The 1990s were not the decade originally associated with the phrase "culture of narcissism," but the concept was still alive and well when *Executive Orders* appeared in late 1996. It was not unusual for daytime television talk shows like *Oprah Winfrey*, with their confessional and voyeuristic style, to be cited as culturally defining; personal traumas and intimacies had become all too public, went the complaint, while serious public and political issues were ignored, trivialized, or reduced to personalities and gossip.[43] Very soon, political events took a turn that seemed to bear all this out. The Monica Lewinsky scandal, which first broke in January 1998 and dominated the news for more than a year—ultimately leading to only the second presidential impeachment trial in American history—touched many of the same issues as the period's fictions: the personal relationships of presidents; secrecy, conspiracy, and intrigue; and, of course, the dignities and possible indignities of high office.[44] Indeed there may be few stories more inherently "novelistic" than the story of a president's mistress. Rolling together sex, power, love, and transgression, such stories cannot help but offer the kind of salacious mix that the novel form was originally invented (and criticized) for telling. At its center will be a flawed hero, a public figure whose private secrets create the kind of doubleness from which vivid, realistic characters are made.[45] And since the story's key events will have occurred with only two people present, their (re-)construction will depend entirely on one of those two. That fact all but guarantees a distinctive narrative voice and storytelling style.

Before Clinton-Lewinsky in the 1990s, alleged presidential or pre-presidential affairs of the 1920s, 1940s, and 1960s had provided varying degrees of scandal and titillation once they were brought to light in novel-like "mistress memoirs." The history of this little genre almost recapitulates that of the novel form itself, and it's instructive to regard the Lewinsky story as the latest stage in that evolution. Nan Britton's *The President's Daughter*, the 1927 exposé of her affair with the much older Warren G. Harding, reads very much like nineteenth-century sentimental fiction. Maybe that is just the idiom that Britton knew best as a writer, or maybe, like Emma Bovary, she viewed love in the first place through a gauzy haze of sentimental notions she got from books. Her "sweet intimacies" with "Mr. Harding," as she calls him, disappear behind flowery euphemisms, just as she claims the two of them were wont to disappear into a White House closet. Even as she frets about practical matters, like securing child support for the daughter she says Harding fathered, Britton writes rhapsodically of "my beloved," the handsome "darling sweetheart" whom she thoroughly idealized. Despite the fact that she was only one of several Harding mistresses, her book tells a familiar tale of love finding a way—of impossible barriers nearly overcome, until death tragically intervenes (albeit Harding's, not the heroine's, as a Victorian novelist would likely have preferred).[46]

Unfortunately Lucy Mercer wrote no memoir of FDR, so after Britton we skip many years ahead to the memoirs of Kay Summersby Morgan and Judith Campbell Exner. These appeared at about the same time in the mid-1970s, and while they both contrast with Britton's, they do so in strikingly different ways. Summersby, author of *Past Forgetting: My Love Affair with Dwight D. Eisenhower* and a military aide to Ike during World War II, writes like the practical-minded career woman she was.[47] (Her earlier, nonromantic account of the war had been titled, simply, *Eisenhower Was My Boss.*) Heroines like Summersby were well known at the time of the events she describes. In the screwball comedies of the 1930s and 1940s, Barbara Stanwyck, Jean Arthur, Irene Dunne, Katherine Hepburn, Carole Lombard, and Rosalind Russell all played savvy, spunky women who found themselves thrown together in intimate circumstances with some lovable but inarticulate lug of a man. Summersby's story, though, is not a comedy. It's more like a wistful wartime romance, a distant memory of poignant moments—like driving down a moonlit road as the first planes take off for Normandy. "I did not believe for a moment that love conquers all," Summersby insists, even while admitting that she had hoped it somehow would.[48] Unlike Nan Britton, who apart from the inconvenience it causes her seems oblivious to the fact that her darling sweetheart is the president, Summersby's feelings for the Supreme Allied Commander are both bound up with and thwarted by the work that the two of them share. Eisenhower, like Harding, comes across as an emotionally distant figure, but that seems less a consequence of Summersby's writing style than a reflection of the man and the circumstances themselves. The fact that *Past Forgetting* is part war memoir has an odd effect, as if Summersby sometimes wished that Ike would pay a little less attention to the Wehrmacht and a little more to her. But it also echoes the *Casablanca* theme: people's private problems don't amount to a hill o' beans in this crazy world. The book's title borrows a lyric from the sorrowful "I'll See You Again," a song that Noël Coward wrote for the musical *Bitter Sweet* and that Summersby says she and Ike, like so many wartime couples, made their own.

Although it was already widely assumed that President Kennedy had had girlfriends, Judith Campbell Exner caused a sensation when she claimed to have been one of them. Exner was one of many long-held state secrets exposed by congressional investigators in the aftermath of Watergate, and the memoir she then published tells the amazing tale of a modern courtesan, a plaything of powerful men who wound up in a roundelay with Frank Sinatra, JFK, and mob boss Sam Giancana. (A protégé of Al Capone's, Giancana was involved in the Kennedy administration's efforts to assassinate Fidel Castro. Campbell played a small role as a go-between.) Like Britton, Campbell registers her paramour's elevation to high office mainly in terms of how hard it then becomes to get dates with him. The difference is that when they do get together she carries the narration beyond the bedroom door, foregoing the discreet fade-outs of the earlier memoirists. This does not heighten the romance. Campbell, in fact, is as cynical as Britton was sentimental. As she tells it, Kennedy treated girlfriends rather less well than a man with a seriously bad back would treat his masseuse. Britton and Summersby may have lamented the obstacles to love, but Campbell's complaints don't even rise to the level of a lament. The impossibility of true love with a powerful, married, and very preoccupied man does not make her wistful so much as just irritated. Campbell's *My Story*, which was adapted into the 2002 docudrama *Power and Beauty* for USA cable network, is finally a cynical account, and its raciness seems of a piece with that cynicism. It deglamorizes the affair, as if Campbell were intent on warning off other young women who might be thinking of dating a president: Don't, they make frustrating boyfriends.

If anyone failed to get that message it was Monica Lewinsky. Sporting cigars, stained dresses, and thong underwear, her story takes the next big leap in explicitness—granted, with the help of a very strange crew of prosecutors, political hatchet men, one amateur wiretapper and other obsessives. And with its references to Clinton as "that schmucko" and "the Big Creep," it's about as far from Nan Britton's rapt sentimentality as one could imagine. There is only one thing less romantic than a grand jury question like "Was there other physical intimacy performed?" and that's the answer. It would be tempting to say that if Britton's story is a Victorian novel, Lewinsky's is a French farce—one in which the many doors the characters keep running in and out of just happen to lead to the Oval Office. It trades in the same absurd comedy of furtive desire, not just deglamorizing love but making everyone, including the keyhole-peeping gumshoes on the couple's trail, look more and more crazed the more seriously they insist on taking the whole tacky business. In French farce, a stained blue dress would be the perfect maguffin.[49]

But what most clearly marks the story as a saga of recent times is its heavy overlay of pop psychology and the jargon of self-help. These, not surprisingly, are the categories to which Lewinsky herself assigned the experience. While she was probably no more narcissistic than other presidential mistresses—or presidents, for that matter—she was the first to have grown up in the culture of narcissism, and she spoke its language like a native tongue. The impossibility of lasting romance with the world's most closely watched man moves her to reflect that

> at the crazy place I was emotionally in my head, I mean, I was willing to sort of risk it all for my love for the president, I mean, which is just so fucking stupid. . . . I have personal issues that resulted in why I allowed myself to get into a relationship with a married man that were not OK, and that I've dealt with now. And I can't speak to whether the president's dealt with his issues.

These remarks come from *Monica in Black and White,* a 2002 HBO documentary filmed around a personal appearance at which Lewinsky answered questions from a live audience (not unlike the format of daytime confessional-talk television). The session is a train wreck of colliding discourses, as both Lewinsky and her questioners alternate between traditional and more contemporary ways of explaining events and assigning responsibility for them. To be fair, Lewinsky does not simply try to excuse herself or deflect all moral concerns with assurances that the inevitable therapy is going well. She recalls an inner debate over whether the affair was something she was "comfortable with" versus whether it was "right." When a friendly questioner describes her experience as "victimization," she does not readily embrace the term; and although she floats the idea that a "male-dominated society" was to blame for her mistreatment, she treats this as at best an interesting hypothesis.

But she also keeps older concepts like "responsibility," "remorse," and "wrong" at arm's length, prompting one questioner to accuse her of having "made this more about you and your pain and not about your own agency." Another member of the audience then jumps to her defense—"I don't think anyone should judge you unless they've gone through it"—and Lewinsky agrees that "I made the best decisions I could" and that some criticisms are best withheld "until someone has walked in my shoes, and walked through this":

> I didn't choose it. I didn't choose to become a public person. The way I came into the public spotlight was pretty tragic for me and for my family and friends. . . . I'm struggling and trying to balance, really, what this new life is, and what it's like to lose your anonymity, and just to, to move on, I guess.

In terms of the word's traditional meanings, it's an odd kind of "tragedy" that ends with its heroine saying, "I'm doing OK. I'm doing OK. . . . I have my bad days, but my good days far outweigh them." But that inflation of the term—or rather, its continued use in a culture not partial to the tragic vision, a culture that views misfortune in terms of personal "growth" and that believes in "struggling" with one's "issues" before "moving on"—is not Monica Lewinsky's doing.

Romantic love is, among other things, a mode of expression, a discourse with its own familiar terms, conventions, and images. Of all the mistress-memoirists, Nan Britton seems the most conversant with that language. Kay Summersby knew but tried to avoid using it, and Judith Campbell largely ignored it. But it surfaced again in the Lewinsky affair. Among the gifts that President Clinton gave Lewinsky was a copy of Walt Whitman's *Leaves of Grass.* The extremely well-read Clinton apparently recognized that the situation called for poetry, and unlike Warren Harding he had the good sense to rely on a master and not to try to write his own.[50] Like everything else about the affair, this detail was reduced both to a comic punch line and to the ultra-prosaic language of grand jury testimony and investigators' reports.[51] In one of the innumerable satires the scandal produced, a little book titled *Poetry Under Oath* took snippets of that testimony and recast them as free verse:

"Blah, Blah, Blah"

"Bob Nash is handling it"
"Marsha's going to handle it"
And "We just sort of need to be careful"

You know
And "Oh, I'll—"
He would always sort of—

What's the word I'm looking for?

Kind of validate
What I was feeling
By telling me something
That I don't necessarily know
Is true

"Oh, I'll talk to her"
"I'll—you know, I'll see
blah blah blah"

And it was just
"I'll do," "I'll do," "I'll do"
And didn't, didn't, didn't . . . [52]

Transposing genres like this pointed up how unpoetic the whole affair
had become. Clinton and Lewinsky were no Abélard and Héloïse, but
even the most lyrical terms of endearment would wither and die under
cross-examination from lawyers and FBI agents. Part of what makes romance romantic is that it's private: Its language and gestures allow two
people to constitute a world unto themselves. The very different lan-
guages of publicity and authority destroy that little world's coherence,
which is why the affair can't be described in news reports and congressional hearings without looking ridiculous. But producing this effect can
make the investigators look ridiculous themselves. When their pursuit of
Clinton and Lewinsky failed to win public acclaim, the scandal became
a national debate over the meaning, importance, and limits of privacy.
Historically, the fear of totalitarianism has focused on the power of
leaders to probe every nook and cranny in the private lives of citizens.
In the Lewinsky affair, some argued, the totalitarian gaze was turning
back on the leader himself.[53]

Besides whatever it was in the zeitgeist that encouraged this, it was a
development to which Clinton was especially vulnerable—or, put another way, it grew from the same roots as Clinton's political success. He
was president in part because voters believed that he could "feel their
pain," and they consistently gave him high ratings on the question of
whether he understood and shared the concerns of "people like me."
This had peculiar consequences even before the Lewinsky scandal. In
one remarkable new way of fictionalizing a president, Julia Anderson-
Miller and Bruce Joshua Miller put together a collection of *Dreams of
Bill*—ordinary citizens' accounts of Clinton's appearances in their
dreams. The book's concept itself arose out of a dream:

> I was at my Macintosh formatting a book about a Japanese concentra-
> tion camp in the Philippines during World War II. I was feeling rather
> fatigued, having been bent over like a button hook for hours. Then, out
> of the blue, Bill Clinton walked through the door and rubbed my neck
> therapeutically. It was one of those dreams where I could feel the thick-
> ness of his hands and smell the fragrance of his after-shave (sea breezy).
> He told me to keep working. When I woke up my neck felt better and I
> wondered if other people had dreamed of Bill Clinton.[54]

Apparently they had; the Millers catalogued several hundred examples under such categories as "Romance," "Weddings," "Nightmares," "Science Fiction," and "My Dad Bill." *Dreams of Bill* appeared before the Lewinsky scandal, and only a few of its dreams involved sex. But by the end of the Clinton years there were racier entries in the genre. One author published a book called *My Erotic Dreams With Bill Clinton,* and the New York City Opera performed a "pocket opera," *Dream President,* featuring a dominatrix whose Clinton dreams were based on the female composer's own.[55]

In themselves, dreams are the most private narratives there are. Americans no doubt have had dreams about presidents since George Washington, but publishing them or appropriating them for art is laying claim to an imagined intimacy (and an intimate imagining) that in the past would have seemed either irrelevant or presumptuous. With the Lewinsky scandal, though, the last barriers of decorum seemed to give way. The most amazing evidence of this was *American Rhapsody,* a collection of essays and vignettes by Joe Eszterhas, one of Hollywood's most successful screenwriters. Heedless of any boundaries between fiction, political commentary, and celebrity gossip, Eszterhas's book blends all three modes in highly idiosyncratic ways, analyzing Clinton through the imagined interior monologues of various close observers—including "Willard," a character whose identity can be inferred from remarks like these: "Billy's worked me hard his whole life, but I'm not tired. I've never been inoperative. I've always had a lot of get-up-and-go. He's never had to eat shark-fin soup or oysters or mandrake root or rhino horn." In the spirit of another of the book's essays, "The President is Black," Willard's commentary ends with a rap lyric directed at Clinton:

> You make a speech, I pluck a peach
> You tell a lie, I poke your fly
>
> . . . .
>
> You're a Lefty, I'm hefty
> You're a boomer, I boom her
>
> . . . .
>
> You think you've got me in your hand
> But I'm the one who's in command.[56]

Over the years there have been other strange and surprising entrées to the White House, including memoirs written from the viewpoints of a dressmaker, a dog trainer, a dog, a parrot, a group of rats and mice, Lincoln's ghost, Lincoln's son's ghost, JFK's ghost, JFK's father's ghost, and a different ghost of JFK who is less gossipy and more paranoid than the first. The 1999 film comedy *Dick* parodied both conspiracy tales and behind-the-scenes exposés by suggesting that "Deep Throat," the secret Watergate informant, had actually been a pair of giggly teenage dog-sitters.[57] *Dick* also recalled just how recently people could be shocked by the notion that presidents—as the Watergate tapes had revealed—might use four-letter words in the Oval Office, let alone do things there that four-letter words could be used to describe. By the late 1990s, though, the language of scandal had become a default mode of political discussion; few expected anything edifying from revelations about presidents past or present. Even so, *American Rhapsody* marked the outer bounds of imagined candor. If there was a secret source who knew more than Willard, most Americans would not want to hear it.

"Just Folks" (or Not): Virtue and Weakness in *The West Wing*

The developments that began with *Tanner '88* and continued through the 1990s culminated in *The West Wing*, the popular prime-time drama series about a fictional president and his closest aides that debuted on NBC in September 1999. While neatly summarizing most of the narrative themes of the period, the series was also a determined effort at realism, which it strove to achieve in part by docu-dramatizing the political issues of the moment. Like *Tanner*, *The West Wing* was never formally grouped in the increasingly popular genre known as alternate history, but for its seven-season run—the rough equivalent of two presidential terms—that is effectively what it provided: "a virtual presidency set in an ongoing alternate universe," in one reviewer's words.[58] Beginning in the midst of Democratic President Josiah "Jed" Bartlet's first year in office, that imagined history extended through the real-life handover of the White House to Republicans in 2001. Notwithstanding this, *The West Wing*'s fourth season depicted Bartlet (Martin Sheen) winning re-election on schedule. After his second term, the series ended in May 2006 with Bartlet yielding the office to his successor, Democrat Matt Santos (Jimmy Smits). In its most notable effort to mimic real events, *The West Wing* had Santos and his Republican opponent (Alan Alda) debate each other in a live episode, with a real-life news anchor hosting the broadcast and the actors improvising dialogue the way actual debaters might.[59] Santos then went on to win a close election, which—like the real elections of 2000 and 2004, though in the opposite direction—was decided by a single state.

In the mode of most contemporary television dramas, *The West Wing* followed continuing storylines (or "arcs"), soap-opera style, over several episodes and in some cases several seasons. This allowed the characters and issues to develop histories of their own, and the series thus became a virtual world: time passed at the same rate it did in reality, developments in the real world were acknowledged, and real-life political problems became the basis of stories. We might say the series "paralleled" reality, but the pattern was more like a zigzag, with events of the virtual world weaving in and out of conformity with the real. Terrorism, for example, became an important issue for *The West Wing*'s characters after September 11, 2001, although the Bartlet administration did not respond to it the way the Bush administration did. In general, Bartlet was very different from George W. Bush, and we were given to believe that America would have been better off if things had gone Bartlet's way. But Bartlet was constrained from doing whatever he liked by a Republican Congress and other pressures from the right, and these constraints kept the series within hailing distance of real-life politics.

As a character, Jed Bartlet has some similarities to Tom Clancy's Jack Ryan: He's a Catholic and a onetime academic whose wife is a doctor, and he seems to be just as personally straitlaced and incorruptible as Ryan. He also resembles another professor-president—fellow Democrat Andrew Shepard of *The American President,* a movie written by *The West Wing*'s creator, writer, and original executive producer Aaron Sorkin. (Martin Sheen, who played Bartlet, had appeared in that film as Shepard's chief of staff.) But by no means is Bartlet another Mr. Smith. True, he has deep roots in the American mythos; his distinguished ancestors include a signer of the Declaration of Independence. But this former governor of New Hampshire is also a professional politician. And, as much as any fictional president ever created, he is unapologetically an intellectual: a habitué of antiquarian bookshops, a Nobel laureate in economics with undergraduate degrees in American Studies and theology, and a bit of a pedant who delights in regaling his staff with historical and scientific trivia, whether about the origins of chess or the difference between rivers and tidal estuaries. When, on one occasion, Bartlet insists that he really is "folksy" and not a snob, one of his aides sets him straight: "You're not 'just folks.' You're not 'plain-spoken.' Do not—do not—*do not* act like it!"[60] Were he not *politically* a friend of the common people, Bartlet's electoral success would be hard to account for. But he's a liberal Democrat in the mold of FDR, another elite northeasterner whose warmth and egalitarian politics made him appealing to voters despite his obvious differences from them.

For all this, Bartlet was not *The West Wing's* star—at least no more so than the other main characters on this "ensemble" series. Many storylines referred to him only peripherally; the people whose shoulders we mostly found ourselves looking over were his senior staffers, the close aides whose working days are spent alongside the president in the title section of the White House. In this *The West Wing* resembled *Tanner '88*— one character's name even seemed to be a direct homage—and also called to mind *Primary Colors,* journalist Joe Klein's originally anonymous 1996 novel and Mike Nichols's 1998 film about the people running a presidential campaign for a charming, undisciplined, Clintonesque southern governor. Like *Primary Colors, The West Wing* dealt with the frustrations and disillusionments involved in translating liberal politics into governing victories and, thus, national policy. Jack Stanton, the soon-to-be president in *Primary Colors,* was himself the source of those frustrations to a greater degree than Jed Bartlet, but the Bartlet West Wing was, if anything, even more crisis-ridden than the Stanton campaign. Just about all that Bartlet's staffers could do in most episodes was try to make the best of one hard decision or unforeseen problem after another. Their typical conversations—good-natured but very fast, dense with facts, and often conducted on the run as they scurried through office-space labyrinths that gave new meaning to the phrase "corridors of power"—implied an endless rush of daunting new challenges, a level of pressure forever threatening to crush even people this knowledgeable and skilled.[61]

That, too, was another way in which *The West Wing's* leftward orientation was made safe for prime-time network TV. The staffers were easy to sympathize with, both because they were well-meaning idealists and because they were constantly beleaguered. They may have been running the executive branch of the world's most powerful government, but in an age of conservative politics they were underdogs, hard-pressed to get what they wanted—what the nation needed—in the exasperating battles they were forced to fight. The immense difficulty of their jobs, and the dogged skill with which they earned the right to do them, also ensured that they would not become any kind of cabal. Yes, they were political professionals, but only the very best kind.

And although Jed Bartlet had his own family, including yet another pair of anxiety-inducing presidential daughters (the younger of whom, in one storyline, is kidnapped while on a date), the senior staff—like most groups of co-workers on long-running TV series—was unmistakably a kind of family as well. This greatly expanded the range of ways in which familiar themes of presidential fiction could be translated into particular stories. Secrets and scandal, for instance, could attach to characters other than the president, threatening without truly compromising him. For example, while the Bartlets' own marriage was solid, at various times his chief speechwriter was seeing a woman who turned out to be a high-priced call girl, and his deputy chief of staff got involved with an outspoken political activist whose interest in administration policy raised the old issue of public loyalties versus private. Bartlet's communications director would eventually be convicted of a crime (albeit one of conscience, prompting a pardon as Bartlet's last act in office), and his first-term chief of staff struggled with various addictions—while, though, valiantly keeping them in check with secret help from Alcoholics Anonymous. Again and again the series artfully managed to push the Bartlet administration toward scandal while keeping its main characters essentially innocent. If anything, their struggles with their own weaknesses and mistakes had the effect of humanizing and ennobling them further.

In the most important of these storylines and the one that directly concerned Bartlet, it eventually came out that he was slowly being incapacitated by multiple sclerosis. Because, in the "backstory," he had hidden this fact from the public, its disclosure generates the familiar panoply of presidential scandal: special prosecutor, congressional hearings, and eventually a resolution of censure. These political struggles overlap with struggles within Bartlet's family, since his M.D. wife is implicated in the "cover-up." At bottom, though, they reflect less on Bartlet's character, let alone his politics, than on his—and any president's—bodily frailty, a condition also brought home when he is wounded in an assassination attempt. (And, for that matter, in the bicycle accident he suffers in the pilot episode. Bartlet's very first appearance in the series has him hobbling in on crutches, physically impaired but full of righteous anger over right-wing attacks that have forced him, like other fictional presidents of the time, to come to the defense of his family and staff.)

The medical scandal plot line also opened the way for Bartlet to wrestle with his personal demons. The "Bartlet psychosis," as he jokingly calls it, turns out to be a long-simmering Oedipal struggle with his late, abusive father, who was also the patrician headmaster of young Bartlet's prep school. His ongoing fight with the ghost of that father puts Bartlet in conflict with his staff, his wife, and in one key scene with God, whom he argues with like Job while standing alone in the National Cathedral. It also puts him, reluctantly, into psychotherapy, in search of a cure for a "historic stretch of sleeplessness." For all the griefs brought on by this stubborn superego, Bartlet cannot stop speaking the traditional language of duty, morality, guilt, and expiation—a language so old-fashioned and biblical-sounding that part of his cathedral soliloquy is even delivered in Latin. He resists the contemporary and very different language of therapy; as he explains to his therapist, Dr. Keyworth:

> BARTLET. I don't like the word "stress." It's a Madison Avenue word. It's something that can be cured with flavored coffee and bath bubbles.
> DR. KEYWORTH. So, you don't feel stress?
> BARTLET. I have a job I like, and my family's healthy.
> DR. KEYWORTH. That doesn't mean you're not entitled to feel stress.
> BARTLET. Stress is for other people.

Bartlet, characteristically, prefers a formula borrowed from literature— "Most men lead lives of quiet desperation":

> DR. KEYWORTH. Yeah, but that's *most* men. That's not you. That's the other people, the ones who feel stress. You're destined for something else.
> BARTLET. I have abilities.
> DR. KEYWORTH. And now you have an opportunity to use them.
> BARTLET. I think I *have*.
> DR. KEYWORTH. That room I passed down the hall, on the left, it's got a name, right?
> BARTLET. I think you're talking about the Lincoln Bedroom.
> DR. KEYWORTH. Right. This is a hell of a curve you get graded on now. Lincoln freed the slaves and won the Civil War. "Thank you. Next! And what will you be singing for us today, Mr. Bartlet?" "Well, we've had six straight quarters of economic growth."

Granting that "It can't be easy being you . . . being inside your head," Dr. Keyworth also assures—or warns—Bartlet that "I'll be the only person in the world, other than your family, who doesn't care that you're the president."[62] The therapy scene ends with Bartlet, alone, communing

A psychotherapist (Adam Arkin, *left*) counsels President Jed Bartlet (Martin Sheen) in *The West Wing*.

with portraits of both his father and Lincoln, the two patriarchs presumably doing battle in the depths of his being.

It's interesting that soon thereafter, this storyline was essentially dropped. Just as Americans' approval of Bill Clinton did not seem to depend on whether he had "dealt with his issues," as Monica Lewinsky put ·it, so *The West Wing*'s makers apparently either lost interest in psychoanalyzing Bartlet or concluded that we soon would.[63] Psychotherapy, as Dr. Keyworth says, treats a person's issues as important for their own sake; it "doesn't care that you're the president" because its goal is the well-being of Jed Bartlet the person, not the health of the government or country he leads. But *The West Wing* wasn't about Bartlet the person, it was about the Bartlet presidency. That's why it foregrounded staffers, not therapists or even family and friends. Staffers are there to serve a *president,* not a person. Like other "prime-time soaps," the series often dealt with problems in its characters' personal lives. But in most cases these were believably framed as the problems of smart, overburdened professionals, the kinds of problems that people responsible for running the world might well have.

In the end, therefore, it did not much matter whether Bartlet came to terms with his father. It mattered whether he came to terms with Lincoln, or rather with the public role of which Lincoln is the reigning symbol and standard. What may be going on in his subconscious, or his soul, was of some interest, as it was not, say, in the case of *President John Smith* a century earlier. The depth in that novel, such as it was, belonged to the party-political philosophy that Smith represented; Smith himself had none, though his political achievements also depended on his impeccable personal virtue. Compared to Smith, Jed Bartlet seemed only weakly tied to a party or philosophy. Like real presidents, he and his staff would work through the party's machinery when it served their purpose, but they were also apt to find themselves struggling at cross-purposes to it. (That they were not "party hacks" was another element of their appeal.) And although whatever good Bartlet's administration managed to do was partly an emanation of his personal virtues, it could not be reduced to those virtues. Above all, it was the hard-won product of political and professional expertise. For that, modern presidents rely on skilled and energetic assistants.

Thus, even while braiding together scandal, family drama, bodily weakness and other leading themes of contemporary political fiction, *The West Wing* set itself apart from a long tradition of make-believe leaders, the tradition that stretches from eighteenth-century Patriot Kings to nineteenth-century utopian administrators to the many Mr. Smiths of today. While skeptical toward parties and ideologies, it denied that politics could be dispensed with, that "common sense" will sweep all before it, that good policy arises simply from good intentions, and that "just folks" make better governors than those for whom political leadership is a lifelong pursuit. From the viewpoint of the West Wing (and *The West Wing*), what matters is not how much you *resemble* the "folks" but how well you understand what they need—and how adept you are at moving the levers of power to see that they get it. Those are not personal but *political* virtues. They arise from the second of "the king's two bodies," the political *persona ficta*, which is only obliquely related to the weakening bodies and disturbed inner selves that afflict mere mortals like Jed Bartlet.[64] As they mine those afflictions for drama, storytellers necessarily focus on the mortal person. But the start of the new century would also see increasing interest in the *ficta*, in the public role as a constructed thing—and in storytelling's own, sometimes anxious part in constructing it.

7

Fictitious Times

Imagining Presidents at the Turn of the Millennium

❖

I'd like to thank the Academy for this. I have invited my fellow
documentary nominees on the stage with us, and we would like
to—they're here in solidarity with me because we like nonfiction. We like nonfiction and we live in fictitious times. We live in
the time where we have fictitious election results that elect a fictitious president. We live in a time where we have a man sending
us to war for fictitious reasons. Whether it's the fiction of duct
tape or fiction of orange alerts, we are against this war, Mr.
Bush! Shame on you, Mr. Bush, shame on you!

Michael Moore, Academy Award acceptance speech, March 2003

❖

George W. Bush was not the first president to take office despite
having won fewer votes than his opponent, nor the first whose vic-
tory rested on questionable vote totals and suspiciously partisan rulings.
When similarly dubious results put Rutherford B. Hayes in the White
House after he lost the 1876 popular vote, his opponents nicknamed him
"Rutherfraud" and "His Fraudulency." But Bush was probably the first

president to be accused not merely of relying on fictions, but of *being* one himself.

In leveling this charge, however, in a televised Oscar acceptance speech that made global headlines on the eve of the Iraq invasion, film-maker and activist Michael Moore was evidently speaking for only a fraction of the public.[1] Most Americans had either embraced or ac-quiesced in the results of the 2000 election. After the brief crisis over the Florida recount, normal political life had resumed; voters' faith in the larger constitutional order was strong enough to weather its apparent failure to give them their choice in this one instance. Or, they persuaded themselves that it actually had: In the years following, it was not unusual to hear commentators retrospectively award Bush even the 2000 popu-lar vote. "Americans," in some abstract sense, were often said to have "preferred" him to Al Gore for this or that reason, even though there was no dispute that Gore had won the votes of more actual Americans. But Bush was president, so somehow "we," the American people, must have willed this, even if we rather mysteriously did it by voting for the other guy. Rarely has the faith—or fiction—at the heart of democratic elections simultaneously been nullified and proven so robust.[2]

But if Moore's suggestion that the Bush presidency was fictitious was not conventional wisdom, as time went on there was more sympathy for his literary critique of the war in Iraq. With no Iraqi weapons of mass destruction to be found, and with new questions arising about the uses of prewar intelligence, the narrative that the president and his aides had relied on to justify invading came to look more and more like a fiction of some kind—if not a deliberate lie, then at least a careful and artful con-struction. Indeed it seemed that some in the president's circle wore the charge of fictionalizing as a badge of honor. Insisting that "history starts today," Bush officials had declared the United States free to write its own stories. One of those officials, in a prewar interview, had explained this credo to a skeptical journalist:

> The aide said that guys like me were "in what we call the reality-based community," which he defined as people who "believe that solutions emerge from your judicious study of discernible reality." I nodded and murmured something about enlightenment principles and empiricism. He cut me off. "That's not the way the world really works anymore," he continued. "We're an empire now, and when we act, we create our own reality. And while you're studying that reality—judiciously, as you

will—we'll act again, creating other new realities, which you can study too, and that's how things will sort out. We're history's actors . . . and you, all of you, will be left to just study what we do."

To this celebration of action and will over the dull, static "studying" of reality, Moore's insistence that "we like nonfiction" was one pointed reply.[3]

Another reply, and the most persuasive one, came from dull reality itself, which it was soon clear the U.S. government was not "creating." Presidents certainly are "actors," as the Bush aide had said. Their actions do help make history, in whose narratives they often play leading roles. But as the war demonstrated, they do not write the stories themselves. Like actors in a theater, they work within a limited space, following scripts and stage directions that are largely *not* of their own making. Sheer political will may shape events, but it does not create them. The truth is often the opposite: narrative roles created for presidents act on *them*, obliging them not just to "act" but to act *out* stories that the audience already knows very well.

This, as we have seen, has been true since the beginning. The Patriot King ideal was older than George Washington, and the Cincinnatus legend of the humble, reluctant national savior was even older than that. To some degree the first American president was bound to try to give the public some version of those well-known roles. Of course, not every leader would have understood this as well as Washington, or worked as diligently to develop the role over such a long period. (If presidents are actors, then Washington was a "Method" actor, determined to "become" his character almost from boyhood.) Nor is it always obvious which script is called for given the circumstances of the time. Presidential politics is in part a debate over this: not just a critics' forum on the leading actor's performance, and not just a casting call to decide who plays the lead next, but a competition to choose *which* stories and roles to enact from the many in the nation's repertoire.

That competition has never ended, and, as long democracy functions, it never will. In that sense we are *always* living in "fictitious times." If anything in the new millennium answers to Michael Moore's comment—if anything about recent years is *especially* fictitious—it may be the degree to which the fictions are self-consciously recognized, cultivated, and critiqued. As the repertoire has grown, and as new technologies have come (literally) online, enhanced means for making and distributing complex narratives can increasingly be found in the hands of individual citizens. Fictive or "virtual" realities thus proliferate, and with these come new possibilities for paralleling or doubling the realities we know. Doubling, as we saw in earlier chapters, is a ready instrument of satire—a mode that often aims to ridicule not just national leaders and legends, nor just the conventional reverence for them, but the artifice of the conventions themselves. To expose a received story as phony is also to expose it *as a story,* and one way of doing this is to draw attention to the contrivances involved in making it one.

Before we consider how this happens in fictions of these fictitious times, it is worth recalling one recent moment when those contrivances were suddenly exposed, when the "storymaking" process itself was thrust into view even as it was struggling to work. Normally, which role a president is called on to act within history becomes clear only in retrospect, if then—only as we look back and see how the drama (or comedy) eventually turned out. But when an event that no one saw coming breaks in and changes the whole plot, a performance can suddenly be called for that neither actor nor audience had foreseen. The first great crisis of the Bush years was just such a moment of improvisation. It's ironic that Bush, of all presidents, would have headed an administration that was so sure it could create new realities as it wished. For in that crisis it was someone else who made the reality, and Bush who was forced to step into a role that he was slow to recognize he had suddenly been assigned.

"Around a Big Table": (Mis)Placing the President on September 11

Television viewers in America are used to seeing images of violence and chaos in less fortunate parts of the world. Describing the view from his hotel room in Sarajevo, a newspaper correspondent who covered the Balkan wars of the 1990s wrote: "A journalist could convince himself on a slow afternoon that he was doing his job by peering through a window at people running for their lives." Citing this remark, one critic argues that Sarajevo and the many places like it—Rwanda, Chechnya, Indonesia, the Sudan—have become "pulverized space," the source of interchangeable images of suffering that Western consumers import in much the same way they import other Third World commodities like oil or tin. Whatever local circumstances might lie behind each image, the many scenes of people running for their lives eventually start to blur together.[4]

September 11, 2001, was not what anyone would call a slow afternoon, and not least of what was shocking about it was that these familiar roles were turned upside-down. Suddenly it was anonymous Third Worlders who had the initiative, while most of the people running for their lives were Americans. And the journalists covering the event were anything but detached. The inevitable comparison was to "something straight out of a war zone," as an NBC correspondent put it.[5] But this time the war zone had come to them; the pulverized space was their own home turf. Like Sarajevo under siege, it lay right outside their windows—literally so, in the case of some Wall Street reporters who found themselves first on the scene.[6] The response needed, therefore, was vastly more complex. At "Ground Zero"—a term that itself suggests the disappearance of distance—the task was not just to passively register another image interchangeable with those familiar from places like Sarajevo. For a Western audience, a shocking event in the heart of the West cannot be just a raw commodity. Instead that audience expects *manufactured* goods—a crafted, if mass-produced, *story* in which, as those Wall Street correspondents might put it, there is "value-added": intelligibility and meaning.

Journalists, then, were called on to produce such a story. In this they were at a disadvantage. The suicide hijackings, it seems, had been story-driven themselves, an attempt to act out in real life a "sacred drama" whose narrative could be at least partly reconstructed from documents the hijackers left behind. The point of the attacks was to seize events and violently reshape them along the lines of the terrorists' own lurid imaginings.[7] For news reporters, the problem in the immediate aftermath was the reverse. They began with the chaos of actual events and had to find a story that would fit. They had to select, from a stock of readily available images and narratives, a plotline in which the events would take on some coherence—and a hero able to carry that plot.

This process of "narrative framing," as those who study the news media call it, is usually invisible. As news consumers, we simply accept most of the stories it produces as windows onto reality.[8] But in this case something went wrong. The matter was resistant; the plot did not unfold as planned; and suddenly, the terms of the emerging narrative had to be rethought. There was an unexpected gap in the story, an absence at its center where we would normally expect to find a key narrative element: the protagonist. For those whose job is to tell the story—the news organizations, reporters and anchors, and the officials they rely on as sources—this was a serious problem. It was not the worst of the day's disasters, by any means; collapsing narratives don't pose the same urgent threat as collapsing buildings. But for the storytellers of September 11, it was not just people who needed rescuing but the story itself.

"[C]learly, something relatively devastating [is] happening this morning there on the south end of the island [of] Manhattan." With this understatement a CNN anchor began that network's coverage, expressing a hesitancy characteristic of the first hour. Reporters were remarkably slow even to name the event. Perhaps the second explosion at the World Trade Center was an after-effect of the first. Perhaps, another CNN anchor guessed after video replays clearly showed two aircraft hitting the towers, the event was some bizarre accident, "a navigational equipment failure or some sort of a navigational quirk by beacons or whatever." It was only when they found an unidentified "U.S. official" willing to say that the attack "appeared to be an act of terrorism" that CNN began to use that word itself. Even then, the anchor fretted that he did not know "which department of this—this U.S. official was speaking from, or the authority this official was actually carrying."[9] As we have since learned, U.S. officials at that early stage were getting their own information from TV; in all likelihood, CNN's unnamed source was just describing what he saw on CNN.

Yet once it was established that the relevant genre was "terrorism," other facts were instantly surmised—above all, the identity of the target. Though the perpetrators themselves had offered no explanation and no statement of political aims, it was quickly concluded that the story, at root, was not about an attack on certain buildings (though these were *literally* the targets), or on certain cities, or on Western civilization, "world trade," capitalism, militarism, or any other such entity (though all these figured in later analysis).[10] Instead, in a vivid illustration of the preeminent place of the *nation* as "imagined community," the story of September 11—as expressed in TV news graphics and onscreen titles— was presumed to be "*America* Under Attack."[11]

But the choice of such a master narrative is only the first step. The story cannot fulfill its purpose—it will not be credible, and will need to give way to a different story—unless its various episodes unfold as expected and its characters act in ways appropriate to the genre. Each episode, or subplot, will constitute what has been called "a little system of tension and resolution," a working out of one of the rhetorical contrasts or oppositions implied by such an event.[12] On September 11, one such little system was identified in reporters' frequent use of terms like *paralyzed, immobilized,* and *shut down,* words naming an unnatural condition whose shock value increased in proportion to the size and importance of the thing said to be paralyzed: "our largest city, and most vital financial market," "the heart of the world financial markets," "the heart of our infrastructure . . . a [transportation] system that, frankly, many people thought was impenetrable," "this country, the strongest country in the world," "Manhattan, the nerve center of America," and "the nation's capital, the most powerful center in the world."[13] This rhetoric of power, center, and "heart" versus immobility and paralysis identified a tension, and resolving that tension would produce a storyline, or at least an episode of one. Somehow, things would have to be recentered.[14]

From this point on September 11 itself, two narrative lines diverged. The New York narrative, as we might call it, mainly involved a different tension (people in danger, missing, trapped) and, therefore, different tasks (escape, search and rescue), and a cast consisting to a large degree of local and collective agencies (firefighters, police, rescue workers, anxious bystanders). The larger task of recentering was *national* business, the business of Washington, where there was an obvious candidate for the role of principal actor—a person whose own centrality could, perhaps, decide just *how* paralyzed the world's strongest country and most powerful center would turn out to be. But that individual himself was conspicuous by his absence. As luck would have it, he was just then in the middle of a "photo op" at a grade school in Florida.

That displacement was immediately noticed. "You have got to let people know there is a government," New York Mayor Rudolph Giuliani said later, explaining his ad hoc assumption of a role that won him praise as "mayor of America" and "the nation's paterfamilias."[15] But a "mayor" of America is at best a fill-in, a placeholder for the usual paterfamilias. Until word was received from the *real* central authority, reporters would hesitate, unsure even whether to report the facts right in front of them. The CNN correspondent traveling with President Bush fretted that there was "no confirmation here from White House officials about what this in fact is, whether it's accident or terrorism." Tacitly, though, it was acknowledged that the attacks were deliberate—hence the urgent need for Bush to "return immediately to Washington."[16]

There was no question, then, what the president would do next: reoccupy the center by returning to the White House. So strongly was this assumed that reports of it were placed, incongruously, alongside reports that the White House and most other government buildings had been evacuated. NBC's reporter gave these conflicting statements in almost the same breath, assuring viewers that "he's coming back directly, and you figure it's about a two-hour flight, so you—you can do the math."[17] On National Public Radio, anchor Bob Edwards noticed the contradiction ("If the White House has been evacuated and they're worried about possible terrorist action, maybe they don't want him at the White House"), but he quickly suggested a way around it: "Do they still have the alternative White House in the Blue Ridge Mountains?" That at least would put Bush nearby. NPR's White House reporter, though, seemed not to know what Edwards was talking about.[18]

Meanwhile, CNN's reporter acknowledged that the scene around Bush was "a bit confused," but explained that "Clearly this morning, with a crowd of children, he wanted to keep an even keel, keep the situation under control as best as possible." Even the president's initial hesitation, that is, could be read as an exercise of "control." Better still, it could be construed as a kind of action: Bush was already "marshaling all the resources of the federal government" and "trying to gather whatever information, all the information he can from various White House sources, make a statement, and then get aboard Air Force One, and get back to Washington just as soon as he can" in order to "convene a National Security Council meeting."[19] In Washington, reporters learned from a senior official that Bush would indeed be hurried back there, in part "to send the signal that the president is back on the job back at the White House." Apparently feeling that the tension of an immobilized center required a stronger assurance than this, CNN anchor Aaron Brown took it upon himself to state the further "symbolic" reason why the president's return was imminent: to let the terrorists know that "what you haven't done is shut down the American government."[20]

But what followed was a new and unexpected development. Warned of a possible security risk, Bush abruptly flew off in a different direction entirely: first to Louisiana, then Nebraska, before finally returning to the White House that evening. Throughout these long hours, reporters and officials visibly struggled for some way to encompass this fact too—to fit it into some kind of coherent storyline. Their confused, convoluted language suggests how hard this was to do. Judy Woodruff told CNN viewers that "The president was on his way back to Washington from Florida. His plane touched down at an air force base in Louisiana, Barksdale Air Force Base near Shreveport." Somehow, a plane on its way from

Florida to Washington "touched down" at a point some 750 miles west of that route. On ABC, similarly, Peter Jennings said Bush had "made it as far as" Louisiana, as if this represented progress *toward* Washington rather than a course designed to avoid it. Apparently concerned that such motiveless explanations made no sense, Woodruff tried again: "That was an unplanned stop that the president made at that place in order to talk with reporters, meet with others."[21] This phrasing at least reassigned agency from the plane to the president. But the notion that Bush flew to western Louisiana "in order to" talk with reporters was absurd—members of the press are either traveling with him or in Washington—and the idea that he would go there to "meet with others" merely restated what was causing the tension. "The White House Situation Room," as CNN had earlier reported, "in the view of White House officials, is the best place from which to monitor events and direct any operations."[22] Then why wasn't the president going there?

Later reports were increasingly at pains to straighten out these narrative tangles. It was belatedly noted that the president's first layover was at "a military installation"—one of several "that is equipped, we were told, with a very sophisticated command and control bunker, very much like the equipment that would be available to the president here at the White House, in the White House Situation Room," and while there, "He was briefed." Even while airborne, Bush "has been in constant contact with officials back here, including members of the congressional leadership."[23] (On ABC Peter Jennings speculated that he was running a Cold War–style "command center in the sky."[24] What officials aboard Air Force One were actually doing, it later came out, was trying to get news from TV sets with spotty inflight reception.) And the White House, "of course, is fully operational, whether the president is there or not."[25] Granted, the complex had become "a virtual ghost town," but nonetheless the center was not left vacant: "national security team members are still in the White House Situation Room. And earlier today, at least, as of a little more than an hour ago, Vice President Cheney, as well, [was] directing operations and monitoring things from there."[26] A bit later this report was embellished with significant additional details:

> Vice President Dick Cheney has been in the White House, underground, in the White House operations center, the Situation Room, which is a fortified command and control structure, throughout the day, with other national security officials, receiving information from around the country and directing U.S. operations from there.

Though not actually in this fortified "command and control structure," Bush was present as well, in a sense: "We are told he is participating in a National Security Council meeting by telephone."[27]

The story as its characters themselves told it followed a similar line of development. In his first remarks, while still in Florida, Bush said that he had "spoken to the vice president, to the governor of New York, to the director of the FBI"—not to any immediate purpose, but "to help the victims and their families and to conduct a full-scale investigation." But goals like those were not immediately pressing.[28] His next statement, from Louisiana, was in a different key. Re-describing those same discussions, the president now stressed that they were immediate and urgent:

> I've been in regular contact with the vice president, the secretary of defense, the national security team and my Cabinet. . . . Our military at home and around the world is on high alert status, and we have taken the necessary security precautions to continue the functions of your government. We have been in touch with the leaders of Congress and with world leaders to assure them that we will do whatever is necessary to protect America and Americans.[29]

Later, a senior Bush aide in Washington raised the urgency level still further, changing the verb tense to present progressive: "President Bush *is conducting* a meeting of the National Security Council as we speak . . . he is in continuous communication with the vice president and key members of his Cabinet and national security team." Around the capital, a "secure facility," a "command center," and the Pentagon were all in use. But the reality of displacement—that people still were not really "in place"—reasserted itself as the spokeswoman stumbled: "[Officials] are meeting President Bush from his location and other members from different locations in Washington and other locations."[30]

A few days after the attacks, journalist Nicholas Lemann interviewed another senior aide, Karl Rove. The notes that Rove kept while traveling with Bush came close to giving a president's-eye view of the day:

> There's lots of fog-of-war rumors. There's a plane down near Washington, approaching from the south. The Pennsylvania plane. The plane in Kentucky. A Korean Air Lines plane forced down in the Black Forest. A hijacked plane down on the ground in Amsterdam. There's lots of this stuff. A car bomb at the State Department. . . .
>
> [Bush] Talks to [Defense Secretary] Rumsfeld. That's where it emerged that it was an American Airlines plane. Before that, there was

some question of whether it was a smaller plane, or whether it was a helicopter. One-oh-five, we get some intel from StratCom [intelligence from the Strategic Air Command] about a high-speed object that is headed toward the [Bush] ranch [in Texas].

Listening to this, "I was thinking that the Presidential party not only did not have better information than was available to those of us who were watching television at that moment but had worse information—or, anyway, more misinformation," Lemann wrote. Glib talk of control and disarray is common in political discussion, he added, but "[t]his time, that was a real question."[31]

In a moment of crisis like this one, what would *control* really mean? In no small part, it would be a matter of language—of finding words that seemed adequate to the shock of what was happening. This would include an appropriate language of moral condemnation, which also took a few days to settle into place.[32] But in the thick of events on September 11 itself, reporters and officials were fumbling just for a language of description, for words they could use with confidence in simply getting the story told. The terms and meanings they usually relied on seemed to be causing further confusion. For instance, *the White House* and *Washington* are casual shorthand for the administration and government, entities through which the nation normally exercises its power—as in "The White House announced today that . . ." or, "In Washington, officials have been meeting to . . ." But suddenly these stock metaphors had ceased to function. The terms reverted to literality, becoming for the moment mere place-names or, worse, targets—not capabilities but vulnerabilities. Anxious to have the conventional meanings restored, the "managers of meaning," as one critic called them, looked to Bush.[33] And despite, or because of, this deference to him, their exasperation when *he* proved hard to manage was palpable. With "freedom" seemingly undefended and the United States "on the run," ABC's Peter Jennings asked "whether or not the president is going to be seen in command in a more vigorous way." It is the president we look to "for some sense of political national stability," Jennings lectured, and therefore "the country is going to expect him to be back in Washington. . . . the president needs to be on station to talk."[34] On CBS, Dan Rather pointedly promised an update "on what President Bush has and has not been doing."[35] A leading character who fails to play the role the narrative assigns him will seem, in a sense, not to be doing anything at all.

After all this confusion, it was plainly a relief when Bush did eventually arrive back at the White House. The image of what had been missing now came into focus; reporters finally could describe in detail the scene that, in their earlier comments, had been struggling to emerge. Bush "will likely be joining the vice president and the national security advisor, Condoleezza Rice, in a room—what's referred to as a Situation Room—in the White House," said Campbell Brown, an NBC reporter, who then went on to explain:

> This is a wood-paneled room, extremely secure, in the basement of the West Wing. And in that room is a giant conference room. Around a big table there are ten chairs, there are about twenty chairs around the perimeter of the room, and there are two giant video screens that can open up where the president and his team can meet and essentially watch all of the communications coming in from around the country there—or around the world, rather. Right next to that conference room is a special communications center where four people are on staff twenty-four hours a day; military, State Department, intelligence, who are sifting through all the cables, all the information, providing them instantly to the president and his team. That's where the vice president has been all day with the national security advisor and other key personnel. In all likelihood, the president is joining there now—joining them there now to get an update before he addresses the nation.[36]

Here at last was that powerful center: the president in a room with a big table and giant video screens, surrounded by advisors and a constant stream of instant communications and other official activity. It was the image that had not been available earlier in the day, the one that reporters instead had labored to glue together like a mosaic from broken fragments—from all those vague assurances that Bush was still in charge despite his puzzling relocations and changes of plan.

Missing a Beat: September 11 and the Operations of Storymaking

Of course, those assurances had a basis in fact: presidents *do* have intelligence and communications facilities available almost anywhere they go. And reporters had repeatedly insisted that Bush had been in constant communication with those at the center. What, then, was so important about this further step, this mind's-eye ability to situate the president in the Situation Room? Just why *was* it such a source of anxiety when Bush and his aides were scattered instead at "various" and "other" locations? If we look again at the description above, we notice—along with the video screens and twenty-four-hour cable traffic—some curious details: the numbers of chairs, the room's wood paneling. If the point of this description is to reassure us that the president is back in charge, details like these are gratuitous; they don't add anything to the room's functional capabilities. And that is assuming that reporters even have the right room, which it seems that most of them did not: The big table where top officials actually gathered on September 11 was in the Presidential Emergency Operations Center, a different part of the White House complex altogether.[37]

What all this suggests is that *Situation Room* was not a physical place so much as a kind of stage direction, the name for a particular narrative setting. The term was used not to pinpoint a given room but to fill out the picture it made possible, a picture with the main character finally in place. For such purposes, nonfunctional details like wood paneling serve just as they would in a novel or screenplay. They add verisimilitude, helping to bring the scene to life. They are essentially *fictive* details, and the narratives they help construct are literary products:

> **Tuesday, September 11**
>
> Shortly after 9:30 p.m., President Bush brought together his most senior national security advisers in a bunker beneath the White House grounds. It was just 13 hours after the deadliest attack on the U.S. homeland in the country's history.
>
> Bush and his advisers sat around a long table in the conference room of the Presidential Emergency Operations Center, or PEOC. Spare and cramped, the bunker was built to withstand a nuclear attack, with sleeping berths and enough food for a few people to survive for several days.

Thus begins a long, multipart series in the *Washington Post*, "Ten Days in September," co-authored by the famous investigative reporter Bob Woodward.[38] It is striking that even though the series chronicles events beginning in the predawn hours of September 11, the narrative leads with the later image of the president and his advisors "around a long table." And again we are given purely scene-setting details, like sleeping berths and "built to withstand a nuclear attack." By the time Bush got there, and certainly by the time this later article reimagined the scene, these details were as irrelevant as wood paneling; no one was thinking in terms of nuclear attack. But the details were included to conjure an image and create a mood—a feeling of high-stakes urgency of the kind we expect from a good suspense thriller.

Indeed, the suspense thriller is a literary model on which narratives like these plainly drew. The Blue Ridge–based "alternative White House" that NPR's Bob Edwards had in mind was probably the Federal Emergency Management Agency (FEMA) compound at Mount Weather, Virginia, a massive 1950s-vintage nuclear bunker designed to house government leaders in a major crisis (and which was, in fact, activated on September 11). Since the government does little to publicize this facility—all reference to it was apparently removed from FEMA's website after the terror attacks—it is best known from fictions like *Seven Days in May* and, more recently, *The Sum of All Fears*, the film adaptation of a Tom Clancy novel.[39] Likewise the "command center in the sky" and other appurtenances of presidential crisis that reporters kept invoking on September 11. "It reminds one a little bit of what it was like in the Cold War," said Peter Jennings—or more accurately, what it's like in Cold War novels, movies, and TV dramas.[40] The president in crisis, the president hearing advice and taking charge at the head of the big table, are part of our cultural stockpile of images, members of a genre nearly as familiar to moviegoing and TV-watching Americans as paintings of the Last Supper were to Renaissance Christians.

Though examples reach back to the 1960s, several works containing variants of the big-table image bracketed the events of September 11. Four months earlier, NBC's drama *The West Wing* had concluded its season with episodes featuring President Jed Bartlet's management of a developing crisis in Haiti. The feature film *Thirteen Days*, in theaters during early 2001, had re-created John F. Kennedy's 1962 response to Soviet missiles in Cuba.[41] Both *The Sum of All Fears* and Chuck Norris's CBS-TV movie *The President's Man: A Line in the Sand* had "wrapped" production during the summer and appeared in the months following the attacks; both featured fictional presidents managing terrorist crises from Situation Rooms, bunkers, or airborne command posts. And in one especially interesting variant, the snowbound president in Rod Lurie's 1999 *Deterrence* had been forced to commandeer a Colorado diner for use as a makeshift Situation Room. Here was an image of displacement not unlike that of September 11—and, as would later happen in life, the displacement itself was treated as a problem; it was the circumstance that motivated most of the story's events.[42] The combined message of these

and many similar narratives was clear: A situation had better have a Situation Room. There is a certain orderly way that presidential crisis management is supposed to look, and any arrangement that does not match that expectation is, itself, a part of the crisis.

Americans' responses to crises had not always gravitated to that image. On those past occasions most closely analogous to September 11, things had been imagined quite differently. The al-Qaida attack was not the first on America or its capitals; in addition to Pearl Harbor and the British invasion of 1814—the parallels typically cited—the event conventionally known as "the Lincoln assassination" was more like the September 11 attacks than is usually recalled. Though the murder of Lincoln turned out to be its centerpiece and the only part that succeeded, the Booth conspirators' plot actually called for "decapitating" the U.S. government, as observers at the time quickly grasped (and as officials also feared on September 11).[43] Hence the attack was supposed to include simultaneous, coordinated strikes at multiple locations. The perpetrators, members of a cell operating in secret amid the vulnerable population, were fanatical adherents of an ideology and way of life to which, in their view, U.S. power was a mortal threat. And at the moment they struck, they appeared at least as seriously menacing to the United States as al-Qaida later would. Not only did they kill the president, but they attacked in the latter days of a vicious war, when the enemy's troops were still in the field and victory over them was not yet secure. Confederate agents had already been discovered trying to burn down New York City with "Greek fire," and Union forces had in fact recently burned Richmond, the Confederate capital. It was, then, at least as easy as it would be on September 11 to believe that much larger plots were afoot, that the survival of whole cities (at least) hung in the balance. On the night of April 14, 1865, New York indeed was placed on military alert, and Washington was put in a state of armed lockdown very similar to that of September 11, though patrolled by cavalry rather than fighter jets.[44]

That earlier crisis, too, had seemed to threaten chaos and loss of control. General William T. Sherman, a man at that moment in command

Left top and center: two dramas from early 2001; President John F. Kennedy (Bruce Greenwood) is informed of Soviet missiles in Cuba in *Thirteen Days*, and President Jed Bartlet (Martin Sheen) manages a fictional crisis in Haiti in *The West Wing*; *left bottom*: confusion in the real White House in the president's absence on September 11, 2001. (White House photo by David Bohrer)

of a huge army, had the sickening feeling he was "powerless" and wondered who "was left on this continent to give order and shape to the now disjointed elements of the government."[45] But here is where the two crises differ. Back then, news coverage and official statements all but ignored the question of who was available to give orders. The new president-apparent, Andrew Johnson, was not even mentioned until the last paragraph of the *New York Times* report. Government officials were depicted as neglecting him to conduct a vigil around the dying Lincoln, and the only "big table" decision making that the secretary of war's dispatch saw fit to mention was that which had taken place hours *before* the attack:

> At a Cabinet meeting, at which General Grant was present, the subject of the state of the country and the prospect of a speedy peace were discussed. The President [Lincoln] was very cheerful and hopeful, and spoke very kindly of General Lee and others of the confederacy, and of the establishment of government in Virginia.[46]

Strikingly, the narrative logic here is almost the reverse of that seen on September 11. Instead of seeking the calm, commanding center that would *answer* the chaos, this choice of gratuitous detail emphasizes the calm before the storm—as if worried that the reader might not fully appreciate how great the upheaval really was.

The president also figures quite differently in early twentieth-century crisis reports, including "news" of the Martian invasion of New Jersey on October 30, 1938. In this famous Mercury Theatre/CBS radio production, which Orson Welles modeled all too accurately on the news reporting styles of the day, the voice of governmental authority is not the president or White House, it's the secretary of the interior. Three years later, the real news broadcasts of December 7, 1941, followed a similar logic. If ever a president was apt to be looked to for calming words in a crisis, it was Franklin D. Roosevelt. Yet, in that day's improvised narratives, FDR seems like an afterthought. One early bulletin on

Left top: President Walter Emerson (Kevin Pollack, *seated center*) struggling to manage a global crisis from a snowbound diner in *Deterrence*; *left center*: President George W. Bush working from temporary headquarters in a Florida schoolroom at the outset of the September 11 crisis; *left bottom*: Bush finally back in place in the White House twelve hours after the attacks, as re-created (with Timothy Bottoms playing Bush) for the docudrama *DC 9/11: Time of Crisis*. (White House photo by Eric Draper)

CBS relied on a White House press release yet said surprisingly little about the president; its emphasis was on cabinet secretaries or generic "officials," and it spoke of actions "being taken," mostly in passive voice.[47] Somewhat more in the style of today's narratives was the next day's *New York Times* banner story, which said that the news of Pearl Harbor "fell like a bombshell on Washington" and mentioned the president's order to put the country on a war footing. Even there, though, the focus soon shifted to other agencies:

> This was disclosed after a long special Cabinet meeting, which was joined later by Congressional leaders. These leaders predicted "action" within a day.
>
> After leaving the White House conference Attorney General Francis Biddle said that "a resolution" would be introduced in Congress tomorrow. He would not amplify or affirm that it would be for a declaration of war.
>
> Congress probably will "act" within the day, and he will call the Senate Foreign Relations Committee for this purpose, Chairman Tom Connally announced.[48]

Further paragraphs listed measures taken by the secretaries of the treasury, war, and the navy, and even by the Civil Aeronautics Authority and one undersecretary, as if these agents were expected to act without central direction.

And even when the story finally returned to the White House, the reporter's focus was not on the president. It was on other high officials, the ones who made their way there to advise him. Whereas in post–September 11 stories the initiative was the president's (Bush "*brought together* his most senior national security advisers"), reporters in 1941 apparently assumed that Americans would want reassurance from government leaders in general: "Cheering crowds lined Pennsylvania Avenue to see them arrive, another evidence of the national determination to defeat Japan and her Axis allies which every official is confident will dominate the country from this moment forth." The president was seen in correspondingly passive terms, "closeted" with various officials and, in one case, unable to reach one who "was too busy to talk to the President even by telephone."[49]

Obviously, some of these narrative differences reflect real changes in political organization and the distribution of power since those earlier times.[50] However much the innovator, FDR himself was necessarily still viewed through expectations developed under earlier, less centralized regimes. The post–New Deal presidency was still taking shape, and the Cold War "imperial presidency" had not yet come into being. All that said, though, it still seems that more is required to account for a paragraph like this:

> Others present [at the special Cabinet meeting] were Speaker Rayburn, Representative Jere Cooper of Tennessee, representing Representative John W. McCormack, the House Majority Leader, who was not able to reach Washington in time for the conference; Chairman Sol Bloom of the House Foreign Affairs Committee and Representative Charles A. Eaton, ranking minority member; Vice President Wallace, who flew here from New York; Senator Allen W. Barkley, majority leader; Senator McNary and Senator Warren R. Austin, ranking minority member of the Foreign Relations Committee.[51]

It is very hard to imagine a reporter today doing so little to visualize the scene—simply listing participants, like some Old Testament chronicler, without at least trying to *picture* them as they deliberate around the big table. But the collective imagination had not yet been stocked with the requisite fictional and filmic images. What *was* available by way of marking important public moments were other images—for example, parades: the "cheering crowds" that materialized in the same story to greet the arriving officials.

On September 11, attention centered on a quite different drama of arrival. Narrating Bush's return to the White House "under very heavy guard," NBC's Tom Brokaw waited for the doors of the presidential helicopter to open:

> We do expect that momentarily he'll be exiting that helicopter and moving briskly into the Oval Office. . . . Secret Service detail exiting first. There were Secret Service offices and a number of other government offices in the World Trade Center. There's the president now walking to what will prove to be one of the longest and most important nights of his presidency back into the White House Oval Office. We do expect him to address the nation later.

In this silent parade across the White House lawn, what the news anchor's imagination substitutes for cheering crowds is a supposed interiority of character utterly absent from the Pearl Harbor reports. There is solicitude for a man who has had a "long and challenging day," as Brokaw puts it, together with an inventory of what might be in his mind, or even in his oedipal unconscious:

These are the kinds of days that you know in the back of your mind may occur when you become the president of the United States and the commander in chief when you're on the campaign trail. But the cold, hard reality has been visited on this president, one of the greatest national security crises this country has faced in many, many years within his first year in office. . . . His father, obviously, was president during the Operation Desert Storm, the Persian Gulf War. His father had been the ambassador to the United Nations, director of the CIA and vice president of the United States for eight years before he occupied the Oval Office.

Brokaw's narration concludes in the second person, rhetorically putting the viewer in the president's place: "There is very little in your experience as governor of Texas or even as a senator of the United States or almost any other job to prepare you for these kinds of occasions."[52]

However prepared or not he may have been, George W. Bush himself evidently did grasp the rhetoric of the narrative that had been constructed around him and the anxiety on which it turned. Worried because "the TV shows [that] our nation has been blasted and bombed," Bush explained later that he had seen his job as minimizing Americans' "angst"—in part by reassuring them "that I was safe . . . not me, George W., but me the president; reassuring that our government was functioning, and that we're going to take care of the American people." The tension, as Bush saw it, was between this "care"-ful functioning and a blasted, bombed nation, and by noon on September 11 he knew what he had to prove: "Government is not chaotic. It's functioning smoothly."[53] Since governing is the opposite of chaos by definition, Bush might seem here to be speaking in tautologies—expressing the same urge ("to let people know there *is* a government") that Mayor Giuliani had expressed more bluntly and acted on sooner. But what he may have grasped, if not as quickly as Giuliani, was that whatever might actually be happening, a government that has no existence within the narrative—that is not embodied in characters—will have no visible agency and, therefore, will seem not to be functioning at all. And to this he added the idea that proving otherwise was *his* function uniquely. Reimagining the day with himself at the center, Bush would later strangely claim that he had seen the attacks with his own eyes and had launched "emergency response plans" at a moment when he manifestly could not have.[54] His own post mortems on the event came close to equating "me the president" with government itself. Rhetorically, at least—and encouraged in this by spokespeople, commentators, and news anchors—he allowed the two to merge in a single, or single-handed, defense against chaos.

The difficulties of getting the story told on September 11 briefly brought the operations of storymaking to the surface. To review news coverage from that day is therefore to get a rare glimpse of those operations, to see what they look like as they unfold in "real time." The question was not just who was in charge in the immediate crisis or whether the government was functioning. Modern presidents can get advice and give orders from wherever they happen to be, and in any case, most of the decisions that had to be made on the day itself were in the hands of police and fire chiefs. The president's presence or absence, his correct placement where the received narrative said he should be, meant something else. It was quite explicitly cast as symbolic, as a proxy for what Peter Jennings called "political national stability"—the best chance for the nation "to create an impression, at least, of a quick return to normalcy," as a CBS correspondent put it (strangely invoking the spirit of Warren G. Harding).[55] Normalcy in this case meant, in part, a certain way of associating leaders with the nation and its people, a fictive equivalence in which the nation is conjured into being and then said to act through the agency of particular persons who metaphorically "represent" it—a term with both political and artistic meanings that, in the case of presidents, intersect. On September 11, this imagined equivalence of leader/ people/nation suddenly became a problem. The danger was not that the fiction would be exposed as such or the metaphor cease to function; in the 2000 election Bush had already survived a crisis of that kind.[56] The real danger was that it would function too well: A president on the run, it was feared, would mean that the nation itself was running for its life.

Returning to normalcy, then, depended on reasserting *artistic* control, the kind we expect at the hands of skilled storytellers. Such control is a matter of successfully negotiating the demands of a genre. When events "read" like the beginning of a kind of story we have seen before, we expect them to proceed from then on in a certain way. The clever novelist or filmmaker might play with such expectations, raising, manipulating, and thwarting them as needed to make a point or achieve an effect. But unless the work is self-consciously experimental, the genre exerts a pressure that keeps further story developments within a predictable range. Without this the story will seem to make no sense at all.[57]

The critic who aptly labeled news reporters and anchors "managers of meaning" also called September 11 "a day on which reality bested every representation of it."[58] But that is not quite correct. The machinery of representation, above all TV news, went to work at once, literally *media*-ting the horror through prevailing and well-known genres. Many observers were quick to compare the events to "something out of a Hollywood action movie"—a better description of their own active storymaking than those observers probably realized.[59] The problem was that the movie in question was a "bad" one. Defying the conventions of the genre, it failed to show the good guys winning or even to sound a Churchillian call to arms.[60] As those who drew such comparisons said, September 11 lacked the usual movie climax, the last-second thwarting of the evil plot by an action star like Bruce Willis or Arnold Schwarzenegger. In Hollywood, producers and screenwriters call such plot points "beats." What happened on September 11 was that the story was missing a beat.[61]

Or rather, it was missing two beats—the heroic climax and, for most of the day, a beat that might have read as follows in the outline for a film or TV thriller: "*At the White House, the president reviews the crisis with his top advisors and military chiefs. Warned of the likely dangers but determined to strike boldly, he gives the order to . . .*" Deprived of that beat, reporters and officials found the story of September 11 harder to "write" and "produce" than expected. When this happens, a storyteller has a couple of options. Since life might not imitate art, the choice of a genre through which to narrate real events must always be provisional, subject to change in light of further developments. If events prove recalcitrant and the first choice doesn't work, it might be possible to switch to some other genre. On September 11, though, other options were few. A president's misplacement or absence can itself be a story premise; fiction writers had furnished many examples before September 11. But the beats in those stories include good explanations—secret missions and the like—that also were not forthcoming in this case. Another possible story type, "Evil triumphs," was even worse. If that plotline was considered it was quickly abandoned, for obvious reasons: An incoherent story might cause some anxiety, but evil triumphing would cause even more.[62]

Unless incoherence itself is embraced, then, as it is in some avant-garde writing and art, the remaining option is to somehow fill in the missing beats. What we have seen here is how resourceful in doing this the managers of meaning can be, how rapidly they can renegotiate and even invent plot points in a dynamic interplay of teller and tale. If needed, the president's presence at the big table can simply be manufactured; he can be there at any time virtually, regardless of when he got there in fact. The efforts to manufacture this image in the hours of crisis itself were, at best, fitful and ad hoc. But later retellings managed the feat in a more polished way. For the first anniversary of September 11, an ABC News documentary reconstructed officials' response to the attacks using digital datelining and titling effects—the same effects often used in fictional thrillers to create minute-by-minute suspense. With the long day compressed into less than an hour, the problem of the president's whereabouts was cured; he was always in the next shot, just a camera angle or quick cut away. And for the second anniversary, a made-for-cable movie produced with White House cooperation took the final step, restaging the whole event with Bush in command throughout. Thus the cycle was complete: an image best known in the first place from films and fiction returned, in the end, to its source.[63]

"How Do We Model This?"
Narrowcasting, Recasting, and Virtual Realities

Those who struggled to assemble the story on September 11 by way of reporting it for television, or who re-created the events for TV and film docudramas in the years following, were working under what many analysts at the time liked to call an "old-media paradigm." By 2001, film and even TV qualified as traditional or "old" media, and the paradigm in question centered on the assumption that the media's contents would be manufactured at a few central sites—TV networks and Hollywood studios—and then delivered prepackaged to large masses of viewers/consumers, all of whom would absorb them in essentially the same passive ways. New media, it was often said, changed all of this, creating a new paradigm based on new and more complex transactions between consumers and media "content providers." By late 2001, "[t]he splintering of media platforms has companies scrambling to deliver entertainment and information on television, radio, the Internet, video game platforms, wireless hand-held devices and cell phones," the *New York Times* reported, while a review of media scholarship found widespread agreement that "the shift of symbolic representation to a global digital information network" was as pervasive and consequential as the shift from handwritten to printed text.[64]

In new media as in old, the September 11 attacks closed a circle:
planned in part using computer simulations, they inspired new simulations and video games in turn. The director of one U.S. military project
to develop "artificial intelligence" war games for use in anti-terrorist
training said that when he saw the attacks on television, "I started thinking right then, 'How do we model this?'" Already in the military's ar-
senal by 2001 was a complex multimedia role-playing game that "uses
storytelling techniques such as plot twists and compelling characterizations" to mimic political and military crises, complete with fictional TV
newscasts and presidential press conferences.[65] What was new about
such fictions (and what made them useful as training devices) was the
game-like element, the fact that the user's own decisions affected the
way the story unfolded. "Interactivity" of this kind, made possible by
computers' immense and rapidly growing capacity for storing and pro-
cessing data, was one leading feature of the new digital media.

Another was the greatly expanded access to information, and the sophisticated means for finding it, made possible by the Internet. Scarcely
known when the 1990s began, this vast, computerized communication
and distribution system was so heavily relied on by decade's end that
there were real fears—groundless, it turned out—that one simple pro-
gramming "bug" could wreak worldwide havoc when the calendar advanced to 01/01/00. As more and more undertakings of all kinds continued to move "online," there was no way to know how many new
capabilities would eventually arise from the Internet and its ubiquitous
interface, the World Wide Web. But one thing the new medium proved
to be as soon as it appeared was a powerful new means of "narrowcasting": tailoring artistic, political, and commercial messages to the small
but select audiences most likely to be interested in them.

Narrowcasting predated the Web; the term was popularized during the previous media "revolution," the spread of cable television and
home video in the 1980s. These were not new media but new models for
financing and distributing the old. Like public and "educational" television before them, and like the government-subsidized systems common
in other countries, cable and premium TV networks could support pro-
gramming that did not draw the huge mass audiences and high-paying
sponsors required on traditional broadcast TV. This allowed greater
scope for content that was commercially unpromising, whether because
it was politically controversial or irreverent, because it was experimental
or offbeat, or simply because it was worn-out (like reruns of old

commercial-TV series) or nonprofessionally produced (as on "public access" cable channels).

The World Wide Web carried these possibilities further. By radically lowering the costs of production and distribution, thus eliminating most "barriers to entry," it enabled narrowcasting of an ever narrower kind. Small companies and even individuals could now produce complex works and find audiences for them just large enough to make the effort worthwhile. At the same time, search engines could pluck even very obscure items out of billions of Web pages, fans could pass them around through links on personal websites or in expanding chains of e-mail, and buyers could find them in the same online marketplaces they visited in search of "big-media" books, movies, and music. And because the Internet is a "distributed network" with little central authority, it benefits, or at times suffers, from a complete lack of what traditional broadcast networks call "standards and practices," i.e., censorship. There are, therefore, essentially no limits on content. A video game that features aircraft attacking the World Trade Center and similar targets might prompt a boycott if sold through normal commercial outlets, yet a game like *New York Defender* can be produced and made available directly to "gamers" via the Web—as could *JFK Reloaded*, an "edutainment" product that allowed the player to try his own luck firing Lee Harvey Oswald's rifle at a simulation of the Dallas motorcade.[66]

Giving even the most idiosyncratic products a chance of finding a niche audience creates a big incentive for making them in the first place, and already by the mid-1990s the Web had inspired a proliferation of do-it-yourself literature and art in both traditional and new-media forms. Fictions written from otherwise marginalized perspectives could be sold as "shareware" to a market that existed only online, as one writer did with his gay-themed dystopian novel about a dangerous homophobe running for president. Other unconventional political writings were also published as "e-books," including one that claimed to be psychically channeled from interviews with the late John F. Kennedy.[67] As an open forum for all manner of personal confessions and obsessions, the Web was a medium well suited to the intimate political imaginings of the time—a quality put to many uses in the Monica Lewinsky affair, which became an early paradigm case of the new media's impact on American politics. The first bulletins of the scandal appeared on *The Drudge Report*, a Web log, or "blog," that would grow into a one-man, self-published online newspaper and gossip sheet. Pioneering a role that innumerable bloggers would soon embrace, *Drudge* claimed to be dishing dirt that the mainstream media knew about but were refusing to cover—thus pushing the scandal into the mainstream through a back door, as attention to it on websites and in Internet "newsgroups" and "chat rooms" prompted coverage in the conventional media. In the months following, further rumors, comments, hourly updates, and countless jokes, including many based on digitally doctored photos and artwork, continued to spread via the Net. The release of the special prosecutor's salacious report and accompanying documents online—"a $50 million peep show," as one prominent Democrat called it—caused overloads on the computer servers that managed the government's Web traffic.[68] Even a traditionally published book like *Poetry Under Oath,* the collection of "found poetry" composed from bits of grand-jury testimony, seemed very much an Internet-age product. It could appear in "real time," amid the scandal, and virtually alongside the grand jury transcripts it drew from thanks to their prompt Web posting. And it could inspire further Web-based efforts in turn—like Steve Hilton's *Under Oath: A Political Cantata for Tenor, Mezzo-Soprano and Independent Counsel,* an even more faux-dignified use of the scandal's verbal banalities.[69]

For all its technical sophistication, in some ways the Internet is not really new. Fast, cheap distribution, especially of political information, has "print culture" antecedents in the penny press of the nineteenth century and the political pamphleteering and committees of correspondence of the eighteenth. And even before that, quickly made mass copies or, we might now say, "printouts" of Luther's Ninety-Five Theses managed to spread from the church door at Wittenberg to the rest of Europe within a matter of weeks. Still, the Web seems to lend itself to creative if odd combinations of the political with the private and esoteric. Blogs can serve equally well as published personal diaries and as political broadsides, and inevitably the two uses sometimes fuse. Nothing that depends on print, moreover, can travel as fast as the political samizdat that now flies around the world by electronic mail. E-mail can also "hyperlink" to websites, and websites to each other, rapidly creating chains of reference and association that run through sources of the most varied kinds. These can range from the most respected and well established to the most dubious. In cyberspace everything is right next door to everything else, from the *New York Times* and the Library of Congress to the Ku Klux Klan (www.kkk.com) and the local neighborhood crackpot. The Web's "associative ethos," as it has been called, encourages promiscuous uses of information, a mixing and matching of ideas based not on how accurate they are but on how well they reinforce each other.[70] The Web is therefore an excellent medium for conspiracy theories and overheated caricatures. "The Clinton Body Count," for instance, which was popular on politically far-right websites in the 1990s, offered a portrait of the forty-second president more lurid than most pulp fiction. When they weren't watching underground videos about this cunning criminal mastermind, devotees could trade rumors or check the Web for updates on the dozens of murders he had orchestrated to cover his arms-dealing, cocaine-smuggling tracks.

The Internet was likewise friendly to intense political mockery. This, too, has a long pre-Internet pedigree; the comic playwrights of ancient Athens wrote on scrolls, not screens. But no earlier medium produced anything quite like "The George W. Bush Dance," a long string of goofy quasi-animated ("dancing") images of George W. Bush under the heading "dance and snort the night away." This website, presumably the work of the same anonymous auteurs who had earlier created www.cowdance.com, www.Jesusdance.com, and other such variants on the same gimmick, showcased the Web's contribution to the age of mechanical reproduction: the reproducibility of images, their gratuitous copying so they could be lined up like high-kicking chorus girls, was itself part of the joke.[71] Only slightly more conventional was *Hard-Drinkin' Lincoln,* Mike Reiss and Xeth Feinberg's series of Web-posted animated shorts. The episodes in this series followed a standard cartoon format, but harnessed that familiar structure to highly irreverent content. Hard-Drinkin' Lincoln was a horribly vulgar, comic-drunk Abraham Lincoln given to lounging around in his underwear and watching TV while his many stovepipe hats hung on a nearby coat rack. A typical episode from 2000, "Robot Trouble," has our antihero visiting a theme park that features an animatronic Lincoln like Disneyland's. Finding the portentous exhibit *"borrring!"* he decides to liven it up by pouring his bottle of firewater down the robot's throat. Unfortunately this blows the mechanism to bits, forcing Hard-Drinkin' Lincoln to stand in and improvise his own version of the patriotic spectacle for some visiting tourists. His quick succession of vaudeville turns includes an impression of Al Jolson, and thus we get the astonishing image of the Great Emancipator performing in blackface. The tourists are suitably scandalized, but they finally get something to applaud when, in the joke that would close every episode, John Wilkes Booth steps from the wings, derringer in hand, and drills a bullet hole through Lincoln's stovepipe-high forehead.[72]

Cartoon short subjects have been around since the days of silent movies, but it's hard to imagine *Hard Drinkin' Lincoln* absent the World Wide Web. Its distributor, Icebox Inc., provided this and other pay-per-view short features for tiny contributions on the order of 25 cents per download. Even more than theatrical shorts, the forerunners of this business model were the peep shows of bygone days. Indeed one thing the Web is proving to be is a latter-day penny arcade, an electronic version of the low-end emporia that once offered cheap access to an array of games, pornography, and other attractions. But now the arcade itself is not needed; the peep shows can be instantly located, accessed from any home or office, and spread "virally" through the electronic equivalent of word of mouth. They also invite interactivity: viewers or readers of online works can be given a chance to respond to them, whether by e-mailing the creator, rating or voting on the work, or posting reviews and comments. Viewers can even make their own creative changes: the Web is a readily searched profusion of text, photos, videos, and computer applications that, with the help of digital authoring tools that automate multimedia design and animation, can be manipulated, recombined, and put to new uses with relative ease. The movement to create "open source" games and software actively promotes such re-authoring, as do "wiki" sites that invite all comers to pool information and to judge or edit each other's work.

All this makes the Web fertile territory for collaborative production and creative recasting. Multiple-author fictions have been written before, but someone had to get them organized (as President Franklin Roosevelt himself did on one occasion).[73] Now a website can take on that task, and such texts can appear through gradual accretion from authors who may not even know each other's identities. At least one Cold War political thriller has been generated in this "write-a-long" fashion.[74] And in the hope that dispirited citizens might be re-engaged and campaigns for office democratized, there have been attempts to carry the same principle into real-life politics. Besides online fundraising, an increasingly important factor in major election campaigns, experiments in this vein have included "virtual primaries," a spoof TV program featured on a Democratic Party website, and Web competitions to develop home-brewed TV ads.[75]

Hard Drinkin' Lincoln relaxing at home (*top*) and doing a vaudeville turn in blackface (*bottom*).

Hosting as it does so many of these imitations, borrowings, parodies, and creative re-uses, the Internet can feel like a world of its own—one that touches the real world at countless points but is not identical to it. In this virtual world one can imagine recasting not just individual works, but reality itself. Again, the underlying concept is not new; fiction of all kinds has been creating virtual realities for thousands of years. But the Web allows for fictions that previously could not have existed or been carried to such lengths. An important example is the pseudo- or joke presidential campaign. This type of "work" is hard to classify by medium or genre because it can manifest itself in many ways. Sometimes an absurd imagined candidacy will provide the satirical premise for a specific short story ("The Cat in the Hat for President"), novel (*Hank Harrison for President*), movie (*Linda Lovelace for President*), cartoon ("Betty Boop for President"), or song ("Christ for President," "Snoopy for President"). Other campaigns are running jokes, as it were, used to fill out some serial form like a magazine column ("Will Rogers for President," *Life* magazine, 1928), radio show ("Eddie Cantor for President," NBC and CBS radio, 1930s and 1940s), comic strip ("Pogo for President," Walt Kelly's *Pogo*, 1950s), or TV series ("Pat Paulsen for President," *The Smothers Brothers Comedy Hour*, CBS, 1968). Once in a while the conceit spills over into reality. Cable-TV comedian Stephen Colbert, whose comic shtick is mimicking right-wing talk-show hosts under the watchwords *truthiness* and *wikiality*—meaning a preference for "virtual" (i.e., politically convenient) truths notwithstanding the fact that they happen to be wrong—declared that he would appeal to citizens' "Amero-centric passions" by campaigning for the 2008 presidential nomination in both major parties. While welcoming the possibility that "I could lose twice," in the end Colbert narrowed his sights to South Carolina's Democratic primary (because Republican filing fees were too high), and then was kept off the ballot altogether when the state's Democrats decided that he wasn't a legitimate candidate. Meanwhile, however, his fellow comedian Al Franken, a *Saturday Night Live* veteran who had become a host of left-wing political talk radio—and who had written a joke presidential memoir, *Why Not Me?*, imagining his own ignominious White House tenure—launched a serious campaign that made him the Democratic nominee for a U.S. Senate seat from Minnesota.[76]

Countless other comedians, nonpolitical celebrities, and fictional and cartoon characters have been teasingly touted for president over the years.[77] Even when no hats are thrown into actual rings, the joke has a way of growing more elaborate and, in its own way, politically serious. W. C. Fields's "campaign" may have been simply an excuse for his trademark one-liners (like "Political baby-kissing must come to an end—unless the size and age of the babies be materially increased"), but with the 1939 *Fields for President* it helped launch a now-familiar genre, the mock campaign manifesto.[78] The cartoon character Pogo's campaigns featured campaign buttons and comic press releases, and political jester Pat Paulsen launched his first campaign on *The Smothers Brothers Comedy Hour* with jokes that were also commentaries on the divisive issues of the late 1960s. ("A good many people feel our present draft laws are unjust," he once opined. "These people are called soldiers.") Before it canceled the dovish variety show, CBS-TV aired a mock campaign documentary, *Pat Paulsen for President*, with Henry Fonda narrating, in the weeks preceding the 1968 election. And Paulsen continued "running" and producing joke campaign paraphernalia for nearly three decades, including an assortment of materials released on digital compact disk.[79]

Digital media take mimicry like this a step or two further. Nothing stops a fake campaign or company from creating an "Internet presence" identical to that of a real one. In 2000 a D.C. Comics website promoting the presidential candidacy of Lex Luthor, the reformed ex-arch-villain of the *Superman* comic books, included a cartoon ad done in the familiar style of campaign TV spots.[80] The "Duke 2000" campaign, featuring a character from Garry Trudeau's comic strip *Doonesbury*, copied most of the features of real campaign sites: press releases, a video archive, updates on the campaign's progress, and photos in which the cartoon candidate "appeared" alongside real public figures like the Dalai Lama. A related collection of computer-animated shorts distributed via Web and DVD included Duke's similarly faked appearances on real television interview programs. These were made using 3-D animation and motion-capture technology; as one of the creators explained:

> We put together a very elaborate campaign with a couple million dollar budget through his inauguration speech (we're assuming he gets elected), and what you're seeing now is the beginning of the television part of that. Prior to the Larry King show we did a 35-city tour to major television markets of all their good[-]morning shows. Duke did three minutes on each of their shows, a live interview with the hosts, and a lot of the hosts did not understand that this was real and they didn't understand what his positions were going to be, and it was very funny, dangerous television. Being a Web company, we can take that material and

put it right back on the Web very quickly. We get to play off Web and
television.[81]

As the surreal possibilities multiply, one pseudo-candidate might even
challenge another. In a particularly strange instance of multimedia
synergy, two joke campaigns followed the lead of recent real-life presidential candidates by taking their contest to federal court. Riffing on
Budweiser beer's longtime slogan "the king of beers," the SABMiller
company mounted a 2004 ad campaign in which its competing Miller
brand "ran" for "president of beers." In addition to a series of TV commercials in which the "candidates" were seen in debate, the Miller campaign included events—at least one local radio station promoted Miller
by staging a live campaign rally—as well as various materials posted to
the Web, where at least two different "polling places" offered ballots listing not just Budweiser and Miller but some "minor-party" beers as well.

As the campaign spread, it was not always clear where the add-ons
and ancillary efforts were coming from. They may have been instances
of "stealth marketing"—illusions of spontaneous public enthusiasm actually concocted at corporate headquarters. Ironically, the Web's anonymous quasi-democracy had made such counterfeits easier to create; on
the Net, corporate marketing departments can easily pose as individual
fans or put up websites that look like the work of amateurs. Still, it's possible that some ordinary consumers had spontaneously decided to join
in on the joke. Either way, the gimmick took on a life of its own when
Anheuser-Busch, the brewer of Budweiser, responded with an unusual
attack. In a counter-campaign, it ran a series of ads on TV, radio, and
the Web that tried to discredit Miller's candidacy while accepting
Miller's basic conceit—that there is such a thing as an election for president of beers, and that Budweiser and Miller were the two opposing
nominees for that office. In one of these counter-ads, Budweiser's animated "spokeslizards" snidely critiqued the Miller debate commercials
as if they had been watching an actual candidates' debate. Miller
couldn't be eligible for the presidency of beers, they complained, because its South African parent company does not meet the constitutional requirement that presidents must be native-born citizens. This
claim provoked a real-life lawsuit from SABMiller, which tried to block
Anheuser-Busch from publicizing Miller's links to South Africa. (SAB
stands for "South African Breweries," which acquired the Miller brand
in 2002.) When a federal judge cleared the way for the campaign to

continue by ruling mostly in favor of Anheuser-Busch, the clashing statements from the two companies' spokespeople—in press releases posted, again, to their websites—also seemed straight out of real political campaigns. "In the end," said one, "America's beer drinkers are the ones to decide this issue, not the court."[82]

Two competing companies colluding to create an elaborate joint fiction may be a commercial advertising first. But it illustrates what can happen to truth in fictitious times. In an age of stealth marketing and the even more fraudulent "astroturfing"—the faking of grassroots political movements by new-media and other corporate lobbyists—the Miller/Budweiser face-off was a bit of comic relief. In essence, the federal court was asked to stop two talking lizards from declaring Miller ineligible for the presidency on the narrow grounds of national origin. That Miller might also be ineligible *because it's a beer* was not at issue, nor did anyone dispute the importance of opinions uttered by talking lizards. The case was not a challenge to the larger fiction but was conducted within it. And although it occurred in the shadow of a real presidential contest between two very conventional candidates, it implicitly posed the same question that comedian Al Franken had insisted Americans answer. If even a beer can run for president, well, then, *Why Not Me?*

Conclusion

{Your Name Here} *for President*

Throughout this book we have noted how new media and new modes of storytelling make possible new ways of imagining, yet without entirely replacing the older ways—which may still be called upon as a storyteller's taste or political purpose requires. The framers of the Constitution may have gestured toward realism, yet George Washington could still be viewed through heavy layers of neoclassical hyperbole. Abraham Lincoln's story may have called for character development and depth, yet later novelists could still construct presidents who were little more than walking, talking political manifestos. Incongruities like these are rife in the American political imagination. On the one hand, the United States was founded on a repudiation of divine right; on the other, it maintains the most theocratic politics of any Western nation, with presidents who are quick to claim God's favor and who describe their government in terms the Bible reserves for the deity.[1] Today's Americans can seem, at times, as politically mystified as ancient Egyptians convinced that society's chief task is building pharaoh a gigantic tomb. Yet they can also shop for bargains on bathroom tile at a "HUGE PRESIDENT'S DAY SALE!!!" or download computer images of the president digitally "morphed" into a pin-up girl. The wildly irreverent and the solemnly mythic, the old-fashioned and the multimedia-enhanced, all sit side-by-side within the artist's or citizen's easy reach.

The speed with which new possibilities emerge today from the cultural imaginary is well illustrated by the evolution of "President Barbie," a series of increasingly sophisticated repackagings of the Mattel toy company's iconic female doll. Barbie first appeared in the late 1950s and, for a long time, was primarily a one-foot-tall fashion model. But her changeable attire early on included nurse, flight-attendant, and student-teacher outfits, and as the years went by she acquired a broader and less stereotyped range of wardrobe-mediated careers, including astronaut, surgeon, business executive, and Marine Corps officer. By 1990 Barbie had been a UN diplomat and "ambassador for world peace," and in 1991 she was marketed for the first time as a possible president. Still, the original "Barbie for President Gift Set" emphasized Barbie's traditional role of facilitating young girls' dreams of grown-up glamour: Its Barbie had immensely long blonde curls and came dressed in a "star-spangled" inaugural ball gown with a big hoop skirt that made her look a bit like an American flag. A red suit was also included as an accessory, but even this was trimmed in unpresidentially flashy gold lamé.

A few years later a new set of Barbie for President accessories, including another suit, a campaign sign, and a doll-sized microphone, was added to a line of "Barbie Cool Career Fashions." Running for office thus joined a list of "fashion"-able Cool Careers that by this point included firefighter, judge, and ballerina. But by 2000 the campaign had become fully developed and multidimensional, with elements drawn from media both old and new. The Barbies that ran for president in 2000 and 2004 were packaged wearing business suits and working-day hairstyles; now it was the inaugural ball gown that was the add-on. There were African American and Latina as well as white versions of President Barbie, and the package included printed materials—a "Girls' Action Agenda," a "Girls' Bill of Rights," and quotes from a Barbie "speech" urging girls to aspire to be leaders. Developed in coordination with nonprofit groups that advocate for girls and promote women in politics, the campaigns also included publicity events modeled on political conventions, a real-life eleven-year-old girl serving as Barbie's campaign manager, and an elaborate website where Barbie's fans could vote to help decide on her platform, "track and follow the campaign's progress, learn the basics of campaigning and the electoral process, receive information about female political role models [and] possible leadership activities, and much more."[2] Barbie even had an opponent: In another example of competing marketers colluding in a shared fiction, a small startup company called the Get Set Club responded to Barbie's 2000 campaign by announcing the candidacy of its own doll, Vanessa, whose entourage included a racially diverse group of female dolls offered as a prospective vice president and cabinet. "We are against dolls that focus their achievement on looks and wardrobe," said the Get Set Club's founder by way of political attack on the front-running Barbie.[3]

Here again we see how new media lend themselves to the making of complex fictions, and even metafictions—newly imagined ways and means of doing the imagining. As a toy doll, Barbie is an example of one of the world's oldest and simplest mimetic devices. But she can also anchor a new kind of imagined universe, an expanding realm of stories impossible to locate in any one place or medium. Translated into, say, a video game, she can become an "avatar" or electronic virtual persona, standing in for and responding to commands from a player who can make her way through a developing story in the roles of author, reader, and main character all at the same time. Computer gamers and participants in digital simulations can watch events unfold under their influence but not their exclusive control, responding to imagined experiences while also, as in life, making decisions that expand or limit the routes through which the experience will play out.[4] By 2006 it was even possible for an actual presidential hopeful, Mark Warner, to send his avatar into virtual precincts in search of real votes.[5] Like a newly discovered continent, "cyberspace" had become a region of new and growing colonies, frontier provinces annexed to real life but also bordering the wider worlds of pure imagination.

Reinforced and accelerated with the help of the new digital technologies—but following, too, their own demystifying logic—the trajectories we have traced through the preceding chapters have brought us to a point at which the presidency seems available for reshaping to any imagined form and purpose. In theory, nothing had ever stopped Americans from imagining presidents in any way they wished. But the dialectic through which the fictions of authority operate, the slow process by which its mystique is constructed and deconstructed, seems to have kept the presidency unavailable for certain imaginative uses until now. It was a long time before presidents could readily be made "real" even in the very conventional terms of fictive realism, and a still longer time before they were fully embodied in fiction, with all the messy intimacy that the term *body* implies. But, ironically, imagining them as fully human freed them to become anything at all. A child, an animal, an android, a

Buddhist, a ghost, a detective, an agent of Satan, a talking head preserved in a glass jar—all these have been depicted as presidents, while the scheming cabal has been played by invading space aliens, by scientists cloning a lost president, and by political techno-wizards channeling public opinion through a microchip in the president's brain. President Barbie is just an exceptionally literal instance of a trend toward the ever more *plastic*, a condition in which nothing is beyond imagining and fictions can be made to order in pursuit of the most idiosyncratic visions and aims.

Equally eccentric and eclectic are the new uses of real-life presidents. Recent works have reimagined John F. Kennedy as a crusty old cynic in a wheelchair, Warren G. Harding as a leather-suited rock-opera singer doing battle with a giant crab (not to mention snorting cocaine in the Oval Office with Alexander Hamilton and Napoleon Bonaparte), and George W. Bush as a black "brother" re-enacting Iraq War lowlights in trash-talkin' hip-hop argot.[6] Genre conventions and boundaries have also been challenged: Karen Finley's *George & Martha*, with its explicitly imagined affair between George W. Bush (wearing stars-and-stripes body paint) and homemaking entrepreneur Martha Stewart, was conceived as a musical, then produced as a "transgressive performance," and published as an illustrated novella. The Imagination Liberation Front's *I'm Going to Kill the President* was subtitled *A Federal Offense* because that is what it literally claimed to be; the stage play was enveloped inside a work of performance art, with audience members conducted to it in secret and, at one point in the show, encouraged to shout the title threat over an open cell-phone line to the White House.[7]

But if, as its creators declared, *I'm Going to Kill the President* was "punk post-modernist," so in a sense are any number of works today even if they don't lay claim to that label. *Postmodernism* is sometimes defined as a ransacking of the cultural storehouse, a playful willingness to make artistic use of whatever comes to hand. Retrieved, remixed, and applied to new uses and contexts, older styles become raw material for contemporary pastiche. Thus Irving Berlin's *Mr. President*, the 1962 Broadway musical that eschewed actual politics and made little impression in its time, was rewritten and revived Off-Broadway as politically topical satire for the Clinton era, while its musical motifs were borrowed for Phyllis Lind's *I Love You, Madam President*, which crossed them with the gender-switching premise of another vintage comedy, *Kisses for My President*. And *Kisses* was mined again a few years later for the short-lived TV drama *Commander in Chief*, which cast Polly Bergen—who had starred in *Kisses* as President McCloud—to play the mother of Geena Davis's President Mackenzie Allen.[8]

The urge to tweak, twist, and refashion reality also manifests itself in the vogue for "alternate history," fiction devoted to imagining the world as it might be if the past had gone differently or could somehow be changed. Such works have been popular enough in recent years to generate a very long list of possible alternative realities, many of which involve reimagined presidents. Some of these, like the short stories in the 1992 anthology *Alternate Presidents*, are primarily intellectual exercises— thought-experiments like "What if Benjamin Franklin had been the first president?" and "What if Victoria Claflin Woodhull, the suffragist and first woman to run for president, had actually won in 1872?" Others aim to underscore the importance of some real event by contrasting it "counterfactually" with what might have happened instead, and still others are frolics in historical irony, attempts to posit startling yet logical differences that might follow from a change at a single historical flash point. On the 1995–2000 Fox TV series *Sliders*, for example, a group of adventurers sucked by accident into a hyperdimensional portal of some kind found themselves "sliding" each week from one parallel world to the next, in the process discovering present-day alternate Americas ruled by British kings, Soviet commissars, and President Oliver North of Iran-Contra fame.

Likewise but far more elaborately, one leading alternate "historian," Harry Turtledove, has written a multivolume series of novels chronicling the South's victory in the Civil War and its many twentieth-century consequences, among them the election of Virginia native Woodrow Wilson as president—of the Confederate States of America. Other alternate histories have posited alternative Cold Wars, pitting Germany against Japan (after an Axis victory), or a Germany that vanquished the Soviets against a United States led in the early 1960s by "President Kennedy" (who, it turns out, isn't JFK but his *father*, Joseph P. Kennedy, a soft-on-Hitler seeker of détente). In still other such flights of fancy, JFK survives his attempted assassination, FDR survives an attempted assassination thanks to a young JFK, and JFK and Bill Clinton switch places in history, with Clinton the assassinated martyr and JFK the disgraced womanizer. Kennedy seems to be a particular fascination of alternate historians, as are the Civil War and World War II. The imaginative replaying of World War II has become such an industry that a 2005 survey, *The World Hitler Never Made,* catalogued no fewer than 116 fictions, films, TV productions, and nonfiction books and essays in this vein.[9]

With their suggestion that history itself is endlessly plastic, alternate histories hand the Oval Office keys to historical might-have-been presidents ranging in plausibility from Aaron Burr and Davy Crockett to Elvis Presley and Marilyn Monroe. They are also obvious vehicles for making political points. R. Emmett Tyrrell's 1997 *The Impeachment of William Jefferson Clinton,* for instance, was as much a political tract as a novel, imagining—a year before the actual impeachment—how the "vast right-wing conspiracy" that Tyrrell had helped mount against Clinton might finally succeed. From the other side, Peter Delacorte's 1998 *Time on My Hands: A Novel with Photographs* spun a tale of two present-day political liberals, a writer and a physics professor, scheming to save the nation from Ronald Reagan's presidency by time-traveling to 1930s Hollywood and derailing the young Reagan's early career. And in his 2004 *The Plot Against America,* Philip Roth offered his own childhood memoir with a startling twist. In this imagined young Philip's America, Charles Lindbergh becomes president in 1940, cozies up to Hitler, and enacts his own frightening but not-quite-final solution to America's "Jewish problem." Roth's and Delacorte's novels were especially intriguing examples of recent efforts to revisit the question prominent in fiction from the decades they describe: What difference can a president make in ordinary people's lives, and how can their concerns affect him? *The Plot Against America* focused on the tensions a President Lindbergh might have caused within one extended family and ethnic enclave, while *Time on My Hands* suggested that a president's dire effect on the country needs to be addressed long before his presidency occurs. And for that, a time machine really comes in handy.

As noted in chapter 6, the popular TV series *The West Wing* was in essence an alternate history—the saga of a fictional presidency written and told in real time over a seven-year period. As such it developed its own internal past, a history parallel to and intertwining with the history we know. In one episode in early 2004, a documentary film crew followed President Bartlet's press secretary through a typical White House workday. The result was a program within a program: scenes alternated between the "reality" being filmed and bits of the finished TV documentary, with voice-overs by the narrator of the real PBS documentary series *Frontline.* Like *Tanner on Tanner* that same year, the episode told the story of a story being told, with one fiction purportedly "documenting" another. Self-referential tricks like this are an old device, but they mark a new phase in the fictionalizing of presidents. At some point the fictions take on their own history. In another variant of the so-called postmodern turn, it becomes possible to take an imagined look back on events that were wholly imagined in the first place. History can be rewritten, in retrospect, with bits of fiction inserted here and there. *Tanner on Tanner* pretended that the 1988 Democratic primaries had actually included a candidate named Jack Tanner (as chronicled in its predecessor series *Tanner '88*); *The West Wing*'s pseudo-documentary situated Jed Bartlet's White House within a real history reaching back to Dwight D. Eisenhower's; and the WB network's *Jack & Bobby* framed its present-day story of two teenage brothers as a preview of what the world of the future would regard as history after one of the brothers had grown up to be president.[10]

Along the same lines, fictions of the past can be treated as history for purposes of a story to be told now. Actor-director Robert Redford, who played a young Senate candidate in Michael Ritchie's 1972 satire *The Candidate*, reportedly had plans to make a sequel depicting the same character's presidency in the 2000s. And inevitably the fictions and jokes become subjects of fiction themselves. One character in Michael Crichton's 2004 novel *State of Fear* is a politically liberal Hollywood actor who, as it happens, plays the president in a TV series. That is, he is obviously modeled on *The West Wing*'s Martin Sheen. Given how often Crichton's novels get made into movies, there was a good chance that Americans would have a chance to see a movie actor playing the novel's actor based on a TV actor who played a president. In the meantime, Barry Levinson's 2006 film comedy *Man of the Year* offered comedian Robin Williams playing a comedian whose gimmick is mimicking a political news commentator, and whose joke campaign for the White House—unlike the "real" joke campaigns mounted by comedians playing political commentators—miraculously wins, making him the real president-elect. Or so it seems, until this, too, turns out to be (probably) another illusion.[11]

In themselves, criss-crossings and mutual borrowings between reality and fiction are not postmodern or even, for that matter, new. We have seen versions of this same interrelationship as far back as Alexander Hamilton's complaint that criticisms of the proposed presidency were coming "from the regions of fiction." It might not altogether surprise

Hamilton that the White House would one day be occupied by a former actor, a man who sometimes confused real events with scenes from movies; or that a presidential candidate would make TV ads featuring a fictional president in a mini-docudrama; or that retired politicians would write novels, including alternate histories, with one ex-president having recently fictionalized another; or that a novelist would imagine a dummy figure of Lincoln coming to life and having to learn who he is by reading his own mythic story in books; or that Michael Crichton would be called to testify before Congress as an expert on global warming because he had written a novel on that theme.[12] Even run-of-the-mill political campaigns, to a large degree, have long been exercises in fashioning characters and framing an opponent's claims as so many made-up stories.

If anything has recently changed, if we have now entered a postmodern moment—or "hypermodern," which would really be the better word—it's in the sense that the realities to be represented or fictively manipulated are, themselves, already permeated by fictions. When Howard Dean ran for the Democratic presidential nomination in 2003–4, for instance, it did not go unnoticed that he bore some resemblance to the fictional President Bartlet. At Dean's campaign rallies,

> actor Martin Sheen takes the stage to introduce Dean. Sheen plays President Josiah Bartlet on NBC's *The West Wing*, which the Dean campaign has adopted as its model. Bartlet was a brainy, hard-nosed governor of New Hampshire; Dean was a brainy, hard-nosed governor of Vermont. Bartlet's campaign called itself "Bartlet for America." Dean's campaign calls itself "Dean for America." Lately, Sheen has been stumping for Dean, as though Bartlet's imaginary presidential authority should carry weight in the real world. "As the acting president of the United States," Sheen begins, and the crowd whoops with delight.[13]

Dean was also widely viewed as the first Internet candidate, a pioneer in the use of new, high-tech methods for raising funds and helping supporters connect with each other. This "peer-to-peer politics," one commentator suggested, "could narrow-cast the Dean message, doing to the Dean campaign what fan fiction does to *Harry Potter*: [Supporters] could create their own narratives and highlight their own issues and points of emphasis." But the danger, he added, was that candidates could also lose control of their own strategies, with arguments arising about which campaign messages were "authentic." Newly empowered voters might be inclined to ignore the candidate's own intentions and assume that

"It's all about us!" as one "Deaniac" recruited through the Internet was quoted insisting.[14]

Dean's campaign eventually fell short, and as the first decade of the new century wore on, it seemed unwise to bet that presidential politicking would change very abruptly—yet equally wrong to suppose that it wouldn't ultimately change, just as it had earlier changed under the impact of television. "Web culture" encouraged consumers to voice their opinions and consult those of other "users" on products and experiences of all kinds, and political opinions were bound to be swept into the same streams. But the new technologies may not have been causing the change so much as ushering it along, mediating the emergence of new assumptions toward which other cultural developments were also pointing. It had long been an article of American faith that any kid could grow up to be president, but by the 2000s there seemed to be a growing interest in imaginative enactments of this notion, in stories and other mediated experiences based on the premise that we can no longer know with any confidence what qualities are and are not "presidential." Uncertainty on that point was the whole premise of *Jack & Bobby*, which treated the question of which teen brother would grow up to be president as a toss-up—not because we didn't know the kids, but because we could not say which contrasting personality type would lend itself better to the future role. Similar questions lay behind *American Candidate*, a Showtime cable network "reality" show, also from 2004, that featured ten contestants "running for president" through a series of weekly contests and elimination rounds. The eventual winner was a white male Republican, but the original group was diverse enough that at least four of the ten did not even meet the eligibility requirements to run in real life.[15]

So when Barbie campaigned on the slogan "You Can Be President!" she was expressing a general cultural message of the time. Barbie's role had always been to help children imagine their own grown-up futures, and "president" joined her menu of offerings at the same time that children's books were asking young readers *So You Want to Be President?*, telling the tale of *The Kid Who Became President*, and offering the means to *Make Your Own President*.[16] In an age when tourists at the White House can become "President for a Day," or deliver their own "inaugural addresses" at Philadelphia's National Constitution Center, it was not surprising that one of the Web's many new "social networking" sites would call itself "U4Prez.com" and propose to bring users together not just to chat or flirt, but to debate and compete in the imagined guise of presidential candidates. "It's all about us!" was more than a political assertion—it was a philosophical one, part of a new claim to the reality and authority of private imaginings even apart from their relationship to the mechanisms of power.

Whether such claims were an advance for democracy or merely narcisstic was another question. In a quote that gained new currency by circulating through blogs and e-mail, H. L. Mencken had once observed that aligning the presidency with "the inner soul of the people" would mean turning it over to a downright moron.[17] Complaints like that were widespread by 2008. One critic expressed annoyance at the "bizarre" obsession with how candidates really felt: "I want a president who is better than I am, not one who makes me feel better about myself. That's what Oprah's for." Another complained of "me fatigue" and berated voters for thinking and talking about themselves like adolescents on a first date. "But enough about us, what about the candidates?" she wisecracked.[18] The hip, Internet-powered candidate of 2008 was Barack Obama, and satirists had particular fun with Obama's supporters— who were seen, for all their new-media savvy, as pathetically dependent on fantasized intimacies with their hero:

> BARACK OBAMA FOLDED YOUR LAUNDRY
> BARACK OBAMA BOOKMARKED YOUR WEBSITE
> BARACK OBAMA SET YOUR VOICE AS HIS RINGTONE
> BARACK OBAMA CARRIES A PICTURE OF YOU IN HIS
>   WALLET
> BARACK OBAMA LEFT A COMMENT ON YOUR BLOG

Rotating through a website called *Barack Obama Is Your New Bicycle*, these and similar reassurances quietly mocked the conflating of political and private affiliation, the tendency to confuse endorsement with endearment, that appeared to be playing at least some role in Obama's early success.

With less irony, another website also inspired by the 2008 Democratic primaries invited visitors to describe dreams they had had about the candidates: "I had a dream that Hillary Clinton was trying to seduce me, and it worked a little. I was thinking, she's never looked more beautiful, her eyes shining in the light. Eventually, we went shopping for Tupperware." Dozens of other such dreams poured into the site by e-mail. Recording political dreams had been done before, but the blogger who sponsored *I Dream of Hillary . . . I Dream of Barack* presented the effort as the "world's first metaphysical poll," an exploration of what the candidates' role in the "collective unconscious" could reveal "about where they might lead us"—as if the voting franchise had now been extended to the id.[19]

Back in the actual heyday of Tupperware, the inaptly named Marx Toys manufactured a line of American presidents in plastic: tiny, stiffly posed mini-statues that were distributed for a while as grocery store promotions, like dish sets and volume-a-week encyclopedias. The idea was to collect all the presidents and display them on a miniature Styrofoam rostrum ringed with neoclassical columns. Today it's almost as hard to imagine playthings like these as it would have been in the 1950s and 1960s to imagine President Barbie, let alone the public posting of candidate-inspired dreams. The Marx figurines were presidents you went shopping *for*, not with, and then only so you could put them (literally) on a pedestal. Their message certainly was not that *you* could be president; it was that these particular middle-aged men already *had* been, leaving the rest of us just to install and admire them in their pint-sized pantheon. What "completed" the presidency was not projecting yourself into it but merely assembling the whole set.

Today citizens receive a very different message, an invitation to make of the presidency what they will. Even granting how tightly actual power in the United States is still tied to wealth and class, this is a dramatic change in just one generation. But it is also not the work of just one generation. The shape-shifting, "user-defined" plastic presidency we see today is the product of more than two centuries, the latest phase in Americans' long history of staking imaginative claims on the office— and, thus, on the nation itself. The framers who first conceived of the presidency placed it within a larger constitutional design, within which they thought it would have well-defined aims and limits. But the process of imagining, once begun, is open to all. And the limits on it are largely self-imposed. We may not all wish to be president, even in our imaginations. But because we have imaginations, we are all framers.

Notes

Introduction

1. Leopold, "Learning from the Masters."
2. Whitman, "Death of Abraham Lincoln."
3. Anderson, *Imagined Communities,* especially chaps. 2 and 3.
4. Auerbach, *Mimesis.*
5. E. S. Morgan, *Inventing the People,* 13, 14.
6. Among selected examples of the cultural histories I'm referring to are D. Greenberg, *Nixon's Shadow*; Peterson, *Jefferson Image in the American Mind* and *Lincoln in American Memory*; and Schwartz, *George Washington.* See also Spragens, *Popular Images of American Presidents.* Cultural-historical studies of events or institutions include Schudson, *Watergate in American Memory*; Biel, *Down with the Old Canoe*; and Kammen, *Machine That Would Go Of Itself.* Some recent examples of cultural histories focused on character types are Nash, *American Sweethearts*; Harkins, *Hillbilly*; Prothero, *American Jesus*; and Huhndorf, *Going Native.* Since *cultural studies* has come to refer to a wide range of projects, I should also note that my use of the term is modest and refers merely to an interest in the interconnections among various literary forms, media products, and social and political phenomena. It is not meant to invoke the more extreme claims—about the radical constructedness of all reality, the illegitimacy of science, the ubiquitousness of power and oppression, and so forth—that are sometimes included under that label or imputed to it.
7. See the discussion of this point in chap. 1.
8. Kantorowicz, *King's Two Bodies,* 3–5, and chap. 7, sec. 2. See also E. D. Morgan, *Inventing the People.*
9. *Bush v. Gore,* 538 U.S. 98, 121 (2000).
10. Recent lists of fictional presidents and candidates on *Wikipedia,* the online encyclopedia, run to dozens of pages and are the work of many contributors, yet even so are nowhere close to complete. See the links at http://en .wikipedia.org/wiki/Fictional_Presidents.
11. These novels are discussed further in chap. 5 and the conclusion.

292 ❖ *Notes to pages 11–18*

12. Other current terms for the objects of critical study include "signify-ing" or "discursive practices," "cultural productions," "performances," and "social texts." Mikhail Bakhtin—whose landmark work on "carnival" will come into play in chap. 2—offered theories and methods meant to apply not just to literature, but to "consciously parodic representations across a range of signifying practices." Graham Pechey, quoted in Dentith, *Bakhtinian Thought*, 84.

Chapter 1. Imagining a President

1. See Leo Marx, "Shakespeare's American Fable," 34–72.

2. Swift is quoted in Kramnick, *Bolingbroke and His Circle*, 212. On the office of prime minister see Keir, *Constitutional History of Modern Britain*, chap. 5. The Tory opposition attached the term *prime* minister to Walpole by way of criticiz-ing his alleged arrogation of power. Keir notes (282) that the term was occa-sionally used earlier, but standard lists of prime ministers—like the one at the British prime minister's official website—begin with Walpole in 1721.

3. Bolingbroke is quoted in Kramnick, *Bolingbroke and His Circle*, 28, 34, 212, 228. The quote is from Bolingbroke's "Dissertation Upon Parties" of 1733–34.

4. Bolingbroke, "Idea of a Patriot King," December 1, 1738. The Tories' view of parties was complex; they were themselves a party, and Bolingbroke was an early advocate for the notion of a regular, organized parliamentary op-position. But the still higher ideal was the Patriot King. See Kramnick, *Boling-broke and His Circle*, 153–63.

5. Walpole was the target of any number of satirists of the period, includ-ing others besides John Gay who wrote stories paralleling him to famous crim-inals. Swift and Henry Fielding both made him tiny, Swift by placing a Wal-polean character in Lilliput, and Fielding, in one of several attacks, by likening him to the mythical Tom Thumb. In a counter-satire, one pro-Walpole pamph-let complained that "Railing at Great Men" had become an art form in itself, and Walpole's government responded to the continued irreverence by cracking down on stage plays with the 1737 Licensing Act. See Beasley, "Portraits of a Monster," 406–31; and Bywaters, "Gulliver's Travels," 717–40.

6. C. F. Burgess, introduction to Gay, *Beggar's Opera*, x–xi. See also Schultz, *Gay's Beggar's Opera*, 63, 108; and Hoile, *Wholenote Magazine*. For a discussion of the "Robinocracy" as it was perceived in America, see Duban, "Robins and Robinarchs," 271–88.

7. Burgess, introduction, xi.

8. Quoted in Kramnick, *Bolingbroke and His Circle*, 31. Although its roots are in Jewish mysticism, the term *cabal* acquired its now-common meaning from English Restoration politics, partly because of its similarity to "cabinet" and partly as an acronym: Its five letters were also the initials of five prominent royal councilors of the 1670s.

9. Bolingbroke, "Idea of a Patriot King."

10. Bernard Bailyn argues that the Tory opposition's "ideas, these beliefs, fears and perceptions, became primary elements of American politics in its original, early eighteenth-century form: primary in the sense of forming assumptions and expectations, of furnishing not merely the vocabulary but the grammar of thought, the apparatus by which the world was perceived . . . the colonists soaked up the protest literature of the opposition and incorporated its main propositions into their basic perceptions of public life." Bailyn, *Origins of American Politics*, 53–54; see also 31–58; and Bailyn, *Ideological Origins of the American Revolution*, chaps. 2 and 3. According to Bailyn, the notion of a cabal or "conspiracy" against liberty had, if anything, "heightened meaning" in America. *Origins of American Politics*, 13, and chap. 1. Daniel Lazare agrees that Bolingbroke's "Country" party (the opposition to Walpole's "Court" party) was even more influential in America than in Britain. Bolingbroke "was considered essential reading by John Adams and Thomas Jefferson" and "the crucial intellectual figure in this period," and his Patriot King idea "would prove highly important in the creation of the American presidency." Lazare (citing Kramnick, *Bolingbroke and His Circle*, 262), *Frozen Republic*, 25, 27, 28. (Lazare's book is largely a critique of this influence and its consequences.) According to Ralph Ketcham, "Most important in determining the shape of the early presidency, the moral and public philosophy articulated by Pope, Swift, Bolingbroke, and their allies in opposition to Walpole became standard opinion among those in power in the new United States and loomed large in American consciousness until well into the nineteenth century, as we have noted." Ketcham, *Presidents Above Party*, 207, and chap. 10. For detailed reconstructions of the framers' concerns, see also Thach, *Creation of the Presidency*; and Rakove, *Original Meanings*, esp. chap. 9, "Creating the Presidency."

11. James Madison [Publius, pseud.], "The Conformity of the Plan to Republican Principles: An Objection in Respect to the Powers of the Convention Examined" [*Federalist* 39], in Rossiter, *Federalist Papers*, 241.

12. James Madison, "Vices of the Political Systems of the United States" (spring 1787), quoted in E. S. Morgan, *Inventing the People*, 52n27.

13. These notions were controversial and much debated at the time; it was not clear, for instance, whether hereditary or elected rulers were more likely to be "sufficiently neutral," whether neutral power was more or less likely to become absolute, and, as Madison himself acknowledged (and famously discussed in *Federalist* 10), whether large republics like America were more or less given to these vices than smaller ones. For one discussion of these issues, see E. S. Morgan, *Inventing the People*, especially chap. 2, "The Enigma of Representation." For relevant documents of the time, helpfully introduced and annotated, see Kurland and Lerner, *Founders' Constitution*.

14. Discussions of these changing traditions and differing styles in literature and oratory can be found in Fliegelman, *Declaring Independence*, especially

28–35; Gebauer and Wulf, *Mimesis,* especially chap. 9; Cmiel, *Democratic Eloquence,* especially chap. 1; and Watt, *Rise of the Novel,* especially 9–30.

15.   Watt, *Rise of the Novel,* 18, 28, 15.

16.   Cobley, *Narrative,* 77–81. Rachel Carnell has recently traced the conventions of realistic characterization in English fiction to specific rhetorical devices used in Whig and Tory political theorizing and pamphleteering during the early eighteenth century. The prevailing mode of realism, she argues, reflects the victory of Whig conceptions over Tory. Carnell, *Partisan Politics.*

17.   Benjamin Franklin, June 2, 1787, in Madison, *Notes of Debates,* 51–55.

18.   Elbridge Gerry, July 25, 1787, in Madison, *Notes of Debates,* 368.

19.   Franklin, in Madison, *Notes of Debates,* 55.

20.   The Federal Farmer [pseud.], *Poughkeepsie* [NY] *Country Journal,* January 17, 1988, Letter 14, *Anti-Federalist Papers,* http://www.constitution.org/afp/fedfar14.txt.

21.   An Old Whig [pseud.], "The Powers and Dangerous Potentials of His Elected Majesty," *New-York Journal,* December 11, 1787, in Kurland and Lerner, *Founders' Constitution,* vol. 3.

22.   "Debate in the Virginia Ratifying Convention, June 5, 1788," in Kurland and Lerner, *Founders' Constitution,* vol. 3, emphasis added.

23.   Alexander Hamilton, "Concerning the Constitution of the President: A Gross Attempt to Misrepresent This Part of the Plan Detected" [*Federalist* 67], in Rossiter, *Federalist Papers,* 407, 408, 411.

24.   Ibid.

25.   Alexander Hamilton, "The Duration in Office of the Executive" [*Federalist* 71], in Rossiter, *Federalist Papers,* 431, 434–35.

26.   Alexander Hamilton, "The Same Subject Continued, and Re-Eligibility of the Executive Considered" [*Federalist* 72], in Rossiter, *Federalist Papers,* 437.

27.   Hamilton, "Same Subject Continued," in Rossiter, *Federalist Papers,* 438.

28.   Hamilton, "The Duration in Office of the Executive" [*Federalist* 68], in Rossiter, *Federalist Papers,* 414.

29.   Scholes and Kellogg, *Nature of Narrative,* 88, emphasis added.

30.   This development has been much discussed, for instance in Watt, *Rise of the Novel*; Cobley, *Narrative* (see notes above); and Auerbach, *Mimesis,* especially chaps. 16–20. Auerbach's views, in turn, are discussed and critiqued in Gebauer and Wulf, *Mimesis,* chap. 1.

31.   Auerbach, in Gebauer and Wulf, *Mimesis,* 292, 434.

32.   Ketcham, *Presidents Above Party,* 29, 207: "Although [Alexander] Hamilton mustered a powerful interest on behalf of his Walpolean programs and was himself quite comfortable with their ethic, oppositionist ideas remained strong, even among Federalists."

33. Cope, "How General George Outlived His Own Funeral Orations," 93.

34. Ibid., 81–82.

35. Corry, *Life of George Washington*, 193.

36. Humphreys, *David Humphreys' "Life of General Washington,"* 54–56. Humphreys' biography had never been published in its entirety, although parts of it appeared in various sources as early as 1789 (see Rosemarie Zagarri, introduction, xxvii.).

37. Ramsay, *Life of George Washington*. Chaps. 11 and 12 deal with Washington's presidency; the quote is from chap. 12.

38. Ibid.

39. Ibid.

40. Marshall, *George Washington*, 5:67.

41. Ibid., 5:93–95.

42. Sparks, *Life of George Washington*, 451, and 450–52.

43. Irving, *George Washington*, 674, 685, 689. The most notable exception is Washington's "ungovernable burst of passion" on hearing of the failure of General St. Clair's expedition against the Indians, but even this story concludes with the assurance that no further sign of this "storm" of emotion was ever afterward heard or seen. Irving, *George Washington*, 668–669.

44. Holcombe, "Sermon Occasioned by the Death of Washington," 1408.

45. Corry, *Life of George Washington*, 237–38; Humphreys, *David Humphreys' "Life of General Washington,"* 56.

46. Kitman, *Making of the President*, 271.

47. Weems, *Life of Washington*, 145, 112.

48. Ibid., 2, emphases in original.

49. Ibid., 134, 135, emphases in original.

50. Dunlap, *André*, 86.

51. See Ellis, *After the Revolution*, 123, also 141–44 and chap. 5. The emotions that the André affair aroused were still close enough to the surface that Dunlap misjudged them; after hearing boos from his opening-night audience, he added lines aimed at excusing the scene in which Washington is most angrily challenged.

52. Dunlap, *André*, 103.

53. Fliegelman, *Declaring Independence*, 104.

54. Dunlap, *André*, 96, emphasis added. Contrast this play with *The Littlest Rebel*, the 1935 Shirley Temple film based on a play about Lincoln pardoning a Confederate spy. See chap. 3, note 81.

55. Ibid., 76.

56. Snowden, *History of the American Revolution*. The text lacks page numbers but divides passages by "chapter" and "verse" as in typical editions of the Bible. Those references are used here. All emphases are in the original.

57. Matthias Bartgis, "To the Public," in Snowden, 3rd and 4th inside pages, emphasis in original.

58. Bartgis, "To the Public," 4th inside page.

59. Onuf, introduction to Weems, *Life of Washington*, xvii.

60. Glass, *Georgii Washingtonii*; Thistlethwaite, "'Our Illustrious Washington,'" 9–10; Smithsonian Institution, "George Washington, Sculpture by Horatio Greenough, 1840," http://www.smithsonianlegacies.si.edu/object description.cfm?ID=66; "Who Is That Man, Anyway? A Photographic Tour of the Statues, Monuments, and Memorials of Washington DC," KittyTours, http://www.kittytours.org/thatman2/. After various relocations, the statue is now in the Smithsonian's National Museum of American History.

61. The term *opaque*, like the term *illustrative*, is Scholes and Kellogg's. See *The Nature of Narrative*, chaps. 4 and 5, esp. 84–89.

62. J. F. Cooper, *Spy*, 1:9.

63. Ibid., 2:221.

64. Thistlethwaite, "Our Illustrious Washington."

65. James Madison, "The Conformity of the Plan to Republican Principles" [*Federalist* 39], in Rossiter, *American Presidency*, 241; and Madison, "The Same Subject [Separation of the Departments of Power] Continued with the Same View and Concluded" [*Federalist* 51], ibid., 323. By "essential" Madison seems to have meant "necessary," as in the familiar philosophical distinction between necessary and sufficient conditions. (The sufficient condition of republican government was having administrators appointed by the people for specified terms.)

66. Goodrich, "Principles of Civil Union," 927.

67. Langdon, "Republic of the Israelites," 1:960.

68. Clinton [Cato, pseud.], "Various Fears Concerning the Executive Department," *New-York Journal*, November 8, 1787, *The Antifederalist Papers*, WEPIN Store, http://www.wepin.com/articles/afp/afp67.html.

69. Watt, *Rise of the Novel*, 13.

70. Weems, *Life of Washington*, 4, 13, 15, and 19, emphases in original.

71. On this point see Cope, "How General George Outlived His Own Funeral Orations," 94–95.

72. Langdon, "Republic of the Israelistes," 946–47.

73. For an extended discussion of this problem, see Ketcham, *Presidents Above Party*.

74. Irving, *George Washington*, 718, emphasis added.

75. Scholes and Kellogg, *Nature of Narrative*, 125, 126.

76. Internet banner ad, Hilo Hattie: The Store of Hawaii, accessed November 2002, http://www.hilohattie.com.

77. George Washington's Mount Vernon Estate and Gardens, "Two New Facilities Opening October 27, 2006: Discover the Real George Washington,"

news release, http://www.mountvernon.org/visit/plan/index.cfm/pid/822/; Mount Vernon Ladies Association, "Mount Vernon Launches $85 Million Campaign"; Copeland, "Buffing Up the Image of George Washington," C01. The executive director was also quoted saying that he wanted the Spielberg-produced museum film to be "as exciting and action-packed as [Spielberg's] 'Indiana Jones.'" Trescott, "Mount Vernon Plans $85 Million Addition," A01. *Washington the Warrior*, a 2006 documentary aired on the History Channel (which was also involved in producing the Mount Vernon film), likewise billed Washington as "America's first action hero," and already in the 1990s a toy Washington had been added to the "GI Joe" line of "action figures." And the new Mount Vernon educational center also aimed at presenting Washington as a savvy entrepreneur, especially of whiskey. Distilled Spirits Council of the United States, "History Channel Documentary Features Famous Distillers Making George Washington's Whiskey," Distilled Spirits Council of the United States newsletter 4, no. 1 (Summer 2004), 1–2, http://distilledspirits.org. Efforts like these exemplify the "plasticity" of presidential images in recent years: see the discussion of that topic in this book's conclusion.

Chapter 2. Seeing Double

1. The period quotations are reproduced in Schreiber, "Sponsors of American Culture," 79–86; and Hofstadter, "Paranoid Style in American Politics," 10–14.

2. Chateaubriand, *Travels in America and Italy*, 100.

3. The cabinet discussion was recorded in Thomas Jefferson's private diary, August 2, 1793, which is quoted at length in Ford, *Washington and his Colleagues*.

4. See the discussion of this concept in chap. 1.

5. Hofstadter, "Paranoid Style in American Politics," 14.

6. Irving [Diedrich Knickerbocker, pseud.], *History of New York*, 1:197, 217, 201, 204.

7. Ibid., 1:224.

8. Ibid., 1:246–47.

9. Story, letter to Mrs. Joseph Story, March 7, 1829, in *Life and Letters of Joseph Story*, 563; M. B. Smith, *First Forty Years of Washington Society*, 262, 296; James Hamilton, letter to Martin Van Buren, March 5, 1829. All emphases, archaic spellings, and punctuation are reproduced from the originals. William Wilberforce, to whom Hamilton alludes, was a prominent abolitionist, while Charles Fenton Mercer was a leader of the "colonization" movement that aimed to repatriate blacks to Africa.

10. *Daily National Intelligencer*, March 6, 1829; M. B. Smith, *First Forty Years of Washington Society*, 296. The letters of Smith's cited here concerning the Jackson years were written on various dates between January 1829 and August 29, 1831.

11. Bakhtin, *Problems of Dostoevsky's Poetics*, 127, emphasis in original.

12. Bakhtin, "From the Prehistory of Novelistic Discourse," 58, 68, 79; Bakhtin, introduction to *Rabelais and His World*, 6.

13. Graham Pechey, quoted in Dentith, *Bakhtinian Thought*, 84.

14. A 1781 ordinance in then-Spanish New Orleans had sought to prohibit "all kinds of masking and public dancing by the Negroes . . . during the Carnival Season." "Digest of the Acts and Deliberations of the Cabildo: Carnival," January 19, 1781, City Archives, New Orleans Public Library, http://nutrias .org/~nopl/inv/digest/digest17.htm. Masking particularly alarmed the authorities, since it encouraged race and gender mixing. But the prohibitions didn't work, and by Jackson's time the anarchic mixing was out in the open: "boys, Negroes, fruit women" followed processions in which "Men and boys, women and girls, bond and free, white and black, yellow and brown, exert themselves to invent and appear in grotesque, quizzical, diabolical, horrible, humorous, strange masks and disguises . . . Everything is license and revelry." See "Blake Pontchartrain," *Gambit Weekly*; and Falzon, "Congo Square." Histories of modern, "official" Mardi Gras often date it to 1827.

15. M. B. Smith, *First Forty Years of Washington Society*, 288–89. Overviews of the affair can be found in Pierce, "Andrew Jackson and the Tavern-Keeper's Daughter," 1–4; and Burstein, *Passions of Andrew Jackson*, 173–80. For more detailed, book-length accounts, see Phillips [pseud. of Noel Bertram Gerson], *That Eaton Woman*; and Marszalek, *Petticoat Affair*. See also P. Eaton, *Autobiography of Peggy Eaton*.

16. M. B. Smith, *First Forty Years of Washington Society*, 252, 282, 289, emphases in original. The remark was a variant of the familiar miscegenation slur: "The nastiest rumors about the couple spread with impunity. One even averred that the war secretary had fathered a child with a 'colored female servant.'" Pierce, "Andrew Jackson and the Tavern-Keeper's Daughter," 4.

17. M. B. Smith, *First Forty Years of Washington Society*, 252, 253, 288–289, emphasis in original. A leading modern biographer of Jackson, Robert V. Remini, interprets the ostracism of Peggy Eaton as part of a "desperate scheme" on the part of John C. Calhoun to undercut Martin van Buren—a scheme that had the opposite of its intended effect. Remini, *Revolutionary Age of Andrew Jackson*, 83.

18. M. B. Smith, *First Forty Years of Washington Society*, 288, 310–11.

19. Floyd, *Diary*, 217–18. Peggy Eaton's *Autobiography* reproduces a statement of Jackson's that probably corresponds to the "defence" Floyd was referring to.

20. Speaking of the Creek Indian baby Jackson adopted after it was orphaned in battle, Eaton wrote that he was "prompted by benevolence, and because, perhaps, its fate bore a strong resemblance to his own, who, in early life, and from the ravages of war, was left in the world forlorn and wretched, without friends to assist, or near relations to direct him on his course." J. H. Eaton,

Memoirs of Andrew Jackson, 334. Eaton's main source of information on Jackson's thoughts and emotions was presumably Jackson himself.

21. This was Johnson Jones Hooper's 1845 *Adventures of Captain Simon Suggs.* See Hopkins, "Simon Suggs," 459–63.

22. M. B. Smith, *First Forty Years of Washington Society,* 252–53, 318–20, emphasis in original.

23. Ibid., 252, 327. Van Buren replaced Calhoun as vice president in Jackson's second term; Eaton became governor of the Florida territory and then American ambassador to Spain.

24. No one but Rachel Jackson had been able to do that. Resembling Peggy Eaton in some ways, Rachel Jackson was her mirror image in this. She was a force for reason and restraint, someone who "could control the violence of [Jackson's] temper." Rachel "not only made him a happier, but a better man," and Smith worried over the harm that her death might do to American politics. M. B. Smith, *First Forty Years of Washington Society,* 5–6, 252–53, 259–60, and 319–20.

25. Maxcy, letter to John C. Calhoun, April 6, 1829, in Calhoun, *Papers,* 11: 17. Editorial brackets in published text omitted.

26. Calhoun, letter to Bolling Hall, October 19, 1831, in Calhoun, *Papers,* 11:482; Calhoun, quoted in "John Henry Eaton," *Virtual American Biographies,* from *Appleton's Cyclopedia of American Biography,* http://www.famousamericans .net/johnhenryeaton/; Calhoun, "Reply to John H. Eaton's Address," October 19, 1831, in Calhoun, *Papers,* 11:477. Calhoun's analogy to the Medes and Persians was an allusion to Daniel 6, where the implicit contrast is between the enlightened, divinely approved laws of Israel and those of gentile alien powers.

27. M. B. Smith, *First Forty Years of Washington Society,* 260, 288, 310, 321. Smith immediately follows her comment on the government with the remark that "One woman [O'Neale] has made sad work here," and she compares Rachel Jackson both to Napoleon's Josephine and to the little boy in the Plutarchan fable who was said to govern all of Greece.

28. F. McConnell, *Storytelling and Mythmaking,* 227, emphasis added.

29. Ibid., 226, 207, 206, 210, and chap. 5. The last of these quotations refers to the satirist, but McConnell uses the terms *satirist* and *wise fool* almost interchangeably; see also 212.

30. For brief accounts of Jack Downing's origins, reception, and influence, see Rourke, *American Humor,* 29–32; Lynn, *Comic Tradition in America,* 81–83; and Veron, *Humor in America,* 63–65, 72. Veron's introductions explicitly place Downing within an American literary tradition of wise fools.

31. S. Smith [Jack Downing, pseud.], Letters 31 and 35, *Life and Writings of Major Jack Downing,* 123–25, 135–38; S. Smith, *Select Letters of Major Jack Downing,* vi. In all quotes from the Downing letters, regional spellings, punctuation, and grammar are preserved from the original.

32. Davis [J. Downing, Major, pseud.], Letter 13, *Letters of J. Downing, Major,* 94.

33. Letter 25, S. Smith, *Select Letters of Major Jack Downing,* 60.

34. Letter 36, ibid., 90.

35. Letter 59, S. Smith, *Life and Writings of Major Jack Downing,* 199–200.

36. Letter 14, Davis, *Letters of J. Downing, Major,* 95.

37. Preface and Letter 65, S. Smith, *Life and Writings of Major Jack Downing,* vi, 215–21.

38. F. McConnell, *Storytelling and Mythmaking,* 202, 225. McConnell discusses these figures in general, not with specific reference to Jack Downing.

39. Letter 55, S. Smith, *Select Letters of Major Jack Downing,* 136.

40. F. McConnell, *Storytelling and Mythmaking,* 225.

41. Trollope, quoting letters from another tourist (with errors in the original) in *Domestic Manners of the Americans,* 119–20.

42. Letter 58, S. Smith, *Life and Writings of Major Jack Downing,* 197. Misspellings in original.

43. On the riverboat incident and nose pulling in general, see K. S. Greenberg, "The Nose, the Lie, and the Duel," 16–23. Floyd's *Diary* (215–20) provides an account from the time sympathetic to the assailant, Lt. Robert Beverly Randolph.

44. *Niles' Weekly Register* 44 (June 22, 1833): 266–67, emphases in original. Eventually Randolph was prosecuted but pardoned at Jackson's request, apparently on the premise that affairs of honor should not be settled by legal proceedings. See Wyatt-Brown, "Andrew Jackson's Honor," 77–80.

45. *Niles' Weekly Register* 43 (September 29, 1832): 78.

46. *Cherokee Nation v. State of Georgia,* 30 U.S. 1 (1831).

47. *Niles' Weekly Register* 44 (June 8, 1833): 256; "Black Hawk," *Frankfort Commonwealth,* July 2, 1833; "Black Hawk Upstages the President," emphasis in original.

48. Catlin, *Letters and Notes on the Manners, Customs, and Conditions.* See Letters 8, 10, and 55. The story continues that Wijunjon's fellow Assiniboines, convinced he had fallen victim to "lying medicine," finally arranged to have him killed.

49. M. B. Smith, *First Forty Years of Washington Society,* 401, emphasis in original.

50. The rebellion itself was easily put down. In one U.S. military history that runs to nearly 500 pages, the entire war is covered in just two pithy sentences: "The overwhelming effects of white population growth were demonstrated in 1832, when old Black Hawk of the Sacks and Foxes attempted to lead a band of his people from exile west of the Mississippi back into their old country, in Illinois east of the river. Black Hawk had only about 400 warriors, and a

motley white force consisting largely of untrained militia, but aggregating about 4,000, was able to crush him and slaughter many of his followers." Weigley, *American Way of War*, 154.

51. *Niles' Weekly Register* 43 (September 29, 1832): 79; 44 (May 18, 1833): 182; 44 (July 20, 1833): 348–49.

52. "A Repentant Jacksonman," *Cincinnati Daily Gazette*, August 22, 1834, posted by the Department of American Studies at the University of Virginia, http://xroads.virginia.edu/~CAP/jackson/repent.htm; *Commonwealth*, July 2, 1833; "Phrenological Developments and Character of the Celebrated Indian Chief and Warrior, Black Hawk; With Cuts," *American Phrenological Journal and Miscellany* 1, no. 2 (November 1838): 51–61, Drew E. VandeCreek, "Native American Relations," Lincoln/Net, Northern Illinois University, http://lincoln.lib.niu.edu/nativeamerican.html.

53. Black Hawk, *Black Hawk*, 145; Fulton, "Sketch of Black Hawk," 221.

54. Turner, quoting John Allen Wakefield, in *Red Men Calling*, 94–99. This northeastern tour of Jackson's is the same one referred to in the Jack Downing letters quoted earlier. For a brief recent description of it in the context of Black Hawk's career, see Trask, *Black Hawk*, 297–303.

55. Patrick Shirriff, quoted in Cole, *I Am a Man*, 250, emphasis added.

56. *Niles' Weekly Register* 44 (June 29, 1833): 282; *Commonwealth*, July 2, 1833; "Black Hawk-ism," *Commonwealth*, July 30, 1833. The "Repentant Jacksonman" believed that Jackson had been more fawned upon than Black Hawk (while demanding still more, he argued), but even this judgment indicates how unavoidable the comparison seemed to observers at the time.

57. Turner, *Red Men Calling*, 100, quoting *United States Telegraph*, June 21, 1833.

58. *Commonwealth*, July 2, 1833; Letter 59, S. Smith, *Life and Writings of Major Jack Downing*, 199.

59. Turner, *Red Men Calling*, 99, quoting *United States Telegraph*, June 20, 1833; *Commonwealth*, July 2, 1833. See Robert M. Sully's portrait of Black Hawk in formal dress on page 67.

60. Turner, *Red Men Calling*, 97, quoting *Commercial Herald/United States Telegraph*, June 18, 1833.

61. *Commonwealth*, July 2, 1833.

62. Turner, *Red Men Calling*, 101.

63. *Niles' Weekly Register* 43 (October 27, 1832): 132.

64. *Commonwealth*, July 2, 1833.

65. *Niles' Weekly Register* 45 (August 31, 1833): 11, emphasis added.

66. He had fought not in hopes of winning, he said, but out of fear of seeming "a coward, and no brave," of having his people say that "Black Hawk is a woman; he is too old to be a chief; he is no Sac." Nonbraves, that is, included women, old men, and tribal outsiders, a list almost identical to the "boys,

negros, women, children" that made up the "rabble" at Jackson's inauguration. Turner, quoting Wakefield, in *Red Men Calling*, 92, 259.

67. Quoted in Fulton, "Sketch of Black Hawk," 221.

68. *Niles' Weekly Register* 44 (June 15, 1833): 256.

69. *Niles' Weekly Register* 44 (May 18, 1833): 182.

70. F. McConnell, *Storytelling and Mythmaking*, 235, emphasis in original.

71. "Black Hawk's Arrival," *Commonwealth*, June 1833, emphases in original. The newspaper calls the poem "an extract from the Valedictory of Mr. Durant to the people he left below him, in relation to the savage chieftain." The event was one of Charles F. Durant's celebrated hot-air balloon demonstration flights.

72. Apess, "Indian Nullification of the Unconstitutional Laws," in *On Our Own Ground*, 184.

73. Ibid., 195.

74. Apess, "Eulogy on King Philip," in *On Our Own Ground*, 297, 299, 305–6, 308.

75. One intriguing parallel to Black Hawk is the story of King Kong, which appeared on film exactly one hundred years after Black Hawk's progress. Here an even more alien creature from an even more distant wilderness is taken from his land and dragged to a big eastern city—and not just to show off the giant ape to the public, but to show the captive who's boss. "He's always been king of his world. But we'll teach him fear!" says one of the film's characters, neatly summing up what had been federal Indian policy a century earlier. In this fictional case, too, the creature's nominally civilized captors underestimate the power of the "native," with consequences that lead to one of the best-remembered scenes in the history of movies. If anything, McConnell's analysis of Kong, and of fools as "naturals," better describes Black Hawk, who is actually able to "ape" his captors. F. McConnell, *Storytelling and Mythmaking*, 206–7, 230–35. And it's another interesting not-quite-coincidence that Kong is a popular attraction at Mardi Gras, where he makes an annual appearance in a parade named after the ancient god Bacchus, whose festivals lie at the origins of carnival. New Orleans today is also, strangely, the site of a curious cultural memory of Black Hawk, who has come to be revered as a saint in a religious movement called the "Spiritual Church"—an appropriation of his image that recalls the spontaneous alliance of Indian, Afro-American, and Afro-Caribbean marginalized groups that originally gave rise to American carnival. See Berry, *Spirit of Black Hawk*; and DeCarlo, "Sister Gertrude, a Preacher Who Could Paint."

76. *Commonwealth*, July 30, 1833, emphasis in original.

77. M. B. Smith, *First Forty Years of Washington Society*, 253–54, 280.

78. J. P. Kennedy [Solomon Secondthoughts, pseud.], *Quodlibet*, 128, emphases in original. The word *quodlibet* translates roughly as "whatever you like."

79. James Parton (1860), quoted in "Andrew Jackson (1767–1845): A Brief Biography," From Revolution to Reconstruction: A Hypertext on American History from the Colonial Period until Modern Times, Department of Humanities Computing, University of Groningen, http://odur.let.rug.nl/~usa/P/aj7/about/bio/jack01.htm.

80. "King Andrew the First" was the image and title of a famous political cartoon, and "the majority's slave" was a judgment of Alexis de Tocqueville's. "Andrew Jackson as Image," posted by the Department of American Studies at the University of Virginia, http://xroads.virginia.edu/~CAP/jackson/ima.htm.

81. Meyers, *Jacksonian Persuasion*, 42, 143.

82. Ward, *Andrew Jackson*, 36–38, and chap. 3.

83. Ibid., 38.

84. Trollope, *Domestic Manners of the Americans*, chaps. 12 and 17. The phenomenon Trollope describes recalls Oscar Wilde's wry description of the traditional peerage: "the best thing in fiction the English have ever done." Wilde, *A Woman of No Importance*, Act III (spoken by the character Lord Illingworth).

85. "A Repentant Jacksonman," *Cincinnati Daily Gazette*, August 22, 1834, posted by the Department of American Studies at the University of Virginia, http://xroads.virginia.edu/~CAP/jackson/repent.htm.

86. Freud, "Uncanny," 241, 219–52. Freud credits Friedrich Wilhelm Joseph von Schelling with the particular idea referred to here.

87. Webster, *Discourse in Commemoration*, 36.

88. Tucker, *Partisan Leader*, 208, 210. Variously subtitled "A Tale of the Future"—it forecast events of the 1850s—as well as "An Apocalypse of the Origin and Struggles of the Southern Confederacy" and, in an 1861 reissue, "A Key to the Southern Conspiracy," Tucker's often-reprinted novel was a fiction even on its title page: Published under a pseudonym in 1836, it claimed to be a product of 1856 and to chronicle efforts to rally a wavering Virginia to the Southern cause against the materialistic, majoritarian North. Encouraging his readers to picture an armed Southern revolt, Tucker closes both volumes of *The Partisan Leader* with the words *Sic semper tyrannis*, "Thus always with tyrants," the battle cry that would later be heard from John Wilkes Booth as he leapt from the presidential box at Ford's Theater.

89. Tucker, *Partisan Leader*, 74–75.

90. Meyers, *Jacksonian Persuasion*, 144.

91. See the discussion of *The Spy* in chap. 1.

92. Tucker did come close to guessing the date of the real Civil War's onset, but he badly overrated Van Buren's political skills—as Van Buren himself would no doubt have agreed: he once ruefully said of himself that if he had just one-tenth the "skill in subtle management" and in "the spirit of intrigue" that had earned him the nickname "the Little Magician," he "could

have turned aside the opposition without much difficulty." Quoted in Kunhardt et al., *American President*, 90–95.

93. Jones, *Border War*.

94. W. W. Brown, *Clotel; or, The President's Daughter*, 217–18, 220. That later edition was re-titled *Clotelle: A Tale of the Southern States*.

95. Locke, "[Nasby] Has an Interview with the President (Nov. 1 '63)," in *Nasby Papers*. Still later in the century, Texas humorist Alex Sweet created yet another such character, "Colonel Bill Snort," alleged confidant of Presidents Benjamin Harrison and Grover Cleveland.

96. "Middle Republic" is Bruce Ackerman's term, and Party/Progressive Eras are Michael Schudson's. See Ackerman, *We the People*, chap. 4; and Schudson, *Good Citizen*, chaps. 3 and 4.

Chapter 3. Deep, Yet Transparent

1. "The politics of deference" is Michael Schudson's phrase. See Schudson, *Good Citizen*, 19–24, and chaps. 2 and 3. For related analyses, see Bruce Ackerman on the early republic and America's "three regimes," in *We the People*, chap. 3; Michael J. Sandel on the "procedural republic," in *Democracy's Discontent*, especially chaps. 1 and 9; Richard Sennett, *Fall of Public Man*, discussed further below; and my discussion of the framers and George Washington in chap. 1.

2. Lincoln, "Address to the Legislature of Ohio at Columbus," 5:79.

3. Quoted in Catton, *Coming Fury*, 221.

4. See the discussion of Parson Weems in chap. 1.

5. [Historian] James Madison, interviewed in *Young Lincoln*, 2004. Transcribed from video.

6. Tim Crumrin and Joan Flinspach, interviewed in *Young Lincoln*.

7. For J. G. Holland, the problem was that Lincoln's "whole life had been spent with people without refinement," and that lawyers are inevitably in close contact with the most appalling characters and events. Holland, *Life of Abraham Lincoln*, 83–85. Ward Hill Lamon also thought that Lincoln's humor came "from the lower orders of the country people," which is why it "was not of a delicate quality; it was chiefly exercised in hearing and telling stories of the grosser sort." Lamon, *Life of Abraham Lincoln*, 480. And Edward Dicey, the British correspondent referred to below, found Lincoln's unprintable, "Aristophanic" wit striking even by the undignified standards of American statesmen in general. Dicey, *Six Months in the Federal States*, 217, 226.

8. Carpenter, *Six Months at the White House*, 79–81, 39–42.

9. "We do not believe," said the *Baltimore Sun*, that "the Presidency can ever be more degraded by any of his successors." Quoted in Holzer, "Abraham Lincoln Takes the Heat." *The Diary of a Public Man*, discussed below, also harshly criticized Lincoln and his associates for the ignominy of sneaking him around.

10. Quoted in Catton, *Coming Fury*, 249, 288.

11. Anonymous, *Diary of a Public Man*. See F. Lauriston Bullard's notes to that volume for a discussion of the *Diary's* authorship. The suggestion that Henry Adams was the author is refuted in Ernest Samuels's *Henry Adams*, 108–9. Merrill D. Peterson questions the *Diary's* authenticity in *Lincoln in American Memory*, but Richard N. Current, whose book *Lincoln and the First Shot* deals with the same events as the *Diary*, treats it as a reliable source. It is a small but possibly deliberate irony that the author called himself a "Public" Man while remaining private about who he (or she) is. Irony is consistent with a literary purpose, but of course, in terms of its value as narrative, the question of the book's authenticity isn't really relevant. If in fact the *Diary* represents not a witness's recollections but a fictionalization, then it is that much more useful as an instance of the ways in which storytellers have chosen to imagine Lincoln.

12. Anonymous, *Diary of a Public Man*, 85–87.

13. Ibid., 106.

14. Ibid., 97–98.

15. Browne, *Every-Day Life of Abraham Lincoln*, 529; Nevins, *Statesmanship of the Civil War*, 46.

16. Dicey, *Six Months in the Federal States*, 219–20, 227–28, emphasis in original.

17. Holland, *Life of Abraham Lincoln*, 543, 544.

18. See Peterson, *Lincoln in American Memory*, chap. 1; and Holzer, "'Columbia's Noblest Sons.'" Some images of Lincoln's "apotheosis" not only resembled those of Washington but specifically linked the two, with Lincoln and Washington embracing in the clouds or standing together astride the American continent.

19. Besides Philip Freneau and Hugh Henry Brackenridge's *The Rising Glory of America* (1771–72, rev. 1786), examples include Joel Barlow's 1787 *The Vision of Columbus* and its revised edition, *The Columbiad* (1807), and Timothy Dwight's *The Conquest of Canaan* and *Greenfield Hill*.

20. Blanchard, *Abraham Lincoln*. See 4–5 for Blanchard's explanation of his approach.

21. Carpenter explained that art "cannot dwell always among classic forms, nor clothe its conceptions in the imagery of an old and worn-out world," and in painting *The First Reading*, a mural that became a best-selling 1866 lithograph, he promised to avoid "the false glitter of tapestry hangings, velvet table-cloths, and marble columns." Carpenter, *Six Months at the White House*, 9–11, 25. The image presents Lincoln and his cabinet as if pausing from work around the cabinet table, with books and papers lying askew to suggest what might almost be a candid moment. But the figures are stiffly posed and unrealistic by modern standards: Carpenter had sketched the picture *before* studying his subjects, selecting their placement and painting their expressions to represent their political positions on emancipation as much as what he actually

saw. Ibid., 12–14. On the lithograph's popularity, see Holzer, *Lincoln Seen and Heard,* chap. 1, especially 7–12 and 22–26.

22. Crosby, *Life of Abraham Lincoln,* 387.

23. See the discussion of this point in chap. 1.

24. This is Erich Auerbach's argument in *Mimesis,* 35–43 and 60–66. See also Auerbach's *Dante,* 11–23.

25. Henry J. Raymond, editor of the *New York Times* and a confidant of Lincoln's, quoted in Carpenter, *Six Months at the White House,* 95; Crosby, *Life of Abraham Lincoln,* 387; Holland, *Life of Abraham Lincoln,* 455, 541, 542, 543.

26. Carpenter, *Six Months at the White House,* v.

27. Ibid., vi–vii.

28. Lamon, *Life of Abraham Lincoln,* 475, 480–81.

29. On Lincoln's interest in Weems's Washington, see Wrone, "Lincoln: Democracy's Touchstone."

30. Herndon and Weik, *Herndon's Life of Lincoln,* v–vii. *Herndon's Lincoln: The True Story of a Great Life* was the title of the first (two-volume) edition of 1888. In the epigraph to this chapter (from p. vii), Herndon is quoting the urgings of another friend of Lincoln's.

31. Lamon, *Life of Abraham Lincoln,* 475; Herndon and Weik, *Herndon's Life of Lincoln,* 473.

32. Herndon and Weik, *Herndon's Life of Lincoln,* 111–12.

33. Ibid., 113–15; see also Lamon, *Life of Abraham Lincoln,* chap. 8.

34. Herndon and Weik, *Herndon's Life of Lincoln,* vi–vii.

35. Ibid., 351; Paul M. Angle, "Editor's Preface," ibid., xxxviii.

36. Quoted by Angle in ibid., xxxiv–xxxv, with spelling as in the original.

37. Shenk, *Lincoln's Melancholy.*

38. Douglass, "Oration in Memory of Abraham Lincoln."

39. Strozier, *Lincoln's Quest for Union,* 35–36, citing James G. Randall, *Lincoln the President,* 2:321–42. (A later edition of Strozier's book was subtitled *A Psychological Portrait.*) For an account of Herndon's lecture series and the subsequent life of the Rutledge legend, see Peterson, *Lincoln in American Memory,* 73–81. Richard N. Current, in *The Lincoln Nobody Knows,* 41–42, notes that Lincoln himself never mentioned Ann Rutledge and that Mary Todd Lincoln called the story a "myth." But more recently, John Evangelist Walsh has argued in *The Shadows Rise: Abraham Lincoln and the Ann Rutledge Legend* that Herndon's fact-gathering methods were basically reliable. Reviewing Joshua Shenk's *Lincoln's Melancholy,* Caleb Crain gives an overview of current scholarly opinion on the legend. Crain, "Critic at Large." See also Schwartz, "Ann Rutledge in American Memory."

40. Herndon and Weik, *Herndon's Life of Lincoln,* 380–81; Lamon, *Life of Abraham Lincoln,* 477; Herndon and Weik, *Herndon's Life of Lincoln,* 369.

41. Just twelve years after Lincoln's death, Frederick Douglass declared that "The whole field of fact and fancy has been gleaned and garnered. . . . His personal traits and public acts are better known to the American people than are those of any other man of his age." Douglass, "Oration in Memory of Abraham Lincoln." In the twentieth century a series of books appeared that attempted to chronicle literally every day of Lincoln's life. See Hoffman, "Benjamin P. Thomas."

42. "About the Hay-Adams," Hay-Adams Hotel, http://www.hayadams.com/About/index.htm.

43. H. Adams, *Education of Henry Adams,* 317. This famous autobiography is written entirely in the third person.

44. For one explanation of that view and how it evolved, see Schudson, "Politics of Narrative Form," 97–112.

45. Henry Adams, *The History of the United States of America during the Administrations of Jefferson and Madison,* 138.

46. On these speculations and the novel's contents and reception in general, see Samuels, *Henry Adams,* 68–104.

47. H. Adams, *Democracy,* emphasis in original. All references are to the searchable electronic edition at Eldritch Press.

48. Ratcliffe was likely modeled on James G. Blaine, among others; for a detailed discussion of character parallels see Samuels, *Henry Adams,* 89–93. Though apparently not bound for greatness, the Hoosier Quarryman also bears one or two similarities to the Illinois Railsplitter: Both are examples of the "western" president, the frontier bumpkin who abruptly rises to the top by being just a bit less unacceptable than his rivals.

49. Prominent examples are Frances Hodgson Burnett's *Through One Administration* (1881) and Madeleine Vinton Dahlgren's *A Washington Winter* (1883). Both these novels centered on female Washington socialites and examined the intrigues of senators, and both featured politically clumsy, personally beleaguered presidents not unlike the Hoosier Quarryman.

50. H. James, "Pandora," 37, 17, 29.

51. Arthur Schlesinger Jr. points out that Adams's spokesman in the novel is generally thought to be Nathan Gore, a minor character who takes a sunnier view of democratic politics and urges that same view on Madeleine. But Schlesinger also notes that Adams clearly concurs with Madeleine's despairing rejection of the Washington scene, even if this makes for some thematic inconsistency. Schlesinger, "On Henry Adams' 'Democracy.'"

52. Bellamy, *Looking Backward,* 181–82.

53. Ibid., chaps. 17 and 25. Besides Bellamy's own 1897 sequel, *Equality,* a number of other novels by various writers responded to *Looking Backward,* in some cases borrowing its characters for further adventures. In one sequel,

Solomon Schindler's *Young West*, Julian West's son becomes the utopia's president. Other sequels reimagined Bellamy's world by way of pointing out possible problems it would create or how it might eventually break down. See Nordstrom, "*Looking Backward*'s Utopian Sequels."

54. F. U. Adams, *President John Smith*, 143, 152, 289.

55. Ibid., 247–48.

56. Ibid., especially chaps. 28 and 29.

57. Besides covering labor issues for the Chicago press and working for the Democratic National Committee during the election of 1896, he was a mechanical engineer who invented the ubiquitous single-arm electric lamppost. He also co-edited the *New Time*, a "magazine of social progress" that promoted socialist ideas. Although there were differences between the Socialist, Progressive, and Populist agendas, and although President John Smith is a Populist, I am following the convention here of periodizing the reform movements under the broad heading "Progressive Era."

58. See the discussion of *Clotel* in chap. 2.

59. Griggs, *Imperium in Imperio*. The novel is clearly an important statement of black nationalist thinking and may have helped inspire the later movement, but sources differ as to how widely read it was in its time; having published the book himself, Griggs originally sold it door to door.

60. Seymour, *Intimate Papers of Colonel House*, 114–15.

61. House, *Philip Dru, Administrator*.

62. For a general discussion of utopian literature and Progressive politics, see Bloomfield, *Peaceful Revolution*, especially chaps. 1 and 2.

63. It's also possible, though, for opposition to be ruled out de jure as a condition for bringing the new order into being in the first place. In *Imperium in Imperio* the secret black underground works by unanimity, and after President Belgrave's unanimously approved appointment, all "factional" differences disappear. But where unanimity is demanded, dissent is treason, so Belton's dissent over the plan to seize Texas requires in the end that he be killed.

64. Gilman, *Herland*.

65. Donnelly [writing as Edmund Boisgilbert, M.D.], *Caesar's Column*; London, *Iron Heel*. In *The Iron Heel* the plutocrats are referred to throughout by the title image, which reduces human agency to a giant synecdoche. In *Caesar's Column*, whose author was a congressman, lieutenant-governor of Minnesota, and leading Populist, the plutocracy does have a kind of committee chair: Prince Cabano, aka Jacob Isaacs, "the wealthiest and most vindictive man in the city," i.e., New York. But it is also clear that actual political leaders are part of a mere "sham and form"—that "political parties, courts, juries, governors, legislatures, congresses, presidents are made and unmade" by the secret *über*-cabal. And the "Prince" is also Jewish, reflecting not just the anti-Semitism common in this literature but also the idea that he is less significant as a person than as

a member of a "race," which is held to be in itself a kind of ancient global conspiracy.

66. Albert E. Pillsbury, *Lincoln and Slavery* (1913), quoted in "Book Notes," *Political Science Quarterly* 30, no. 1 (March 1915): 182–83.

67. J. C. Harris, "Kidnapping of President Lincoln."

68. Peterson's phrase, from *Lincoln in American Memory*, 155.

69. Tarbell, "He Knew Lincoln," 27, 28, 23–24, 33.

70. Ibid., 34, 35.

71. Ibid., 39.

72. Herndon and Weik, *Herndon's Life of Lincoln*, 256, 257, 351, 480.

73. Tarbell, introduction to *He Knew Lincoln*, vii, vii–xvi.

74. Isaiah 53:4. Lincoln's identity with the people (and vice-versa) is a conceit freely used in Mark Van Doren's play *The Last Days of Lincoln*. See, for instance, the speeches of "Anonymous I," p. 8; Sumner, p. 13; and Davis, p. 14 in scene 1. Even during Lincoln's lifetime, one supporter had declared that the rails Lincoln had once split "represent the issue in the coming contest between labor free and labor slave; between democracy and aristocracy." Herndon and Weik, *Herndon's Life of Lincoln*, 372–73.

75. The epic was *Lincoln and Ann Rutledge: An Idyllic Epos of the Early North-West* by Denton J. Snider, leader of the St. Louis Philosophical Society, a group of American devotees of German philosophy. The critical summary is from Peterson, *Lincoln in American Memory*, 228.

76. Mitchell, *Youth of Washington*. As it happens, Mitchell had once been Charlotte Perkins Gilman's doctor and had treated her for depression.

77. Freud and Bullitt, *Thomas Woodrow Wilson*, 106 and passim. Although the book wasn't published until the 1960s, work on it began in 1930.

78. The 1920s scrutiny of Harding included Nan Britton's 1927 "mistress memoir," *President's Daughter*, discussed in chap. 6, and the novel *Revelry*, muckraking journalist Samuel Hopkins Adams's lightly fictionalized account of the Harding scandals, which was published in 1926 and adapted for a brief run on Broadway in 1927.

79. Peterson, *Lincoln in American Memory*, 285–91.

80. This "Minor Affair," named for the true authors of the letters, is described in ibid., 291–98.

81. Ford also frames Lincoln in poses evidently based on famous photographs, and his closing shots have the future president walking up a hill into a gathering storm—a bit of deeply conventional symbolism straight out of nineteenth-century engravings. On the subject of reverential treatments of Lincoln, it's also worth briefly noting *The Littlest Rebel*, a Civil War play by Edward Peple originally staged on Broadway in 1911, rewritten later and then made into a 1935 Shirley Temple song-and-dance vehicle at Twentieth-Century Fox. In that film, Lincoln (replacing General Grant, who had been the

figure of authority in the original play) pardons an accused enemy spy after the Confederate's young daughter finds her way to the White House to plead the case—at one point even spending a long scene snuggled up on the president's lap. The story is an interesting counterpoint to *André*, the William Dunlap play (discussed in chap. 1) in which George Washington demonstrates a very different kind of virtue by resisting sentiment and dutifully turning aside such pleas.

82. Sennett, *Fall of Public Man*, 3, 4, 275–76, 281.

83. For one sustained critique, see Wolin, "Rise of Private Man."

84. Carnegie, *Lincoln the Unknown*. On Van Doren's *Last Days of Lincoln*, see note 74.

85. Stewart, *Perfect Behavior*, 181–82.

Chapter 4. A Simple, Honest Man

1. The quote is from the original Dave Fleischer cartoon. (Much later, a compilation of Betty Boop clips plus original songs, edited and dubbed to create a feature-length "musical" and credited to Dan Dalton as producer/director, was released in 1980 as *Betty Boop for President: The Movie*.) In September 1933 another musical short, *Rufus Jones for President*, directed by Roy Mack for Vitaphone and Warner Bros., starred a seven-year-old Sammy Davis Jr. as a singing and dancing child president (albeit in a dream sequence) and Ethel Waters as his mother, the "presidentess." Alluding to numerous racist jokes of the time, young Jones's presidency promises such improvements to everyday life as a federal "watermelon investigator," an end to locked chicken coops, a "dice president" to solve the problem of loaded dice, and a pledge that "From now on pork chops will be free."

2. Lowi, *Personal President*, 51.

3. See the similar argument about America's changing "regimes" in Ackerman, *We the People*, chap. 3.

4. Kuklick, *Good Ruler*, 49.

5. See the discussion of the "Tory Wits" and *The Beggar's Opera* in chap. 1.

6. On *Of Thee I Sing*'s place in American musical history, see Mast, *Can't Help Singin'*, 77–80.

7. A similar premise also figures in *The Scarlet Pimpernel*, which became a United Artists film in 1934; in Charlie Chaplin's 1940 comedy *The Great Dictator*; and, most notably, in Ivan Reitman's 1993 film *Dave*, which is discussed further in chap. 6.

8. Worts, *Phantom President*, 26–27, 124, 74.

9. "There He Is—Theodore K. Blair," a number not used in the finished film but reprinted in *The Complete Lyrics of Lorenz Hart*, 182.

10. Worts, *Phantom President*, 140, 61, 65, 32.

11. Ibid., 272.

12. Ibid., 80, 223–24, 234, 245, 290, 296.

13. Tweed, *Gabriel Over the White House*. In Britain the novel was published under the title *Rinehard*, which was also the president's name. The later reissue, based on the British edition, was published by Fantasy Books/Cherry Tree Novels/Kemsley Newspapers, London, date unspecified. Although Tweed was British, the work seems worth including in this discussion because of the wide attention given the tale in America both in print and on film.

14. *Gabriel Over the White House*, directed by Gregory LaCava, 1933. Roosevelt was elected in November 1932. The novel was published, anonymously, in the United States on February 10, 1933. FDR was inaugurated on March 4. By then, filming was already well underway, and by March 16 a rough cut had been screened for the Production Code–enforcing Hayes Office. After some changes aimed at removing what Will H. Hayes and "a number of film leaders" deemed "subversive" and "invidious" elements, the film was released on March 31, approximately one-quarter of the way through FDR's famous "First Hundred Days." Furthermore, "the British release print contained a different ending from American prints. In the British version, according to modern sources, Huston's character is shown as a dangerous schizophrenic, capable of doing good deeds only in certain phases of his illness." See "Gabriel Over the White House," American Film Institute Catalog, Proquest, http://www.proquest.com/; and "'Gabriel' Film Sent Back to Hollywood," 21. For a detailed account of the film's production, themes, and relationship to the novel, see R. L. McConnell, "Genesis and Ideology," 7–26.

15. See the discussion of this topic in chap. 3.

16. The movie's ending is simpler: Hammond dies just as he completes his great work, melodramatically slumping over the peace covenant he has just signed—with Lincoln's quill pen, which in his earlier incarnation he had mocked as useful mainly for signing a measure dealing with "Puerto Rican garbage."

17. Worts, *Phantom President*, 134–39.

18. Tweed, *Gabriel Over the White House*, 81–83, 225–26, 237–38. Capitalization corrected.

19. Even the movie *Gabriel*, which supplied its president with microphones but no "televisor," envisioned him not so much chatting as speechifying on air, and the only home we see him reach is a leading gangster's. Tweed dutifully corrected himself in a later edition of his novel. Here is the passage rewritten post-FDR:

> . . . it came like a bolt from the blue, the statement that the President was going to talk to the people of the United States, not through the medium of a convention or even an address to the Senate, but by the simple agency of the radio.

... For years past people had not been accustomed to the finer arts of the orator. The development of the loud-speaker at conventions and public gatherings had accustomed the crowd to hearing speech in stentorian, metallic tones devoid of human interest and of personal intimacy. Now, sitting by their own firesides, they heard oratory at its very best. Every subtle inflection, every hesitation for the sake of getting better effect, the warmth and colour of language, the whispered sentence and the loud crescendo of scorn and declamation, soothed, cajoled and roused answering impulses, and with those impulses a real affection and tremendous faith in the man who to most of them had been but a name.

Just like FDR's, these radio addresses also acquire a popular nickname: "Bedtime Stories."

20. Kuklick, *Good Ruler*, 42. Presumably the public's experience with Hoover explains why candidate Betty Boop, in the 1932 cartoon quoted above, assumes that giving voters everything they want includes promising *not* to address them on radio.

21. Tweed, *Gabriel Over the White House*, 119.

22. Levine and Levine, *People and the President*, 42, 46, 51–52. According to Kuklick, the number of White House staffers assigned to answer letters to the president increased from one, under Hoover, to fifty under Roosevelt. Kuklick, *Good Ruler*, 47.

23. Levine and Levine, *People and the President*, 70.

24. Ibid., 43–44.

25. Stout [Anon.], *President Vanishes*, directed on film by William A. Wellman, 1934. Contrast this story's rather blasé view of a president's weakness with the fear and even terror that the same quality would inspire in 1960s presidential fictions, as discussed further below and in chap. 5.

26. See the discussion of antebellum novels in chap. 2 and of Progressive Era novels in chap. 3. As noted above, *Gabriel Over the White House* was similar to Progressive fictions in style and purpose and could well be viewed as the last of the pre–New Deal utopian/socialist novels.

27. Alger wrote many broadly similar novels; among those whose plot elements most closely parallel *A Cool Million*'s is *Bound to Rise*. On West's literary parallels, see Light, "Varieties of Satire," 45–59.

28. On the parallel to Voltaire's *Candide*, see Light, "Varieties of Satire." It might also be apt to compare Shagpoke to Mephistopheles, although Lemuel Pitkin's ambitions are considerably more modest than Faust's.

29. West, *Cool Million*, 13, 11.

30. Ibid., 58.

31. Ibid., 123.

32. The relationship between fascism and capitalism was actively debated in the 1930s. Fascism may have been, as some have argued, an extreme form of capitalism, but it also apparently sought to fill a spiritual void at the heart of modern, materialistic societies and economies. At any rate, for West, the national myths of America—America's counterpart to German fascism's mystical *volk*- and *Führer*-worship—included a myth of capitalism's beneficence. (The slang phrase *a cool million* does not denote an amount of money so much as a dream of wealth and easy living.) By naming his hero "Lemuel," West linked his story to *Gulliver's Travels,* an earlier satire attacking the values of commercial culture; see the discussion in chap. 1 of Lord Bolingbroke and his circle, which included Jonathan Swift. West collaborated on a screenplay treatment for the novel that dropped the Shagpoke Whipple character and focused instead on the story's Algeresque elements, and among the reasons it was never filmed may have been the loss of depth these changes wrought. See West, "'Cool Million': A Screen Story."

33. Lewis, *It Can't Happen Here.* For specific text references, see the searchable text at Project Gutenberg. Vermont was the home state of Calvin Coolidge. The "ironbound Republican" but independent state, as Lewis calls it, proved its political distinctiveness in 1936 when it joined Maine as one of only two states to vote against the landslide re-election of FDR.

34. For an extended discussion of these themes in *1984,* see J. Smith, *Unthinking the Unthinkable,* chap. 6.

35. Among such works are Nathanael West's own *Day of the Locust,* Frank Capra's *Meet John Doe* and *Mr. Smith Goes to Washington,* Fritz Lang's *M* and *Fury* (which was based on a story titled "Mob Rule"), and Charlie Chaplin's *The Great Dictator.* It is perhaps not coincidental that Capra, Lang, and Chaplin, though working in the United States, were all born in Europe, where "it" obviously *could* happen.

36. Sontag, "Fascinating Fascism." Belief in cinema as a propaganda medium figures in *Gabriel Over the White House,* where President Hammond commissions a movie aimed at dramatizing and promoting his reforms. Sure enough, the result is a work not unlike the film version of *Gabriel Over the White House* itself.

37. Mast, *Can't Help Singin'.*

38. Other treatments of the public/private theme on film included *Stand Up and Cheer!* by Fox Films, a 1934 Shirley Temple vehicle in which President Roosevelt tries to cheer up the nation by creating a new cabinet-level Department of Amusement, thus conflating (or punning on) the two meanings of the word *depression*; *Grand Old Girl,* a 1935 RKO film in which a president personally intervenes to resolve a small town's dispute involving the local high school principal (May Robson); and *First Lady,* Kaufman and Katharine Dayton's 1935 Broadway comedy (and a 1937 Warner Bros. film) in which the drawing-room

competition between presidential candidates' wives overshadows the public politicking of the candidates themselves.

39. Examples of this in later years would include Irving Berlin's 1962 *Mr. President* and Phyllis Lynd's 1994 *I Love You, Madam President,* both discussed further below.

40. Quoted in Ketcham, *Presidents Above Party,* 60.

41. From *Marbury v. Madison,* 5 U.S. 137 (1803), 163.

42. The quotations are from James Madison [Publius, pseud.], *Federalist* 51, in Rossiter, *Federalist Papers,* 322.

43. *Abraham Lincoln,* directed by D. W. Griffith, 1930. All quoted dialogue from the films discussed here is the author's transcription.

44. Herndon's work and other early Lincoln storytelling are discussed in chap. 3.

45. This scene may have been inspired by a gravesite scene in Thomas Dixon's 1919 novel *The Southerner: A Romance of the Real Lincoln,* although there the grave in question is Lincoln's mother's, not Ann Rutledge's. Though an admirer of Lincoln, whom he celebrated as a southern-born president, Dixon was better known as the author of several Ku Klux Klan–friendly novels that he and D. W. Griffith adapted into the silent epic *The Birth of a Nation.*

46. It's worth noting that in reality, Lincoln—a Unionist, not an abolitionist—insisted as president and party leader that the law required him *not* to free slaves rather than to free them. At crucial moments, that is, he did treat the virtues of freedom and of law as if they were in conflict. See Wills, *Lincoln at Gettysburg,* 137–47.

47. As noted in chap. 3, stories featuring the Ann Rutledge legend had multiplied rapidly in the 1920s and after. Although Griffith's film makes for the more striking contrast with John Ford's, it's worth acknowledging at least one other treatment the tale received at the time: Robert Sherwood's 1938 Pulitzer-winning Broadway play *Abe Lincoln in Illinois,* directed for RKO by John Cromwell in 1940. In this telling, Abe (Raymond Massey) must come to *Ann's* defense against local ruffians and gossip, so his emergence as a civilizing force and a leader are due in part to old-fashioned chivalry.

48. More succinctly and certainly more sunnily, this idea is also put forward in another 1939 film, Garson Kanin's *The Great Man Votes.* After all the hoopla from both sides, a mayoral election comes down to the single vote of one hard-luck citizen. *Mr. Smith* differs from that movie in treating the issue not as a parable of democracy in general, but specifically as a question about the viability of *American* government and the political health of the United States. It is also the considerably darker story—an element of Capra's vision not well captured by the familiar term *Capraesque.* The wishful sentimentality to which that term usually refers may apply to *Mr. Smith's* emphasis on the noble and sincere as opposed to the practical and effective, but as Capra well understood, it's

a two-edged sword: The appealingly guileless everyman can also be the demagogue's best weapon, a point that Gary Cooper's character demonstrates in Capra's *Meet John Doe*.

49. That climactic scene, and the movie, had famous echoes in real-life politics. Resisting the bosses' effort to cut off his microphone and stop the speech, Matthews barks, "I'm paying for this broadcast!" Running in the 1980 New Hampshire primary, candidate Ronald Reagan upbraided the moderator of a debate he had funded: "I'm paying for this microphone!" Many, including Reagan himself, believed that this remark brought him from behind to win the primary and thus put him on course to the White House. See the excerpt from Reagan's autobiography at "Discover Reagan/The 1980 Primaries," http://www.ronaldreagan.com/primaries.html. It has also been noted that Ross Perot's independent 1992 campaign bore several similarities to Matthews's.

50. *Mr. President* ran for less than eight months, while *I Love You, Madam President* was apparently performed only as a studio recording.

Chapter 5. The Human Element

1. The epigraph quotes from the following websites: "Great Moments with Mr. Lincoln," http://www.geocities.com/oooketchup/lincoln.htm; Just Disney, "The Walt Disney Story, Featuring 'Great Moments with Mr. Lincoln,'" http://www.justdisney.com/Features/great_moments_with_mr_lincoln/; Intercot West: Disneyland Inside and Out, "The Walt Disney Story, Featuring 'Great Moments with Mr. Lincoln,'" http://www.intercotwest.com/theme Parks/dlMsTheWaltDisneyStory.asp; and the vacation travel site ThrillMoun tain.com (http://www.thrillmountain.com/disneyland1.asp?page=24&att=39 and http://www.thrillmountain.com/disneyland1.asp?page=27&art=50; no longer functioning).

2. Dallek, "Medical Ordeals of JFK."

3. J. F. Kennedy, "Address to a Joint Convention." To note a couple of other examples: Martin Luther King Jr.'s "I Have a Dream" speech spoke of the need "to stand up for freedom together," and in his last presidential address to the Southern Christian Leadership Conference, on August 16, 1967, King argued that "we must stand up and say, I'm black and I'm beautiful, and this self-affirmation is the black man's need, made compelling by the white man's crimes against him." King, "The Southern Christian Leadership Conference Presidential Address," *Martin Luther King, Jr., On Racism, Poverty, Capitalism, and other big questions*, Hartford Web Publishing, http://www.hartford-hwp.com/archives/45a/628.html.

4. An especially elaborate—and contrived—list of such parallels has been used to argue that Kennedy was Lincoln's reincarnation. See "The Reincarnation of Abraham Lincoln into John Kennedy," *Near-Death Experiences and the*

Afterlife, International Association for Near-Death Studies, http://www.near-death.com/experiences/reincarnation08.html. Lincoln automobiles—which have included a long line of presidential limousines—were originally named after the sixteenth president.

5. J. F. Kennedy, "Commencement Address at American University." That we all breathe the same air was important to Kennedy's point, since he went on to call for an end to "atmospheric" (above-ground) nuclear tests.

6. Ibid.

7. Mills, *Causes of World War Three,* 20. Mills's own view, however, was that the widespread feelings of "historical inevitability" and "fatalistic resignation" were illusions born of a genuinely powerful elite's "default and incompetence." Mills, 6, and part 1.

8. Eldredge, *Second American Revolution,* 327.

9. Neustadt, *Presidential Power,* xi, 140–43, 158–63, 203, 208. For other warnings about presidential weakness, see the following and the sources they cite: Lerner, "Presidency and Demos" and "Wounded Titans," in *Wounded Titans,* 16–17, 31–45; Rossiter, *American Presidency,* 272, 274, and chap. 8; D. B. James, *Contemporary Presidency,* 171–72; Buchanan, *Presidential Experience,* 6–8, 11n10, 13n12, 122–23, 155; Lammers, *Presidential Politics,* 264–65; and "TRB from Washington," quoting Thomas E. Cronin and Godfrey Hodgson on this point. Eventually, weakness and limits simply came to be taken for granted. Thus, for instance, Theodore J. Lowi, writing about "the crisis of public authority," titled one section "Why Effective Urban Policies Cannot be Made by Modern Presidents." Lowi, *End of Liberalism,* 211.

10. R. Marx, *Health of the Presidents.*

11. Neustadt, *Presidential Power,* 122–23.

12. Hughes, *Ordeal of Power,* 3, 115, and chap. 7.

13. Ibid., 19, emphases in original.

14. For instance Vaughn Meader, whose satirical record album *The First Family* (Cadence Records), spoofing the Kennedys, sold four million copies within a month of its release in late 1962 and more than seven million overall, making it for a long time the fastest-selling LP album "on record." Though they are beyond the scope of this study, politically themed comedy albums—cross-fertilized with nightclub acts and TV variety-show appearances, and often featuring comedians doing impressions of presidents—were a popular source of semi-fictional light commentary in this period.

15. Sorenson, *Decision-Making in the White House,* xii, xvi, 12; Reedy, *Twilight of the Presidency,* 1st ed., 36; see also 127, 132–33, 138, 150–51, 160–85. All subsequent citations are to this edition unless otherwise noted.

16. L. B. Johnson, *Choices We Face,* 3, 7.

17. Neustadt, *Presidential Power,* 143.

18. Reedy, *Twilight of the Presidency*, 36, 160, and chap. 12; see also Buchanan, *Presidential Experience*, 6, 11n10, and 47–48.

19. Woodward and Bernstein, *Final Days*. For examples of this image of Nixon in later works, see Oliver Stone's movie *Nixon* and Russell Lees's stage play *Nixon's Nixon*, both 1995.

20. Roberts, *Truth About the Assassination*.

21. Skolnick et al., *Assassination and Political Violence*, 93–94.

22. Warren et al., "Lee Harvey Oswald: Background and Possible Motives," chap. 7 of the *Report of the President's Commission on the Assassination of President Kennedy*.

23. See the discussion of the 1930s in chap. 4.

24. In reality, Wilson's stroke had left him barely able to fold a letter into an envelope. Yet the final scene of *Wilson* has him leaving office by walking away upstage, i.e., into the past, a politically broken but more or less physically able man. *Sunrise at Campobello*, by contrast, closes with FDR as a physically lame but politically confident rising star, aware of the possible indignity but nonetheless determined to step *forward* (downstage) to claim leadership.

25. "A game object that has no inherent significance except to be a focal point of the action. Alfred Hitchcock defined 'maguffin' as 'the thing that the protagonist has, the antagonist wants, and the audience doesn't care.'" From From *FAQ #28: A Glossary of Game Biz Terms*, Sloperama Productions, http://www.sloperama.com/advice/lesson28.html.

26. The mold appears to be metal and has an unfortunate resemblance to a bedpan. In *Manchurian Candidate* the change in faces is achieved more adroitly, through an implanted memory of a ladies' garden club. When this image in Marco's nightmares slips sideways, we see that the "ladies" are really the dour apparatchiks who ordered the brainwashing.

27. Brian W. Fairbanks, "Richard Widmark: The Face of Film Noir," http://www.angelfire.com/oh2/writer/widmark.html.

28. Knebel and Bailey, *Seven Days in May*, 35, 38–39, 47.

29. "His face was colorless and an unnatural puffiness hung about his eyes. . . . [T]he middle-aged man of 52 . . . seemed almost old. . . . The hunch of his shoulders bore the imprint of resignation, almost defeat." Ibid., 119, 219, 245–49, 297–98, 301–2. In the film, Lyman is seen at one point gulping down pills.

30. Reedy, *Twilight of the Presidency*, 162.

31. The best example comes from *Night of Camp David*, the 1966 novel in which Knebel takes the next step and imagines a president whose close associates come to fear that he has actually gone insane. Confronted about his erratic behavior—he will shortly be forced to resign—President Hollenbach explains, "Gentlemen, this office does change the man. The President is in

command so constantly. He is Number One. He is never denied. He is king for his term. So, it is only natural that a President begins to think of himself as the country. . . . You all help to foster that attitude, by your kowtowing to the President. . . . Every one of you helps build the power complex of the White House, gentlemen, every one of you" (297). Note the striking similarity between this passage and the analysis in Reedy, *Twilight of the Presidency,* 165–66; and Buchanan, *Presidential Experience,* especially chaps. 2 and 4.

32. Knebel and Bailey, *Seven Days in May,* 6.

33. Scott in this case is Michael Goodwin. It's also indicative of the difference between the film and the radio play that Lancaster/Scott is top-billed in the film, while top billing in the L.A. Theatre Works radio play goes to Asner/Lyman.

34. Yet another spin on the *Seven Days* theme is John Calvin Batchelor's 1994 novel *Father's Day,* which borrows many elements of the earlier work but makes the current (acting) president one of the chief plotters—along with, again, a popular chairman of the Joint Chiefs. The rightful President Jay, having suffered a mental breakdown, has temporarily relinquished office under the 25th Amendment (a provision for presidential disability that itself came out of the mid-'60s). The conspirators' aim is to keep him from taking it back. It's plainer here than in *Seven Days* that they may even be right on the merits; as one critic put it, "President Jay is still battling depression and sounds like a total wet noodle throughout the book. You start to wonder who is the better guy to have in the White House" (John J. Rust, "Good Characters, But Needed Better Execution," reader's comment posted March 24, 2002, Amazon.com). Regardless, the plot is foiled. But in the meantime Jay attempts suicide and winds up partly paralyzed, so he can't stay in office anyway. This extreme heightening of the president's debility seems inversely proportioned to the story's political stakes: No great danger looms like the Soviet threat, so the storyteller tries to compensate by making the president progressively sicker.

35. Sellers would have played a fourth character, the bomber pilot, if not for an actual disability: He broke his leg while the movie was being filmed, which led to the brilliant recasting choice of Slim Pickens—an actor known for his roles as a cowboy.

36. The publishers of *Red Alert* were apparently concerned to make clear that it was the earliest treatment of the theme. A later printing of the original paperback, probably from late 1963, carries this text on the front cover: "Is FAIL-SAFE foolproof? red alert [*sic*] by Peter Bryant *is the original* novel about an unauthorized H-bomb attack on the USSR by American B-52s despite our Fail-Safe system. Can our President prevent Russian retaliation?" (emphasis in original). The back cover also carries a January 24, 1963, quote from the *New York Chronicle* attesting that the novel *Fail-Safe,* its film adaptation, and a then-untitled Stanley Kubrick film project were all derived from *Red Alert.*

37. Bryant, *Red Alert*, 78, 178.

38. Guthrie, "'Fail-Safe' Compels."

39. For a more detailed discussion of *Dr. Strangelove's* philosophical orientation and context, see J. Smith, *Unthinking the Unthinkable*, chap. 3.

40. Bryant, *Dr. Strangelove*, 29–32.

41. Shadows and "mood" lighting are now common on prime-time television; they were a very noticeable feature of NBC's *The West Wing* (discussed in chap. 6), where it sometimes looked as if the president's staff could deal with all manner of international crises but could not remember to pay the electric bill. In B-movies, a good example of this aesthetic is *Chain of Command*, made in 2000 with Roy Scheider as the fictional president—and, like other B-movies today, distributed exclusively to domestic cable TV, video/DVD, and theaters abroad. One viewer describes *Chain of Command* as a "Poorly done political actioner. Badly photographed, acted, and directed. Every single scene is underlighted, including those very few that are shot during the daytime. It doesn't matter what the location is. At an important conference in the White House, no lights are on, and the only available lighting is a gloomy blue that is filtered through a few windows. The pr[e]mier of China conducts an earth-shattering phone conversation under conditions of such intense chiaroscuro that he should be contemplating a bust of Homer in a Rembrandt painting. Honest. It's as if he had a tiny spotlight on his face and was otherwise in total darkness." Robert J. Maxwell, "It's Lonely at the Bottom," user comment posted August 16, 2002, *Internet Movie Database*, http://www.imdb.com/title/tt0207377/user comments?start=10. Like other B-movies, *Chain of Command* is a collection of genre motifs from both its own and earlier eras: the system out of control, the hostage president, the womanizing president, the inadequate substitute suddenly thrust into power.

42. A "black" in live theater is a backdrop curtain, usually defining the edge of the stage, but the term can also describe the fact of being outside the available light.

43. The phrase "virulent hypermasculinity" is from Kimmel, *Manhood in America*, 33. See also chap. 2 above.

44. Cortright, *Apollo Expeditions to the Moon*. For an extended study of the "gendered" quality of Cold War political rhetoric and its concern with emasculation and effeminacy, see Cuordileone, *Manhood and American Political Culture*.

45. Kimmel, *Manhood in America*, 263, 271.

46. While a "subtle and sensitive" leader might find the right course, "the more probable outcome of our current difficulties will be a 'man on horseback'—a George Wallace with a broader appeal or a Ronald Reagan with greater depth." Reedy, *Twilight of the Presidency*, 1st ed., 181–82; 2nd ed., 171. As it turned out, the actual Ronald Reagan who served in the 1980s was less a Napoleon than a Louis Napoleon, in Reedy's view (2nd ed., 169–80).

47. Zaretsky, " Culture Wars of the 1960s," 12–13, 15, 25, 26, 29.

48. "If 'youth' is not the word we are going to use to cover this obstreperous population, then we may have to coin another. But undeniably the social grouping exists with a self-conscious solidarity." Roszak, *Making of a Counter Culture*, 30.

49. Cuordileone, *Manhood and American Political Culture*, especially chap. 3.

50. Later in the decade, Fletcher Knebel's *Vanished* (1968), which became the TV miniseries in which Richard Widmark played a president, again raised the specter of creeping unmanliness in the Oval Office. The president's closest friend and advisor mysteriously disappears at the same time as a prominent physicist with whom he has been secretly meeting, and the ensuing scandal includes rumors that he was "a secret fag." In this case, though, the issue is a red herring; the two men were actually on a mission for the president, concluding a top-secret nuclear arms pact. As to the dying president, that image appears not only in *Advise and Consent* but in several Allen Drury novels. In a series of sequels published between 1962 and 1975, Drury has several presidents violently or mysteriously killed—including one character who is killed two different ways in different books.

51. Russell, *Shadow of Blooming Grove*. The political color barrier was, if not breached, at least tested in 1972, when Congresswoman Shirley Chisholm ran for the Democratic nomination and was prominently featured at the Democratic National Convention. See also the comments on *Rufus Jones for President* in the first endnote to chap. 4.

52. Wallace, *Man*. A token member of the Senate leadership, Dilman begins the story as Senate president pro tem, a purely ornamental post that in 1947 was placed just three heartbeats away from the presidency (an oddly high placement that probably reflects the fact that it's an office mentioned in the Constitution, unlike the more powerful and politically meaningful position of majority leader). On Capra's *Mr. Smith Goes to Washington*, see the discussion in chap. 4; on other "Mr. Smiths," see the discussion in chap. 6. Drew Pearson, the longtime Washington reporter and columnist, wrote two novels—*The Senator*, 1968, and *The President*, 1970—telling the tale of a senator who is part Kiowa Indian and becomes president amid the civil disorders that Pearson expected to continue into the 1970s, and whose liberalism runs afoul of the old guard and eventually gets him impeached. The influence of *The Man* on this story seems obvious, even though President Ben Hannaford is an adept, self-confident politician more reminiscent of LBJ than Douglass Dilman. But *The President* can claim one distinction: it may be the first instance in American political fiction in which *both* sides in conflict declare the other to be a "cabal."

53. Wallace, *Man*, 251, 375. In the film version, a newly sworn-in Dilman drops and breaks a drinking glass because his hands are trembling, then begins to cry when he sees himself in a mirror and tries to utter the words "Mr. President."

54. Wallace, *Man*, 516–17, 545–46.

55. Ibid., 600–601, 765–66.

56. Knebel, *Trespass*, 107–8, 119–20, 146, 151. Among the many examples of essentially that same ideal are the presidents in the TV series *The West Wing*, *24*, and *Commander in Chief*, which are discussed in the chapters following.

57. Quoted in "Pigasus the Immortal and the 1968 Chicago Democratic Convention," *Porkolopis*, http://www.porkopolis.org/ftr/pigasus.htm. In this connection it's also worth mentioning *MacBird!*, Barbara Garson's faux-Shakespearean spoof of the Johnson administration, which began as an idea for a skit accompanying the 1965 International Days of Protest and became a minor cult classic. See "Notes about MacBird" (from the preface to the 1967 Grove Press edition), brumm dot com, http://www.brumm.com/MacBird/MacBirdNotes.html. Elevating contemporary politicians to the stature of blank-versifying Shakespearean heroes makes them seem especially absurd—as does telling their story in pseudo-biblical language, a gimmick used on the Orson Welles–narrated comedy record album *The Begatting of the President* (Hollywood, CA: Mediarts, 1969), about the fall of Johnson and the rise of Nixon.

58. Without citing a source, *Wikipedia* claims that "*Super President* came under fire from critics and TV watchdog groups for its depiction of a national leader who was an invincible superhuman; many found this tasteless, especially in the wake of President John F. Kennedy's assassination just four years earlier." If so, this would suggest that it was perceived at the time as a response to the problem of presidents' bodily weakness. "Super President," *Wikipedia*, http://en.wikipedia.org/wiki/Super_President.

59. *Prez: First Teen President*, no. 4, February/March 1974. The quote is from a reader's letter.

60. For instance, the term appears in the title of Berger and Luckmann's *Social Construction of Reality*. The term *deconstruction* and the foundational works of Michel Foucault were also appearing in these years.

61. L. Marx, "Technology," 971. Marx traces this line of thought back through Howard Scott and the 1930s, Frederick Winslow Taylor, and Thorstein Veblen to Daniel Webster in 1847.

62. Roszak, *Making of a Counterculture*, chap. 1, and *Where the Wasteland Ends*, 32–38.

63. Eldredge, *Second American Revolution*, 326, and chap. 12. Compare this remarkable description of how NASA went about its work in this period: "Systems engineering and systems management were developed to high efficiency. So was project management. New ways to achieve high reliability in complex machines were worked out. . . . The best of large-scale management theory and doctrine was used to bring together both organizational (or administrative) optimization and join it to responsibility to work within the constraints of accepted organizational behavior." Cortright, *Apollo Expeditions to the Moon*, chap. 1.4.

64. Youngblood, *Expanded Cinema*, 55, 45.

65. "Age of Aquarius" was common usage, most famously popularized by the hit song "Aquarius" from the Broadway musical *Hair*. "Consciousness III" was Charles A. Reich's term, explained in his bestselling book *The Greening of America*. The terminology of "Apollonian" and "Dionysian" can be found in, among others, Norman O. Brown (*Life against Death* and *Love's Body*), Theodore Roszak (*Making of a Counter Culture* and *Where the Wasteland Ends*), and William Braden (*Age of Aquarius*). It was fitting that the era's single biggest high-tech undertaking, an effort that at the same time was *literally* cosmic, was known as Project "Apollo." For that matter, as Bruce Kuklick notes, even the Kennedy version of the technocratic ideal was not simply a matter of intellect but a sexualization thereof. Kuklick, *Good Ruler*, 121, 125. And, of course, we now know that there was an element in Kennedy himself of Dionysian excess.

66. *The Christine Jorgensen Story*, directed by Irving Rapper, 1970, also juxtaposed imagery drawn from transsexual Jorgensen's trip-like dreams with a long clinical description of how the body can be re-engineered.

67. Youngblood, *Expanded Cinema*, 139–56, 45. See also McLuhan, *Understanding Media*.

68. See the essays in Rosenthal, *McLuhan: Pro and Con*. At best, McLuhan's famous formula depends on an unusual definition of terms. Clearly, different "messages" in the ordinary sense of that word can be conveyed through the same medium, and the same message through different media. McLuhan, though, defines "message" as something other than information or propositional content. The message he is referring to is a kind of medium-specific overlay on that content. But insofar as this overlay is identifiable with the medium, "The medium is the message" becomes a tautology.

69. Gilbert Seldes (1952) and Jack Gould (1956), quoted in Spigel and Jenkins, "Same Bat Channel, Different Bat Times," 121.

70. Besides this direct influence, there were other ways in which TV images seemed to inspire storytellers in other media. Without the televised Army-McCarthy and organized-crime hearings of a few years earlier, it would be hard to imagine a story like *Advise and Consent* whose drama is built around a Senate hearing—or, for that matter, the scenes in *The Manchurian Candidate* and *Seven Days in May* that are set in congressional committee rooms.

71. Swift, *Gulliver's Travels*, part 2 ("A Voyage to Brobdingnag"), chap. 1. Gulliver has discovered this, along with the "great Holes in my [own] Skin . . . and my Complexion made up of several Colours altogether disagreeable," by virtue of his changing sizes relative to the Lilliputians and Brobdingnagians.

72. Mason, *Hostage*, 206. In Richard Z. Chesnoff, Edward Klein, and Robert Littell's novel *If Israel Had Lost the War* (1969), a fictional "alternate history" of the Six-Day War, Israel is destroyed after America fails to intervene to save it, in part because Lyndon Johnson happens to have a bad cold that week.

There are similar passages in Hank Searls's novel *The Pilgrim Project,* Larry Collins and Dominique Lapierre's *The Fifth Horseman,* and others.

73. Examples include Robert J. Serling's *President's Plane Is Missing,* discussed further below, and the ABC-TV series *Voyage to the Bottom of the Sea,* specifically episode 16, "Hail to the Chief," broadcast in December 1964. Serling's novel is the source of the line "the patient is the nation," and it opens with the president waking up "with his usual hangover—fashioned not of liquor but of tensions and worries that sleep had failed to dissolve."

74. For example, Nancy Freedman's novel *Joshua Son of None* (1973) imagines the life story of a new JFK, "Joshua Francis Kellogg," cloned from the salvaged genetic code of the dying original and raised in circumstances designed to copy his prototype's. The story's main actor is the physician who oversees this dubious project, and who pays for it in a "nightmare of repetition": His complex experiment in resurrection through body doubling unfolds "as programmed and foreordained as a Greek tragedy," right up to the inevitable second assassination. The mythic figure explicitly invoked in *Joshua Son of None* is Thor, the god who "shrove and hallowed the dead that they would rise," as the novel puts it. JFK likewise seems to have inspired *The President's Doctor,* a 1975 novel by William Woolfolk. Here the question was what kind of crisis might arise if a young, charming, vigorous president's treatment for neck pain went haywire, gradually addicting him to painkillers whose unfortunate side effects included paranoid psychosis. In this novel the role of Rasputin is played by another crazed general—this one the head of an internal security force who exploits the doctor's efforts, taking advantage of the president's intensifying illness in his own bid to seize power.

75. Rossiter (*American Presidency,* 274) and D. B. James (*Contemporary Presidency,* 171), among others, described modern presidents as prisoners of one kind or another. Garry Wills, looking back on the era, saw the struggles of one president and his brothers as examples of *The Kennedy Imprisonment,* as explained in his book of that title.

76. Templeton, *Kidnapping of the President,* directed on film by George Mendeluk, 1980.

77. In a climactic scene, the newly freed president also grabs a machine gun and does some of his own shooting. The image of a president physically taking over his own protection would recur in such 1990s movies as *Air Force One, First Target,* and others. See the discussion in chap. 6.

78. In *The Wild Wild West Revisited,* a 1979 CBS-TV sequel to the offbeat adventure series of the late 1960s, President Grover Cleveland turns up locked in a cell alongside Queen Victoria and Tsar Nicholas. It seems that an evil genius—one bent on world domination, as evil geniuses usually are—has been kidnapping world leaders and replacing them with perfect doubles. Other examples of captive presidents include those in the novels *The Fifth Horseman, Hostage One,*

and *We Are Holding the President Hostage,* and in the films and TV movies *Counterstrike, The Alternate, 2001: A Space Travesty, Chain of Command,* and *Deterrence.* In still other variants the hostage could be the vice president (*Sudden Death*), a member of the president's family (*First Daughter, The West Wing*), and other associated characters. Typically the protagonists of such stories are their rescuers—agents or operatives of some kind who are free to act while the president himself is out of commission. The president's role, in other words, is as often as not that of maguffin, a device discussed further in chap. 6.

79. Lerner, *Wounded Titans,* 38.

80. Serling, *President's Plane Is Missing,* 5, 8, 15, 26–30, 87–89, 103, 248, directed for ABC-TV by Daryl Duke, 1973. Allen Drury's 1968 *Preserve and Protect* was also premised on the loss of the president in an Air Force One crash. Other absent-president stories included Sherwin Markman's 1970 *The Election,* which imagined unrest in the streets during a long struggle in Congress to resolve a deadlocked three-candidate race, and Fletcher Knebel's 1972 *Dark Horse,* about an obscure candidate picked to fill a vacancy after a nominee dies just before the election.

81. Milton, *President Is Missing.*

82. Prochnau, *Trinity's Child*; *By Dawn's Early Light,* directed by Jack Sholder, 1990. This film is discussed further in chap. 6.

83. The first of White's *Making of the President* series appeared in 1961 and dealt with the campaign of 1960. And in a related trope, presidents were also seen as manufactured products, things to be bought and sold. This was the premise of John G. Schneider's 1964 novel *The Golden Kazoo* and Joe McGinnis's *The Selling of the President,* a nonfiction chronicle of Richard Nixon's 1968 campaign.

84. Reedy, *Twilight of the Presidency,* 185. Unlike Neustadt, whose proposed reforms were based on some hope of raising the level of presidents' expertise, Buchanan (*Presidential Experience,* 177) offered reforms with the caveat that "none is likely of adoption."

85. Serling, *President's Plane Is Missing,* 47–48.

86. D. F. Jones's *Colossus,* the 1966 novel on which the TV movie was based, explicitly draws the parallel with Frankenstein. Likewise, the film's Dr. Forbin is played by Eric Braeden, a native German whose hint of an accent is reminiscent of both Frankenstein and Strangelove. At the same time, the novel—by contrast with the movie—makes both Forbin and the president hot-blooded, hot-tempered, and highly emotional. The president is also exhausted and has developed a nervous tic. That character note aligns him with other fictional presidents of the time, but the fact that it's left out of the movie serves the further purpose of helping recast both Forbin and the president as bloodless technocrats, characters of such limited affect they almost seem cryogencially frozen.

87. Roth, *Our Gang.* Another noteworthy example of the mocking of Nixon, though set in his vice presidential years, is Robert Coover's 1977 *The*

Public Burning. In part a fictional memoir of Nixon, the novel includes an imagined but explicit account of his lust for Ethel Rosenberg after she is convicted in the celebrated atomic-spying case. It also presents Uncle Sam as a superhero battling his Communist counterpart, "the Phantom."

88. In the late 1970s *Saturday Night Live* also aired such comedy skits as "Carter Held Hostage: Day 154" and a spoof of the film *The China Syndrome*, the latter featuring an action-hero President Carter whose efforts to stop a radioactive meltdown turn him into a grinning, one-hundred-foot-tall mutant.

89. The quality and, perhaps, intent of this "campy" work has been aptly expressed by one viewer, who called it "an immensely enjoyable party film that gets better the deeper you get into the 12 pack sitting in the cooler." Mike [no last name], "Blood Suckers: Bad, in a fun way," user comment posted November 18, 2001, *Internet Movie Database,* http://www.imdb.com/title/tt0086980/ usercomments. Other examples of absurdism include Robert Coover's 1980 *A Political Fable,* expanded from a 1968 short story and satirically promoting "The Cat in the Hat for President," and Richard Brooks's 1982 film *Wrong Is Right,* which tried without much success to turn nuclear terrorism and Middle Eastern revolution into another *Dr. Strangelove.* This time the media was one target of the spoof; *Wrong Is Right* starred Sean Connery as a globe-trotting journalist, George Grizzard as the beleaguered president (whose favorite pastime, incidentally, seemed to be working out on exercise machines), and pseudo-suave comic Leslie Nielsen as the candidate running to replace him.

90. See the discussions in earlier chapters, especially 1 and 4.

91. Compared to *Blood Suckers from Outer Space,* however, *First Family* is high art. That may have been part of its problem: it's not quite stupid *enough* or poorly enough made to qualify as "camp." A similar problem in striking the right note of seriousness or absurdity might have afflicted *1600 Pennsylvania Avenue,* an Alan Jay Lerner/Leonard Bernstein Broadway musical that became "one of the greatest flops in Broadway history," closing after just seven performances in 1976 and not even released as a cast recording. See Warren Hoge, "Bernstein's Singing Presidents: A Recount," *New York Times,* theater section, March 31, 2008.

Chapter 6. Who Am I?

1. Other examples of such satires include Trudeau's own *Rap Master Ronnie,* a musical spoof originally written for the 1984 election and produced for the HBO and Cinemax cable TV networks in 1988, and the 1989 *Mastergate: A Play on Words,* a stage play—later adapted for Showtime cable—by Larry Gelbart, the writer/producer who turned *M*A*S*H* into a hit television series after Altman's 1970 film had made the story a touchstone of antiwar sentiment. In *Mastergate* the Iran-Contra scandal, a complex politico-military undertaking

that President Reagan and his aides all agreed he had done little to control, is lampooned as a conspiracy to use a big-budget Hollywood movie production as a front for illegal arms shipments.

2. When the British series *Spitting Image*—a comedy sketch program that used puppet caricatures to stage what amounted to live-action political cartoons—briefly tried to cross over to American network television in 1986–87, one episode imagined show-biz impresarios, like Bill Cosby and Ed McMahon, as kingmakers plotting to seize the White House for their (literal) puppet, Sylvester Stallone, an actor whose tough-guy characters are easily spoofed as even more vapid than Reagan.

3. See the discussion of alternate history in this book's conclusion.

4. See the discussions in chaps. 4 and 5, respectively.

5. Barbara Brenner's *Saving the President: What If Lincoln Had Lived?* is focused on an eighteen-year-old heroine, Lavinia "Vinnie" Ream, an artist who in real life sculpted Lincoln at the White House. Part alternate history—Vinnie manages to thwart Lincoln's assassination—this "young adult" novel was basically a coming-of-age story. Wolfgang Petersen's 1993 film *In the Line of Fire* recalled an even older genre. It was a story of personal trial and redemption, a distant echo of the ancient Christian "lives of the saints." Still tormented decades later over having failed to save President Kennedy, aging Secret Service agent Frank Horrigan (Clint Eastwood) struggles against a new would-be assassin, a taunting projection of his worst fears like the demons in the stories of old. Killing the president seems less important to this assassin—played by John Malkovich, an actor whose trademark is demonic intensity—than putting Horrigan to the test; the film's real interest isn't the president's safety so much as the struggle for Horrigan's soul.

Other works have turned the focus from those who might save the president to those who want to kill him. Here, too, the president is the perfect maguffin, motivating the would-be assassin while possibly not appearing in the story at all. Cultural and character studies of real or fictional assassins in recent fiction have included Don DeLillo's novel *Libra*, about Lee Harvey Oswald; Stephen Sondheim's 1990 musical *Assassins*, Niels Mueller's 2004 film *The Assassination of Richard Nixon* (in which Nixon himself appears only in archival footage), and Sarah Vowell's *Assassination Vacation*. The Imagination Liberation Front's 2003 play *I'm Going to Kill the President* and Nicholson Baker's 2004 novella *Checkpoint* both arose from widespread anger at George W. Bush yet presented assassination as something to ponder philosophically, an understandable if possibly nutty response to political stress whose impact on the individuals contemplating it matters to the writers as much as its impact on the nation. By contrast, the 2006 British fictional documentary *Death of a President*, which imagined the future assassination of Bush, was focused on the political *effects* of the act more than on its political or personal causes, and its implied claim was precisely that

Americans and their government would be more interested in scapegoating—in forcing the event into an established narrative of "terrorism"—than in finding or understanding the real assassin.

In one curious case, filmmakers dramatizing the efforts of assassins had to imagine *two* possible presidents. *Black Sunday*, a 1977 thriller about a terrorist plot to bomb the Super Bowl from a blimp while the president is in the crowd, was filmed before the outcome of the 1976 election was known—so brief glimpses of both Gerald Ford *and* Jimmy Carter look-alikes were filmed. Here was an especially pointed reminder that maguffin presidents are interchangeable plot devices, not important in and of themselves.

6. Thanks to the film, the old expression *wagging the dog* became common political shorthand for a president's use of military or other crises as pretexts for diverting attention from situations that might damage him politically. It points up how unimportant the president was in *Wag the Dog* that he wasn't named, even though Larry Beinhart's *American Hero*, the 1993 novel on which the film was based, made him George H. W. Bush—prompting *Kirkus Reviews* to remark, "What a terrific movie this book is never, ever going to make." Quoted on Amazon.com, http://www.amazon.com/gp/product/0345366638/qid=1148868253/sr=2-3/ref=pd_bbs_b_2_3/002-1737158-8568820?s=books&v=glance&n=283155.

7. Joe Weber, *Defcon One*, 65, 93, 257. In another typical technothriller, *Nimitz Class*, author Patrick Robinson all but forgets that there *is* a president. *Nimitz Class* is focused on a Navy investigator's frantic search for a nuclear-armed Russian submarine that has been stolen by terrorists and used to vaporize an American aircraft carrier. The president in this story is simply absent; given how and by whom the key decisions are made, a reader who didn't know better might think that America's highest official is its chief of naval operations.

8. See the discussions of realism and its conventions in earlier chapters.

9. On the terms *cycle* and *genre*, see Cavell, *World Viewed*, especially chap. 5. My usage expands the concepts from film to storytelling media in general.

10. See the discussions of these themes in chaps 4 and 5.

11. Besides *Wag the Dog* and *Primary Colors*, which is further discussed below, examples include *The Absolute Truth, Majority Rule, No Safe Place, Protect and Defend, Primary Motive*, and two different TV movies called *Running Mates*, to name a few.

12. This focus on the personal persisted as other dangers came to replace the nuclear threat. In the made-for-TV *Quarantine*, terrorist threats and the possible destruction of humanity by a mystery virus become occasions for a president to stop neglecting his teenage daughter. See also *By Dawn's Early Light, First Target*, and *Counterstrike*, the source of the tag line quoted. Among works not involving presidents, Steven Spielberg's 2005 film remake of H. G. Wells's *The War of the Worlds* demonstrates this reflexive preoccupation with the personal almost as if it were the result of a controlled experiment. The narrator of Wells's

1898 novel was a writer anxious to report what he saw; the narrators of the 1938 Orson Welles radio play were newscasters trying to warn the public; and the hero of the 1953 Byron Haskin film was a scientist struggling to understand what was happening. Only Spielberg's version gives us a hero who has family responsibilities: Tom Cruise's character is a single dad whose main concern is to save his children and reunite them with their mother.

13. The works mentioned in this paragraph are discussed in chaps. 3, 4, and 5.

14. For fictional presidents, daughters function much more commonly than sons as sources of anxiety, both serious and comic. Other examples include *Escape from L.A.*, discussed above; novelist Jack Higgins's 1997 thriller *The President's Daughter*, in which the title character is both a kidnap victim and the basis of a career-threatening secret; two teen-oriented TV film comedies, *My Date with the President's Daughter* (1998) and *Mail to the Chief* (2000); *The West Wing*, discussed further below; David Mamet's 2004 film *Spartan*, in which apparent danger to the president's daughter sets the story's events in motion; and the 2006 NBC-TV disaster miniseries *10.5 Apocalypse*.

15. A similar but more elaborate instance is Tim Green's 2002 suspense novel *The Fourth Perimeter*, which made family vengeance its central conceit. A retired Secret Service agent with intimate knowledge of how presidents are protected hatches an elaborate plot to kill the incumbent, who, he believes, is criminally responsible for the death of his son.

16. *Nixon*, directed by Oliver Stone, 1995. *Jack & Bobby*, a 2004–5 WB network series, was entirely devoted to early development: Chronicling the high school years of two quite different teenage brothers, it teased the audience with the question of which of them would wind up as president by the mid-twenty-first century. As to earlier works in which presidents' family pressures figure importantly, one exceptional case was *Kisses for My President*, discussed in chap. 5. That president, however, was a woman, and part of the source of the comedy was the new idea of a "mom" becoming president and her husband redefining First Lady–hood.

17. The first approach was tried twice in the 1980s, once with former sitcom star Patty Duke as the president (*Hail to the Chief*, ABC-TV, 1985) and once with George C. Scott in the role (*Mr. President*, Fox TV, 1987). Neither effort succeeded with either viewers or critics. The second approach yielded the short-lived American edition of *Spitting Image* mentioned above, the 1998 UPN-TV series *The Secret Diary of Desmond Pfeiffer* (about Abraham Lincoln and his fictional black servant), and the Comedy Central cable network's 2001 *That's My Bush!* Other curiosities in this vein have included the 2002 Fox TV movie *The Brady Bunch in the White House*, in which the well-known characters from a popular 1970s sitcom became the First Family, and the 2002–3 MTV series *Clone High*, an animated "high-school sitcom" that differed from other members of

that familiar genre in one key respect: the main characters were teenage clones of famous people, including Abraham Lincoln and JFK. Presidents have also made "guest" appearances on animated sitcoms; cartoon versions of George H. W. and Barbara Bush have appeared on Fox Network's *The Simpsons,* and Bill Clinton and George W. Bush on Comedy Central's *South Park.*

18. *My Fellow Americans* was originally supposed to co-star Walter Matthau, who had also played opposite Lemmon in *The Odd Couple* but who by this time was in failing health.

19. It should be noted that *My Fellow Americans* appeared before the real-life parties in effect switched positions on the issue of balancing the federal budget.

20. On *State of the Union,* see the discussion in chap. 4. Interestingly, *The American President* evolved from a project called *The President Elopes,* originally developed several years earlier as a 1940s-style screwball comedy starring Robert Redford. In one early telling, the widowed president's dalliance helps lift the depression brought on by his wife's death, a psychic impairment that has "rendered him useless as a president." The story changed tenor as the project changed hands, and while a dispute later arose over whom to credit for the final screenplay, it would seem that at least part of the credit lay with the times themselves and the changing genre pressures we've been considering: by the 1990s the salient issue was no longer a president's incapacity but his personal and romantic life as such, which the storytellers had come to see as a subject calling for serious treatment in its own right. See William Richert, "The Grand Theft President: The Internet Trial of Aaron Sorkin," *William Richert—West Wing Unauthorized,* http://www.williamrichert.com/page17.php.

21. The sketch aired on October 19, 1996. In other works of the period, too, physical action was needed from presidents. At one point in *Quarantine,* Harry Hamlin's President Kempers saves an irreplaceable vial of serum by diving through the air to catch it. And in *First Target* President Jonathan Hayes (Gregory Harrison), a onetime battalion commander in Operation Desert Storm, lends his Secret Service protectors a hand at the climactic moment by wrestling with, disarming, and finally shooting a would-be assassin.

22. See the discussion of this point in chap. 5.

23. The presidents' bodyguards are themselves important characters in many recent fictions. The uneasy relationship between a president, his family members, and their protectors has been played for both suspense and laughs, depending on who makes trouble for the agent: If it's kidnappers or assassins, we have a thriller; if it's the First Family member him- or herself, we have a comedy. Movies based on such a premise in recent years have included *Assassination, Guarding Tess, First Kid, Chasing Liberty,* and the cable-TV trilogy *First Daughter, First Target,* and *First Shot.* A similar premise also generated at least two "story arcs" on *The West Wing,* and variants of it can be found in *Spartan* and in the 2006 film *The Sentinel.*

24. *Air Force One* opens with President Marshall giving a speech that commits the United States to abandon realpolitik and side with the forces of truth and justice everywhere. That could be called a policy, and it does link Marshall's personal heroics to a larger national concern. But it's so sweeping and unqualified a promise that it sounds more like movie dialogue than a real speech—or did until 2001, when a real-life president took to promising to "rid the world of evil" and the like.

25. Brubaker and Shanower, *Prez: Smells Like Teen President*, 1995. The original *Prez* is discussed in chap. 5.

26. Compare this with *The Kidnapping of the President* and *Twilight's Last Gleaming*, discussed in chap. 5, as well as *Escape from New York*, in all of which a president is immobilized or somehow trapped in a way that forces him to submit wholly to the actions of others. In *Twilight's Last Gleaming* he is compelled literally to "step down" to meet his antagonist in a missile silo.

27. Where a president cannot stand up to the threat himself—where the looming disaster is plainly beyond his control—dignity may have to be reaffirmed in other ways. President Tom Beck in the 1998 disaster film *Deep Impact* obviously can't do personal battle with an asteroid heading straight for Earth. But, probably for that very reason, the filmmakers have him played by Morgan Freeman, an actor whose voice and bearing are as dignified as they come.

28. *Reagan's Raiders*, 1–3.

29. McCloud, *New Adventures of Abraham Lincoln*.

30. Smigel and McKay, *X-Presidents*.

31. Examples are the stuffy T. K. Blair of *The Phantom President* and the beatific Judson Hammond of *Gabriel Over the White House*, each of which had a back-slapping alter ego. See the discussions of those and related works in chap. 4.

32. See the discussion of *Mr. Smith Goes to Washington* in chap. 4.

33. *Commander in Chief*'s President Allen had a few policy goals, but trying to keep her above politics obliged this series—in contrast to *The West Wing*—to rely heavily on nonpolitical family issues, threats from ambitious rivals, and various emergencies often borrowed from earlier works: her own illness, a hostage incident involving Air Force One, a husband who accidentally gets photographed in a seemingly compromising position.

34. Compare the main characters in *Bulworth* and *Head of State* with Bill McKay (Robert Redford) in Michael Ritchie's *The Candidate* (1972). McKay is another honest outsider tapped to fill a vacancy (in a Senate race) and expected to lose because he tells the truth. When he wins, though, it's taken as a grim sign of the system's victory over *him*, not vice-versa.

35. See the discussions of these points in chaps. 1 and 3.

36. Gross, *Man of Destiny*. Pages referred to in this discussion include 58, 89–90, 141, 201–2, 237, 277, 282–91, 305, 306, 394, 406–7. Gross has written a number of nonfiction books promoting this same view, and in 1986 he had also

published a novel about a president who was the opposite of Charlie Palmer: As a Soviet agent, *The Red President*'s title character was about as staunch a "party man" as it's possible to be.

37. The films are *The Hunt for Red October* (1990), starring Alec Baldwin as Jack; *Patriot Games* (1992) and *Clear and Present Danger* (1994), with Harrison Ford in that role; and *The Sum of All Fears* (2002), in which Ben Affleck stars as a younger Jack (in an episode out of sequence with the others).

38. This fictional incident was among examples noted in rebutting claims of President Bush and others that the attacks of September 11, 2001, were unforeseeable—like National Security Advisor Condoleeza Rice's remark on May 16, 2002, that no one could have imagined hijacked aircraft being used as missiles to attack buildings.

39. Clancy, *Executive Orders*, 1216, 621, 159. In all quotations from *Executive Orders*, emphases are in the original.

40. See the discussion of F. U. Adams's *President John Smith* in chap. 3.

41. Clancy, *Executive Orders*, 435, 488–93, 235.

42. Ibid., 469. For the writers in question, what appears to join self-interest and ideology in a common critique—despite the fact that self-interest is narrow and inwardly focused, and ideology is large and diffuse—is the assumption that ideologies do not arise from sincerely held social visions and critiques but instead are merely cynical masks for self-interest. The true patriot cares about individuals, not abstract ideas, but the individuals he cares about are family members and perhaps fellow citizens, not himself.

43. See, for instance, Atlas, "Confessing for Voyeurs," Herman, "The Culture of Narcissism." Historian and social critic Christopher Lasch's bestselling *Culture of Narcissism* appeared in 1979, and the phrase quickly entered common use as a shorthand description of both the 1970s and contemporary America in general.

44. During the scandal, charges of conspiracy came from different directions. The official investigation, special prosecutor's report, and ensuing impeachment treated the matter as a criminal conspiracy, while the president's largely successful defense included Hillary Clinton's famous charge that he was the victim of a "vast right-wing conspiracy" among his political opponents.

45. See the discussion of these issues in chap. 3.

46. Nan Britton, *President's Daughter*, 203–4, 226, 241. Other authors besides those discussed here have claimed affairs with presidents, especially in recent years, but none of those claims has been as well substantiated or had nearly the public impact of these four.

47. K. S. Morgan, *Past Forgetting*; Exner, *My Story*. In the text I refer to these memoirists by their maiden names, Summersby and Campbell, respectively, because that's how they were known at the time of the events in question.

48. K. S. Morgan, *Past Forgetting*, 152.

332 ❖ *Notes to pages 233–238*

49. In fact, Eugène Labiche's play *Un chapeau de paille d'Italie,* twice adapted to film and once to ballet, does make a maguffin of the title Italian straw hat, and one of its characters complains repeatedly about a soiled shirt.

50. Anthony, "President Of the Peephole." Based on the example this article quotes, Harding's poetic style might kindly be described as "erotic doggerel."

51. For example, here is footnote 161 of Part III, "Grounds [for impeachment]," of the special prosecutor's report to the House of Representatives, commonly known as *The Starr Report* ("GJ" refers to transcripts from the grand jury, and "Depo." to sworn depositions): "Ms. Lewinsky testified that *Leaves of Grass* was 'the most sentimental gift he had given me.' Lewinsky 8/6/98 GJ at 156. Ms. Lewinsky made near-contemporaneous statements to her mother, her aunt, and her friends Ms. Davis, Ms. Erbland, and Ms. Raines that the President had given her *Leaves of Grass.* Davis 3/17/98 GJ at 30–31; Erbland 2/12/98 GJ at 40–41; Finerman 3/18/98 Depo. at 15–16; Marcia Lewis 2/10/98 GJ at 51–52; Marcia Lewis 2/11/98 GJ at 10 ('[S]he liked the book of poetry very much.'); Raines 1/29/98 GJ 53–55."

52. Simon, *Poetry Under Oath,* 106. The "poem" here is quoted in full.

53. A conception of romance similar to the one here, and tied to its uses in film comedy, can be found in Stanley Cavell's *Pursuits of Happiness.* In George Orwell's *1984* a love affair is the locus of resistance to state authority, and the state's ability to defeat and redirect love is the measure of its totalitarian power. See the discussion of *1984* in chap. 4 above.

54. Anderson-Miller and Miller, *Dreams of Bill,* ix.

55. Samon, *My Erotic Dreams*; Griffith, *Dream President,* May 2004. The Lewinsky scandal also inspired two Broadway-style stage musicals, Blank Theater Company's *Starr Struck: A Musical Investigation,* which was based on investigators' transcripts, and Page 73 Productions' *Monica! The Musical* (2005)— as well as at least one pornographic film, aired on the premium-cable Playboy Channel and featuring, as it were, a Clinton body double. Two mainstream works that should also be mentioned in this connection are Merchant Ivory Productions' *Jefferson in Paris,* a 1995 film inspired by Thomas Jefferson's alleged affair with the slave Sally Hemings, and *The Secret Diary of Desmond Pfeiffer,* the satirical and short-lived 1998 UPN-TV sitcom about randy goings-on in the Lincoln White House. Within a few more years a fictionalized memoir, Curtis Sittenfeld's *American Wife: A Novel* (New York: Random House, 2008), was imagining the sexually explicit marital confessions of a first lady obviously modeled on Laura Bush.

56. Eszterhas, "Willard Comes Clean," 425–32.

57. Other examples of presidents in this period's farce comedies include Lloyd Bridges in Jim Abrahams's *Hot Shots! Part Deux* (1993); Jack Nicholson in Tim Burton's *Mars Attacks!* (1996), a send-up of old sci-fi and alien-invasion thrillers; and David Zucker's *Scary Movie 3* (2003) and *4* (2006), which made

their president a master *farceur,* Leslie Nielsen. Another Zucker satire, *The Naked Gun 2½: The Smell of Fear* (1991), as well as *2001: A Space Travesty* (2000), both of which starred Nielsen in his trademark role as a bumbling cop, also featured comic actors playing real presidents—George H. W. Bush and Bill Clinton, respectively. And George W. Bush, of course, would be treated farcically in a number of works, beginning with Comedy Central's 2001 *That's My Bush!*

58. Hoberman, "Lights, Camera, Exploitation."

59. *West Wing* episode 139, "The Debate," NBC-TV, November 6, 2005.

60. *West Wing* episode 58, "Hartsfield's Landing," February 27, 2002. The speech begins, "You're a good father, you don't have to act like it. You're the president, you don't have to act like it. You're a good man, you don't have to act like it"—a striking contrast to the advice given Clancy's Mr. Smith, Jack Ryan, in the epigraph to this chapter.

61. The very fast dialogue is a trademark of Aaron Sorkin's writing, and figures in TV series he has set in other very high-pressure, high-stakes work environments, like television production companies. It also seems well suited to— perhaps even impossible without—the widespread use of home video recording, which by the 1990s allowed most viewers to play back individual scenes as needed to catch anything they had missed.

62. *West Wing* episode 57, "Night Five," February 6, 2002. Transcribed from video, with emphasis added to indicate how the scene was performed.

63. Dr. Keyworth (Adam Arkin) makes only a couple of further brief appearances, in one case when Bartlet is struggling over a decision that might involve breaking the law—and that therefore can't be discussed with Keyworth anyway.

64. See the discussion of "the king's two bodies" and related concepts in the introduction. According to Edmund S. Morgan, the two-bodies theory reached the point "where [the king's] body politic might lose touch with his body natural": claiming to know what the king "must" want, seventeenth-century British Parliaments sometimes declared even measures that the real king supported to be contrary to "the king's" true will. Morgan, *Inventing the People,* 25–34.

Chapter 7. Fictitious Times

1. Michael Moore, speaking at The 75th Annual Academy Awards, ABC-TV, March 23, 2003. "Duct tape" and "orange alerts" were references to Bush administration terrorism warnings that critics charged were political scare tactics. The notion of war for fictitious reasons was an old one for Moore, whose 1995 film satire *Canadian Bacon* imagined an unpopular president (Alan Alda) seeking to boost his political fortunes by manipulating public opinion into a bogus conflict with Canada.

2. Syndicated columnist Richard Cohen, for example, wrote that "George Bush won last time out because Al Gore lost. . . . He won because he seemed the more genuine man, an aw-shucks guy who we could take a chance on. We took the chance." Cohen, "Amateurs and Zealots," *Washington Post*, September 11, 2003, A23. On the fictive quality of concepts like "the people," "representation," and "consent," see the discussions earlier in this book. Of course, it could simply be that Americans in 2000 had no illusions; perhaps they acquiesced in Bush's victory because they decided after voting that they preferred him after all, or because they agreed with the complex legal theories used to justify the Supreme Court's decision: that for purposes of choosing a president, the peoples of the states play only what amount to advisory roles, and the people of the nation, as such, play no role at all. But this would just be another way of saying that Americans accept the fiction of another, higher-ranking entity, "We, the People," along with the related ideas that this entity's will can be divined through convoluted constitutional mechanisms and that it trumps the wishes of the actual people.

3. Suskind, "Faith, Certainty and the Presidency of George W. Bush," ellipsis in original. (Although nicely counterposed against this view, Moore's was not a direct reply because the interview was not published until the following year.) The official who spoke to Suskind was not named, but "history starts today" were the words of Deputy Secretary of State Richard Armitage and probably others; see *Anderson Cooper 360 Degrees*, September 22, 2006, CNN Transcripts, http://transcripts.cnn.com/TRANSCRIPTS/0609/22/acd.01 .html.

4. Hozic, "Making of the Unwanted Colonies," 228–40. See especially 238.

5. "President Bush returns to White House."

6. Thanks to their base on Wall Street, some of the first news people on the scene at the World Trade Center were financial reporters—who, suddenly, found themselves reassigned from covering market "panics" to covering the real thing.

7. For attempts to reconstruct the terrorists' imaginings, see Mneimneh and Makiya, "Manual for a 'Raid,'" and L. Harris, "Al Qaeda's Fantasy Ideology." Like many of the most destructive deeds, the September 11 attacks apparently relied on an instrumentalism closely allied to the aesthetic: The pain and death of actual people was rated less important than the story these helped complete or the theory they helped "prove."

8. For a discussion of news framing with specific reference to September 11, see Uricchio, "Television Conventions." Framing in general has been described this way: "Now, each [fact] is a fragment of information that a reporter confronts. Somehow the reporter has to take those fragments and shape them into something coherent that can be transmitted in a way that a reader or listener or

viewer can easily follow and understand. To do that, they reach for a *narrative frame*. The narrative frame is like the skeleton for the body: everything cascades outward from that choice. It determines what is good news and what is bad, what information then looks relevant and what becomes meaningless and gets left out." Dauber, "Choosing a Narrative Frame," emphasis in original. By fitting events to one of a limited number of predictable patterns, narrative frames serve roughly the same purpose in newswriting that genre conventions do in fiction; one study has even identified thirteen basic types. See "Framing the News."

9. See the coverage from both CNN and WNYW-TV in New York: "Terrorist Attack on United States," CNN.

10. On other possible ways of defining the event, see Uriccho, "Television Conventions" (suggesting "an attack on the West"), or this first-anniversary comment: "The loss of life and property in lower Manhattan was massive almost beyond comprehension, but New York is a place apart from much of America, and it could be argued that this tragedy was less an attack on one nation than an attack on worldwide financial markets. It was the World Trade Center, not the American Trade Center." Dinty Moore, "White House as target."

11. "Imagined communities" is Benedict Anderson's phrase; see the discussion of Anderson's *Imagined Communities* in this book's introduction. By way of contrast to "America Under Attack," the 1995 Oklahoma City bombing, which was plainly aimed at the national government, occurred outside the capitals and was the work of Americans. It, therefore, was assigned a specific geography: "Terror in the *Heartland*," as the typical TV-news caption had called it.

12. Scholes and Kellogg, *Nature of Narrative*, 239. See also Kenneth Burke's definition of "rhetorical form" as "creation of appetite and the fulfilling of the desires. The listener anticipates, participates in, and is gratified by the sequence. Identification results from an interaction of form and content. Through participation in its form, a rhetorical work induces tensions and expectations." Burke, *Rhetoric of Motives*, 69.

13. The quotes are from the following Lexis-Nexis transcripts: *NBC News Special Report: Attack on America* (8:00 p.m. ET); *NBC News Special Report: Attack on America* (10:00 a.m. ET); *CBS News Special Report*, "Airplanes crashing into American institutions" (8:48 a.m. ET); *Today*, "White House evacuated; President Bush en route from Florida," NBC News (7:00 a.m. ET).

14. In this lay one criterion for judging later efforts. If, for example, plans for rebuilding downtown Manhattan fell short—like the first round of official proposals, unveiled to near-universal disfavor—that would reflect "a crisis of inspiration," as one critic put it: "Rebuilding downtown is about rebuilding New York as *a seat of useful power for action* in the world," and any plan would fail that did not embrace "New York City's unique position of power" and the World Trade Center's role in representing that power. Byard, "Global City Rebuilt," A23, emphasis added.

15. Johnston, "The mayor's report," 17; Rich, "De Facto Capital."

16. *CNN Breaking News*, "Terrorist Attack on United States." The failure of reporters to speculate on whether Bush would head to New York is telling because, in most disasters, the expected response of presidents—as was later made amply clear in the case of Hurricane Katrina—is to travel to the *site* to inspect relief efforts and comfort victims. Since at this point on September 11 the Pentagon had not yet been attacked, Washington was not such a site; its only relevance was as a military command center and symbolic seat of national leadership. To assume that the president would go there was, therefore, to grant that the event was both national and military—a terrorist attack, not a freak convergence of airline accidents.

17. Ibid.

18. *NPR Morning Edition*, "Possible Terrorist Attacks."

19. *CNN Breaking News*, "Terrorist Attack on United States" and "Planes Crash Into World Trade Center."

20. *CNN Breaking News*, "White House Personnel and Officials Are Safe."

21. *CNN Breaking News*, "America Under Attack: Bush Holds Press Briefing"; *ABC News Special Report*, "America Under Attack."

22. *CNN Breaking News*, "White House Personnel and Officials Are Safe."

23. *CNN Breaking News*, "America Under Attack: President Bush Stops."

24. *ABC News Special Report*, "America Under Attack."

25. *CNN Breaking News*, "Terrorism Strikes In The United States."

26. *CNN Breaking News*, "America Under Attack: President Bush Stops" and "America Under Attack: Former National Security Adviser."

27. *CNN Breaking News*, "America Under Attack: President Bush Stops."

28. *CNN Breaking News*, "President Bush Addresses Possible Terrorist Attacks."

29. *CNN Breaking News*, "America Under Attack: Former National Security Adviser."

30. Karen Hughes (counselor to the president), quoted on *CNN Breaking News*, "America Under Attack: Karen Hughes Delivers Remarks," emphasis added.

31. Lemann, "Letter from Washington."

32. "In the wake of the attacks," Geoffrey Nunberg, a linguist and dictionary editor, observed later that week, "official America needed . . . language that would reassert control of a world that had gotten terrifyingly out of hand." The language of moral judgment that Nunberg was referring to was largely absent on September 11 itself, but was heavily deployed soon thereafter as the president and others rhetorically threw down the gauntlet to al-Qaida's "evildoers." Nunberg, "When Words Fail."

33. Wieseltier, "Washington Diarist." Wieseltier called reporters' inarticulateness a sign that "the managers of meaning, the anchors and the reporters

and the commentators, were themselves too shocked to set to work." I would say, to the contrary, that it revealed the very difficulties that were making them work all the harder. CNN's Aaron Brown probably spoke for most newspeople when he looked back on the media's performance and pronounced it good: "we proved that we were very much prepared to handle the biggest story of our lives." Brown also called September 11 "the defining moment for my generation of journalists" and said he was "incredibly proud" of how they performed. It was the words themselves, not reporters, that failed to work as expected. Brown, quoted on *All Things Considered*, "Rise and Decline in Popularity."

34. *ABC News Special Report*, "America Under Attack."

35. *CBS News Special Report*, "Major Terrorist Attack."

36. *NBC News Special Report: Attack on America*, "The situation room in the White House."

37. This center, abbreviated PEOC, is "the White House's deepest sanctum," compared to which "the Situation Room is like the front lawn." It seems the PEOC was the "fortified structure" reporters meant to identify, even as they persisted in calling it the Situation Room. See Sanger and Van Natta, "After the Attacks"; Safire, "Plan from PEOC"; *Today*, "Day in the life of the president"; *CNN Breaking News*, "White House Personnel and Officials Are Safe."

38. Balz and Woodward, "Ten Days in September." The same reporting, which administration officials actively facilitated, later became Woodward's book *Bush at War*.

39. *Seven Days in May* is discussed in chap. 5.

40. *ABC News Special Report*, "America Under Attack."

41. On *The West Wing*, see chap. 6; the episodes referred to here were "18th and Potomac" and "Two Cathedrals." The website for *Thirteen Days*, which is no longer active, had invited viewers to put *themselves* at the big table in video-game versions of the crisis. The site's features included a "Cabinet Room" and an "Operations Center" where visitors could receive "debriefings" on the Cuban situation, review a "War Simulation," and conduct a "Strategic Military Exercise," i.e., play a simulated nuclear war game. *Thirteen Days*, directed by Roger Donaldson, 2000.

42. *The President's Man*'s original title, *Ground Zero*, was changed after September 11. On *Deterrence*, see the discussion in chap. 6.

43. "Cheney was worried the terrorists might be trying to decapitate the government, to kill its leaders. Bush agreed." Balz and Woodward, "Ten Days in September." In interviews broadcast on the first anniversary, Cheney and the president's press secretary and national security advisor all confirmed this. See *ABC Specials and Breaking News*, "9/11."

44. For a recent summary of these events, see Winik, *April 1865*, 224–29, and Wyatt-Brown, "Anatomy of a Murder," 22.

45. Quoted in Winik, *April 1865*, 311.

46. Secretary of War Edwin M. Stanton in "Official Despatch," 1.

47. "The meeting between Secretary Hull and the Secretaries of War and Navy this morning was an example of the plans that are being laid. It would be a mistake for Japan to believe that these preparations are any kind of bluff. Although officials in Washington are silent on what would be the definite consequences of a Japanese attack on Hawaii or an attack on Thailand, there are indications of what is being considered, and the steps which may be taken this very afternoon." Albert Warner, reporting from Washington on CBS radio, 2:37 p.m. Eastern time, Dec. 7, 1941. "Radio Days/The Bombing of Pearl Harbor," http://www.otr.com/r-a-i-new_pearl.shtml.

48. Kluckhohn, "Japan Wars on U.S. and Britain."

49. Ibid.

50. For an interesting study linking changes in newswriting conventions to changes in the presidency, see Schudson, "Politics of Narrative Form," 87–112. From a longitudinal analysis of reports of State of the Union addresses, Schudson charts a complex relationship that includes, in the terms I'm using, changes in the way presidents are imagined: "The news story . . . not only describes a world 'out there,' but *translates a political culture into assumptions of representation* built into the structure of the story itself." Schudson, 108, emphasis added.

51. Kluckhohn, "Japan Wars on U.S. and Britain."

52. *News Special Report: Attack on America,* "President Bush returns to White House."

53. Balz and Woodward, "Ten Days in September." The last of these quotes is reportedly what Bush told the vice president in a phone conversation from Louisiana, the first of his unscheduled stops.

54. Contradicting his own statements and other records, Bush claimed to have seen the first World Trade Center attack live on television (when in fact no one had), and then to have immediately launched emergency response plans—a claim the White House later dropped. For a detailed reconstruction, see Wood and Thompson, "Interesting Day."

55. *CBS News Special Report,* "Terrorist attacks on the World Trade Center."

56. For discussions of these and related points, see the introduction and chaps. 1 and 6.

57. "Without extraordinary imaginative energy, or profound historical crisis, it becomes nearly impossible to view life except as it has been mediated by the prevailing genres." Reilly, "Reconstruction of Genre," 3–6. Reilly was speaking of the emergence of African American literature as African Americans ceased to be "merely objects of history" and entered "the realm of conscious history-making"—in the process freeing themselves from the "system of dominations" of received literary forms. And while September 11 was a crisis, it was not a "profound" one in Reilly's sense, which may be why expectations remained strong that it could somehow be made to fit within known genres.

58. Wieseltier, "Washington Diarist."

59. This quote, for instance, is from a television critic's column in a newspaper that appeared that afternoon: Pennington, "Television Viewers Watch Attacks Unfold." A few days later the analogy was discussed at greater length in Gabler, "This Time, the Scene Was Real." Gabler saw the "movie" continuing in a struggle between the terrorists and the American public to see who would control the "final cut."

60. Hozic, "Making of the Unwanted Colonies," 229.

61. The terminology of "beats" is used in early stages of story development—for instance, in analyzing "treatments," the written narratives en route to becoming screenplays. Beats are the individual plot developments that carry a story from one point to the next. The beats that make up stories in the familiar genres are so well established that it is even thought possible to generate them automatically: There is scriptwriting software on the market today that guides aspiring scenarists through "the nine beats of the thriller" and "the fifteen beats of the horror film."

62. On fictions of absent or misplaced presidents, see the discussions in chaps. 5 and 6. As noted above, the September 11 hijackers had their own ideas about what the story was, and a Hollywood version of events from their point of view might have produced a story like "Plucky band of warriors for Allah succeed against all odds and bring Great Satan to its knees." Obviously this, too, was an option that American news personnel neither did nor should have seriously considered.

63. *ABC Specials and Breaking News,* "9/11"; *DC 9/11: Time of Crisis.* Based on the access and assistance it provided, the Bush administration should probably be credited as a co-producer of *DC 9/11.* Ironically, the film—originally titled *The Big Dance*—was made in Canada to take advantage of Canadian tax breaks and government subsidies; and the actor starring as a decisive and heroic Bush, Timothy Bottoms, had previously played Bush as a clueless idiot on another cable TV production, the short-lived Comedy Central sitcom *That's My Bush!* Discussing the film's production history and relationship to real events, one critic said the "shameless propaganda vehicle" marked "a new stage in the American cult of personality: the actual president as fictional protagonist," proving that "[i]n the end 9-11 turned out to be a made-for-TV movie, or rather, the basis for one." Hoberman, "Lights, Camera, Exploitation."

64. Warner, "Computable Culture."

65. The speaker who said "How do we model this?" was Michael Zyda of the Naval Postgraduate School's Modeling, Virtual Environments and Simulation Institute in Monterey, California. Quoted in Kaplan, "Sims Take on Al Qaeda," A1. The game that models international crises, "Final Flurry," is a product of the Defense Modeling and Simulation Office and the Industrial

College of the Armed Forces; the quoted description is from Daukantas, "DOD is game for teaching crisis strategy."

66. Both *New York Defender* and *JFK Reloaded* were foreign-made products of companies in France and Scotland, respectively, and in both cases their makers claimed that the games advanced legitimate political discussion—*Defender* by dramatizing the uselessness of seeking foolproof measures against terrorism (the human player/"defender" always lost), and *Reloaded* by allowing users to test the lone-gunman theory of the Kennedy assassination by re-enacting it themselves. *Reloaded* was eventually abandoned, but *Defender* was updated with a second release in late 2007. See "Staten Island 9/11 survivor disgusted by 'tasteless' Internet video game," and Tuohey, "JFK Reloaded Game Causes Controversy."

67. Boughner, *Advent Project,* and Novan and Cooper, *Madame President,* the story of the first lesbian president, which appeared in print only after its Web publication. Other examples include Robert Burrows's 2003 anti-Bush satire *The Great American Parade,* and Rochelle Sparrow's *JFK Is Still Alive,* Lulu Marketplace: Religion & Spirituality, http://www.lulu.com/content/96789. "Fan fiction," in which fans write their own stories based on television series and their characters, existed earlier but has proliferated as the Web has made finding readers for it easier. Where the series has a large following and involves a president, like *The West Wing,* "fanfic" and the related but racier "slash fiction" generate literally thousands of new and often startling do-it-yourself variants on the ways in which that president can be imagined.

68. The source for this remark is itself a weblog kept by one Sherry Sylvester, reprinting a news report that in turn quotes an open letter to Clinton from Hudson County (NJ) Executive Robert Janiszewski, then a member of the Democratic National Committee. "Clinton Has a Friend in North Jersey," blog entry posted September 9, 1998, Sherry Sylvester, http://sherrysylvester.com/septembe.htm.

69. This work's credits read: "Music by Steve Hilton, Texts from the sworn testimony of William Jefferson Clinton and Monica Lewinsky, Edited by Tom Simon" (i.e., in *Poetry Under Oath*). The composer's own website was evidently meant to be the distribution outlet, although a brief note in *Time* magazine on March 29, 1999, said the cantata was also available on CD. In any case, it has since disappeared—but that itself exemplifies the ephemeral nature of the Web, which is the flip side of the medium's quick responsiveness to topical developments. For more on *Poetry Under Oath,* see chap. 6.

70. The term "associative ethos" comes from Boxer, "Blogs."

71. The original site is defunct, but its contents were saved at least for a time at *The George W. Bush Dance,* http://www.geocities.com/dubyahump/old site/index.html. Another site gave the viewer control of "Bush's" dance steps and styles, http://www.dancingbush.com/. Still other sites allow the Web surfer to choose or manipulate what a satirized figure "says"—for instance, the

"online comic generator" George Says . . . , http://george.says-it.com/. Regarding "The Work of Art in the Age of Mechanical Reproduction," see Benjamin's famous 1935–36 essay of that title.

72. *Hard-Drinkin' Lincoln*, episode 6 ("Robot Trouble"). The difficulties that material like this faces in the larger old-media market, where a mass audience and advertising base are required, were pointed up by the rapid failures of the American version of *Spitting Image*, imported from the United Kingdom in 1986; of *The Secret Diary of Desmond Pfeiffer*, a sitcom parody resembling *Hard-Drinkin' Lincoln*, on broadcast TV in 1998; and of *That's My Bush!* on Comedy Central in 2001. Conversely, *Yes, Minister* appeared on the BBC, which is subsidized by government-mandated user fees, and *Tanner '88* on the subscription cable service HBO. See the discussions of these works in chap. 6.

73. Roosevelt et al., *The President's Mystery Plot*. The story of how FDR prompted the project in 1935 is told in Arthur Schlesinger Jr.'s introduction, iii–x. With Phil Rosen directing and Nathanael West co-credited on the screenplay, Republic Pictures released a 1936 film version titled *The President's Mystery*, although there is no president in the story.

74. See "We wrote a Cold War novel! The Cold War 'write-a-long,'" CNN Interactive, 1998[?], http://www.cnn.com/SPECIALS/cold.war/experience/culture/write.along/content.html.

75. The Web-based advocacy group MoveOn.org sponsored a virtual primary to choose which candidate to support for the 2004 Democratic presidential nomination, and an affiliated group allowed entrants to submit and choose among television ads for use in that year's presidential campaign. "Republican Survivor," a parody of the popular CBS-TV reality/game show *Survivor* but featuring Republican candidates, was featured on the website of the Democratic Congressional Campaign Committee, May 31, 2004. Similar efforts resumed in 2008. MoveOn is itself an interesting case: an advocacy group that carries out some political party–like functions, and that first arose out of a petition drive conducted by e-mail during the Clinton impeachment.

76. Kaufman, "If Stephen Colbert Can't Get On A Presidential Ballot, Who Can?"; Franken, *Why Not Me?*

77. The fictional characters Jack Downing, Simon Suggs, and Col. Gracchus Vanderbomb, mentioned in earlier chapters, all ran for president, and an 1880 comic novel by Edward Goodman Holden touted *A Famous Victory: Brewster for President*. But overall it's difficult to find examples of the phenomenon before about 1930. Not surprisingly, it seems to be connected to the rise of the "personal presidency" discussed in chap. 4. Will Rogers's 1928 "Anti Bunk Party" campaign, which was conducted in a series of *Life* magazine columns and won "endorsements" from Henry Ford, Babe Ruth, William Allen White, and other luminaries, championed measures resembling those of the later New Deal—although Rogers's principal pledge was that if elected, he would resign.

78. Fields, *Fields for President*, 12. Michael Taylor identifies the difficulty that joke candidacies pose for defining genre: "The problem was that [the book was originally] received as an ordinary book written by a novelist, which it definitely is not. It is an anthology of humorous gags, sketches, and comic situations laced together with a hint of a plot line, only for appearances." Taylor, introduction to *Fields for President*, xxii.

79. "Pat Paulsen's 1960's Television Editorials" ["Draft Laws"], Pat Paulsen for President, http://www.paulsen.com/pat/. *Pat Paulsen for President* was also the title of a book of political jokes and monologues published in 1968 and of a CD-ROM issued in 1995. A later, more elaborate political "mockumentary" like *Tanner '88*, discussed in chap. 6, would seem descended from *Pat Paulsen for President*, with the joke broadened to include the machinery of electoral politics. We might say that the "comedian" showcased in *Tanner* isn't the candidate, but the film itself and its makers.

80. Superman himself had already run for president in a 1991 D.C. Comics graphic novel. In the story, his eligibility depended on a Supreme Court ruling that he had technically been "born" in Kansas, not on the planet Krypton.

81. Danielson, president of Protozoa.com, quoted in John Townley, "Duke2000."

82. The spokeswoman's quote appears in "Anheuser-Bush wins two of three ad challenges by SABMiller," press release, *Anheuser-Bush News*, May 29, 2004, http://www.anheuser-busch.com/news/millerrelease.htm. Compare this account of the court's action with Miller's press release, "U.S. District Court Grants Preliminary Injunction against Anheuser-Busch Marketing Tactics," *Newsroom Archive*, May 28, 2004, Miller Brewing Co., http://www.miller brewing.com/home.asp (Newsroom).

Conclusion

1. For example: In remarks at Ellis Island on the first anniversary of the September 11 attacks, President George W. Bush said: "This ideal of America is the hope of all mankind. That hope still lights our way. And the light shines in the darkness. And the darkness will not overcome it." The last two sentences quote John 1:4–5, where the "light" in question is Christ. In his 2003 State of the Union address, Bush declared that "there's power, wonder-working power, in the goodness and idealism and faith of the American people." This language comes from "There is Power in the Blood," an old revival hymn that ascribes the "wonder-working power" to "the precious blood of the Lamb," which again means Christ.

2. "Barbie® Announces a Surprise Bid for the 2004 Presidency; Barbie® to Represent Popular 'Party of Girls,'" Mattel, Inc. press release, August 12, 2004.

See also *The White House Project—Change Culture*, http://www.thewhitehouse project.org/culture/change/index.php. Further reflecting how seriously Barbie's "candidacy" was taken, mild protests were lodged against the fact that Mattel's gesture toward racial diversity did not extend to an Asian American President Barbie. (Mattel appealed to market research suggesting that Asian American girls preferred playing with "white" dolls.) In all, a considerable distance had been traveled since a much earlier Barbie "ran" only for student-body president, and then with the help of her "boyfriend" doll, Ken.

3. Alimurung, "Offbeat: Barbie's Revenge." Compare these competing campaigns with the Miller/Budweiser contest for "President of Beers," discussed in chap. 7.

4. Video games and digital/interactive devices involving presidents or politics have included Take 2 Interactive's *Political Tycoon*, PortaBush/Eruptor Entertainment's "PortaBush," and Konami's *Metal Gear Solid 2: Sons of Liberty*, a game loosely based on the rescue-the-president plot of *Escape from New York* (discussed in chap. 6). The official website advertising the 2001 movie *Thirteen Days*, a docudrama about the Cuban Missile Crisis, mimicked presidential decision-making with the viewer as president, receiving "briefings" and playing out possible war scenarios. But as one critic has noted, these early experiments have not yet realized the potential of digitally simulated politics. S. Johnson, "SimCandidate."

5. Before withdrawing from the 2008 race, former Virginia Gov. Mark Warner introduced himself to potential voters in a Web-based virtual world called "Second Life" (http://secondlife.com/) by sending in his avatar to interact with their avatars. See Au, "Second Life of Governor Mark Warner"; and Cillizza, "The Fix: Mark Warner the Avatar."

6. The play that imagines a meeting between Nixon and an aging JFK, who lives on a Greek island and resembles Aristotle Onassis, is Donald Freed's *American Iliad*. Harding, who may have died of seafood poisoning, fights the giant crab in *President Harding Is a Rock Star*. George W. Bush is imagined as black in Dave Chapelle's "Black Bush," *Chapelle's Show*, Comedy Central, http://www.comedycentral.com/motherload/index.jhtml?ml_video=11923.

7. According to *Publishers Weekly*, Finley's performance piece (and its spinoff book), whose title *George & Martha* also plainly alludes to the original First Family, "depicts domination, rather lackadaisical fellatio, spanking, cocaine abuse, diaper play and baby wipes, and much pop psychoanalysis." At one point Martha discovers that George is speaking literally when he says, "I have [Osama] bin Laden up my ass." See the listing for *George & Martha* on Amazon.com, and David Bowman, "Karen Finley smears Bush all over," *Salon*, April 22, 2006, http://www.salon.com/books/int/2006/04/22/finley/. *I'm Going to Kill the President: A Federal Offense* was written by "Hieronymous Bang" [pseud.] and

produced by the Imagination Liberation Front at undisclosed locations in New York City, 2003.

8. On Berlin's *Mr. President*, see the discussion in chap. 4. As noted in chap. 6, *Commander in Chief*, which was no doubt pitched to ABC as "a female *West Wing*," was—like creator Rod Lurie's earlier fish-out-of-water presidential tale *Deterrence*—far less interested in actual policy, at least until near the end of its brief run. ABC publicity billed it as "a woman president who has the world on her shoulders and her children on her back," and its numerous parallels to *Kisses for My President* gave it a distinctly pre–*West Wing* feel (although, like *The West Wing*, it inspired a growing body of "fan fiction" that borrowed its characters and storylines and circulated via the Web). The ready resort to nontraditional presidential types also shows up frequently in the casting of African American presidents; examples include the movies *The Fifth Element* (1997) and *Deep Impact* (1998), the Fox TV series *24*, and Louis Gossett Jr.'s appearance as presidents in both the 1995 TV-movie *Solar Strike* and *Left Behind: World at War*, a 2005 entry in the series of film adaptations of the very popular, evangelical-Christian-themed apocalyptic novels. Usually the race of these characters is treated as normal and does not function in the plot, although one imaginative barrier seems to remain: nontraditional presidents are typically conceived as flawless—modest, incorruptible, and inspiring, especially compared to their mostly white male antagonists. (The many disasters over which they have fictionally presided, however, prompted the satirical newspaper *The Onion* to reply to Barack Obama's candidacy with the question, "Do We Really Want Another Black President After the Events of *Deep Impact*?" Kevin Henry [pseud.], *The Onion*, February 13, 2008, http://www.theonion.com/content/opinion/do_we_really_want_another_black.)

9. Resnick, *Alternate Presidents* and *Alternate Kennedys*; Turtledove, *Great War*. Possible consequences of Southern victory are presented through the device of a mock present-day documentary in Kevin Willmott's 2004 *CSA: The Confederate States of America*, cablecast on the Independent Film Channel. A Germany-Japan Cold War is imagined in an early alternate history, Philip K. Dick's 1964 *The Man in the High Castle*. A possible Hitler-Kennedy détente is the backdrop of the British novelist Robert Harris's *Fatherland*, adapted for HBO cable television in 1994. Other works referred to here are Bernau, *Promises to Keep*; Poyer, *Only Thing to Fear*; Silver, *Naked Presidents*; and Rosenfeld, *World Hitler Never Made*. An even more comprehensive list of "Divergences" from real history, with the date of each and the work in which it's imagined, takes up several pages of *Uchronia: The Alternate History List*, http://www.uchronia.net/bib.cgi/diverge.html, from 4.5 billion years ago ("What if the sun were more massive?") to the present ("What if Al Gore had won in Florida?").

10. *West Wing* episode 106, "Access," March 31, 2004. *Tanner on Tanner* actually included two levels of self-referentiality, with the documentary-in-the-making itself becoming the subject of a student film. And *Jack & Bobby* also

included pseudo-documentary features, with its final episode, "Legacy" (no. 22, May 11, 2005) framing the brothers' (and future president's) whole story that way and with veteran presidential fictionalizer Gore Vidal playing the documentary's "host." See the further discussions of these series in chap. 6.

11. On comedians' joke campaigns generally, see chap. 7. *Man of the Year* was not a commercial hit or an artistic success, perhaps in part because of its convolutions: The question of whether the Williams character's victory is real hinges on a possible fraud involving voting machines, and this in turn leads to an uneven plot turn from comedy to suspense. A better-plotted, more persuasive satire, also worth mentioning in this connection, is Paul Weitz's 2006 movie *American Dreamz*, in which an intellectually unimpressive chief executive apparently modeled on George W. Bush is recruited to guest-judge a TV talent show.

12. When Senator Richard Lugar of Indiana ran for the 1996 Republican presidential nomination, his TV ads included a four-part mini-docudrama in which a fictional president confronted nuclear terrorism (but not as effectively, the ads implied, as would a President Lugar). Newt Gingrich and William Forstchen's *Gettysburg: A Novel of the Civil War* and *Never Call Retreat: Lee and Grant: The Final Victory* provide an alternate Civil War history. Jimmy Carter's *The Hornet's Nest: A Novel of the Revolutionary War* is not primarily about George Washington but does deal with events in which he played a role. The brain-damaged Lincoln who can't remember his own life, and who must therefore rely on Carl Sandburg's hagiography, is one of the museum figures who comes alive in the *Smithsonian Institution* in Gore Vidal's 1998 novel of that title, another entry in the alternate history and time-travel genre (discussed in chap. 6). And Michael Crichton's *State of Fear*, which presents global warming as a massive liberal hoax, got Crichton invited to testify on that issue before the Senate Committee on Environment and Public Works in September 2005.

13. Saletan, "I See Dean People." For a more detailed list of parallels between Bartlet and Dean, see McCarthy, "Candidacy of Howard Dean Takes 'Wing.'" The 2008 race would also draw comparisons with *The West Wing*'s final season, in which an ethnically distinctive Democrat defeats both parties' more experienced warhorses. Peter Funt, "A Race Straight Out of a 'West Wing' Rerun," *Washington Post*, May 26, 2008, A17. And as noted above, *The Onion* newspaper satirically framed Barack Obama's candidacy within a checkered "history" of black presidents constructed from movies. By 2008, fiction was "lapping" reality in projects like Oliver Stone's *W.*, the first White House "biopic" to appear while its subject was still in office (unless one counts *PT-109*, which did not deal with JFK's presidency). One reviewer of *W.* saw it as registering a new relationship between reality and storytelling: "There's a misapprehension abroad that *W.* is an Oliver Stone movie about George W. Bush. That gets it exactly backward. The life and presidency of George W. Bush were an Oliver Stone movie well before the director of *JFK* and *Wall Street* arrived on

the scene. *W.* merely records that unassailable fact." Timothy Noah, "Dubya, Stoned," *Slate*, October 17, 2008, http://www.slate.com/id/2202341/.

14. Suellentrop, "Peer-to-Peer Politics." Borrowing and extending Dean's techniques, the Barack Obama campaign in 2008 created what one analyst analogized to the DINUs, or "Deeply Immersive Narrative Universes," of some video games and movie franchises. Rick Leibling, "Barack Obama: DINU Brand," EYECUBE: Insight, Innovation & Ideas, April 21, 2008, http://eyecube.wordpress.com/2008/04/21/barack-obama-dinu-brand/.

15. It's also worth noting that the winning "American Candidate," Park Gillespie, tried to run for a South Carolina congressional seat in 2006, but the Republican Party shunted him aside for a better-funded contender. (Real-life American candidates depend on having to raise and spend enormous amounts of money, a condition that the game could not do much to simulate.) Meanwhile, some citizens have aimed higher than the presidency—Don Lautenbach, for instance, who offered himself for emperor, and performance artist Vermin Supreme (http://www.verminsupreme.com/), who has variously claimed to be running for the Republican presidential nomination, mayor of the United States, and "emperor of the new millennium." There had been other fictions of American emperors, including a 1929 Sax Rohmer/Fu Manchu yarn (Rohmer also created a *President Fu Manchu* in 1936) and Richard Condon's 1990 *Emperor of America,* a satirical novel in which the author of *The Manchurian Candidate* imagines a homegrown Napoleon. The strangest example, though, was probably Emperor Joshua A. Norton, a nineteenth-century San Franciscan whose fantasy of power may have inspired the character of the king in *Huckleberry Finn.* Norton's two decades of performance art and/or mental disturbance made him a celebrity and were widely indulged, despite the fact that he had to issue handwritten edicts instead of "blogging" them as such characters do today.

16. See Gutman, *Kid Who Ran for President* and *Kid Who Became President*; Williams, *How to Be President*; St. George, *So You Want to Be President*; and Pastan and McKnight, *Make Your Own President,* a 2006 Smithsonian-sponsored activity book that encouraged mixing and matching of real presidents' facial features and political characteristics to create, potentially, millions of imagined new characters. Barbie, meanwhile, was joined on toy shelves by soldier-president versions of her macho male counterpart, "GI Joe": between 1995 and 2000 the Hasbro toy company produced versions of this "action figure" that were modeled on Gen. George Washington, Gen. Dwight D. Eisenhower, and Lt. John F. Kennedy USN, commander of PT-109.

17. The quote was from a July 26, 1920, column reprinted in Mencken's collection *On Politics: A Carnival of Buncome.* Mike Judge's 2006 film *Idiocracy* spun a similar idea into an elaborate satire: an unimpressive citizen of the present,

transplanted to a distant, culturally devolved future, proves to be comparatively the world's smartest person and, of course, eventually becomes president.

18. Michelle Cottle, "Schedules, Shmedules: Hil's Still an Enigma," blog entry, *New Republic*, March 20, 2008, http://blogs.tnr.com/tnr/blogs/ the_plank/archive/2008/03/20/schedules-shmedules-hil-s-still-an-enigma.aspx; Lithwick, "Me Fatigue."

19. Anonymous, *Barack Obama Is Your New Bicycle*, http://barackobamais yournewbicycle.com/. Sheila Heti, *I Dream of Hillary . . . I Dream of Barack*, http://www.idreamofhillaryidreamofbarack.com/about.

Bibliography

Archival Sources

"Black Hawk Upstages the President." *Odd Wisconsin Archive*. Wisconsin Historical Society. http://www.wisconsinhistory.org/odd/archives/000857.asp.

"Digest of the Acts and Deliberations of the Cabildo: Carnival." January 19, 1781. *City Archives*. New Orleans Public Library. http://nutrias.org/~nopl/inv/digest/digest17.htm.

Douglass, Frederick. "Oration in Memory of Abraham Lincoln." Washington, D.C., April 14, 1876. Ashbrook Center for Public Affairs, Ashland University. http://teachingamericanhistory.org/library/index.asp?document print=39.

"Eyewitness Accounts." *The Rise of Jacksonian Democracy*. White House Historical Association. http://www.whitehousehistory.org/04/subs/1828_c.html.

Hamilton, James. Letter to Martin Van Buren. March 5, 1829. *American Memory*. Library of Congress. http://www.memory.loc.gov/ammem/pihtml/pihome.html.

Kennedy, John F. "Address to a Joint Convention of the General Court of the Commonwealth of Massachusetts." January 9, 1961. John F. Kennedy Presidential Library and Museum. http://www.jfklibrary.org/Historical+Resources/Archives/Reference+Desk/Speeches/JFK/003POF03 GeneralCourt01091961.htm.

———. "Commencement Address at American University." June 10, 1963. John F. Kennedy Presidential Library & Museum. http://www.jfklibrary.org/Historical+Resources/Archives/Reference+Desk/Speeches/JFK/003POF03AmericanUniversity06101963.htm.

Internet Sources

Antifederalist Papers, The. *WEPIN Store*. http://www.wepin.com/articles/afp/.

Anti-Federalist Papers. *Liberty Library of Constitutional Classics.* The Constitution Society. http://www.constitution.org/afp.htm.

Au, Wagner James. "The Second Life of Governor Mark Warner." *New World Notes* 31 (August 2006). http://nwn.blogs.com/nwn/2006/08/the _second_life.html.

Boughner, Terry. *The Advent Project.* Distributed through the Gay/Lesbian International News Network. N.p.: GLINN, 1995. http://www.glinn.com.

Burrows, Robert. *The Great American Parade.* http://www.lulu.com/content/4380.

Bush in 30 Seconds. MoveOn.org Voter Fund. http://www.bushin30seconds.org/.

DancingBush.com. June 1, 2006. http://www.dancingbush.com/.

Dauber, Cori. "Choosing a Narrative Frame." *Rantingprofs: Media Coverage of the War on Terror* [weblog], March 9, 2004. http://rantingprofs.typepad.com/rantingprofs/2004/03/choosing_a_narr.html.

Falzon, Gary. "Congo Square." *19th Century New Orleans.* David J. Popalisky/Performance Studies 62/162. http://itrs.scu.edu/students/winter03/gfalzon/congosquare.htm.

Floyd, John. *Diary of John Floyd.* Chap. 6, part C. http://www.webroots.org/library/usabios/ladojfo6.html.

"Framing the News: The Triggers, Frames, and Messages in Newspaper Coverage." July 13, 1998. *Project for Excellence in Journalism.* http://www.journalism.org/node/445.

George Washington's Mount Vernon Estate and Gardens. "Two New Facilities Opening October 27, 2006: Discover the Real George Washington." News release. http://www.mountvernon.org/visit/plan/index.cfm/pid/822/.

Hard-Drinkin' Lincoln. Directed and designed by Xeth Feinberg. Written and created by Mike Reiss. Mishmash Media and Icebox.com. 2000. http://www.icebox.com/index.php?id=show&showid=s3.

Johnson, Steven. "SimCandidate." *Slate,* December 16, 2003. http://slate.msn.com/id/2092688/.

Kaufman, Gil. "If Stephen Colbert Can't Get on a Presidential Ballot, Who Can?" *MTV News,* November 2, 2007. http://www.mtv.com/news/articles/1573404/20071102/id_0.jhtml.

Leopold, Todd. "Learning from the Masters." *CNN Interactive,* November 7, 2000, updated December 28, 2000. http://archives.cnn.com/2000/books/news/12/28/presidential.books/index.html.

Lithwick, Dahlia. "Me Fatigue." *Slate,* March 8, 2008. http://www.slate.com/id/2186141/.

Moore, Dinty W. "The White House as Target." *Salon,* September 10, 2002. http://dir.salon.com/storynews/feature/2002/09/10/whitehouse/index.html.

Mount Vernon Ladies Association. "Mount Vernon Launches $85 Million Campaign to Restore National Understanding of George Washington." April 23, 2002. http://www.mountvernon.org.

"The Reincarnation of Abraham Lincoln into John Kennedy." *Near-Death Experiences and the Afterlife.* International Association for Near-Death Studies. http://www.near-death.com/experiences/reincarnation08.html.

Saletan, William. "I See Dean People: Howard Dean's Fatal Echo Chamber." *Slate,* January 26, 2004. http://slate.msn.com/id/2094443/.

Suellentrop, Chris. "Peer-to-Peer Politics: Should Howard Dean Be a Little Bit Afraid of the Internet?" *Slate,* July 14, 2003. http://slate.msn.com/id/2085610/.

Swift, Jonathan. *Gulliver's Travels.* 1726. http://www.enotes.com/gullivers-travels/.

Thistlethwaite, Mark. "'Our Illustrious Washington': The American Imaging of George Washington." February 21, 2000[?]. McConnell Center for Political Leadership, University of Louisville. http://www.mcconnellcenter.org/pdf/lectures/thistlewaite.pdf.

Townley, John. "Duke2000: Virtual Cartoon Comes 'Alive.'" *Streaming Media World,* March 24, 2000. http://www.streamingmediaworld.com/video/voices/duke2000/.

Uricchio, William. "Television Conventions." *Re:constructions: Reflections on Humanity and Media after Tragedy,* September 16, 2001. http://web.mit.edu/cms/reconstructions/interpretations/tvconventions.html.

Wood, Allan, and Paul Thompson. "An Interesting Day: President Bush's Movements and Actions on 9/11." Center for Grassroots Oversight. http://www.historycommons.org/essay.jsp?article=essayaninterestingday

Media Sources

ABC News Special Report. "America Under Attack." ABC-TV. 12:00 Noon ET, September 11, 2001. Lexis-Nexis.

ABC Specials and Breaking News. "9/11." ABC-TV. 7:00 p.m. ET, September 11, 2002. Lexis-Nexis.

Abraham Lincoln. Directed by D. W. Griffith. Written by Stephen Vincent Benet et al. United Artists, 1930.

Absolute Power. Directed by Clint Eastwood. Written by William Goldman. Malpaso Productions. Castle Rock Entertainment and Sony/Columbia Pictures, 1997.

Advise and Consent. Directed by Otto Preminger. Written by Wendell Mayes. Sigma Productions and Columbia Pictures, 1962.

Air Force One. Directed by Wolfgang Petersen. Written by Andrew W. Marlowe.

Beacon Communications, Radiant Productions, and Columbia Pictures, 1997.

All Things Considered. "Rise and Decline in Popularity of the American News Media in the Year since 9/11." National Public Radio. September 6, 2002. Lexis-Nexis.

American Candidate. Directed by Michael McNamara. Actual Reality Pictures and Showtime Networks, 2004.

American Dreamz. Directed and written by Paul Weitz. Depth of Field. NBC Universal Television and Universal Pictures, 2006.

American President, The. Directed by Rob Reiner. Written by Aaron Sorkin. Castle Rock Entertainment, Wildwood Enterprises, Columbia Pictures, and Universal Pictures, 1995.

Being There. Directed by Hal Ashby. Written by Jerzy Kosinski. Lorimar Film Entertainment et al. United Artists, 1979.

Best Man, The. Directed by Franklin J. Schaffner. Written by Gore Vidal. Millar/Turman Productions and United Artists, 1964.

Betty Boop for President. Directed by Dave Fleischer. Fleischer Studios/Paramount Pictures, 1932.

Blood Suckers from Outer Space. Directed and written by Glen Coburn. Warner Home Video, 1996, orig. released 1984.

Bob Roberts. Directed and written by Tim Robbins. Miramax Films et al. and Paramount Pictures, 1992.

Brady Bunch in the White House, The. Directed by Neal Israel. Written by Lloyd J. Schwartz and Hope Juber. Based on the series created by Sherwood Schwartz. Paramount Television and Fox Network, 2002.

Bulworth. Directed by Warren Beatty. Written by Warren Beatty and Jeremy Pikser. Twentieth Century Fox, 1998.

By Dawn's Early Light. Directed by Jack Sholder. Written by Bruce Gilbert. Home Box Office, 1990.

Candidate, The. Directed by Michael Ritchie. Written by Jeremy Larner. Redford-Ritchie Productions and Warner Brothers, 1972.

CBS News Special Report. "Major Terrorist Attack in the US." CBS-TV. 8:48 a.m. ET, September 11, 2001. Lexis-Nexis.

CBS News Special Report. "Terrorist Attacks on the World Trade Center and the Pentagon." CBS-TV. 8:48 a.m. ET, September 11, 2001. Lexis-Nexis.

Chasing Liberty. Directed by Andy Cadiff. Written by Derek Giuley and David Schneiderman. Alcon Entertainment et al. and Warner Brothers, 2004.

Christine Jorgensen Story, The. Directed by Irving Rapper. Written by Robert E. Kent and Ellis St. Joseph. Based on the autobiography of Christine Jorgensen. Edward Small Productions and United Artists, 1970.

Clear and Present Danger. Directed by Phillip Noyce. Written by Donald Stewart, Steven Zaillian, and John Milius. Paramount Pictures, 1994.

Clone High. Created by Phil Lord and Chris Miller. Nelvana Limited. MTV, 2002–2003.

CNN Breaking News. "America Under Attack: Bush Holds Press Briefing." CNN. [No time.] September 11, 2001. Lexis-Nexis Transcript # 091135CN.V00.

CNN Breaking News. "America Under Attack: Former National Security Adviser Richard Holbrooke and Former U.N. Ambassador Discuss Terrorist Situation." CNN. 1:10 p.m. ET, September 11, 2001. Lexis-Nexis Transcript #091119CN.V00.

CNN Breaking News. "America Under Attack: Karen Hughes Delivers Remarks on Terrorist Attacks." CNN. 3:47 p.m. ET, September 11, 2001. Lexis-Nexis Transcript #091152CN.V00.

CNN Breaking News. "America Under Attack: President Bush Stops at a Military Installation in Nebraska." CNN. 3:25 p.m. ET, September 11, 2001. Lexis-Nexis Transcript #091144CN.V00.

CNN Breaking News. "Planes Crash Into World Trade Center And Pentagon Also On Fire." CNN. 9:31 a.m. ET, September 11, 2001. Lexis-Nexis Transcript #091102CN.V00.

CNN Breaking News. "Terrorism Strikes In The United States in a Massive Attack." CNN. 09:42 a.m. ET, September 11, 2001. Lexis-Nexis Transcript #091103CN.V00.

CNN Breaking News. "Terrorist Attack on United States." CNN. 8:48 a.m. ET, September 11, 2001. Lexis-Nexis Transcript #091101CN.V00.

CNN Breaking News. "White House Personnel and Officials Are Safe." CNN. [No time.] September 11, 2001. Lexis-Nexis Transcript #091114CN.V00.

CNN Live Event/Special. "President Bush Addresses Possible Terrorist Attacks." CNN. 9:30 a.m. ET, September 11, 2001. Lexis-Nexis Transcript #091101CN.V54.

Colossus: The Forbin Project. Directed by Joseph Sargent. Written by James Bridges. Universal Pictures, 1970.

Commander in Chief. Created by Rod Lurie. Battleplan Productions, Touchstone Television, and James Works Entertainment, 2005–2006.

Counterstrike. Directed by Jerry London. Written by J. B. White. Lions Gate Television and TBS Superstation, 2003.

Dayton, Katherine, and George S. Kaufman. *First Lady.* Music Box Theatre, New York, November 26, 1935.

Daukantas, Patricia. "DOD Is Game for Teaching Crisis Strategy." Government Computer News. 6:30 p.m. ET, September 13, 1999. http://resources.bandwidthmarket.com/corporate/www.gcn.com/print/vol18_n30/649-1.html.

Dave. Directed by Ivan Reitman. Written by Gary Ross. Donner/Shuler-Donner Productions, Northern Lights Entertainment and Warner Brothers, 1993.

DC 9/11: Time of Crisis. Directed by Brian Trenchard-Smith. Written by Lionel Chetwynd. Lionel Chetwynd Productions and Showtime Networks, 2003.

Deterrence. Directed and written by Rod Lurie. Battleplan Productions, Moonstone Entertainment and Paramount Classics, 1999.

Dick. Directed by Andrew Fleming. Written by Fleming and Sheryl Longin. Phoenix Pictures et al. and Columbia Pictures, 1999.

Dr. Strangelove, or: How I Learned to Stop Worrying and Love the Bomb. Directed by Stanley Kubrick. Written by Stanley Kubrick, Terry Southern, and Peter George. Hawk Films and Columbia Pictures, 1964.

Enemy Within, The. Directed by Jonathan Darby. Written by Rod Serling, Darryl Ponicsan, and Ron Bass. Vincent Pictures Productions and Home Box Office, 1994.

Escape from L.A. Directed by John Carpenter. Written by John Carpenter, Nick Castle, Debra Hill, and Kurt Russell. Rysher Entertainment and Paramount Pictures, 1996.

Escape from New York. Directed by John Carpenter. Written by John Carpenter and Nick Castle. AVCO Embassy Pictures et al, 1981.

Fail-Safe. Directed by Sidney Lumet. Written by Walter Bernstein. Columbia Pictures, 1964.

Fail Safe. Directed by Stephen Frears. Written by Walter Bernstein. Maysville Pictures, Warner Bros. Television and CBS-TV, 2000.

Fatherland. Directed by Christopher Menaul. Written by Stanley Weiser and Ron Hutchinson. Eis Film and Home Box Office, 1994.

Feed. Directed by Kevin Rafferty and James Ridgeway. Video Democracy and Original Cinema, 1992.

Finley, Karen. *George & Martha.* Collective: Unconscious, New York, September 17, 2004.

First Daughter. Directed by Armand Mastroianni. Written by Chad Hayes and Carey Hayes. Columbia TriStar Television et al., TBS, and Turner Network Television, 1999.

First Daughter. Directed by Forest Whitaker. Written by Jerry O'Connell, Jessica Bendinger, and Kate Kondell. New Regency Pictures et al. and Twentieth Century Fox, 2004.

First Family. Directed and written by Buck Henry. F. F. Associates, IndieProd Company Productions, and Warner Bros., 1980.

First Lady. Directed by Stanley Logan. Written by George S. Kaufman, Katherine Dayton, and Rowland Leigh. Warner Bros., 1937.

First Target. Directed by Armand Mastroianni. Written by Chad Hayes and Carey Hayes. Columbia TriStar Television et al. and TBS Superstation, 2000.

Freed, Donald. *American Iliad.* Victory Theatre, Burbank, CA, May 31 [?], 2001.

Gabriel Over the White House. Directed by Gregory LaCava. Written by Carey

Wilson and Bertram Bloch. Cosmopolitan Productions and Metro-Goldwyn-Mayer, 1933.

Gelbart, Larry. *Mastergate: A Play on Words.* Criterion Center Stage Right, New York, October 12, 1989.

George & Martha. Written by Karen Finley. Rollins/Joffe Productions and Showtime Networks, 1992.

Griffith, Jennifer. *Dream President.* VOX: Showcasing American Composers. New York City Opera, May 2004.

Hail to the Chief. Directed by J. D. Lobue. Created by Susan Harris. Witt/Thomas/Harris Productions and ABC-TV, 1985.

Head of State. Directed by Chris Rock. Written by Chris Rock and Ali LeRoi. DreamWorks, 3 Art Entertainment, and United International Pictures, 2003.

"Hundred Days of the Dragon, The." Directed by Byron Haskin. *The Outer Limits,* season 1, episode 2, September 23, 1963.

I Love You, Madam President. Music and lyrics by Phyllis Lynd. Greenwich, CT: Original Cast Records, 1994.

I'd Rather Be Right. Book by George S. Kaufman and Moss Hart. Music by Richard Rodgers. Lyrics by Lorenz Hart. Alvin Theater, New York, November 2, 1937.

In the Line of Fire. Directed by Wolfgang Petersen. Written by Jeff Maguire. Castle Rock Entertainment and Columbia Pictures, 1993.

Independence Day. Directed by Roland Emmerich. Written by Roland Emmerich and Dean Devlin. Centropolis Entertainment and Twentieth Century Fox, 1996.

Jack & Bobby. Created by Greg Berlanti, Steve Cohen, Brad Meltzer, and Vanessa Taylor. Warner Bros. Television et al. and WB Network, 2004–2005.

Kidnapping of the President, The. Directed by George Mendeluk. Written by Richard Murphy and Charles Templeton. Presidential Films, Sefel Films, and Crown International Pictures, 1980.

Kisses for My President. Directed by Curtis Bernhardt. Written by Robert G. Kane and Claude Binyon. Perlayne and Warner Brothers, 1964.

Lees, Russell. *Nixon's Nixon.* Manhattan Class Company, New York, September 29, 1995.

Let 'em Eat Cake. Book by George S. Kaufman and Morrie Ryskind. Music by George Gershwin. Lyrics by Ira Gershwin. Imperial Theater, New York, October 21, 1933.

Lindsay, Howard, and Russel Crouse. *State of the Union.* Hudson Theater, New York, November 14, 1945.

Mail to the Chief. Directed by Eric Champnella. Written by Eric Champnella and Jack Thomas. Walt Disney Pictures, Buena Vista Television, and ABC-TV, 2000.

Man, The. Directed by Joseph Sargent. Written by Rod Serling. ABC Circle Films, Lorimar Television, and Paramount Pictures, 1972.

Manchurian Candidate, The. Directed by John Frankenheimer. Written by George Axelrod and John Frankenheimer. M.C. Productions and United Artists, 1962.

Man of the Year. Directed and written by Barry Levinson. Morgan Creek Productions and Universal Pictures, 2006.

Mastergate: A Play on Words. Directed by Michael Engler. Written by Larry Gelbart. Imagination Productions and Showtime Networks, 2002.

Mr. President. Book by Howard Lindsay and Russel Crouse. Music and lyrics by Irving Berlin. St. James Theater, New York, October 20, 1962.

Mr. President. Produced by Gene Reynolds. Carson Productions and Fox Network, 1987.

Mr. Smith Goes to Obscuristan. Directed by Michael Gene Sullivan and Keiko Shimosato. Written by Michael Gene Sullivan and Josh Kornbluth. Produced by the San Francisco Mime Troupe at various locations. 2003.

Mr. Smith Goes to Washington. Directed by Frank Capra. Story by Lewis R. Foster. Screenplay by Sydney Buchman. Columbia Pictures, 1939.

Monica in Black and White. Directed by Fenton Bailey and Randy Barbato. World of Wonder Productions and Home Box Office, 2002.

Murder at 1600. Directed by Dwight H. Little. Written by Wayne Beach and David Hodgin. Regency Enterprises and Warner Bros., 1997.

My Fellow Americans. Directed by Peter Segal. Written by E. Jack Kaplan, Richard Chapman, and Peter Tolan. Peters Entertainment, Storyline Entertainment, and Warner Bros., 1996.

NBC News Special Report: Attack on America. NBC-TV. 10:00 a.m. ET, September 11, 2001. Lexis-Nexis.

NBC News Special Report: Attack on America. NBC-TV. 8:00 p.m. ET, September 11, 2001. Lexis-Nexis.

NBC News Special Report: Attack on America. "President Bush returns to White House on Marine One." NBC-TV. 6:30 p.m. ET, September 11, 2001. Lexis-Nexis.

NBC News Special Report: Attack on America. "The situation room in the White House as Bush returns." NBC-TV. 6:30 p.m. ET, September 11, 2001. Lexis-Nexis.

Nixon. Directed by Oliver Stone. Written by Oliver Stone, Stephen J. Rivele, and Christopher Wilkinson. Cinergi Pictures Entertainment et al. and Buena Vista Pictures, 1995.

NPR Morning Edition. "Possible Terrorist Attacks on the World Trade Center and Pentagon." National Public Radio. September 11, 2001.

Of Thee I Sing. Book by George S. Kaufman and Morrie Ryskind. Music by George Gershwin. Lyrics by Ira Gershwin. Music Box Theatre, New York, December 26, 1931.

Pat Paulsen for President. Produced by Ken Kragen and Ken Fritz. Directed by Bob Collins. CBS-TV. October 1968. Distributed on video by Paul Brownstein Productions.

Phantom President, The. Directed by Norman Taurog. Written by Walter DeLeon and Harlan Thompson. Paramount Pictures, 1932.

President Harding Is a Rock Star. Music and text by Kyle Jarrow. Produced by Les Freres Corbusier. HERE Arts Center, New York, July 11, 2003.

President's Analyst, The. Directed and written by Theodore J. Flicker. Panpiper Productions and Paramount Pictures, 1967.

President's Plane Is Missing, The. Directed by Daryl Duke. Written by Mark Carliner and Ernest Kinoy. ABC Circle Films, ABC-TV, 1973.

President Vanishes, The. Directed by William A. Wellman. Written by Lynn Starling, Carey Wilson, Cedric Worth, Ben Hecht, and Charles MacArthur [uncredited]. Walter Wanger Productions and Paramount Pictures, 1934.

Primary Colors. Directed by Mike Nichols. Written by Elaine May. Award Entertainment et al. and MCA/Universal Pictures, 1998.

Quarantine. Directed by Chuck Bowman. Written by Lawrence C. Horowitz, Steven Salzburg, and Audrey Salzburg. Greengrass Productions, Selby Lane Productions, and ABC-TV, 1999.

Rap Master Ronnie. Book and lyrics by Garry Trudeau. Music by Elizabeth Swados. Village Gate, New York, October 3, 1984.

Rap Master Ronnie. Directed by Jay Dubin. Written by Garry Trudeau. Home Box Office, 1988.

Schary, Dore. *Sunrise at Campobello.* Cort Theater, New York, January 30, 1958.

Secret Diary of Desmond Pfeiffer, The. Created and written by Barry Fanaro, Jim Gerkin, and Mort Nathan. United Paramount Network [UPN], 1998.

Seven Days in May. Directed by John Frankenheimer. Written by Rod Serling. Paramount Pictures, 1964.

Seven Days in May. Radio adaptation by Kristin Sergel. Produced by LA Theatre Works. KPCC Public Radio, Los Angeles, May 18, 2002.

Shadow Conspiracy. Directed by George P. Cosmatos. Written by Adi Hasak and Ric Gibbs. Paramount Pictures and Buena Vista Pictures et al., 1997.

Sliders. Created by Tracy Tormé and Robert K. Weiss. Universal TV et al. and Fox TV, 1995–1997. Sci-Fi Channel, 1998–2000.

Sorenson, Theodore. *Decision-Making in the White House: The Olive Branch or the Arrows.* April 18 and May 9, 1963. Gino Speranza Lectures. Columbia University. New York: Columbia University Press, 1964.

Spitting Image: Down and Out in the White House and *The Ronnie and Nancy Show.* Spitting Image Productions, David Paradine TV, and NBC-TV, September 1986 and January 1987.

State of the Union. Directed by Frank Capra. Written by Lindsay Crouse, Myles Connolly, and Anthony Veiller. Liberty Films and Metro-Goldwyn-Mayer, 1948.

Sunrise at Campobello. Directed by Vincent J. Donehue. Written by Dore Schary. Schary Productions and Warner Bros., 1960.

Super President. DePatie-Freleng Enterprises [DFE]. NBC-TV, 1967–68.

Tanner '88. Directed by Robert Altman. Written by Garry Trudeau. Home Box Office, 1988.

Tanner on Tanner. Directed by Robert Altman. Written by Garry Trudeau. Sandcastle 5 Productions, the BBC, and the Sundance Channel, 2004.

That's My Bush! Created by Trey Parker and Matt Stone. Important Television and Comedy Central, 2001.

Today. "Day in the life of the president of the United States." NBC-TV. January 23, 2002. Lexis-Nexis.

Today. "White House evacuated; President Bush en route from Florida." NBC-TV. September 11, 2001. Lexis-Nexis.

Tricia's Wedding. Directed by Milton Miron. Written by Milton Miron, Robert Patteson, and Kreemah Ritz. Independently distributed, 1971.

Twilight's Last Gleaming. Directed by Robert Aldrich. Written by Ronald M. Cohen and Edward Huebsch. Lorimar Productions et al. and Allied Artists Pictures Corporation, 1977.

2001: A Space Odyssey. Directed by Stanley Kubrick. Written by Stanley Kubrick and Arthur C. Clarke. Polaris and Metro-Goldwyn-Mayer, 1968.

24. Created by Joel Surnow and Robert Cochran. Real Time Productions et al. Fox TV, 2001–continuing.

Vidal, Gore. *The Best Man.* Morosco Theater, New York, March 31, 1960.

Wag the Dog. Directed by Barry Levinson. Written by David Mamet and Hilary Henkin. Baltimore Pictures et al. and New Line Cinema, 1997.

Welcome to Mooseport. Directed by Donald Petrie. Written by Doug Richardson and Tom Schulman. Mooseport Productions et al. and Twentieth Century Fox, 2004.

West Wing, The. Created by Aaron Sorkin. John Wells Productions, Warner Bros. Television and NBC-TV, 1999–2006.

Wild in the Streets. Directed by Barry Shear. Written by Robert Thom. American International Pictures, 1968.

Wilson. Directed by Henry King. Written by Lamar Trotti. Twentieth Century Fox, 1944.

World War III. Directed by David Greene and Boris Sagal. Written by Robert L. Joseph. NBC-TV, 1982.

Wrong Is Right. Directed and written by Richard Brooks. Columbia Pictures, 1982.

Yes, Minister and *Yes, Prime Minister.* Created by Antony Jay and Jonathan Lynn. BBC-TV, 1980–84 and 1986–87.

Young Lincoln. Written and produced by Todd Gould. WFYI-TV and the Indiana Historical Society, 2004.

Young Mr. Lincoln. Directed by John Ford. Written by Lamar Trotti. Twentieth Century Fox, 1939.

Published Sources

Ackerman, Bruce. *We the People.* Vol. 1, *Foundations.* Cambridge, MA: Harvard University Press/Belknap Press, 1993.

Adams, Frederick Upham. *President John Smith: The Story of a Peaceful Revolution.* 1897. New York: Arno Press, 1971.

Adams, Henry. *Democracy: An American Novel.* New York: Henry Holt, 1880. Eldritch Press, http://ibiblio.org/eldritch/hadams/democ.htm.

———. *The Education of Henry Adams.* Edited by Ernest Samuels. Boston: Houghton Mifflin, 1973.

———. *The History of the United States of America During the Administrations of Jefferson and Madison.* Abridged and edited by Ernest Samuels. Chicago: University of Chicago Press, 1967.

Adams, Samuel Hopkins. *Revelry.* New York: Boni and Liveright, 1926.

Alimurung, Gendy. "Offbeat: Barbie's Revenge." *LA Weekly,* August 2, 2000. http://www.laweekly.com/news/offbeat/barbies-revenge/11347/.

Anderson, Benedict. *Imagined Communities: Reflections on the Origin and Spread of Nationalism.* Rev. ed. London: Verso, 1991.

Anderson-Miller, Julia, and Bruce Joshua Miller, eds. *Dreams of Bill: A Collection of Funny, Strange, and Downright Peculiar Dreams about Our President, Bill Clinton.* New York: Citadel Press/Carol Publishing Group, 1994.

Anonymous. *The Diary of a Public Man.* New Brunswick, NJ: Rutgers University Press, 1947. Orig. serialized in *North American Review,* August–November 1879.

Anthony, Carl Sferrazza. "A President Of the Peephole." *Washington Post,* June 7, 1998. http://www.washingtonpost.com/wp-srv/style/features/harding.htm.

Apess, William. *On Our Own Ground: The Complete Writings of William Apess, a Pequot.* Edited by Barry O'Connell. Amherst: University of Massachusetts Press, 1992. See esp. "Indian Nullification of the Unconstitutional Laws of Massachusetts Relative to the Mashpee Tribe; or, The Pretended Riot Explained, 1835," and "Eulogy on King Philip. As Pronounced at the Odeon, in Federal Street, Boston, January 8, 1836."

Atlas, James. "Confessing for Voyeurs: The Age of the Literary Memoir Is Now." *New York Times Magazine,* May 12, 1996.

Auerbach, Erich. *Dante: Poet of the Secular World.* 1929. Translated by Ralph Manheim, 1961. New York: New York Review Books, 2007.

———. *Mimesis: The Representation of Reality in Western Literature.* Translated by Willard Trask. New York: Anchor Books, 1957.

Bailyn, Bernard. *The Ideological Origins of the American Revolution.* Enlarged ed. Cambridge, MA: Belknap/Harvard University Press, 1992.

———. *The Origins of American Politics.* New York: Vintage Books, 1968.

Baker, Nicholson. *Checkpoint.* New York: Alfred A. Knopf, 2004.

Bakhtin, M. M. "From the Prehistory of Novelistic Discourse." In *The Dialogic Imagination: Four Essays.* Edited by Michael Holquist. Translated by Caryl Emerson and Michael Holquist. Austin: University of Texas Press, 1981.

———. Introduction to *Rabelais and His World.* Translated by Helene Iswolsky. Bloomington: Indiana University Press, 1984. Stetner's Excerpt Mill. http://phoenixandturtle.net/excerptmill/bakhtin2.htm.

———. *Problems of Dostoevsky's Poetics.* Edited and translated by Caryl Emerson. Minneapolis: University of Minnesota Press, 1984.

Balz, Dan, and Bob Woodward. "Ten Days in September. Part 1: America's Chaotic Road to War." *Washington Post,* January 27, 2002, A1.

Batchelor, John Calvin. *Father's Day.* New York: Henry Holt, 1994.

Beasley, Jerry C. "Portraits of a Monster: Robert Walpole and Early English Prose Fiction." *Eighteenth-Century Studies* 14, no. 4 (Summer 1981): 406–31.

Bellamy, Edward. *Looking Backward: 2000 to 1887.* 1888. N.p.: Vanguard, 1917. The EServer Fiction Collection. http://eserver.org/fiction/bellamy/17.html.

Benjamin, Walter. "The Work of Art in the Age of Mechanical Reproduction." In *Illuminations* (New York: Schocken Books, 1968), 217–51. Marxists Internet Archive. http://www.marxists.org/reference/subject/philosophy/works/ge/benjamin.htm.

Berger, Peter L., and Thomas Luckmann. *The Social Construction of Reality: A Treatise in the Sociology of Knowledge.* New York: Doubleday, 1966.

Bernau, George. *Promises to Keep.* New York: Warner Books, 1989.

Berry, Jason. *The Spirit of Black Hawk: A Mystery of Africans and Indians.* Jackson: University Press of Mississippi, 1995.

Biel, Steven. *Down with the Old Canoe: A Cultural History of the Titanic Disaster.* New York: W. W. Norton, 1996.

Black Hawk. *Black Hawk: An Autobiography.* Edited by Donald Jackson. Urbana: University of Illinois Press, 1964.

"Black Hawk." *Commonwealth.* Frankfort [Kentucky?], July 2, 1833.

"Black Hawk-ism." *Commonwealth.* Frankfort [Kentucky?], July 30, 1833.

"Black Hawk's Arrival." *Commonwealth.* Repr. from the *New York Commercial Advertiser.* Frankfort [Kentucky?], June 1833.

"Blake Pontchartrain." *Gambit Weekly,* February 25, 2003. http://www.bestof neworleans.com/dispatch/2003-02-25/blake.html

Blanchard, Rufus. *Abraham Lincoln; The Type of American Genius: An Historical Romance.* Wheaton, IL: R. Blanchard, 1882.

Bloomfield, Maxwell. *Peaceful Revolution: Constitutional Change and American Culture from Progressivism to the New Deal.* Cambridge, MA: Harvard University Press, 2000.

Bolingbroke, Henry St. John, Viscount. "The Idea of a Patriot King." December 1, 1738. In *Bolingbroke: Political Writings,* ed. David Armitage (Cambridge: Cambridge University Press, 1997). http://socserv.mcmaster.ca/~econ/ugcm/3ll3/bolingbroke/king.html.

Boxer, Sarah. "Blogs" [review of several books]. *New York Review of Books* 55, no. 2 (February 14, 2008). http://www.nybooks.com/articles/21013.

Braden, William. *Age of Aquarius: Technology and the Cultural Revolution.* Chicago: Quadrangle Books, 1970.

Braxton, Greg. "Blacks in Hollywood's White House." *Los Angeles Times,* June 22, 2008. http://articles.latimes.com/2008/jun/22/entertainment/ca-president22.

Brenner, Barbara. *Saving the President: What If Lincoln Had Lived?* New York: Julian Messner/Simon and Schuster, 1987.

Britton, Nan. *The President's Daughter.* New York: Elizabeth Ann Guild, 1927.

Brown, Norman O. *Life against Death: The Psychoanalytical Meaning of History.* Middletown, CT: Wesleyan University Press, 1970.

———. *Love's Body.* New York: Random House, 1966.

Brown, William Wells. *Clotel; or, The President's Daughter: A Narrative of Slave Life in the United States.* London: Partridge and Oakey, 1853. Documenting the American South. University of North Carolina Library. http://docsouth.unc.edu/southlit/brown/menu.html.

———. *Clotelle: A Tale of the Southern States.* Boston: J. Redpath, 1864.

Browne, Francis Fisher. *The Every-Day Life of Abraham Lincoln: A Narrative and Descriptive Biography.* Chicago: Browne and Howell, 1913.

Brubaker, Ed, and Eric Shanower. *Prez: Smells Like Teen President.* Vertigo Visions series/D.C. Comics, 1995.

Bryant, Peter [Peter George, pseud.]. *Dr. Strangelove, or: How I Learned to Stop Worrying and Love the Bomb.* New York: Bantam Books, 1964.

———. *Red Alert.* New York: Ace, 1958.

Buchanan, Bruce. *The Presidential Experience: What the Office Does to the Man.* Englewood Cliffs, NJ: Prentice-Hall, 1978.

Burdick, Eugene, and Harvey Wheeler. *Fail-Safe.* New York: Dell, 1962.

Burke, Kenneth. *The Rhetoric of Motives.* Berkeley: University of California Press, 1969.

Burstein, Andrew. *The Passions of Andrew Jackson.* New York: Alfred A. Knopf, 2003.

Bush v. Gore. 538 U.S. 98. 2000.

Byard, Paul Spencer. "A Global City Rebuilt." *New York Times,* August 22, 2002, A23.

Bywaters, David. "Gulliver's Travels and the Mode of Political Parallel during Walpole's Administration." *ELH* 54, no. 3 (Autumn 1987): 717–40.

Calhoun, John C. *Papers.* Vol. 11. Edited by Robert L. Meriwether. Columbia: University of South Carolina Press for the South Carolina Society, 1959.

Carnegie, Dale. *Lincoln the Unknown.* New York: Century, 1932.

Carnell, Rachel. *Partisan Politics, Narrative Realism, and the Rise of the British Novel.* New York: Palgrave Macmillan, 2006.

Carpenter, F. B. [Francis Bicknell]. *Six Months at the White House with Abraham Lincoln: The Story of a Picture.* New York: Hurd and Houghton, 1866.

Carter, Jimmy. *The Hornet's Nest: A Novel of the Revolutionary War.* New York: Simon and Schuster, 2003.

Catlin, George. *Letters and Notes on the Manners, Customs, and Conditions of North American Indians.* London, 1844. Library of Western Fur Trade Historical Source Documents. http://www.xmission.com/~drudy/mtman/html/catlin/index.html.

Catton, Bruce. *The Coming Fury.* Vol. 1 of *The Centennial History of the Civil War.* New York: Pocket Books, 1971.

Cavell, Stanley. *Pursuits of Happiness: The Hollywood Comedy of Remarriage.* Cambridge, MA: Harvard University Press, 2004.

———. *The World Viewed: Reflections on the Ontology of Film.* Cambridge, MA: Harvard University Press, 1980.

Chateaubriand, François-René. *Travels in America and Italy.* London: H. Colburn, 1828.

Cherokee Nation v. State of Georgia. 30 U.S. 1. 1831. Carl Vinson Institute of Government. University of Georgia. January 21, 2005. http://www.cviog.uga.edu/Projects/gainfo/cherovga.htm.

Cillizza, Chris. "The Fix: Mark Warner the Avatar." *Washington Post,* August 31, 2006. http://blog.washingtonpost.com/thefix/2006/08/mark_warner_in_cyberspace.html.

Clancy, Tom. *Executive Orders.* New York: Berkeley Books, 1997.

Cmiel, Kenneth. *Democratic Eloquence: The Fight over Popular Speech in Nineteenth-Century America.* New York: William Morrow, 1990.

Cobley, Paul. *Narrative.* London: Routledge, 2001.

Cole, Cyrenus. *I Am a Man: The Indian Black Hawk.* Iowa City: State Historical Society of Iowa, 1938.

Commonwealth, The. Frankfort [Kentucky?], July 2, 1833, July 30, 1833.

Cooper, James Fenimore. *The Spy: A Tale of the Neutral Ground.* Vol. 1. New York: Wiley and Halsted, 1821.

Coover, Robert. *A Political Fable.* New York: Viking Press, 1980.

Cope, Kevin L. "How General George Outlived His Own Funeral Orations." In *George Washington in and as Culture,* ed. Kevin L. Cope. New York: AMS Press, 2001.

Copeland, Libby. "Buffing Up the Image of George Washington: Mt. Vernon Creates a Toothsome Teen." *Washington Post*, August 30, 2005, C01.

Corry, John. *The Life of George Washington*. Bridgeport, CT: Lambert Lockwood, 1815.

Cortright, Edgar M., ed. *Apollo Expeditions to the Moon*. Publication SP-350. Washington, DC: Scientific and Technical Information Office. National Aeronautics and Space Administration. 1975. Chapter 1.5. NASA History Division/NASA Headquarters. http://www.hq.nasa.gov/office/pao/History/SP-350/ch-1-5.html.

Crain, Caleb. "A Critic at Large: Rail-Splitting." *New Yorker*, November 7, 2005.

Crichton, Michael. *State of Fear*. New York: HarperCollins, 2004.

Crosby, Frank. *The Life of Abraham Lincoln, Sixteenth President of the United States*. Philadelphia: John E. Potter, 1865.

Cuordileone, Kyle A. *Manhood and American Political Culture in the Cold War*. New York: Routledge, 2004.

Current, Richard N. *Lincoln and the First Shot*. Philadelphia: J. B. Lippincott, 1963.

———. *The Lincoln Nobody Knows*. New York: Hill and Wang, 1981.

Daily National Intelligencer, The. Washington, DC, March 6, 1829.

Dallek, Robert. "The Medical Ordeals of JFK." *Atlantic Monthly*, December 2002. http://www.theatlantic.com/doc/200212/dallek-jfk.

Davis, Charles Augustus [J. Downing, Major, pseud.]. *Letters of J. Downing, Major, Downingville Militia, Second Brigade, to His Old Friend, Mr. Dwight, of the New York Daily Advertiser*. New York: Harper and Brothers, 1834. Early American Fiction Collection. University of Virginia Library. http://etext.lib.virginia.edu/eaf/.

DeCarlo, Tessa. "Sister Gertrude, a Preacher Who Could Paint." *New York Times*, Arts and Leisure section, February 22, 2004.

Delacorte, Peter. *Time on My Hands: A Novel with Photographs*. New York: Scribner, 1997.

Dentith, Simon. *Bakhtinian Thought: An Introductory Reader*. New York: Routledge, 1995.

Dicey, Edward. *Six Months in the Federal States*. London: Macmillan, 1863.

Donnelly, Ignatius ["Edmund Boisgilbert. M.D."]. *Caesar's Column: A Story of the Twentieth Century*. Chicago: F. J. Shulte, 1890. Project Gutenberg, 2004. http://www.gutenberg.org/etext/5155.

Drury, Allen. *Advise and Consent*. Garden City, NY: Doubleday, 1959.

Duban, James. "Robins and Robinarchs in 'My Kinsman, Major Molineaux.'" *Nineteenth-Century Fiction* 38, no. 3 (December 1983): 271–88.

Dunlap, William. *André; A Tragedy, in Five Acts: As Performed by the Old American Company, New-York, March 30, 1798*. Edited by Jeffrey H. Richards. New York: Penguin Classics, 1997.

Eaton, John Henry. *Memoirs of Andrew Jackson, Late Major-General and Commander in Chief of the Southern Division of the Army of the United States, Compiled by a Citizen of Massachusetts*. Boston: Charles Ewer, 1828.

Eaton, [Margaret] Peggy. *The Autobiography of Peggy Eaton*. Edited by Annette K. Baxter. New York: Arno Press, 1980.

Eldredge, H. Wentworth. *The Second American Revolution: The Near Collapse of Traditional Democracy*. New York: Washington Square Press, 1966.

Ellis, Joseph J. *After the Revolution: Profiles of Early American Culture*. New York: W. W. Norton, 2002.

Eszterhas, Joe. "Willard Comes Clean." In *American Rhapsody*. New York: Vintage Books, 2000.

Exner, Judith, with Ovid Demaris. *My Story*. New York: Grove Press, 1978.

Fields, W. C. *Fields for President*. Edited by Michael M. Taylor. New York: Dell, 1971.

Finley, Karen. *George & Martha*. London: Verso Books, 2006.

Fliegelman, Jay. *Declaring Independence: Jefferson, Natural Language, and the Culture of Performance*. Stanford. CA: Stanford University Press, 1993.

Ford, Henry Jones. *Washington and His Colleagues: A Chronicle of the Rise and Fall of Federalism*. New Haven. CT: Yale University Press, 1918. Project Gutenberg, 2004. http://www.gutenberg.org/etext/11702.

Franken, Al. *Why Not Me? The Inside Story*. New York: Random House/Delacorte, 1999.

Freedman. Nancy. *Joshua Son of None*. New York: Delacorte Press, 1973.

Freud, Sigmund. "The Uncanny." In *The Standard Edition of the Complete Psychological Works of Sigmund Freud*, vol. 17. Translated and edited by James Strachey. London: Hogarth, 1953.

Freud, Sigmund, and William C. Bullitt. *Thomas Woodrow Wilson, Twenty-eighth President of the United States: A Psychological Study*. Boston: Houghton Mifflin, 1966.

Fulton, A. R. "Sketch of Black Hawk." In *The Red Men of Iowa: Being a History of the Various Aboriginal Tribes*, ed. Edith Fulton Stone. http://yawp.com/redmen/.

Gabler, Neal. "This Time, the Scene Was Real." *New York Times*, September 16, 2001, sec. 4, 2.

"'Gabriel' Film Sent Back to Hollywood; Hays and Metro Officials Frown on Motion Picture 'Dramatizing' White House Story." *New York Times*, March 17, 1933, 21.

Gay, John. *The Beggar's Opera and Companion Pieces*. Edited by C. F. Burgess. Northbrook, IL: AHM, 1966.

Gebauer, Gunter, and Christoph Wulf. *Mimesis: Culture—Art—Society*. Translated by Don Reneau. Berkeley: University of California Press, 1995.

Gilman, Charlotte Perkins. *Herland*. 1915. Project Gutenberg, 1992. http://www.gutenberg.org/etext/32.

Gingrich, Newt, and William Forstchen. *Gettysburg: A Novel of the Civil War.* New York: Thomas Dunne Books/St. Martin's Press, 2003.

———. *Never Call Retreat: Lee and Grant: The Final Victory.* New York: Thomas Dunne Books/St. Martin's Press, 2005.

Glass, Francis. *Georgii Washingtonii, Americae Septentrionalis Civitatum Foederatum Praesidis Primi, Vita.* Edited by J. N. Reynolds. New York: Harper and Brothers, 1835.

Goodrich, Elizur. "The Principles of Civil Union and Happiness Considered and Recommended." In *Political Sermons of the Founding Era, 1730–1805,* vol. 1. Edited by Ellis Sandoz. Indianapolis, IN: Liberty Fund, 1998.

Greenberg, David. *Nixon's Shadow: The History of an Image.* New York: W. W. Norton, 2003.

Greenberg, Kenneth S. "The Nose, the Lie, and the Duel." In *Honor and Slavery.* Princeton, NJ: Princeton University Press, 1997. Excerpted at http://www .onealwebsite.com/onealpeggy.htm.

Greenberg, Martin H., and Francis M. Nevins, eds. *Mr. President, Private Eye.* New York: iBooks, 2004.

Griggs, Sutton E. *Imperium in Imperio: A Study of the Negro Race Problem/A Novel.* Cincinnati: Editor, 1899. Project Gutenberg, 2005. http://www.gutenberg .org/etext/15454.

Gross, Martin L. *Man of Destiny.* New York: Avon Books, 1997.

Guthrie, Marisa. "'Fail-Safe' Compels, but Pales in Film's Shadow." *Boston Herald,* April 10, 2000, 31.

Gutman, Dan. *The Kid Who Became President.* Caledonia, MN: Turtleback Books/Demco Media, 1999.

———. *The Kid Who Ran for President.* New York: Scholastic, 1996.

Haas, Peter J., and Terry Christensen. *Projecting Politics: Political Messages in American Films.* Armonk, NY: M. E. Sharpe, 2005.

Harkins, Anthony. *Hillbilly: A Cultural History of an American Icon.* Oxford: Oxford University Press, 2003.

Harris, Joel Chandler. *The Kidnapping of President Lincoln and Other War Detective Stories.* Garden City, NY: Doubleday, Page, 1909.

Harris, Lee. "Al Qaeda's Fantasy Ideology." *Policy Review* 114 (August and September 2002). http://www.hoover.org/publications/policyreview/3459646 .html.

Harris, Robert. *Fatherland.* New York: HarperTorch/HarperCollins, 1992.

Hart, Lorenz, et al. *The Complete Lyrics of Lorenz Hart.* New York: Random House, 1988.

Herman, David. "The Culture of Narcissism—Contemporary Books." *New Statesman* 126, no. 4332 (May 1997): 124–27.

Herndon, William H., and Jesse W. Weik. *Herndon's Life of Lincoln.* 1888. Cleveland: World, 1949. (Originally published as *Herndon's Lincoln: The True Story of a Great Life.*)

Hill, Doug, and Jeff Weingrad. *Saturday Night: A Backstage History of Saturday Night Live.* New York: William Morrow, 1986.

Hoberman, J. "Lights, Camera, Exploitation," *Village Voice,* August 27–September 3, 2003. http://www.villagevoice.com/news/0335,hoberman,46558,1.html.

Hoffman, John. "Benjamin P. Thomas." *Journal of the Abraham Lincoln Association* 19, no. 2 (Summer 1998): 21. http://www.historycooperative.org/journals/jala/19.2/hoffmann.html.

Hofstadter, Richard. "The Paranoid Style in American Politics." In *The Paranoid Style in American Politics and Other Essays.* New York: Vintage Books, 1967.

Hoile, Christopher. *Wholenote Magazine,* March 2004. http://www.thewholenote.com/wholenote_mar_04/opera.html.

Holcombe, Henry. "A Sermon Occasioned by the Death of Washington." In *Political Sermons of the Founding Era, 1730–1805,* vol. 2. Edited by Ellis Sandoz. Indianapolis, IN: Liberty Fund, 1998.

Holden, Edward Goodman. *A Famous Victory: Brewster for President.* Chicago: Jansen, McClurg. 1880.

Holland, J. G. *The Life of Abraham Lincoln.* Springfield, MA: Gurdon Bill/Republican Press/Samuel Bowles, 1866.

Holzer, Harold. "Abraham Lincoln Takes the Heat." *Civil War Times,* February 2001. http://www.historynet.com/culture/social_history/3704871.html.

———. "'Columbia's Noblest Sons': Washington and Lincoln in Popular Prints." *Journal of the Abraham Lincoln Association* 15, no. 1 (Winter 1994). http://www.historycooperative.org/journals/jala/15.1/holzer.html.

———. *Lincoln Seen and Heard.* Lawrence: University Press of Kansas, 2000.

Hopkins, Robert. "Simon Suggs: A Burlesque Campaign Biography." *American Quarterly* 15, no. 3 (Fall 1963): 459–63.

House, Edward Mandell. *Philip Dru, Administrator: A Story of Tomorrow, 1920–1935.* New York: BW Huebsch, 1912. Project Gutenberg, 2004. http://www.gutenberg.org/etext/6711.

Hozic, Aida A. "Making of the Unwanted Colonies: Un-Imagining Desire." In *Cultural Studies and Political Theory.* Edited by Jodi Dean. Ithaca, NY: Cornell University Press, 2000.

Hughes, Emmet John. *The Ordeal of Power: A Political Memoir of the Eisenhower Years.* New York: Atheneum, 1963.

Huhndorf, Shari M. *Going Native: Indians in the American Cultural Imagination.* Ithaca, NY: Cornell University Press, 2001.

Humphreys, David. *David Humphreys' "Life of General Washington."* Edited by Rosemarie Zagarri. Athens: University of Georgia Press, 1991.

Irving, Washington. *George Washington: A Biography.* Edited and abridged by Charles Neider. Garden City, NY: Doubleday, 1976.

——— [Diedrich Knickerbocker, pseud.]. *A History of New York, From the Beginning of the World to the End of the Dutch Dynasty*. Vol. 1. New York: Inskeep and Bradford. 1809. Electronic Text Center, University of Virginia Library. http://etext.lib.virginia.edu/.

James, Dorothy Buckton. *The Contemporary Presidency*. New York: Pegasus, 1969.

James, Henry. "Pandora." 1884. In *Daisy Miller; Pandora; The Patagonia; and Other Tales* (New York: Scribner's, 1937). http://www.literaturepage.com/read/henry-james-pandora.html.

Johnson, Lyndon Baines. *The Choices We Face*. New York: Bantam Books, 1969.

Johnston, Damon. "The Mayor's Report." *Herald Sun* [Australia], September 25, 2001, 17.

Jones, J. B. *Adventures of Col. Gracchus Vanderbomb, of Sloughcreek, in Pursuit of the Presidency*. Philadelphia: A. Hart, 1852. Wright American Fiction 1851–1875. Library Electronic Text Resource Service. Indiana University. http://www.letrs.indiana.edu/

———. *Border War: A Tale of Disunion*. New York: Rudd & Carleton, 1859. Early American Fiction Collection. University of Virginia Library. http://etext .virginia.edu/eaf/authors/jbj.htm.

Kahn, Herman. *Thinking about the Unthinkable*. New York: Horizon Press, 1962.

Kammen, Michael. *A Machine That Would Go of Itself: The Constitution in American Culture*. New York: Alfred A. Knopf, 1986.

Kantorowicz, Ernst H. *The King's Two Bodies: A Study in Medieval Political Theology*. Princeton, NJ: Princeton University Press, 1957.

Kaplan, Karen. "The Sims Take on Al Qaeda." *Los Angeles Times*, November 2, 2001, A1.

Keir, Sir David Lindsay. *The Constitutional History of Modern Britain since 1485*. 9th ed. New York: W. W. Norton, 1969.

Kennedy, John Pendleton [Solomon Secondthoughts, pseud.]. *Quodlibet: Containing Some Annals Thereof: With an Authentic Account of the Origin and Growth of the Borough*. Philadelphia: Lea and Blanchard, 1840.

Ketcham, Ralph. *Presidents Above Party: The First American Presidency, 1789–1829*. Chapel Hill: University of North Carolina Press, 1987.

Kimmel, Michael S. *Manhood in America: A Cultural History*. New York: Free Press, 1996.

Kitman, Marvin. *The Making of the President 1789: The Unauthorized Campaign Biography*. New York: HarperPerennial, 1989.

Klein, Joe. *Primary Colors*. New York: Random House, 1996.

Kluckhohn, Frank L. "Japan Wars on U.S. and Britain; Makes Sudden Attack on Hawaii; Heavy Fighting at Sea Reported." *New York Times*, December 8, 1941.

Knebel, Fletcher. *Night of Camp David*. New York: Bantam Books, 1966.

———. *Trespass*. New York: Pocket Books, 1970.

Knebel, Fletcher, and Charles W. Bailey II. *Seven Days in May.* New York: Harper & Row, 1962.

Kramnick, Isaac. *Bolingbroke and His Circle: The Politics of Nostalgia in the Age of Walpole.* 1968. Reprint, Ithaca, NY: Cornell University Press, 1992.

Kuklick, Bruce. *The Good Ruler: From Herbert Hoover to Richard Nixon.* Piscataway, NJ: Rutgers University Press, 1989.

Kunhardt, Philip, Jr., et al. *The American President.* New York: Riverhead Books, 1999.

Kurland, Philip B., and Ralph Lerner, eds. *The Founders' Constitution.* Chicago: University of Chicago Press, 1987. http://press-pubs.uchicago.edu/founders/.

Lammers, William W. *Presidential Politics: Patterns and Prospects.* New York: Harper & Row, 1976.

Lamon, Ward Hill, and Chauncey F. Black [uncredited]. *The Life of Abraham Lincoln; From His Birth to His Inauguration as President.* New York: James R. Osgood, 1872.

Langdon, Samuel. "The Republic of the Israelites an Example to the American States." In *Political Sermons of the Founding Era, 1730–1805,* vol. 1. Edited by Ellis Sandoz. Indianapolis, IN: Liberty Fund, 1998.

Lazare, Daniel. *The Frozen Republic: How the Constitution Is Paralyzing Democracy.* New York: Harcourt, Brace, 1996.

Lemann, Nicholas. "Letter from Washington: The Options." *New Yorker,* October 1, 2001.

Lerner, Max. *Wounded Titans: American Presidents and the Perils of Power.* New York: Arcade, 1996.

Levine, Lawrence W., and Cornelia R. Levine. *The People and the President: America's Conversation with FDR.* Boston: Beacon Press, 2002.

Lewis, Sinclair. *It Can't Happen Here.* New York: Doubleday, 1935. Project Gutenberg Australia. http://gutenberg.net.au/ebooks03/0301001h.html.

Light, James F. "Varieties of Satire in the Art of Nathanael West." *Studies in American Humor* 2, no. 1 (April 1975): 45–59. http://www.compedit.com/var_of_satire.htm.

Lincoln, Abraham. "Address to the Legislature of Ohio at Columbus [February 13, 1861]." In *The Writings of Abraham Lincoln, Constitutional Edition,* vol. 5. Edited by Arthur Brooks Lapsley. New York: G. P. Putnam's Sons, 1905. Project Gutenberg, 2004. http://www.gutenberg.org/etext/2657.

Locke, David Ross. *The Nasby Papers: Letters and Sermons Containing the Views on the Topics of the Day, of Petroleum V. Nasby.* Indianapolis: C. O. Perrine, 1864. Online Books Page, University of Pennsylvania Library. http://onlinebooks.library.upenn.edu/webbin/book/lookupid?key=olbp32840.

London, Jack. *The Iron Heel.* New York: Macmillan, 1908. Jack London Online Collection. Sonoma State University Library. http://london.sonoma.edu/Writings/IronHeel/.

Lowi, Theodore J. *The End of Liberalism: Ideology, Policy, and the Crisis of Public Authority.* New York: W. W. Norton, 1969.

———. *The Personal President: Power Invested, Promise Unfulfilled.* Ithaca, NY: Cornell University Press, 1985.

Lynn, Kenneth S., ed. *The Comic Tradition in America: An Anthology of American Humor.* New York: Doubleday Anchor Books, 1958.

Madison, James. *Notes of Debates in the Federal Convention of 1787 Reported by James Madison.* New York: W. W. Norton, 1987.

Marbury v. Madison. 5 U.S. 137 (1803), 163.

Marshall, John. *George Washington.* Vol. 5, *1804–7.* New York: Chelsea House/American Statesman Series, 1983.

Marszalek, John F. *The Petticoat Affair: Manners, Mutiny, and Sex in Andrew Jackson's White House.* New York: Free Press, 1997.

Matviko, John W. *The American President in Popular Culture.* Westport, CT: Greenwood Publishing Group, 2005.

Marx, Leo. "Shakespeare's American Fable." Chap. 2 of *The Machine in the Garden: Technology and the Pastoral Ideal in America,* 34–72. New York: Oxford University Press, 2000.

———. "Technology: The Emergence of a Hazardous Concept." *Social Research* 64, no. 3 (1997): 965–88.

Marx, Rudolph, M.D. *The Health of the Presidents.* New York: Putnam, 1960.

Mason, Colin. *Hostage.* New York: Pinnacle Books, 1973.

Mast, Gerald. *Can't Help Singin'.* New York: Overlook Press, 1987.

McCarthy, Sheryl. "The Candidacy of Howard Dean Takes 'Wing.'" *Newsday,* July 3, 2003. http://www.fightingdemocrat.com/dean/archives/000124.html#more.

McCloud, Scott. *The New Adventures of Abraham Lincoln.* La Jolla, CA: Homage Comics/Aegis Entertainment, 1998.

McConnell, Frank. *Storytelling and Mythmaking: Images from Film and Literature.* New York: Oxford University Press, 1979.

McConnell, Robert L. "The Genesis and Ideology of 'Gabriel Over the White House.'" *Cinema Journal* 15, no. 2 (Spring 1976): 7–26.

McLuhan, Marshall. *Understanding Media: The Extensions of Man.* New York: McGraw-Hill, 1965.

Meyers, Marvin. *The Jacksonian Persuasion: Politics and Belief.* Stanford, CA: Stanford University Press, 1960.

Mills, C. Wright. *The Causes of World War Three.* New York: Simon and Schuster, 1958.

Milton, Henry A. *The President Is Missing.* New York: Banner/Hearst Corp, 1967.

Mitchell, S. Weir. *The Youth of Washington: Told in the Form of an Autobiography.* New York: Century, 1904.

Mneimneh, Hassan, and Kanan Makiya. "Manual for a 'Raid.'" *New York*

Review of Books 49, no. 1 (January 17, 2002). http://www.nybooks.com/articles/15106.

Morgan, Edmund S. *Inventing the People: The Rise of Popular Sovereignty in England and America.* New York: W. W. Norton, 1988.

Morgan, Kay Summersby. *Past Forgetting: My Love Affair with Dwight D. Eisenhower.* New York: Simon and Schuster, 1975.

Nash, Ilana. *American Sweethearts: Teenage Girls in Twentieth-Century Popular Culture.* Bloomington: Indiana University Press, 2006.

Neustadt, Richard E. *Presidential Power: The Politics of Leadership from FDR to Carter.* New York: John Wiley and Sons, 1980.

Nevins, Allan. The *Statesmanship of the Civil War.* New York: Macmillan/Collier Books, 1962.

Niles' Weekly Register. Vols. 43–45, October 1832–August 1833.

Nordstrom, Justin. "Looking Backward's Utopian Sequels: 'Fictional Dialogues' in Gilded-Age America." *Utopian Studies* 28, no. 2 (March 2007): 193–222.

Novan, T., and Blayne Cooper [Advocate, pseud.]. *Madame President.* [New Orleans?]: Jane Doe Press, 2001.

Nunberg, Geoffrey. "When Words Fail: The Stilted Language of Tragedy." *Los Angeles Times,* September 16, 2001, 2.

"Official Despatch, The [to Major General Dix. New York]. War Department. Washington. April 15. 1:30 a.m." *New York Times,* April 15, 1865, 1.

Pastan, Amy, and Linda McKnight. *Make Your Own President.* Smithsonian/HarperCollins, 2006.

Pennington, Gail. "Television Viewers Watch Attacks Unfold." *St. Louis Post-Dispatch,* September 11, 2001, Tuesday Extra edition, A10.

Peterson, Merrill D. *The Jefferson Image in the American Mind.* Oxford: Oxford University Press, 1992.

———. *Lincoln in American Memory.* Oxford: Oxford University Press, 1995.

Phillips, Leon [Noel Bertram Gerson]. *That Eaton Woman: In Defense of Peggy O'Neale Eaton.* Barre, MA: Barre, 1974.

Pierce, J. Kingston. "Andrew Jackson and the Tavern-Keeper's Daughter." *American History,* June 1999, 1–4. http://www.historynet.com/andrew-jackson-and-the-tavern-keepers-daughter-june-99-american-history-feature.htm

Poyer, David. *The Only Thing to Fear.* New York: Tor Books, 1996.

Prez: First Teen President. Nos. 1–4. New York: DC Comics/National Periodical. August/September 1973–February/March 1974.

Prochnau, William. *Trinity's Child: A Novel.* New York: Putnam, 1983.

Prothero, Stephen. *American Jesus: How the Son of God Became a National Icon.* New York: Farrar, Straus & Giroux, 2003.

Rakove, Jack N. *Original Meanings: Politics and Ideas in the Making of the Constitution.* New York: Alfred A. Knopf, 1996.

Ramsay, David. *The Life of George Washington.* 1807. Archiving Early America. http://www.earlyamerica.com/lives/gwlife/.

Ratcliffe, David T. *Understanding Special Operations and Their Impact on the Vietnam War Era.* Santa Cruz, CA: rat haus reality press, 1999. http://www.ratical.org/ratville/JFK/USO/.

Reagan's Raiders. Vols. 1–3. Created by Monroe Arnold and Rich Buckler. Brooklyn, NY: Solson, 1986–87.

Reedy, George E. *The Twilight of the Presidency.* 1st ed. New York: Mentor/New American Library, 1970. *The Twilight of the Presidency: From Johnson to Reagan.* 2nd ed. New York: Mentor/New American Library, 1987.

Reilly, John M. "The Reconstruction of Genre as Entry into Conscious History." *Black American Literature Forum* 13, no. 1 (Spring 1979): 3–6.

Remini, Robert V. *The Revolutionary Age of Andrew Jackson.* New York: Avon Books, 1976.

Resnick, Mike, ed. *Alternate Kennedys.* New York: Tor Books, 1992.

———. *Alternate Presidents.* New York: Tor/Tom Doherty Associates, 1992.

Rich, Frank. "The De Facto Capital." *New York Times,* Editorial/Op-Ed, October 6, 2002.

Roberts, Charles. *The Truth about the Assassination.* New York: Grosset and Dunlap, 1967.

Rollins, Peter C., and John E. O'Connor, eds. *Hollywood's White House: The American Presidency in Film and History.* Lexington: University Press of Kentucky, 2003.

———, eds. *The West Wing: The American Presidency As Television Drama.* Syracuse, NY: Syracuse University Press, 2003.

Rosenfeld, Gavriel D. *The World Hitler Never Made.* Cambridge: Cambridge University Press, 2005.

Rosenthal, Raymond, ed. *McLuhan: Pro and Con.* Baltimore: Penguin Books, 1968.

Rossiter, Clinton. *The American Presidency.* 1956. New York: Time, 1960.

———, ed. *Federalist Papers.* New York: Mentor Books/New American Library, 1961.

Roszak, Theodore. *The Making of a Counter Culture: Reflections on the Technocratic Society and Its Youthful Opposition.* New York: Doubleday/Anchor Books, 1969.

———. *Where the Wasteland Ends: Politics and Transcendence in Postindustrial Society.* Garden City, NY: Doubleday/Anchor Books, 1972.

Roth, Philip. *Our Gang.* New York: Random House, 1971.

———. *The Plot Against America: A Novel.* New York: Houghton Mifflin, 2004.

Rourke, Constance. *American Humor: A Study of the National Character.* New York: Doubleday/Anchor Books, 1953.

Russell, Francis. *The Shadow of Blooming Grove: Warren G. Harding in His Times.* New York: McGraw-Hill, 1968.

Safire, William. "The Plan from PEOC." *New York Times*, June 10, 2002, A25.

St. George, Judith. *So You Want to Be President*. Illustrated by David Small. New York: Scholastic, 2004.

Samon, Celin. *My Erotic Dreams With Bill Clinton*. N.p.: Impact, 2000.

Samuels, Ernest. *Henry Adams: The Middle Years*. 1958. New York: History Book Club, 2003.

Sandel, Michael J. *Democracy's Discontent: America in Search of a Public Philosophy*. Cambridge, MA: Harvard University Press, 1998.

Sanger, David E., and Don Van Natta Jr. "After the Attacks: The Events; In Four Days, a National Crisis Changes Bush's Presidency." *New York Times*, September 16, 2001, 1.

Schlesinger, Arthur, Jr. "On Henry Adams' 'Democracy.'" *New York Review of Books* 50, no. 5 (March 27, 2003). http://www.nybooks.com/articles/article-preview?article_id=16160.

Scholes, Robert, and Robert Kellogg. *The Nature of Narrative*. Oxford: Oxford University Press, 1979.

Schreiber, Lee L. "Sponsors of American Culture: A Social Profile of Philadelphia's Federal Party Activists." *Journal of American Culture* 10, no. 1 (Spring 1987): 79–86.

Schudson, Michael. *The Good Citizen: A History of American Civic Life*. Cambridge, MA: Harvard University Press, 1999.

———. "The Politics of Narrative Form: The Emergence of News Conventions in Print and Television." *Daedalus* 111, no. 4 ["Print Culture and Video Culture"] (Fall 1982): 97–112.

———. *Watergate in American Memory: How We Remember, Forget, and Reconstruct the Past*. New York: Basic Books, 1992.

Schultz, William Eben. *Gay's Beggar's Opera: Its Content, History, and Influence*. New Haven, CT: Yale University Press, 1923.

Schwartz, Barry. "Ann Rutledge in American Memory: Social Change and the Erosion of a Romantic Drama." *Journal of the Abraham Lincoln Association* 26, no. 1 (Winter 2005). http://www.historycooperative.org/journals/jala/26.1/schwartz.html.

———. *George Washington: The Making of an American Symbol*. New York: Free Press, 1987.

Sennett, Richard. *The Fall of Public Man: On the Social Psychology of Capitalism*. New York: Vintage Books/Random House, 1976.

Serling, Robert J. *The President's Plane Is Missing*. Garden City, NY: Doubleday, 1967.

Seymour, Charles. *The Intimate Papers of Colonel House Arranged as a Narrative*. Vol. 1. Boston: Houghton Mifflin, 1926.

Shenk, Joshua. *Lincoln's Melancholy: How Depression Challenged a President and Fueled His Greatness*. New York: Houghton Mifflin, 2005.

Silver, James. *Naked Presidents: An Alternate History.* Lincoln, NE: Writers Club Press/iUniverse.com, 2000.

Simon, Tom, ed. *Poetry Under Oath: From the Testimony of William Jefferson Clinton and Monica S. Lewinsky.* New York: Workman, 1998.

Skolnick, Jerome, et al. *Assassination and Political Violence.* Staff report to the National Commission on the Causes and Prevention of Violence. New York: Ballantine Books, 1969.

Smigel, Robert, and Adam McKay. *X-Presidents.* New York: Random House Comics Group, 2000.

Smith, Jeff. *Unthinking the Unthinkable: Nuclear Weapons and Western Culture.* Bloomington: Indiana University Press, 1989.

Smith, Margaret Bayard. *The First Forty Years of Washington Society.* Edited by Gaillard Hunt. New York: Charles Scribner's Sons, 1906. American Memory. Library of Congress. http://memory.loc.gov/cgi-bin/query/r?ammem/lhbcb:@field(DOCID+@lit(lhbcb40262)).

Smith, Seba [Jack Downing, pseud.]. *The Life and Writings of Major Jack Downing, of Downingville, Away Down East in the State of Maine.* Boston: Lily, Wait, Colman & Holden, 1833. Early American Fiction Collection. University of Virginia Library. http://etext.lib.virginia.edu/eaf/.

———. *The Select Letters of Major Jack Downing.* Philadelphia[?]: R. Withington and H. Davis, 1834. Early American Fiction Collection. University of Virginia Library. http://etext.lib.virginia.edu/eaf/.

Snider, Denton J. *Lincoln and Ann Rutledge: An Idyllic Epos of the Early North-West.* N.p.: Sigma, 1912.

Snowden, Richard. *The History of the American Revolution; In Scripture Style. to Which Is Added, the Declaration of Independence, the Constitution of the United States of America, and the Farewell Address of General Washington.* Frederick Co., MD: M. Bartgis, Pleasant Dale Paper Mill, 1823.

Sontag, Susan. "Fascinating Fascism." *New York Review of Books,* February 6, 1975. Repr. in Sontag, *Under the Sign of Saturn* (New York: Farrar, Straus and Giroux, 1980). *Ressources documentaires sur le génocide nazi et sa négation.* http://www.anti-rev.org/textes/Sontag74a/index.html.

Sparks, Jared. *The Life of George Washington.* Boston: Tappan and Dennet. 1844.

Spigel, Lynn, and Henry Jenkins. "Same Bat Channel, Different Bat Times: Mass Culture and Popular Memory." In *The Many Lives of Batman: Critical Approaches to a Superhero and His Media,* edited by Roberta E. Pearson and William Uricchio. New York: Routledge, 1991.

Spragens, William C., ed. *Popular Images of American Presidents.* New York: Greenwood Press, 1988.

"Staten Island 9/11 Survivor Disgusted by 'Tasteless' Internet Video Game." *Staten Island Advance,* January 1, 2008. http://www.silive.com/news/index.ssf/2008/01/staten_island_911_survivor_dis.html.

Stewart, Donald Ogden. *Perfect Behavior: A Parody Outline of Etiquette.* New York: George H. Doran, 1922. Electronic Text Center. University of Virginia Library. http://etext.lib.virginia.edu/toc/modeng/public/StePerf.html.

Story, Joseph. *Life and Letters of Joseph Story: Associate Justice of the Supreme Court of the United States.* London: J. Chapman, 1851.

Stout, Rex [Anon.]. *The President Vanishes.* New York: Farrar and Rinehart, 1934.

Strozier, Charles B. *Lincoln's Quest for Union: Public and Private Meanings.* New York: Basic Books, 1982.

Suskind, Ron. "Faith, Certainty and the Presidency of George W. Bush." *New York Times Magazine,* October 17, 2004.

Tarbell, Ida M. *He Knew Lincoln and Other Billy Brown Stories.* New York: Macmillan, 1922.

Templeton, Charles Bradley. *The Kidnapping of the President.* Toronto: McClelland and Stewart, 1974.

Thach, Charles C., Jr. *The Creation of the Presidency: A Study in Constitutional History.* 1923. Indianapolis: Liberty Fund, 2007.

Trask, Kerry A. *Black Hawk: The Battle for the Heart of America.* New York: Owl Books/Henry Holt, 2005.

"TRB from Washington: The First 100 Days." *New Republic,* May 2, 1981. Republished June 6, 2004. http://www.tnr.com/doc.mhtml?i=redux&s=trb050281.

Trescott, Jacqueline. "Mount Vernon Plans $85 Million Addition." *Washington Post,* April 19, 2002, A01.

Trollope, Frances. *Domestic Manners of the Americans.* 1832. Project Gutenberg, 2003. http://www.gutenberg.org/etext/10345.

Tucker, Judge [Nathaniel] Beverley. *The Partisan Leader: A Novel, and an Apocalypse of the Origin and Struggles of the Southern Confederacy.* Edited by Rev. Thos. A. Ware. Richmond, VA: West & Johnston, 1862. Documenting the American South. University of North Carolina Library. http://docsouth.unc.edu/imls/tucker/menu.html.

Tuohey, Jason. "JFK Reloaded Game Causes Controversy." *PCWorld,* November 24, 2004. http://www.pcworld.com/article/id,118717-page,1/article.html.

Turner, Katharine C. *Red Men Calling on the Great White Father.* Norman, OK: University of Oklahoma Press, 1951.

Turtledove, Harry. *The Great War: American Front.* New York: Del Rey/Random House, 1998.

Tweed, Thomas F. *Gabriel Over the White House: A Novel of the Presidency.* New York: Farrar and Rinehart, 1933.

Tyrrell, R. Emmett. *The Impeachment of William Jefferson Clinton.* Washington, DC: Regnery, 1997.

Van Doren, Mark. *The Last Days of Lincoln: A Play in Six Scenes.* 1954. New York: Hill and Wang, 1959.

Veron, Enid, ed. *Humor in America: An Anthology*. New York: Harcourt Brace Jovanovich, 1976.

Wallace, Irving. *The Man*. New York: Simon and Schuster, 1964.

Walsh, John Evangelist. *The Shadows Rise: Abraham Lincoln and the Ann Rutledge Legend*. Urbana: University of Illinois Press, 1993.

Ward, John William. *Andrew Jackson: Symbol for an Age*. Oxford: Oxford University Press, 1955.

Warner, William B. "Computable Culture and the Closure of the Media Paradigm." Review of *The Language of New Media*, by Lev Manovich. *Postmodern Culture* 12, no. 3 (May 2002).

Warren, Earl, et al. *Report of the President's Commission on the Assassination of President Kennedy* [The Warren Report]. Washington: U.S. Government Printing Office, 1964. National Archives. http://www.archives.gov/research/jfk/warren-commission-report/index.html.

Watt, Ian. *The Rise of the Novel*. Berkeley: University of California Press, 1964.

Weber, Joe. *Defcon One*. Novato, CA: Presidio Press, 1989.

Webster, Daniel. *A Discourse in Commemoration of the Lives and Services of John Adams and Thomas Jefferson, Delivered in Faneuil Hall, Boston, August 2, 1826*. Boston: Cummings, Hilliard, 1826.

Weems, Mason Locke. *The Life of Washington: A New Edition with Primary Documents and Introduction*. Edited by Peter S. Onuf. Armonk, NY: M. E. Sharpe, 1996.

Weigley, Russell F. *The American Way of War: A History of United States Military Strategy and Policy*. Bloomington: Indiana University Press, 1973.

West, Nathanael. *A Cool Million*. 1934. New York: Berkeley Medallion Books, 1961.

———. "'A Cool Million': A Screen Story." In *Nathanael West: Novels and Other Writings*, edited by Sacvan Bercovitch. New York: Library of America/Penguin Books, 1997.

Whitman, Walt. "Death of Abraham Lincoln: Lecture Deliver'd in New York, April 14, 1879—in Philadelphia, '80—in Boston, '81." 1892. Bartleby.com Great Books Online, 2000. http://www.bartleby.com/229/.

Wieseltier, Leon. "Washington Diarist: A Year Later. *New Republic,* September 2, 2002. http://www.tnr.com/doc.mhtml?i=20020902&s=diarist090202.

Williams, Stephen P. *How to Be President: What to Do and Where to Go Once You're in Office*. San Francisco: Chronicle Books, 2004.

Wills, Garry. *Lincoln at Gettysburg: The Words That Remade America*. New York: Touchstone/Simon and Schuster, 1992.

Winik, Jay. *April 1865: The Month That Saved America*. New York: HarperCollins, 2001.

Wolin, Sheldon S. "The Rise of Private Man." *New York Review of Books* 24, no. 6 (April 14, 1977). http://www.nybooks.com/articles/article-preview?article_id=8541.

Woodward, Bob. *Bush at War.* New York: Simon and Schuster, 2002.

Woodward, Bob, and Carl Bernstein. *The Final Days.* New York: Touchstone/ Simon and Schuster, 1994.

Woolfolk, William. *The President's Doctor.* Chicago: Playboy Press, 1975.

Worts, George F. *The Phantom President.* New York: Jonathan Cape and Robert Ballou, 1932.

Wrone, David R. "Lincoln: Democracy's Touchstone." *Journal of the Abraham Lincoln Association* 1, no. 1 (1979): 83. http://www.historycooperative.org/ journals/jala/1/wrone.html.

Wyatt-Brown, Bertram. "Anatomy of a Murder." *New York Review of Books* 49, no. 16 (October 24, 2002).

———. "Andrew Jackson's Honor." In *The Shaping of Southern Culture: Honor, Grace, and War, 1760s–1890s.* Chapel Hill: University of North Carolina Press, 2000.

Youngblood, Gene. *Expanded Cinema.* New York: E. P. Dutton, 1970.

Zaretsky, Eli. "The Culture Wars of the 1960s and the Assault on the Presidency: The Meaning of the Clinton Impeachment." In *Our Monica, Ourselves: The Clinton Affair and the National Interest,* edited by Lauren Berlant and Lisa Duggan. New York: New York University Press, 2001.

Index